# THE MILITARY AIRFIELDS OF BRITAIN

# Southern England

## Kent, Hampshire, Surrey and Sussex

# THE MILITARY AIRFIELDS OF BRITAIN
# Southern England
## Kent, Hampshire, Surrey and Sussex

KEN DELVE

CROWOOD

First published in 2005 by
The Crowood Press Ltd
Ramsbury, Marlborough
Wiltshire SN8 2HR

www.crowood.com

**British Library Cataloguing-in-Publication Data**
A catalogue record for this book is available from the British Library.

ISBN 1 86126 729 0

**Acknowledgements**
My thanks for help with compiling this series of books goes to the staff of the Air Historic Branch,
London for their usual patience, co-operation and knowledge; to the staff of the Fleet Air Arm Museum,
Yeovilton; Ray Towler, Barry Abraham and other members of the Airfield Research Group,
Geoff Gardiner for the Watton pictures, Aldon Ferguson for advice and a variety of material,
and a large number of individuals who are involved in preserving and presenting particular
airfields or who have a general interest in aviation history and have been happy to share their
research. Finally, to two long-established friends and fellow enthusiasts, Peter Green and
Andy Thomas for their help with photographs and advice.

Typeset by Textype, Cambridge

Printed and bound in Great Britain by Biddles Ltd, King's Lynn, Norfolk

# Contents

Series Introduction                                  6

Airfield Recording                                  12

Introduction – Southern England                     13

Operational Period Matrix                           21

Notes on Using the Series                           22

Airfields                                           23

World War One Airfields and Landing Grounds        250

Abbreviations                                       268

# Series Introduction

This series of books examines Britain's military airfields region by region, covering military aviation from World War One to the present day. There have been two main periods of airfield construction – World War One, when a large number of landing grounds and aerodromes were built for either defensive purposes or training, the majority of offensive operations taking place from airfields in France, and World War Two, when some parts of England housed hundreds of airfields, many of which were 'taking the war to the enemy' on a daily basis. The highpoint of airfields in terms of numbers came in the latter months of 1944, when Britain housed some 1,000 airfields and over 30,000 aircraft, plus a significant number of small or temporary landing strips.

This series is not a detailed history of every airfield but rather a 'user-friendly' reference, which, for each airfield, comprises an outline history along with maps, plans, photographs and data tables containing information such as location, units and memorials. Commercial publishing realities mean that even the entries for major airfields have had to be restricted in size and all airfields and landing strips that had no recorded military usage have been excluded.

## Note on Sources

It is a well-established misunderstanding that military records are precise, comprehensive and accurate; sadly this is far from the truth and the problems inherent in first locating and then checking documents are not for the faint-hearted researcher. In addressing the history of airfields in the UK, the researcher has a variety of primary sources to consult; for the RAF the most in-depth, at least potentially, is the F540 Operational Record Book (ORB), a series of records now classified in the AIR 28 series by the National Archives at Kew, London. There are, however, two problems with this document: firstly, only RAF Stations, i.e. independent locations with a station headquarters, were required to compile and submit this monthly record, and that parameter removed many of the wartime airfields and landing grounds; secondly, the quality of record is very variable. The researcher is invariably frustrated by the way in which such records were kept; the compiling officer was following Air Ministry guidelines, but these took

no account of the desires and interests of future historians! An airfield could, for example, have gone from a grass surface to a concrete runway with no mention at all in its ORB, and when you consider more minor building works the chances of a mention are even slimmer. Movements in and out of units may or may not be recorded – even if mention is made there is no guarantee that the date given is accurate. This might sound strange, however it has to be remembered that these monthly ORBs were not compiled on a daily basis but were invariably put together in retrospect – at best days after the end of the recorded month but perhaps weeks later.

I spent much of my RAF career compiling ORBs at squadron and station level – as a secondary duty that had to be fitted around my primary aircrew task – and the problems of pulling together information in retrospect, especially from units or individuals that were either too busy or disinterested was a major struggle. The net result was a submission that would get past the signatory (squadron or station commander) and satisfy both the higher command that saw it and the final recipients at Air Ministry/MoD. Because such records were sent via higher commands there was also an element of politics in their content, as few commanders would submit a 'warts and all' record that might ruffle feathers further up the chain. However, even with these constraints and problems, the ORB remains the core historical document at all levels of the RAF organization. To put any appreciable level of detail into the overall research of an airfield requires reference to the ORBs of the based units, those for the flying units being particularly helpful – but with the same set of difficulties outlined above. Squadron ORBs are contained in the AIR 27 series. Other unit records, flying and ground, can also be consulted and, indeed, for some airfields, especially major training units, the unit record is essentially the station record.

The SD161 'location on units' record is an excellent source for unit listings at a particular location for a given month. There is one major drawback, in that it is compiled from other inputs that may not, in themselves, be accurate or up to date; for example, the SD161 might list the presence of a particular squadron or other unit in its monthly entry for an airfield but, in fact, the move of that unit, whilst planned and authorized, might not have taken place or might have occurred at a slightly different time. It is a similar picture with the Secret Organizational Memoranda (SOM) files: these documents were the authorization for units to form, move, change command-allegiance, change name, disband, and so on, and as such they can prove very useful – as long as they are used with care. A planned and authorized action might subsequently be modified or cancelled and the researcher might not have picked up the amendment. An example of this, in respect to airfields, is the authorization under SOM 79/40 (dated 30 January 1940) for 'the requisitioning of land at Bysshe Court, Surrey as a RLG for Redhill, the site is 2½ miles West of Lingfield'. Two months later, however, SOM 194/40 (dated 11 March) stated 'Redhill is to use Penshurst as an RLG and the site at Bysshe Court is not required'.

For Royal Navy/Fleet Air Arm units the official record system is the Ship's Log, which applies to shore sites as well as floating vessels, and these documents can be even more frustrating, as they vary from diary format, often excellent and including photographs, to minimal factual statements that are of little use.

The USAAF units also submitted regular official reports and, as one airfield usually only housed a single Group, the records of that Group can provide some useful details, although they are primarily concerned with operations and not infrastructure.

It would, of course, be impossible to refer to every one of these sources when compiling a series of books

such as the Crowood 'Military Airfields in Britain' series and the author freely acknowledges his debt to other researchers who have ploughed this field and produced excellent reference works. A great many of these secondary sources (a term that is no insult to these authors) have been used during the compilation of the Crowood series and a selection of the major ones is given below:

Halley, James J, *The Squadrons of the Royal Air Force and Commonwealth* (Air Britain)
Jefford, C G, *RAF Squadrons* (Airlife)
Sturtivant, Ray; Hamlin, John; Halley, James J, *RAF Flying Training and Support Units* (Air Britain)
Lake, Alan, *Flying Units of the RAF* (Airlife)
Sturtivant, Ray; Page, Gordon, *Royal Navy Aircraft, Serials and Units* (Air Britain)
*Airfield Review*, Airfield Research Group magazine (see below)
Freeman, Roger, *The Mighty Eighth* (Arms and Armour Press) – the impressive series of books by Roger on the 8th Air Force
Plus the author's own published works such as, *The Source Book of the RAF* (Airlife)

All good historians will confess that everything that appears in print contains errors; some of these are errors repeated from primary or secondary sources, some are typological (1942 and 1943 are a mere keystroke apart) and some are simply omissions where the author has not been able to fill in the gap or has

Late 1930s map showing positions of airfields.

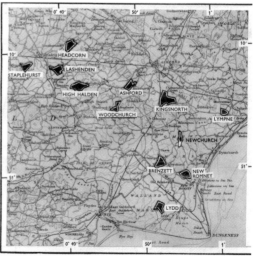

Location map 1944 that shows not only locations but also the approximate shape and size of each airfield; this series of maps highlights the density of airfields, in this example the group of Advanced Landing Grounds in Kent.

completely missed a document. All of these errors will be found in this series – I would welcome feedback so that any future updates can be more accurate and complete.

## Photographs and Plans

Photographs and plans are an essential element of the research and presentation of airfield history and this series attempts to bring together one of the most comprehensive pictorial records yet published. For some airfields there is a plethora of plans, whilst for others the search for a period layout draws a blank. It is a great shame that virtually all of the civilian contractors involved in airfield construction did not maintain, or have subsequently disposed of, their records of this work. Official plans (Air Ministry Drawings) exist for various periods, particularly fine sets being available for late-1944 and the mid-1950s, but in both cases the surviving documents have, in typical military fashion, been amended to the latest issue; for example, airfields no longer in use in December 1944 have been removed from that volume. With the exception of the Air Ministry overall-layout drawings, most plans cover only the main infrastructure of the airfield itself – runways, peri-track, dispersal and hangars, ignoring the off-airfield sites, such as accommodation and technical. Most of the airfield plans used in this volume are Crown Copyright via Air Historical Branch unless otherwise stated. The majority of World War One airfield plans are courtesy of RAY.

Photographs are perhaps an even thornier issue and the quality and number of images varies hugely from airfield to airfield, with training bases being the most poorly represented. The RAF's security-conscious attitude meant that cameras were a real no-no at airfields and, other than occasional official or press sessions and the odd illicit snap, there are massive gaps in the photo coverage. The situation at the USAAF bases was somewhat better, for both official and unofficial photographs; what makes this even easier from the researcher's point of view is the ease of access to this material at the National Archives building in Maryland.

Wartime air-to-ground images are hard to find and, although it seems likely that every airfield in the

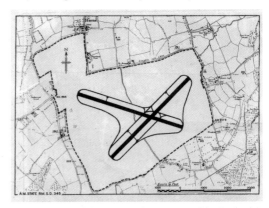

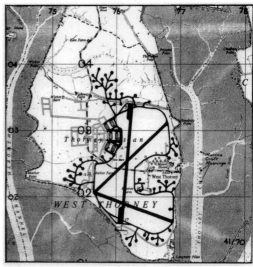

Airfield plans are invaluable historical documents. The three shown here are:
1. Sketch map based on the AIR 1 series of plans for World War One landing grounds (via Ray Sturtivant, drawn by . . .)
2. 1944-series plan of the ALG at Horne; not all airfields are provided with a drawn plan in the 1944 series, some use an overlay on an aerial photograph.
3. 1950s-series plan of Thorney Island; this is an excellent series of plans but sadly it is not complete as with subsequent amendments to the document those airfields removed from the RAF list were removed from the document – a classic case of 'if only' someone had preserved a complete set!

UK was photographed on numerous occasions during the war, unearthing these images is never easy. The Luftwaffe produced excellent target folders, including aerial photos, of many British airfields and this source of material is superb when you can find it.

A number of photographic surveys of the UK have been flown over the past sixty years; indeed, according to some sources, the 7th Photographic Group flew a vertical survey of much of Britain during the war and this material would prove invaluable should it be easy to access, which sadly is not the case. Post-1945, airfields have been popular targets for reconnaissance squadrons to practice both vertical and oblique pinpoint-photography and thousands of negatives would have been exposed – but not necessarily printed or preserved. Keele University is the present home for tens of thousands of air-to-ground photos from World War Two onwards and almost every airfield in Britain is likely to be amongst the collection – if you can locate the individual site. There are three main 'national' collections of aviation images in the UK; the Imperial War Museum and the RAF Museum, both in London, and the Fleet Air Arm Museum at Yeovilton. For the researcher/author this is a somewhat mixed blessing as, whilst the material can usually be studied by prior arrangement, it is often prohibitively expensive to acquire copies for publication. The majority of illustrations used in this series are from private collections and plans/diagrams are from official sources.

## Airfield or Aerodrome?

For the sake of ease I have used the term airfield throughout this series, but have freely mixed it with aerodrome and other terms; the purist will rightly say that this is not technically correct and it is true that, at various times, the RAF (and other Services) had definitions they used for specific types of 'air installation'.

The same problem of nomenclature occurs with individual elements of the airfield; for example, taxiway or perimeter track, runway or landing strip? Different sources will provide different definitions and, indeed, the definitions change with the period in question. It is not the purpose of this series of books to get bogged down in the debate on terminology.

## Pubs

For every airfield there is the question of drinking! All RAF aircrew and ground crew had their favourite pubs, and usually they went to different ones; likewise, different squadrons might adopt their own pub

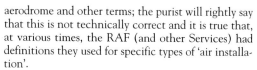

Aerial photographs are a valuable complement to airfield plans but the tracking down period shots can be difficult; some airfields are well represented whilst others are blanks in the record. It is certain that every airfield was photographed from the air in World War Two, the problem is tracking down the material! The series show here comprises:
1. Aerial view of Bekesbourne, c.1918 from the 50 Squadron photo album
2. Wonderful shot of Thorney Island c.mid 1940s.
3. June 2003 shot of Biggin Hill; modern aerial shots always make a useful comparison, especially for disused airfields.

or pubs. Whilst regular drinking took place in the messes and the NAAFI, a trip down to the 'local' was an essential part of squadron life, with frequent reference to the 'boys' climbing into the Boss's car and tearing off to the pub. You only have to read any autobiography from a wartime-RAF chap to find reference to these forays – often with humorous results. The Americans were even keener on making use of local pubs and every airfield will have had one or more favourite watering holes. Although reference is made to pubs in some of the entries in this series, we have not included complete lists, as this information is not available. I would like to have included details of wartime pubs in these records but that level of research relies on people with local knowledge and interest – if you know of any pubs that fit this description then let me know and I will update the file!

## Messes and Headquarters

Pre-war RAF stations included excellent living accommodation; indeed, one of the great advantages of an expansion-period officers' mess, for example, was that they all followed the same pattern and it was easy therefore to stagger from bar to accommodation wing without getting lost, no matter which airfield you were at! However, with the threat of air attack and with many airfields having little or no accommodation, the military adopted the course of 'acquiring' a suitable local establishment, which in many cases meant a stately home or, at least, very large house. This type of building was taken over by HQ staff and also for use as officers' messes, with the frequent addition of a hutted 'village' in the grounds. As with pubs, this information is not always readily to hand, other than for major HQ-units, and I would like to hear from local researchers who can add details of houses taken over in this way. Perhaps the best known in the UK is the Petwood Hotel at Woodhall Spa, Lincolnshire, which was used as a mess by the officers of 617 Squadron, and which hosts numerous RAF reunions and is a great place to spend a weekend.

## Visiting Airfields

The majority of airfield sites are *out of bounds*, either because they are still active military installations or, more commonly, they are in private hands for agricultural or industrial use. While touring the countryside looking for airfields you will come across many variations on the 'KEEP OUT' sign, some couched in pleasant, but firm, tones and others somewhat more vehement in their opinion of any who would dare tread from the public paths. It is worth noting that footpaths exist over many of these airfields and so reference to a good OS map (which is an essential part

of any pack-up for the airfield tourer) will keep you on the straight and narrow. Sadly, the footpaths were not laid out with visiting airfield structures in mind and all too often all that is glimpsed is a building, often partly hidden by vegetation, often at some distance from the marked path. You can always try contacting the landowner to seek permission to enter the airfield site and this is certainly worth a try for a pre-planned visit – although finding contact details for landowners can be tricky. As with all outdoor activities you need to have the right clothing and equipment – stout, waterproof footwear (that is not allergic to mud) is an essential if you plan to walk the ground rather then observe from the side of the road. When it comes to photography, a long lens (up to 300mm) is always worth having, as you may not be able to get close to some structures.

A good military maxim is that 'time spent on reconnaissance is seldom wasted' and this equally applies to the research time you spend before taking to the field – study the maps and diagrams in this book, in conjunction with the OS Landranger map, and you will (hopefully) have a much more productive visit. These books are, of course, equally useful for the 'armchair visitor' and provide a wealth of information for those interested in a particular area or type of airfield.

## Memorials

I have always been a 'people person' when it comes to aviation history and, to that end, I find the question of memorials fascinating, as these are a means of providing a visible link with, and recognition of, those who were involved with operations from the airfields. Any student of memorials will soon realize the variations that exist in this recognition – and it should be pointed out that the majority of airfields do not have a memorial. The regional variation is enormous and in large part reflects the type of organization operating in a region; for example, the USAAF bases are generally well-represented with memorials, often comprising impressive stones complete with inscriptions, and in many cases twin white flag-poles from which to fly the Stars and Stripes and the Union Jack. This is in large part due to the strength of post-war Associations amongst the American Groups and the creation of Anglo-American friendship groups. Likewise, the RCAF units, especially those of No.6 (RCAF) Group in Yorkshire, are well represented with memorials. Of the RAF operational commands only Bomber Command has an appreciable number of memorials at their former airfields, whilst for others, including Fighter Command, the situation is very variable, with some of the London/Kent Battle of Britain airfields having memorials – the one at

Croydon is one of the finest in the UK – but with others having nothing. Taking the country as a whole, there have been two major 'memorial building' phases, the early 1980s and the early 1990s; however, over the last couple of years there has been another burst of activity, although not on the scale of the previous ones. It would be great if every airfield was provided with a memorial that recognized the role it and its personnel played in World War Two, and it is this conflict that memorials commemorate, but this laudable aim is unlikely ever to be achieved, although there are still groups and organizations working towards the creation of such memorials. When looking for memorials it is not always a case of looking in the obvious places, such as the airfield site, as in many cases they are located in the nearby village, either on the village green or in the churchyard (or indeed the church itself). The entries in this airfield series give location details for memorials where appropriate and this will save many an hour of sometimes fruitless searching (been there!); however, I do not claim that I have listed them all or even that they are all where I say they are – so feel free to update our information!

Talking of churches, it is always worth a look in the local church and churchyard – which may not always be the one nearest to the airfield or the village

with the same name as the airfield – for additional memorials, such as Books of Remembrance, and for grave stones. Many parish churchyards in the UK include Commonwealth War Grave Commission grave markers, although these do not always relate to the local airfield but might simply be the grave of a local person who had died whilst in military service. Don't, however, simply look for the CWGC markers, as many graveyards will contain other RAF (and even RFC) stones. Not all graves are in the War Graves plot and not all have the standard stone. I did not visit all local graveyards during this survey and so this information has been omitted – but I would be delighted if researchers were able to piece together these details for their airfields.

## Non-Airfield Sites

Airfields are only part of the military aviation story and a variety of other locations played roles in the overall picture, from HQ units to training establishments and storage units. However, despite the importance of such sites, they have been omitted from this series except for passing reference where appropriate in an airfield entry. This has been done for reasons of space, as to include all the 'other' sites would have added a significant number of pages – and cost.

Many airfields in this region do not have a memorial – some have very impressive memorials, one of the best being the figure and series of plaques (only part of which is shown here) at West Malling.

# Airfield Recording

As part of the on-going research into military airfields there is a vital role for local historians and enthusiasts – by becoming 'local experts' they can help fill in the detail. It is the detail, such as grave records, local pubs, present condition of the airfield and its associated structures, preserved material (museums and local collections) and photographs, that helps provide a more complete picture of the airfield and those who were once based there.

The example form provides a standard record-sheet and in conjunction with the Aviation History Centre we are encouraging individuals to become 'local representatives', in order that the detail can be added for every airfield in the UK. This is not, of course, a permit to go marching over fields claiming right of access! The normal procedures have to be followed, but a local representative can take the time to get to know the airfield and its surrounding area, talking to landowners for access and finding out such lost information as the pubs used by various units. This is a people task – asking questions and chasing up little bits of information with which to build the overall picture.

The Aviation History Centre has agreed to provide basic information as a starting point for anyone wishing to become a local representative and they have also pointed out that you do not actually need to be local – it may be that you have a particular interest in an operational Group, squadron or local area and would like to pursue that interest. Individuals are also not restricted to taking on a single airfield but what is required is a responsible attitude when dealing with the landowners, an interest in finding out accurate information and a desire to share that information.

## Airfield Research Group

It is worth considering joining the Airfield Research Group: this organization consists of individuals with an interest in research into and, to some extent, preservation of airfields in the UK. They publish an excellent magazine (free to members) and the quality of research is superb. For further details contact: Hon. Secretary, Raymond Towler, 33A Earls Street, Thetford, Norfolk IP24 2AB.

| AIRFIELD RECORD | | | | |
|---|---|---|---|---|
| Airfield name | | County | | |
| Lat/Long | | OS Map | | |
| Nearest town/village | | OS Grid | | |
| AIRFIELD SURVEY | | | | |
| Control Tower | | | | |
| Hangars | | | | |
| Runways | | | | |
| Perimeter Track | | | | |
| Dispersals | | | | |
| Technical Buildings | | | | |
| Admin Buildings | | | | |
| Domestic Buildings | | | | |
| Land Ownership | | | | |
| Public Access | | | | |
| ASSOCIATED SITES | | | | |
| Memorial | | | | |
| Church (graves?) | | | | |
| Pubs | | | | |
| House (mess or HQ) | | | | |
| Museum | | | | |
| Other Information | | | | |
| Date of Record | | | | |
| Recorded By | | | | |

NOTES:
1. Permission must be acquired before entering areas that are not public access.
2. Mark positions of buildings, memorials, etc on airfield plan/map.
3. A photo record should also be made.

Aviation History Centre: navman678@hotmail.com; or via Crowood Press

# Introduction – Southern England

The counties in the southern part of England will forever be associated with two events in British aviation history: the Battle of Britain in 1940 and D-Day in 1944; in general terms this simplistic overview is accurate and, without doubt, these were the most significant periods for military aviation in the area covered by this volume of the Crowood series. However, the overall picture is a little more complex and interesting, and the following overview of airfield development in these counties provides a brief synopsis of ninety years of military aviation in southern England.

## World War One

By the outbreak of war in August 1914, this region was home to a variety of landplane and seaplane bases, with roles ranging from aircraft manufacture to training and Home Defence. The latter role was primarily the task of the Admiralty until 1916 and with London a target for the German airships it was vital that an aeroplane defence-network be established. A number of airfields were tasked with this difficult duty and, with inadequate aircraft, pilots struggled into the night sky – and met with little success. The Royal Flying Corps took over the task in late-1916 but met with little more success, especially when the German Air Service switched from airships, which

had become vulnerable and whose losses had risen, to large bomber-aircraft by day and night. Whilst Home Defence was the most public role of aeroplanes during this period, there was far more effort being expended on the training of pilots and a significant number of airfields in this region housed training-units for the RFC, RNAS and, in the latter part of the war, the United States Air Service (USAS). Coastal patrols and anti-submarine work were carried out by aircraft and airships from a number of coastal stations, such as Dover and Capel, whilst other airfields, such as Calshot, played a significant role in development and trials work. By early 1918 the region's aircraft factories were producing large numbers of aircraft and the training schools were turning out the necessary pilots and providing specialist training; however, with the signing of the Armistice Agreement in November this all came to a rapid end and, by mid-1919, military aviation throughout the region was in a major decline. Units disbanded and airfields closed; the build-up of American strength, for which a number of airfields were under construction, had ended and it was not long before most airfields had been dismantled and the sites disposed of.

## Between the Wars

A number of military airfields did, of course, survive, all now in the hands of the RAF, but in most cases it

There were a number of airship stations in this region and anti-submarine/coastal patrols were an important role; SS-type airship over Capel. (Peter Green)

Throwley was one of a number of landing grounds that performed the Home Defence function.

was not until the mid-1920s that the home establishment of squadrons had settled down to permanent locations. Some airfields were used for private or commercial flying, often with only limited success, and it was not until the early 1930s that significant new airfield development took place. Whilst the 1930s expansion period in RAF strength didn't completely pass this area by, it did have far less effect here than in other parts of the UK, as one of the major thrusts of the expansion plans was a re-orientation to face the new 'most likely' air opponent, Germany. With France once more an ally, it seemed the near Continent was seen more as a potential forward-deployment area than a threat zone and, as such, little attention was paid to airfield development, other than a number of improvements in facilities at existing airfields. Fighter Command was formed on 14 July 1936, under the command of Air Marshal Sir Hugh Dowding, as part of a general re-organization of the RAF, and headquartered at Bentley Priory, Middlesex. At this time, Fighter Command had three operational groups – No.11 Group (HQ Uxbridge) covering the south of England and the south Midlands, No.12 Group (HQ Hucknall) covering the north Midlands, north-west England and north Wales, and No.13 Group (HQ Newcastle-upon-Tyne) covering north-east England, Scotland, and the Orkney and Shetland Islands. In addition to its airfields, the Command was developing a network of radar stations and an associated reporting and control system. Much of this effort was focused on the Southern Counties.

## World War Two

With the outbreak of war in September 1939 the main concern was not so much the immediate defence of Britain but rather the positioning of squadrons in France to support the British troops deployed as part of the Expeditionary Force. The air elements comprised the Advanced Air Striking Force of light bombers from No.1 Group and the Air Component of the British Expeditionary Force; it was the latter that drew Hurricane squadrons from airfields in the Southern Counties, as No.11 Group was tasked with providing the bulk of the fighters. Once again this is something of an over-simplification, as the air component was drawn from a number of sources, but the essence of the statement is correct and was soon to become the thrust of the 'no more aircraft to send' stance adopted by Fighter Command's AOC, Hugh Dowding.

In addition to the units deployed to France, the home-based squadrons of Fighter Command flew a large number of missions over France and the adjacent waters. For example, one of the myths of World War Two is the 'lack of RAF fighters over the Dunkirk beaches during the evacuation'. In fact the RAF, and Fighter Command in particular, went to considerable effort to provide both fighter cover and offensive sorties. It was during this period that the Spitfire squadrons first became heavily engaged, enabling the RAF pilots to absorb tactical lessons relating to their formations and the effectiveness of their gunnery.

The German occupation of Norway, the Low

58 Squadron at Worthy Down; this Wessex Bombing Area airfield was one of the main inter-war RAF stations in the region.

When the Fleet Air Arm reformed it took over a number of airfields in this region; this 1939 shot shows a Blackburn Shark at Ford in 1930. (Ray Sturtivant)

Countries and France gave Fighter Command an increased frontage to defend, as the Luftwaffe now had additional bases over a wider geographic area. Consequently, the Command's existing organization had to be modified to provide additional cover for the north-east and south-west of England. The need for additional airfields and a command organization – not to mention aircraft and pilots – put a severe strain on the already limited resources.

## Battle of Britain

The dates for the Battle of Britain are usually accepted as 10 July to 31 October 1940 and during these fifteen weeks the course of the war took a major turn, with the Germans postponing their plans to invade the British Isles. As the Battle intensified, a few hundred RAF fighters operating from twenty or so airfields in south-east England were pitted against an air armada that had previously been unbeaten. The morale of the Luftwaffe, boosted by easy victories over Poland and France, was high, some might even say verging on arrogance – certainly most of the German pilots believed that the RAF would soon be destroyed.

On 16 July Hitler issued Directive No.16,

Operation *Sealion*, the invasion of England, which came with the proviso that 'the British Air Force must be eliminated to such an extent that it will be incapable of putting up any sustained opposition to the invading troops'. In most histories of the Battle the radar stations – Chain Home as they were called – are usually assessed as being one of the key factors in Fighter Command's success. It was the combination of warning systems, including the Observer Corps and ground intelligence, as well as radar, analysed by Filter Rooms and then acted upon by sector controllers, that made the system successful and reasonably robust against attack.

At this opening stage of the Battle, the tactical advantage lay very much with the Germans, as the Luftwaffe could choose the time, place and size of any attack. It was able, on paper, to mass overwhelming force at any one point, whilst maintaining a threat to other areas that would prevent any attempt by the RAF to concentrate its forces. The German bomber force was capable of reaching over the entire UK land-area and surrounding waters; a massive geographic area for the defenders to cover. It was, of course, realized by both sides that the decisive conflict would have to take place in south-east England, but the ability to stretch and weaken the British fighter-force was a significant tactical card to play. The fact that the Luftwaffe failed to take full advantage of this was one of the main factors in the failure of the German air campaign.

On the afternoon of 8 July the British radar stations reported a build-up of enemy aircraft over France. Five squadrons were scrambled to intercept the Dornier Do17s and their escort of Messerschmitt Bf109s and Bf110s that had attacked a convoy near Dover. The dogfight eventually involved over 100 aircraft, the first major air battle over British territory. Convoy attacks of this type, varying in intensity and sometimes limited to small numbers of unescorted raiders using cloud cover, was the pattern of the Battle for the first few weeks. Most activity centred on shipping off Dover. Fighter Command was continuing to evolve its organization and No.10 Group had been formed on 31 May 1940, becoming effective on 13 July.

During July the average number of defensive sorties was 500–600 a day, the highest rate occurring on 28 July when 794 sorties were flown, during which the RAF claimed ten aircraft for the loss of five of their own. Day-fighter strength grew during July, enabling the Command to field forty-nine Hurricane and Spitfire squadrons by early August – the number of Spitfire units remained at eighteen but an additional four Hurricane units were now in the line. There was great variation in the RAF's daily sortie-rates for August, from as few as 288 to a high of 974. The latter took place on 15 August, as part of the Luftwaffe's concerted attacks on the RAF's airfields under the so-called _Adler Tag_ (Eagle Day). This new strategy to destroy Fighter Command's combat potential consisted of a series of attacks on radar installations and fighter airfields and was launched on 12 August. The first raids were on Hawkinge, Manston and Lympne, the latter being hit twice with the result that, by the end of the second attack, the airfield was pockmarked with craters and there was barely a clear space on which to land. Hawkinge was hit at around 17.00, with Ju88s destroying two

hangars, workshops and other buildings, as well as leaving the airfield surface badly damaged. Overnight the craters were filled, the unexploded bombs dealt with and the airfield was declared operational again within twenty-four hours. It was a similar story at Manston, with 65 Squadron's Spitfires taking off as the bombs fell. This pattern of airfield attacks continued to the end of the first week of September but, with a few notable exceptions, there appears to have been little in the way of overall co-ordination of the strategy.

One of the greatest 'debates' at the time, and one that still rages, was that of Fighter Command's Diary for 15 September 1940, recording a communiqué from the Prime Minister addressed to Fighter Command via the Secretary of State for Air:

> . . . yesterday eclipses all previous records of the Fighter Command. Aided by squadrons of their Czech and Polish comrades, using only a small proportion of their total strength, and under cloud conditions of some difficulty, they cut to rags and tatters three separate waves of murderous assault upon the civil population of their native land, inflicting a certain loss of 125 bombers and fifty-three fighters upon the enemy, to say nothing of probable and damaged, while themselves sustaining only a loss of twelve pilots and twenty-five machines. These results exceed all expectations and give just and sober confidence in the approaching struggle.

This is the day that is now celebrated as Battle of Britain Day.

The last of the massed daylight raids took place on 30 September and was given a very rough handling by a Fighter Command that was now much stronger than it had been at any point in the Battle. From then until the end of the accepted Battle period (31 October) the main Luftwaffe effort comprised small formations or lone aircraft (the latter often fighter-bombers) – undertaking as many as 1,000 sorties a day. Whilst the damage they inflicted was small, they represented a major problem for the defending fighters and the Command had to resort to standing patrols. The end date for the Battle is somewhat arbitrary, as these types of raid continued well into 1941.

As the daylight campaign began to wind down in late-summer, the night campaign – the Blitz – was starting in earnest; to counter this, the RAF increased its night-fighter operations and a number of stations received squadrons, or detachments, of aircraft for this purpose. 'The Few', as Churchill described them, had won a stunning victory. The airfields of southern England and the aircraft that flew

Kenley under attack 18 August 1940.

Pilots of 257 Squadron at Gravesend in August 1943.

from them had replaced the wooden walls of the Royal Navy as Britain's main line of defence.

## Preparation for D-Day

Whilst defending the skies over Britain remained the primary task for Fighter Command throughout the war, it was not long before thoughts turned to ways of taking the war to the enemy. The first acknowledged offensive mission was flown on 20 December 1940, when two Spitfires of 66 Squadron attacked Le Touquet airfield; the following day the first intruder mission was flown, Blenheims of 29 Squadron operating over enemy airfields. Under the codename *Circus*, the first of the escort missions was flown on 10 January 1941, with Bomber Command Blenheims to the airfield at Guines.

These *Circus* operations, during which a bomber force would attack targets in France, aimed to 'raise and engage that portion of the Luftwaffe fighter-strength based on the Western Front' (Fighter Command operational memo). This was the logical follow-on to the previous concept of fighter sweeps, which had proved to be a waste of effort because the Luftwaffe had refused to take the bait.

*Circus* operations remained a key element of the

Command's work during 1942, but it is worth noting a special operation that took place in August that year. On 19 August a raid on Dieppe was supported by the largest array of RAF squadrons yet employed on a single operation, some sixty-eight squadrons being airborne; many of these operated from airfields in this region, some deploying for just the few days of the operation. Typical of the new Fighter Command formations charged with this work was No.127 Wing, which formed at Kenley on 11 July 1943, with an initial strength of two Canadian squadrons equipped with Spitfire IXs.

A massive airfield-construction programme was instituted in 1941–42 to cater for the thousands of American aircraft destined for the European theatre; however, the bulk of this activity took place to the north and west of the area under consideration in this book. A number of new airfields were constructed in the west of the area as part of this plan and the main USAAF presence was that of the Troop Carrier Groups of IXth Air Force. However, there is one aspect of the airfield programme that is particularly relevant to the D-Day campaign and the southern counties of England: the construction of a series of Advanced Landing Grounds (ALGs). In the autumn of 1942, work started on a series of ALGs – temporary airfields that would accommodate British and American tactical squadrons for a limited time in the pre-invasion period. With the massive weight of air power being assembled for the invasion, the question of where to base units became increasingly acute and, whilst the construction programme for permanent airfields was accelerated, an even more acute need was for airfields for use by short-range tactical aircraft, so a network of ALGs was constructed in southern England, primarily in Kent, Hampshire and Sussex. A large number of possible sites were surveyed during early 1942 and, once a selection had been made, plans were drawn up for the construction of twenty-three ALGs for use by the RAF's 2nd TAF. Initial work involved the clearing of woodland and the draining of marshland, after which an RAF Airfield Construction Service (ACS) team of three officers and 200 airmen would be given an average of three months to complete the construction of the site. In general terms each airfield was constructed to the same pattern, although local conditions did require some variation, with two metal-track runways, two-and-a-half miles of perimeter track, plus an additional MT track. A typical ALG construction involved:

Levelling of site: 10,000 tons of earth to be shifted

Laying of runways: two runways, each 1,600 × 50 yards, metal track

Aircraft standings: 80 in metal track

Perimeter track and MT road: 2.5 miles perimeter plus 2.5 miles MT road in metal track or hardcore with tarspray cover

Hangars: eight blister type

Petrol installation: sufficient for 18,000 gallons

Other than the blister hangars, and these were not always provided or at least not to the 'standard' scale, very few other buildings would be provided, so tents or requisitioned buildings would be the norm. Each airfield was to be capable of supporting up to fifty day-operational aircraft, i.e. a Wing of three squadrons. Most of the work was carried out by the RAF's Airfield Construction Service, although Royal Engineers, American Engineer Aviation Battalions and civilian contractors all contributed. Target date for completion was March 1943 and eleven of the sites were allocated for USAAF use, the remainder being for the RAF. For a variety of reasons the programme was soon behind schedule and the first airfield to open was Chailey, three miles east of Burgess Hill, in April 1943 but, like many of these airfields, there was no initial attempt to move in operational units. Most of the new airfields had been completed

Medium bombers operated from airfields such as Dunsfold as part of the Tactical Air Force; 98 Squadron Mitchells taxy out.

by the end of 1943 and many had been used by squadrons on evaluation exercises, testing the ability of the squadrons (Wing) to operate from a 'mobile' location and checking that the airfield itself had not major faults. Virtually all the ALGs received further work in the winter of 1943–44, with hangars, usually blister types, taxi-tracks and hardstands being built. By spring 1944 they began to receive their operational units, usually an Airfield (a mobile grouping of usually three squadrons), the nomenclature being changed to Wing in May 1944. After a few weeks of hectic activity the squadrons left and the sound of aircraft engines was replaced by that of agriculture as the land was de-requisitioned, buildings and tracking removed, and the land handed back to its original purpose. Most had been abandoned by September 1944 and were promptly de-requisitioned.

## Second Blitz

With the Allied invasion of France in June 1944 it seemed that the war had entered its final phase and whilst this was, of course, true, it did not mean that the end was going to come quickly or easily. At 04.18 on 13 June 1944, the peace at Swanscombe, near Gravesend, Kent, was shattered by a fierce explosion. The first of Hitler's new 'terror' weapons had landed on English soil. Within an hour, three more of these

V-1 flying bombs had come to earth – one crashing into a railway bridge at Grove Road, Bethnal Green, in London, causing six deaths and a substantial amount of damage.

The revised *Diver* plan of February 1944 called for eight day-fighter squadrons, plus a number of night-fighter units, but for a lower total of anti-aircraft guns. In the 24-hour period from 22.30 on 15 June to 16 June 1944, British records show 151 reported launches, with 144 V-1s crossing the English coast. Of those, seventy-three reached the London area. The defences notched up only a modest score, seven falling to the fighters, fourteen to the guns and one shared, whilst a further eleven were shot down by the guns of the Inner Artillery Zone. The Hawker Tempests of No.150 Wing at Newchurch had been at readiness for defensive patrol since dawn on 15 June.

The first phase of the flying-bomb campaign ended on 1 September 1944, with the Allied capture of those V-1 launching sites within range of London. Although the campaign never resumed with the same intensity, from 4 September 1944 to 14 January 1945 the city was subjected to attack by V-1s launched from Heinkel He 111 carrier-aircraft over the North Sea. Defensive patrols remained in force, but there was even less warning of attack, so the ideal solution was to destroy the parent aircraft before they launched their weapons.

Meteor night-fighters of 85 Squadron at West Malling; the airfield was one of a number of Fighter Command bases in the immediate post-war period.

In the overall campaign the Germans launched some 9,252 flying bombs, of which just under 5,900 crossed the English coast and 2,563 of those reached the London area. The defences claimed 4,262 destroyed – a very respectable 72.3 per cent of those that crossed into England. The threat posed by the V-1 was enormous and it was a weapon the like of which no-one had seen before. That the defences were able to react so quickly and so effectively is a tribute to all concerned.

With the end of the Second Blitz there was almost no significant activity and Fighter Command's role over southern England was one of chasing unknown radar-plots, almost all of which turned out to be Allied aircraft. It would be true to say that for this area, which had twice been the main focus of air activity, the war pretty much petered out. There was a final burst of activity at many of the airfields when squadrons returned from Europe, although in most cases this was simply to disband.

## Cold War and Beyond

With the immediate post-war disposals and disbandment phase over, the RAF and Fleet Air Arm established their presence at a number of permanent airfields, whilst others were taken over for civil use under the auspices of the Ministry of Civil Aviation or by aircraft manufacturers. In regard to the latter, sites such as Brooklands, the Vickers-Armstrong factory and Dunsfold, home of British Aerospace and the Harrier, are well known but others such as Chilbolton, used by Supermarine and Folland as a flight-test centre, are less familiar. Of the civil airfields the most successful was Gatwick, although the early post-war years were a struggle. The 1950s were a final heyday for military aviation, with great Fleet Air Arm stations such as Ford and Lee-on-Solent, and RAF fighter wings at the likes of Tangmere. The birth of the Army Air Corps brought airfields such as Middle Wallop to prominence, whilst the new-fangled helicopters came to dominate at places such as Odiham. By the early 1960s the next phase of decline had set in, a decline that has been pretty constant ever since – until the point has been reached at which there are now very few active military airfields in this region. Indeed, the only significant RAF airfield still operational – and that with helicopters – is Odiham in Hampshire and the only other operational military station, again helicopters, is the Army Air Corps at Middle Wallop. However, a significant number of the airfields in this region are still extant, many as commercial or private airfields (ranging from international airports such as Gatwick to busy private airfields such as Shoreham) and some as traces of old runways and buildings. Many have all but vanished, especially the series of temporary Advanced Landing Grounds. There are a number of very good aviation museums, such as Manston and Tangmere, but in general the wonderful aviation history of counties such as Kent and Hampshire has all but been forgotten.

# Operational Period Matrix

| | World War I | World War II | Post-1950[1] |
|---|---|---|---|
| All Hallows (Kent) | X | — | — |
| Andover (Hants) | X | X | X |
| Appledram (Sussex) | — | X | — |
| Ashford (Great Chart) (Kent) | — | X | — |
| Beaulieu (Hants) | X | X | — |
| Bekesbourne (Kent) | X | X | — |
| Bembridge (IoW) | X | — | — |
| Biggin Hill (Kent) | X | X | X |
| Bisterne (Hants) | — | X | — |
| Blackbushe (Hants) see Hartford Bridge | | | |
| Bognor (Sussex) | — | X | — |
| Brenzett (Ivychurch) (Kent) | — | X | — |
| Brooklands (Surrey) | X | X | X |
| Calshot (Hants) | X | X | X |
| Capel (Kent) | X | — | — |
| Chailey (Sussex) | — | X | — |
| Chattis Hill (Hants) | X | X | — |
| Chilbolton (Hants) | — | X | X |
| Christchurch (Hants) | — | X | X |
| Coolham (Sussex) | — | X | — |
| Cowdray Park (Sussex) | — | X | — |
| Croydon (Waddon) (Surrey) | X | X | — |
| Deanland (Sussex) | — | X | — |
| Detling (Kent) | X | X | X |
| Dover (Kent) | X | — | — |
| Dymchurch | X | — | — |
| Eastbourne (Sussex) | X | — | — |
| Eastchurch (Kent) | X | X | — |
| Eastleigh (Hants) | X | X | X |
| Fairoaks (Surrey) | — | X | X |
| Farnborough (Hants) | X | X | X |
| Ford (Sussex) | X | X | X |
| Foreland (IoW) | X | — | — |
| Friston (Sussex) | — | X | — |
| Frost Hill Farm (Hants) | — | X | — |
| Funtingdon (Sussex) | — | X | — |
| Gatwick (Surrey) | — | X | X |
| Goring By Sea (Sussex) | X | — | — |
| Gosport (Hants) | X | X | X |
| Grain (Kent) | X | — | — |
| Gravesend (Chalk) (Kent) | — | X | — |
| Hamble (Hants) | X | X | X |
| Hammerwood (Sussex) | — | X | — |
| Hartford Bridge (Hants) | — | X | X |
| Hawkinge (Kent) | X | X | X |
| Headcorn (Kent) | — | X | — |
| High Halden (Kent) | — | X | — |
| Holmsley South (Hants) | — | X | — |
| Horne (Surrey) | — | X | — |
| Hurn[2] (Hampshire) | — | X | X |
| Hythe (Kent) see Dymchurch | | | |
| Ibsley (Hants) | — | X | — |
| Kenley (Surrey) | X | X | X |
| Kingsnorth – WWI (Kent) | X | — | — |
| Kingsnorth (Kent) | — | X | — |
| Larks Barrow (Hants) | — | X | — |
| Lasham (Hants) | — | X | X |
| Lashenden (Kent) | — | X | X |
| Lee-on-Solent (Hants) | X | X | X |
| Leysdown (Kent) | X | — | — |
| Lydd (Kent) | — | X | X |
| Lymington (Hants) | — | X | — |
| Lympne (Kent) | X | X | — |
| Manston (Kent) | X | X | X |
| Marwell Hall (Hants) | — | X | — |
| Merston (Sussex) | — | X | — |
| Middle Wallop (Hants) | — | X | X |
| Needs Oar Point (Hants) | — | X | — |
| Newchurch (Kent) | — | X | — |
| Newhaven (Sussex) | X | — | — |
| New Romney (Honeychild) (Kent) | X | X | — |
| Odiham (Hants) | — | X | X |
| Penshurst (Kent) | X | X | — |
| Polegate (Sussex) | X | — | — |
| Pulborough (Sussex) | X | — | — |
| Portsmouth (Hants) | — | X | X |
| Ramsgate (Kent) | — | X | — |
| Redhill (Surrey) | — | X | X |
| Rochester (Kent) | X | X | X |
| Rustington (Sussex) | X | — | — |
| Selsey (Sussex) | — | X | — |
| Sheerness (Kent) | X | — | — |
| Shoreham (Sussex) | X | X | X |
| Slindon (Sussex) (see Polegate) | | | |
| Soberton (Hants) | — | X | — |
| Somerton (IoW) | X | X | — |
| Southbourne (Sussex) | | | |
| Staplehurst (Kent) | — | X | — |
| Stoney Cross (Hants) | — | X | — |
| Swingfield (Kent) | — | X | — |
| Tangmere (Sussex) | X | X | X |
| Telscombe Cliffs (Sussex) | X | — | — |
| Thorney Island (Hants) | — | X | X |
| Throwley (Kent) | X | — | — |
| Tipnor (Hants) | X | — | — |
| Walmer (Kent) | X | — | — |
| Westgate (Kent) | X | — | — |
| Westhampnett (Goodwood) (Sussex) | — | X | X |
| Westenhangar (Kent) | — | X | — |
| West Malling (Kent) | — | X | X |
| Winkton (Hants) | — | X | — |
| Wisley (Surrey) | — | X | X |
| Woodchurch (Kent) | — | X | — |
| Worthy Down (Hants) | X[3] | X | — |
| Wye (Kent) | X | — | — |

Notes:
(1) Post-1950 has been chosen because many airfields were not abandoned until 1946–47 and most sites not actually disposed of until the early 1950s. This refers to airfields operational during the Cold War period of the 1950s to 1970s.
(2) Hurn (Dorset) is included because it was in Hampshire prior to the county-boundary changes.
(3) Worthy Down is listed as 'WWI' because of the airfield's significant inter-war use.

# Notes on Using the Series

## Unit Tables

There was much debate on how to present the unit tables, with some preferring a numerical list and others a chronological list. The 'solution' that has been adopted is as follows: unit tables are presented in four chronological divisions – Pre-1919 (World War One), 1919–1939 (Inter-War), 1939–45 (World War Two) and Post-1945. This is not always ideal but it does show major utilization of a given airfield by period. Where a unit is appropriate to more than one period it appears in each, although where the overlap is a matter of months the periods might overlap with the entry; e.g. the following entry for Biggin Hill:

32 Sqn    Sep 1932–Jan 1940    Bulldog, Gauntlet, Hurricane

In this case the Squadron subsequently re-appeared at Biggin Hill and has a second entry in the 1939–1945 period.

During World War Two, and particularly at fighter and maritime bases, units moved around frequently and often were at an airfield for a matter of days or with brief periods of absence elsewhere. It would be impractical to list all these changes and so for some entries the following symbol appears alongside the entry '+'; this signifies 'not a continuous period', for example, 79 Squadron's entry for Biggin Hill:

79 Sqn    Mar 1940–10 May 1940; 21 May 1940–8 Sep 1940+

The Squadron spent time at Digby, Hawkinge, Sealand and Acklington during the period 21 May 1940–8 Sep 1940 and these dates are bracketed by its appearance at Biggin Hill.

Within these broad division squadrons are listed in numerical order and other units, listed after the squadrons, are in chronological order, as there is less likelihood that readers will scan these looking for a particular unit. All RAF units are listed first, followed by Fleet Air Arm and then USAAF/USAF.

Only the major types on establishment with a unit are listed and the reader will often see reference to 'various': this means that the unit had such a diverse fleet that it has not been practicable to list every type. This is particularly true of training units during World War One, although a glance at the records of a World War Two Spitfire squadron might well reveal a Tiger Moth, Magister or even Hurricane on strength as a 'hack' aircraft.

The region's ALGs saw a short but intense period of activity in summer 1944; pilots of 257 Squadron at Needs Oar Point.

# ANDOVER

**County:** Hampshire

**UTM/Grid:** OS map 185–SU328458
**Lat/Long:** N51°12.30 W001°31.30
**Nearest Town:** Andover 2½ miles to east

Aerial photo of Andover August 1918. (Aldon Ferguson).

## HISTORY

Located close to an extensive area of military ranges (Salisbury Plain) the airfield at Andover has, over the years, been home to a variety of operational and training units as one of the RAF's main bomber air-fields. The original 400-acre site just west of the town was acquired in early 1917 for a major airfield and, as such, work commenced on a series of seven General Service Belfast-truss hangars that for many years dominated the airfield. Andover opened in August 1917, although, like many airfields of this period, it was far from complete when it opened and tented accommodation, along with temporary Bessonneau hangars, was the order of the day whilst construction work continued. The first two units, 104 and 106 Squadron, arrived in September for work-up, being joined by 105 Squadron a few days later. All three used a variety of types but the main aircraft were

RE8s and DH9s. By early January 1918 two more squadrons had arrived and Andover was a very busy airfield, although this was fairly short-lived, as the bomber squadrons began to depart in March, some to active service in France and others to UK bases. By mid-May they had all gone, but in their place came two established bomber-units, 207 and 215 Squadron, both of which had returned from France to Netheravon in April to re-equip with Handley Page 0/400s and now moved to Andover for final work up; both departed back to the Front in early summer. However, by that time the airfield was home to a major training unit, No.2 School of (Aerial) Navigation and Bomb Dropping having formed here during June 1918 with a fleet of various de Havilland bombers plus a few HP 0/400s and assorted other types.

Aerial view of the Andover airfield display 23 June 1929. (Aldon Ferguson)

The end of the war brought a run-down of train- ing, but the school continued to operate on a reduced basis into 1919, becoming the School of Air Pilotage in September that year. However, on 1 April 1920 it was reduced to cadre status and was finally disbanded two years later. This was not the end of the airfield, for although, temporarily, there was no flying unit in residence it had been the HQ of No.7 Group since April 1920, this command organization being respon- sible for Army Co-operation squadrons, and during April 1922 the RAF Staff College had moved in. Flying returned the following year with the arrival, or rather the re-forming, of 11 Squadron and over the next few years a number of squadrons made use of Andover, the situation settling down by spring 1924 with two units, 12 and 13 Squadrons, in residence, although the latter was replaced a few years later by 101 Squadron. The airfield's command unit had changed from No.7 Group to Wessex Bombing Area and, as the RAF gradually re-organized and re- equipped during the early 1930s, the Air Pilotage School (Air Navigation School from January 1935) was reformed at Andover. Further changes of flying and command units took place over the next few years as this re-organization continued and at the

P-38s of the 402nd FS of the 370th FG.

outbreak of World War Two the airfield was in the hands of Fighter Command and was being used for No.22 Group's Army Co-operation role. The Blenheims departed for France as part of the Air Component of the Expeditionary Force and Andover returned to a training role when No.2 School of Army Co-operation formed in October 1939. The Staff College had also departed but, since July 1938, Andover had been home to the HQ of Maintenance Command and this connection, which included the

## AIRFIELD DATA DEC 1944

| | | | |
|---|---|---|---|
| Command: | Fighter Command | Runway surface: | Grass |
| Function: | Operational Training Unit | Hangars: | 5 × B.1, 4 × General Service, 7 Old Belfast |
| Runways: | NE/SW 1,000yd | Dispersals: | 4 × 100ft diameter frying pan |
| | SE/NW 900yd | Personnel: | Officers – 243 (18 WAAF) |
| | *N/S 830yd | | Other Ranks – 1,821 (264 WAAF) |

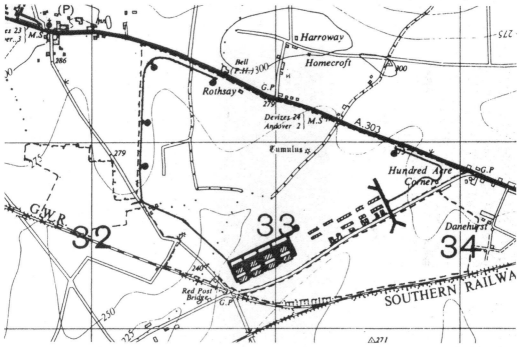

Austers were operated by a number of squadrons at Andover in the latter war years; this is not an Andover-based aircraft as it belonged to 657 Squadron.

Amongst the Army Co-operation types based at Andover during the 1920s was the AW Atlas, as used by 13 Squadron.

formation and initial basing of a number of Groups within the Command was to be an important and invariably unrecognized role of the station for many years.

Like so many RAF airfields in the south, Andover

was on the Luftwaffe target-list in August 1940 and was hit on 13 August by Ju88s from LG1, followed by a solo attack the next day. Not too much damage was caused, but three people were killed and a number of aircraft damaged. However, the most effective

The 370th Fighter Group's three squadrons spent four months operating from here in early 1944.

attacks took place in 1941 when Andover was attacked a number of times, one raid in April destroying two of the hangars. Nevertheless, the training task continued, albeit with a change of name in July 1941 to No.42 Operational Training Unit, this unit remaining in residence for a further year. Andover was also home to a number of AC squadrons during this period and the Fleet Air Arm's 'spotter wing', No.4 Naval Fighter Wing with Seafires, also spent some time here. This hectic period of RAF and naval activity came to an end in the latter weeks of 1943, as the flying units departed in readiness for the airfield's transfer to the United States Army Air Force.

Having spent a few days at Aldermaston, the 370th Fighter Group hopped its P-38s across to Andover on 29 February and continued their work-up under Colonel Howard F Nichols. The Group had trained on P-47s in the States but was issued with P-38s on arrival in England, eventually entering combat on 1 May and from then on flying intensively with the build-up of the air campaign towards D-Day. With the Allies ashore in Normandy the 370th departed for Cardonville at the end of July.

The departure of the Americans was swiftly followed by a return of the RAF, as Andover became home to the primarily Auster-equipped No.43 OTU. For the rest of the war, and indeed beyond, this was very much 'Auster country', as the OTU and a variety of squadrons made use of the somewhat bumpy grass of Andover. In the immediate post-war period the rate of training slowed and the OTU finally moved to Middle Wallop in January 1948, by which time it had become No.227 (AOP) Operational Conversion Unit.

This was not quite the end in terms of flying and Andover was used by a small number of communications types during the 1950s in support of the various Command units, such as Maintenance Command, and the newly returned RAF Staff College. In January 1960 it also became home to the Sycamores and Whirlwinds of 225 Squadron, albeit only for three years, whilst the final based flying-units were Western Communications Squadron, which subsequently became 21 Squadron. The squadron was eventually disbanded at the end of March 1976 and Andover was, to all intents and purposes, closed as an RAF Station. The following year it was taken over by the army as the HQ of the Army Logistic Executive.

In a recent development, part of the site, now referred to as Andover North, has been used for the construction of the new complex of buildings for the Defence Logistics Organization, whilst other parts of the site are scheduled for disposal and commercial development.

# DECOY SITES

| | | |
|---|---|---|
| Q | Hurstbourne | SU401536 |
| Q | Thruxton | SU280458 |

# UNITS

## HQ Units at Andover

| | |
|---|---|
| No.7 Gp | 1 Apr 1920–12 Apr 1926 |
| Wessex Area | 12 Apr 1926–1 May 1936 |
| No.3 Gp | 1 May 1936–Jan 1937 |
| No.2 Gp | Jan 1937–Apr 1938 |
| Maintenance Command | Jul 1938–? |
| No.40 Gp | 1 Jan 1939–Feb 1947 |
| No.42 Gp | Jan 1939–Sep 1939 |
| 71st FW | 1 Mar 1944–4 Jul 1944 |

## Pre-1919

| | | |
|---|---|---|
| 104 Sqn | 16 Sep 1917–19 May 1918 | DH9 |
| 105 Sqn | 3 Oct 1917–19 May 1918 | RE8 |
| 106 Sqn | 30 Sep 1917–30 May 1918 | RE8 |
| 116 Sqn | 1 Dec 1917–1 Apr 1918 | various |
| 119 Sqn | 1 Jan 1918–1 Mar 1918 | various |
| 148 Sqn | 10 Feb 1918–1 Mar 1918 | FE2b |
| 207 Sqn | 13 May 1918–7 Jun 1918 | HP 0/400 |
| 215 Sqn | 15 May 1918–4 Jul 1918 | HP 0/400 |
| SoN&BD | 23 Jun 1918–23 Sep 1919 | DH4, DH6, DH9, 0/400 |

## 1919–1938

| | | |
|---|---|---|
| 2 Sqn | 17 Sep 1923–31 Mar 1924 | F2b |
| 9 Sqn | 15 Oct 1935–15 Jan 1936 | Virginia |
| 11 Sqn | 13 Jan 1923–16 Sep 1923 | DH9a |
| 12 Sqn | 23 Mar 1924–4 Oct 1935; 29 Aug 1936–9 May 1939 | DH9a, Fawn, Fox, Hart, Hind, Battle |
| 13 Sqn | 30 Jun 1924–23 Sep 1929 | F2b, Atlas |
| 44 Sqn | 18 Mar 1937–16 Jun 1937 | Hind |
| 63 Sqn | 15 Feb 1937–3 Mar 1937 | Hind |
| 82 Sqn | 4 Jun 1937–6 Jul 1937 | Hind |
| 101 Sqn | 10 Oct 1929–1 Dec 1934 | Sidestrand |
| 103 Sqn | 10 Aug 1936–26 Feb 1937 | Hind |
| 107 Sqn | 10 Aug 1936–25 Feb 1937 | Hind |
| 142 Sqn | 3 Jan 1935–4 Oct 1935 | Hart |
| 214 Sqn | 15 Oct 1935–6 Oct 1936 | Virginia |
| SoAP/APS | 23 Sep 1919–15 Jan 1923 | various |
| APS | 5 May 1933–25 Jan 1935 | |
| ANS | 25 Jan 1935–6 Jan 1936 | Prefect |
| 11 Gp Pool | 14 Jan 1939–1 Jul 1939 | Hurricane, Battle |

## 1939–1945

| | | |
|---|---|---|
| 16 Sqn | 2 Jan 1943–1 Jun 1943 | Mustang, Tomahawk, Spitfire |
| 53 Sqn | 21 May 1940–1 Jun 1940 | Blenheim |
| 59 Sqn | 11 May 1939–12 Oct 1939; 21 May 1940–9 Jun 1940 | Blenheim |
| 169 Sqn | 21 Jan 1943–25 Mar 1943 | Mustang |
| 170 Sqn | 20 Oct 1942–28 Feb 1943; 13–25 Mar 1943 | Mustang |
| 285 Sqn | 19 Nov 1944–4 Jan 1945 | Hurricane |
| 289 Sqn | 5–26 Jun 1945 | Vengeance |
| 296 Sqn | 25 Oct 1942–19 Dec 1942 | Whitley |
| 613 Sqn | 26 Sep 1941–6 Oct 1941 | Lysander, Tomahawk |
| 660 Sqn | 21 Sep 1943–1 Nov 1943 | Auster |
| 661 Sqn | 27 Nov 1943–18 Feb 1944 | Auster |
| 664 Sqn | 9 Dec 1944–3 Feb 1945 | Auster |
| 665 Sqn | 22 Jan 1945–17 Mar 1945 | Auster |
| 666 Sqn | 5 Mar 1945–18 Apr 1945 | Auster |
| 2 SoAC | 20 Oct 1939–31 May 1941 | Blenheim, Lysander |
| 6 OTU | 1 Jun 1941–18 Jul 1941 | Blenheim |
| 42 OTU | 18 Jul 1941–Oct 1942 | Blenheim, Anson |
| 1526 Flt | Oct 1941–11 Nov 1941 | Anson, Blenheim |
| 15 (P)AFU | 15 Dec 1942–28 Oct 1943 | Oxford |
| 43 OTU | 10 Aug 1944–7 May 1947 | Auster |
| 227 OCU | 7 May 1947–30 Jan 1948 | Auster |
| HTF | 5 Feb 1945–16 Jan 1946 | Hoverfly |

## FAA Units

| | | |
|---|---|---|
| 808 Sqn | 20–30 Jul 1943 | Seafire |
| 809 Sqn | 13–28 Jul 1943; 12 Oct 1943–19 Dec 1943 | Seafire |
| 879 Sqn | 17 Jun 1943–8 Jul 1943; 7 Oct 1943–29 Nov 1943 | Seafire |

## USAAF Units
### 370th FG

| | |
|---|---|
| Squadrons: | 401st FBS, 402nd FBS, 485th FBS |
| Aircraft: | P-38 |
| Dates: | 29 Feb 1944–31 Jul 1944 |
| First mission: | 1 May 1944 |
| Last mission: | 4 May 1945 (from Frankfurt-am-Main) |

## Post-1945

| | | |
|---|---|---|
| 21 Sqn | 3 Feb 1969–31 Mar 1976 | Devon, Pembroke |
| 225 Sqn | 1 Jan 1960–23 May 1960 | Sycamore, Whirlwind |
| 657 Sqn | 26 Jan 1946–19 Jan 1948 | Auster |
| 1900 Flt | 1 Jan 1947–1 Dec 1948 | Auster |
| 1901 Flt | May 1947–1 Feb 1948 | Auster |
| 227 OCU | 7 May 1947–26 Jan 1948 | Auster |
| MRF | 18 Dec 1950–Dec 1952 | |
| 1913 Flt | 13 Feb 1957–1 Apr 1957 | Auster |
| WCS | 1 Apr 1964–3 Feb 1969 | Anson, Pembroke, Devon |

# APPLEDRAM

**UTM/Grid:** OS map 197–SU839018
**Lat/Long:** N50°48.38 W000°48.45
**Nearest Town:** Chichester 2½ miles to north-east

**County:** West Sussex

## HISTORY

Having been surveyed in June 1942 for ALG use, this area of farmland was requisitioned in December and an RAF Airfield Construction Unit arrived on site in February. Construction work, which largely comprised removal of hedges and other obstructions and the laying of two tracked-runways in the shape of a cross – the standard arrangement for these ALGS – was completed within a matter of weeks. Appledram was one of the first batch of airfields constructed in this way and opened on 2 June 1943. The Sommerfeld Track runways were soon in use by the Typhoons of No.124 Airfield, whose three squadrons moved in from Lasham. However, for both airfield and squadrons this was very much an exercise in mobile tactical air-operations.

All personnel lived in tents and aircraft were simply dispersed around the airfield in squadron grouping, hardened dispersals not being required for summer operation. The Typhoons flew their first missions from here on 12 June and over the next two weeks the airfield proved itself capable of supporting operations by this type of aircraft – the Typhoon (and its pilots) likewise presented no problems. All sides being satisfied the squadrons moved out at the beginning of July and Appledram was reduced to Care and Maintenance to await its role in the invasion of Europe.

It was not until April 1944 that the next squadrons arrived, No.134 Airfield arriving with its three Spitfire squadrons. In the intervening period the airfield had undergone some development, including additional hangars of the Extra-Over Blister type plus a number of dispersals, the latter using metal tracking. The Wing settled-in to its tented accommodation and the squadrons, having arrived from Mendlesham, continued their routine of fighter

# AIRFIELD DATA DEC 1944

| | | | |
|---|---|---|---|
| Command: | Fighter Command | Runway surface: | Sommerfeld Track |
| Function: | Advanced Landing Ground | Hangars: | 4 × Extra Over Blister |
| Runways: | 051 deg 1,600yd | Dispersals: | Hardstands of temporary Sommerfield Track |
| | 143 deg 1,400yd | | |
| | 270 deg 2,000 × 50yd | Personnel: | Other Ranks – Tented camp |

sweeps and escort as the pre-invasion air campaign intensified. The Czechs were airborne from Appledram on D-Day, as part of the massive fighter umbrella protecting the invasion area. Like all fighter squadrons on this day, they admired the mass of shipping over which they patrolled but saw no action, as the Luftwaffe flew very few sorties on 6 June 1944. Fighter patrols and ground strafing became the routine for the Spitfires in the weeks following the invasion but on 22 June the Wing was transferred to Tangmere for anti-V-1 patrols.

The final occupants of Appledram were the Poles of No. 131 Wing, who brought three squadrons of Spitfire IXs in from Chailey on 28 June. There was no break in the intensity of operations, as all Allied tactical aircraft were thrown into the battle during these critical weeks. However, on 16 July the Wing departed for Ford and this stretch of Sussex countryside was no longer required. The airfield was derequisitioned in November and before long little was left on site, the last major feature – the runway tracking – being lifted in January for possible future use on the Continent.

Appledram had seen more use than many of the ALGs but, even so, there is now virtually no trace of the part these fields once played in the great air campaign of sixty years ago. With careful observation and a good map you can still work out the lines of the airfield, as not all ditches and hedges have yet returned to their 1944 appearance.

| | | |
|---|---|---|
| 302 Sqn | 28 Jun 1944–16 Jul 1944 | Spitfire |
| 308 Sqn | 28 Jun 1944–16 Jul 1944 | Spitfire |
| 317 Sqn | 28 Jun 1944–16 Jul 1944 | Spitfire |
| 310 Sqn | 3 Apr 1944–22 Jun 1944 | Spitfire |
| 312 Sqn | 4 Apr 1944–22 Jun 1944 | Spitfire |
| 313 Sqn | 4 Apr 1944–22 Jun 1944 | Spitfire |

## MEMORIALS

Rose garden at Museum of D-Day Aviation, Shoreham; the museum is no longer open (2004) but it is believed that the rose garden is still accessible.

Appledram's Spitfire Wing was part of the massive Allied air armada assembled for D-Day; this is not an Appledram aircraft.

## UNITS

### HQ Units at Appledram

| | | |
|---|---|---|
| No.124 Airfield | 2 Jun 1943–2 Jul 1943 | 175, 181, 182 Sqn |
| No.131 (Polish) (F) Wing | 28 Jun 1944–16 Jul 1944 | 302, 308, 317 Sqn |
| No.134 Airfield/ (Czech) (F) Wing | 3 Apr 1944–22 Jun 1944 | 310, 312, 313 Sqn |

### 1939–1945

| | | |
|---|---|---|
| 175 Sqn | 2 Jun 1943–1 Jul 1943 | Typhoon |
| 181 Sqn | 2 Jun 1943–2 Jul 1943 | Typhoon |
| 182 Sqn | 2 Jun 1943–2 Jul 1943 | Typhoon |

Typhoon of 182 Squadron following a landing incident at the ALG; the Squadron was part of No.124 Airfield when this organisation made a brief stay at Appledram in summer 1943. (Peter Green)

# ASHFORD (Great Chart)

**County:** Kent

UTM/Grid: OS map 189–TQ972402
**Lat/Long:** N51°07.15 E000°49.00
**Nearest Town:** Ashford 2½ miles to north-east

## HISTORY

One of a number of Advanced Landing Grounds constructed in the Ashford area, this airfield, also known locally as Great Chart, was the only wartime site to carry the name of the town. An area of farmland to the south-west of the town was requisitioned in January 1943, the site having been approved the previous autumn. Construction was rapid and involved the usual removing of hedges and filling-in of ditches, along with some other minor grading work. Two Sommerfeld Track runways were laid in a 'V' shape, mirroring two local roads, but at this stage little else was provided, although some buildings at Chilmington Farm were identified as suitable for

storage. With construction complete in early spring, the airfield was left virtually unmanned until August, when the two Mustang squadrons of No.129 Airfield arrived from Gatwick. These squadrons continued to operate as part of the Canadian Reconnaissance Wing and there seemed to be few problems operating from Ashford. A test runway using impregnated Hessian was laid by Canadian engineers as part of on-going trials in airfield construction techniques; whilst this type of surface was recorded as unsatisfactory, it later proved to be one of the best options in France.

The Mustangs departed in the first week of October and their place was taken by two Spitfire

# AIRFIELD DATA DEC 1944

| | | | |
|---|---|---|---|
| Command: | RAF Fighter | Runway surface: | Sommerfeld and steel-planking |
| Function: | Advanced Landing Ground | Hangars: | Nil |
| Runways: | 150 deg 1,600yd | Dispersals: | 50 × Loop |
| | 040 deg 1,250yd | Personnel: | Other Ranks – Tented camp |

squadrons from Kingsnorth. Both squadrons continued their operational flying over France and their ten-day stay at Ashford would have been unremarkable except for the fact that two Spitfires were stolen by Canadian pilots on an escape-and-evasion exercise!

The departure of the RAF units freed the airfield to become one of the ALGs allocated to the USAAF's IXth Air Force for fighter-bomber operations. During the winter the airfield was improved, being given a longer – and stronger – runway with steel-planking areas being added to the Sommerfeld Track, plus additional tracked-taxiway and seventy 'hardstands' (mesh). On 8 March 1944 the HQ element of the 303rd Fighter Wing moved in to Ashford, being joined a month later by the Thunderbolt-equipped 406th Fighter-Bomber Group. The three squadrons were declared operational in early May and were soon involved in the fighter-bomber campaign to prepare the Normandy battlefield. The intention was that the IXth Air Force's units would move to France as soon as airfields were available and, whilst the first units were on the move by late-June, it was not until August that the 406th FG finally left Ashford, although they had been using strips in France since July.

The site of the airfield was derequisitioned in autumn 1944 but was still on the RAF books for December 1944 and allocated to Fighter Command. However, by early 1945 the airfield had been dismantled and, although used as storage area by No.42 Group for a short period, it was soon returned to agriculture.

As with most of these ALG sites there is now little to see at Ashford.

## UNITS

### HQ Units at Ashford

303rd FW    8 Mar 1944–31 Jul 1944

### 1939–1945

| | | |
|---|---|---|
| 65 Sqn | 5–15 Oct 1943 | Spitfire |
| 122 Sqn | 5–15 Oct 1943 | Spitfire |
| 414 Sqn | 13 Aug 1943–5 Oct 1943 | Mustang |
| 430 Sqn | 13 Aug 1943–5 Oct 1943 | Mustang |

### USAAF Units
#### 406th FG

| | |
|---|---|
| Squadrons: | 512th FS, 513th FS, 514th FS |
| Aircraft: | P-47 |
| Dates: | 4 Apr 1944–5 Aug 1944 |

Bombing-up a P-47 of the 406th Fighter Group.

May 1944 with one of the ALG's tented area under camouflage.

# BEAULIEU (Station 408)

**County:** Hampshire

**UTM/Grid:** OS map 196–SU350005
**Lat/Long:** N50°48.15 W001°30.15
**Nearest Town:** Southampton 8 miles to north-east

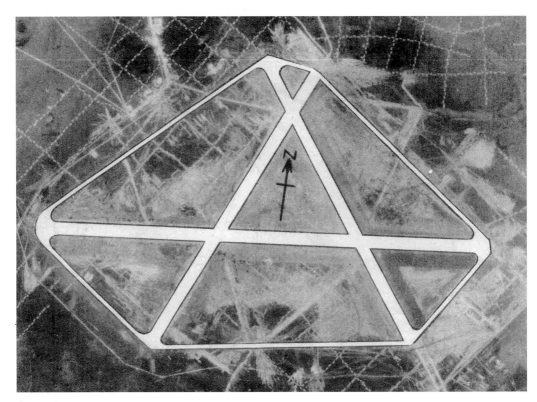

## HISTORY

Flying came early to this part of Hampshire when a small strip was laid out at East Boldre in 1910, although it saw very little use until taken over by the Royal Flying Corps in 1915. Beaulieu housed a variety of units during World War One and was primarily used as a training base, No.16 Training Squadron being formed here in December 1915 and operating a diverse collection of aircraft types. The final units left in late-1919 and, as there was no further use for Beaulieu, the airfield was closed. This site at East Boldre saw some private use in the 1930s but the centre of interest shifted to Hatchet Moor for the RAF's next wartime airfield in the Beaulieu area.

The new airfield was originally intended as a satellite for Thorney Island, some ten miles to the east, and was constructed with three runways and facilities to accommodate two General Reconnaissance squadrons, the initial work being advanced enough for the airfield to open on 8 August 1942. The first opera-

tional unit, 224 Squadron, equipped with Liberators, moved in from Tiree in September to join in Coastal Command's major U-boat offensive over the Bay of Biscay. Operational strength was increased in October with the arrival of Halifax units and Beaulieu was a very busy airfield. Although the number of aircraft fluctuated over the next few months, by spring 1943 the airfield had adopted a training role in addition to its operational commitments, with the arrival of a detachment of No.1 (Coastal) Operational Training Unit to undertake Liberator conversion training. One of the first tasks was to convert the Czechs of 311 Squadron, this unit subsequently taking on the operational mantle from Beaulieu. By this time the airfield infrastructure was well established with a comprehensive array of buildings.

The maritime squadrons departed in early 1944 and were replaced by fighter-bombers in the shape of the Typhoon; two squadrons – 257 and 263 – arrived

# AIRFIELD DATA DEC 1944

| | | | |
|---|---|---|---|
| Command: | Fighter Command | Runway surface: | Tarmac |
| Function: | Forward Airfield, Middle Wallop Sector | Hangars: | 2 × T.2, 1 × B.1 |
| Runways: | 088 deg 1,970 × 50yd | Dispersals: | 50 × 122ft diameter, concrete |
| | 027 deg 1,370 × 50yd | Personnel: | Officers – 191 (10 WAAF) |
| | 151 deg 1,370 × 50yd | Personnel: | Other Ranks – 1,524 (328 WAAF) |

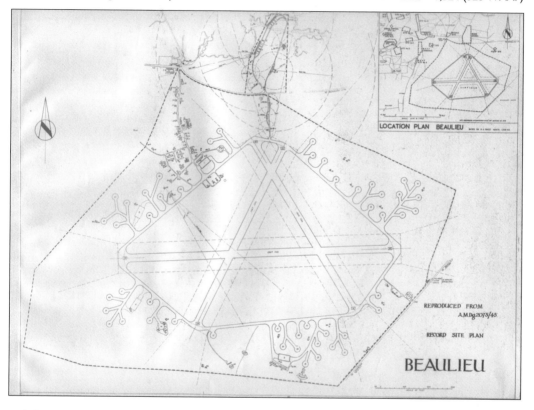

and flew their first operation from Beaulieu on 22 January. The 'Tiffies' flew a range of sorties over France as part of the pre-D-Day campaign, but by March they had all departed in order to leave the airfield for its next occupants.

The Americans arrived in early March, when the P-47s of the 365th Fighter Group moved across from Gosfield, having become operational the previous month. Escort and fighter-bomber work kept the three squadrons busy, especially in the days before and after D-Day. However, on 28 June the Group moved across the Channel to Azeville and for a few weeks Beaulieu was almost deserted. This situation changed in mid-July when the Marauders of the 323rd Bomb Group arrived from Earls Colne; this was an experienced IXth Air Force bomb group and from the day it moved in it continued its attacks on targets

Dolphin C3816 of No.1 Training Squadron at Beaulieu in 1918.

in and around Normandy. It was, however, a short-lived occupation and the Marauders departed for France on 26 August.

The airfield fell quiet for a few months and was not destined to undertake any more operational flying, although it was not the end of flying from Beaulieu; indeed, the next residents were in many respects just as interesting and vital as those that had gone before. The Airborne Forces Experimental Establishment (AFEE) moved in from Sherburn-in-Elmett in December, with its diverse array of aircraft types and vital role of trial and evaluation of aircraft and equipment. Gliders, glider-tugs, helicopters and all manner of other equipment was put through its paces; this work didn't cease when the war ended and the AFEE, although reduced in size, was kept busy with tasks, which included evaluations of German equipment.

The Establishment remained in residence to September 1950, when it was amalgamated with, and moved to join, the A&AEE at Boscombe Down. Beaulieu was reduced to Care and Maintenance and three years later was assigned to the Americans as a reserve airfield. They made very little use of Beaulieu and just over two years later it was handed back to the RAF, who duly shut it for the last time in November 1959. There is now little trace of the airfield's buildings and most of the area is now under the control of the Forestry Commission; however, an aerial view of the airfield shows the outline of runways and taxiways.

## UNITS

### HQ Units at Beaulieu

| | | |
|---|---|---|
| No.17 Wing | 2 Aug 1917–12 Aug 1918 | |
| No.146 Airfield | Feb 1944–10 Apr 1944 | 183, 197, 198, 257, 609 Sqn |
| 84th FW | 4 Mar 1944–19 Jun 1944 | |
| 98th CW | 18 Jul 1944–19 Aug 1944 | |

### Pre-1919

| | | |
|---|---|---|
| 79 Sqn | 8 Aug 1917–20 Feb 1918 | various |
| 84 Sqn | 7 Jan 1917–22 Mar 1917 | BE2c, BE12, BE12a |
| 103 Sqn | 1 Sep 1917–8 Sep 1917 | various |
| 16 TS | 15 Dec 1915–1 Jun 1917 | various |
| 1 TS | 16 Dec 1917–27 Jul 1918 | Avro 504, Camel, Dolphin |
| 70 TS | 1 Jan 1918–27 Jul 1918 | various |
| 81 TS | Jan 1917–Feb 1917 | |
| 87 TS | Feb 1917–? 1917 | |
| 29 TDS | 27 Jul 1918–28 Mar 1919 | Avro 504, Camel, Dolphin |
| 11 TDS | Apr 1919–Jul 1919 | various |

P-47s spent most of the period either side of D-Day on fighter-bomber work, for which a variety of weapons were employed. The three squadrons of the 365th FG operated from Beaulieu from March to June 1944. This is probably not a 365th FG aircraft. (US National Archives)

| | | |
|---|---|---|
| W/T school | May 1919–1 Sep 1919 | |

### 1939–1945

| | | |
|---|---|---|
| 53 Sqn | 25 Sep 1943–3 Jan 1944 | Liberator |
| 158 Sqn det | Oct 1942–Nov 1942 | Halifax |
| 224 Sqn | 9 Sep 1942–25 Apr 1943 | Liberator |
| 257 Sqn | 20–31 Jan 1944 | Typhoon |
| 263 Sqn | 10 Jan 1944–6 Mar 1944 | Typhoon |
| 311 Sqn | 26 May 1943–23 Feb 1944 | Wellington |
| 405 Sqn | 25 Oct 1942–3 Mar 1943 | Halifax |
| 486 Sqn | 31 Jan 1944–28 Feb 1944 | Tempest |
| 1 (C) OTU det | 24 Mar 1943–6 Sep 1943 | Liberator |
| AFEE | 4 Jan 1945–19 Sep 1950 | various |

### USAAF Units

**323rd BG**

| | |
|---|---|
| Squadrons: | 453rd BS, 454th BS, 455th BS, 456th BS |
| Aircraft: | B-26 |
| Dates: | 21 Jul 1944–26 Aug 1944 |
| First mission: | Jun 1943 (from Earls Colne) |
| Last mission: | Apr 1945 (from Denain) |

**365th FG**

| | |
|---|---|
| Squadrons: | 368th FS, 387th FS, 388th FS |
| Aircraft: | P-47 |
| Dates: | 5 Mar 1944–28 Jun 1944 |
| First mission: | Feb 1944 (from Gosfield) |
| Last mission: | Apr 1945 (from Fritzlar) |

### Post-1945

| | | |
|---|---|---|
| 1901 Flt | 1 Jan 1947–May 1947 | Auster |

## MEMORIALS

There is a memorial in Beaulieu Abbey but it commemorates the role of the Special Operations Executive and not the airfield.

# BEKESBOURNE

**County:** Kent

**UTM/Grid:** OS map 179–TR205553
**Lat/Long:** N51°51.3 E000°51.8
**Nearest Town:** Canterbury 4 miles to north-west

## HISTORY

Located close to Canterbury and intended to be part of an air screen for London, Bekesbourne, named after the local village, was in use from 1916 as an emergency landing ground for the Royal Flying Corps. The first based unit was 'B Flight' of 50 Squadron, this Squadron being the main Home Defence unit in the area and operating a diverse fleet of aircraft from a number of landing grounds in the

Canterbury area. As usual with these landing grounds, Bekesbourne was little more than a field, in this case a sloping area of around ninety-eight acres, with few other facilities. Fighter strength was boosted in June 1917 with the arrival of 56 Squadron and its SE5a fighters from France; this short-lived deployment, mirrored in other areas, was in response to the failure of the Home Defence squadrons to counter

The long-term occupant of Bekesbourne during World War One was 50 Squadron, who operated a number of types from here, including the SE5a.

'The Nest'; 50 Squadron's hangar.

the German daylight-bombers. However, there was no improvement, in part due to good German intelligence that kept the bombers away from the enhanced defences, and, in July, 56 Squadron returned to France having achieved nothing.

In February 1918 the rest of 50 Squadron moved to Bekesbourne and completed re-equipment with Camels, it finally having been realized that the antiquated types operated by the HD units had no chance of intercepting the bombers. Additional facilities had been built at the airfield, including Belfast Truss hangars – one of which was named 'the nest' by 50 Squadron – and hutted accommodation to replace tents. The Squadron exchanged the Camel for the SE5a in November but for a number of months had

little to do. With the Armistice, the run-down of the RAF was rapid and, after a hectic social round in the immediate post-war period, 50 Squadron disbanded in June 1919. The airfield site was abandoned the following year, but was brought back into use as Canterbury Aerodrome for civil aviation in the 1920s, being home to the Kent Flying Club. The airfield was closed when war broke out in 1939, but it saw limited emergency use the following year. Two Lysander squadrons made temporary use of the airfield in May–June 1940 as a rear base whilst they operated over France. However, with the fall of France, the airfield was no longer required and was obstructed against enemy airborne-assault. Despite its limited military occupation there are still significant traces of Bekesbourne's former use, a number of buildings having survived.

## Units

### Pre-1919

| | | |
|---|---|---|
| 50 Sqn | Oct 1916–Jun 1919 | BE12b, SE5a, Camel |
| 56 Sqn | Jun 1917–Jul 1917 | SE5a |

### 1939–1945

| | | |
|---|---|---|
| 2 Sqn | May 1940–June 1940 | Lysander |
| 13 Sqn | 29–30 May 1940 | Lysander |

# BIGGIN HILL

**County:** Kent

**UTM/Grid:** OS map 177–TQ415605
**Lat/Long:** N51°19.30 E000°02.00
**Nearest Town:** Biggin Hill 2 miles to South

Aerial shot of the hangar and technical buildings in the corner of the airfield.

## HISTORY

One of the most famous of all RAF airfields, Biggin Hill first opened on 14 February 1917 and played a part in the defence of the London area during the latter stages of World War One. An 80-acre site on the plateau of the North Downs was set out as a simple grass airfield with a number of huts for its first unit, the Wireless Testing Park (or Test Flight) that had actually arrived in January from Joyce Green. It had been realized that a means of communication between the air and ground – other than signals or message drops – would be essential and the work of the Test Flight, which in December became the Wireless Experimental Establishment, paved the way in such developments. For this task it used a variety of aircraft; indeed, its diverse fleet at one stage comprised no less than twenty types. This unit was to continue its role into the post-war period and, for a few months in early 1918, the airfield also housed the Wireless Telegraphy School. However, Biggin's location and the threat of German air attack on London

meant that from late-1917 the airfield also played a role in Home Defence, with a detachment provided by 78 Squadron, followed in February 1918 by the move of 141 Squadron from Rochford to become Biggin's resident fighter-unit, a role they retained into the immediate post-war period.

Biggin Hill survived into the post-war period as a fighter station but, during the early part of the 1920s, it was fairly quiet and it was not until May 1923 and the arrival of 56 Squadron that a full-strength fighter-unit was present. The airfield was also used during this period by a number of specialist units, such as the Instrument Design Establishment and the Night Flying Flight. However, by the late-1920s, the airfield was virtually deserted and the opportunity was taken for a major rebuild. This proved to be a three-year construction programme of hangars and other facilities and it was not until 1932 that the airfield received its next resident squadrons. It was now scheduled as a two-squadron station and, as such, in

## Airfield Data Dec 1944

| | | | |
|---|---|---|---|
| Command: | RAF Fighter Command | Runway surface: | Concrete and asphalt |
| Function: | Sector Airfield | Hangars: | 12 × Blister, 2 × Bessonneau, 1 × F |
| Runways: | 215 deg 1,600yd | Dispersals: | 19 × SE hardstands, 12 × SE protected pens |
| | 235 deg 950yd | Personnel: | Officers – 176 (14 WAAF) |
| | 295 deg 950yd | | Other Ranks – 2,968 (737) |

September 1932 received 23 and 32 Squadrons from Kenley. Biggin was now a well-established airfield with good facilities and for the rest of the decade it remained home to two squadrons as well as a number of specialist flights. The RAF's great Expansion Period construction programme did not pass Biggin by and later, in the 1930s, it was given additional buildings, including married quarters and barracks, followed in autumn 1939 by a tarmac runway of 4,800ft.

At the outbreak of war, Biggin Hill – 'Biggin on the Bump' as it came to be known – was still home to two squadrons of fighters, although for much of the war it was to have a complement of three squadrons. The fighters were in action from late-1939 on convoy patrols, but with one or two exceptions it was a quiet period and it was not until early summer 1940 and

the evacuation of Dunkirk that fighter activity increased. The airfield had been camouflaged as early as autumn 1938, following the Munich Crisis, and like all 'front-line' airfields it had sprouted air-raid shelters, sandbagged buildings, additional aircraft revetments and various other methods of bringing it to operational readiness. The test finally came later, in summer 1940, when Biggin Hill became one of the key stations in the Battle of Britain. By the height of the Battle this was primarily a Spitfire base and a large number of squadrons rotated through the Kent airfield over the next few months. During the Battle, the station's squadrons were often hard-pressed, being repeatedly scrambled to intercept incoming air raids, many of which singled out the airfield for attack. Biggin Hill was heavily damaged in raids during August and September 1940, the first such

BE2e of the Wireless Experimental Establishment (WEE).

Hurricanes of 79 Squadron spent a number of periods at Biggin in 1940.

Spitfire P8342 of the Polish 306 Squadron at Biggin Hill in 1941.

Pilots of 610 Squadron during a break in the Battle of Britain.

significant attack taking place on 18 August, although the series of raids between 30 August and 1 September were more effective in terms of damage, and the airfield was left in very poor state. However, like most Fighter Command stations, Biggin continued to operate, albeit at reduced capacity. Once the Luftwaffe turned its attention towards London and switched to a night offensive, the heat was taken off the airfields and work to repair Biggin Hill was able to get underway. Rotation of squadrons continued to be the routine for the station and, by mid-1941, the emphasis was very much on offensive operations and bomber escort.

For the remainder of the war, many RAF fighter squadrons made Biggin Hill their home, as did Canadian and New Zealand squadrons, most operating the Wing principle and usually comprising three squadrons. Spitfires remained the 'fighter of choice' for Biggin's squadrons, with Mark IXs soon dominating the flight line. By May 1943, the station had notched up its 1,000th confirmed victory – an incredible achievement – and the score board was not yet closed. In the lead up to D-Day the squadrons were heavily involved with escort and fighter-bomber work but, in early June, the start of the V-1 campaign brought a change of role for the airfield when it was taken over by Balloon Command to become part of the London inner barrage-balloon belt, which essentially prevented flying. This phase ended in September; the balloons left and the fighters returned. Transport Command was also now using the airfield for flights to liberated parts of Europe.

The December 1944 survey on extensibility suggested that each of the existing runways, Biggin by this time having three surfaced runways, could be extended but that a proposed fourth runway 'would entail considerable expense'. The survey also showed that Biggin Hill had a particularly high percentage of WAAF personnel; by late-1944 over one-third of 'other ranks' were female.

The transport role increased and the fighter role decreased: to reflect this, the airfield was transferred to Transport Command in June 1945, becoming home to a number of Dakota squadrons. Fighters were back the following year with the formation of two Royal Auxiliary Air Force squadrons: 600 (City of London) and 615 (County of Surrey), both equipped initially with Spitfires but later acquiring

340 Squadron was at Biggin for a few months from September 1942.

Wg Cdr Al Deere taxies in Spitfire EN568. (Andy Thomas)

## DECOY SITES

| | | |
|---|---|---|
| Q/K | Lullingstone | TQ526648 |

## UNITS

### HQ Units at Biggin Hill

| | | |
|---|---|---|
| No.5 Wing | 1 Apr 1923–1924 | |
| No.126 Airfield | 13 Oct 1943–14 Apr 1944 | 401, 411, 412 Sqn |
| No.141 (F) Wing | 18 Oct 1944–5 Nov 1944 | 91, 345, 410 Sqn |
| SE Sector | Nov 1945–1946 | |

### Pre-1919

| | | |
|---|---|---|
| 78 Sqn det | Sep 1917–Dec 1919 | various |
| 141 Sqn | 9 Feb 1918–1 Mar 1919 | BE12, Pup, BE2e, F2b |
| WTP | 1 Jan 1917–14 Dec 1917 | various |
| WEE | 14 Dec 1917–1 Nov 1919 | various |
| W/T School | 2–16 Apr 1918 | |

### 1919–1938

| | | |
|---|---|---|
| 23 Sqn | Sep 1932–Dec 1936 | Bulldog, Demon |
| 32 Sqn | Sep 1932–Jan 1940 | Bulldog, Gauntlet, Hurricane |
| 37 Sqn | Mar 1919–Jul 1919 | Snipe, Camel |
| 39 Sqn | Jul 1919–Apr 1920 | various |
| 56 Sqn | May 1923–Oct 1927 | Snipe, Grebe, Siskin |
| 79 Sqn | Mar 1937–Dec 1939 | |
| IDE | 1 Nov 1919–1922 | various |
| NFF | 1 Jul 1923–22 Oct 1931 | Vimy, F2b, Horsley |
| AACF | 22 Oct 1931–14 Apr 1936 | Horsley, Moth, Wallace |
| AACU | 14 Apr 1936–10 Feb 1937 | Wallace |

Meteors. Between August 1946 and November 1949 Biggin Hill was under the control of Reserve Command but on the latter date it returned to the Fighter Command fold. The auxiliaries operated at Biggin from May 1946, when 600 and 615 Squadrons re-formed here, receiving Spitfire F.XIVs in October. The squadrons operated a number of Spitfire variants before turning to jets, with Meteor F.4s and subsequently F.8s, from March 1950. Sadly, the mass disbandment of the Royal Auxiliary Air Force flying units on 10 March 1957 brought an end to these fine squadrons. The third unit of the Biggin Wing, 41 Squadron, disbanded the following January and fighter operations ceased, with all RAF flying from the airfield ending the following year. The RAF Officer and Aircrew Selection Centre (OASC) continued to use the domestic site (North Camp) for many years, but the main part of the airfield (South Camp) was leased for private and subsequently commercial aviation. The airfield site was eventually acquired by the London Borough of Bromley and, in due course, the RAF pulled out completely, with the final enclave, the OASC, moving to Cranwell in September 1992.

Today Biggin Hill Airport (EGKB) is very much an active airfield, with two hard-surface runways, the longest of which (03/21) is almost 1,700 yards, and extensive facilities. It is operated by Regional Airports Ltd and, like most airports in the London area, markets itself as a London regional airport. Much of the wartime structure remains, especially in the administrative and technical areas, although new buildings have sprung up in recent years. The last RAF element, the OASC and the area by the Chapel has (so far) changed little and plans are well advanced for a memorial museum.

| | | |
|---|---|---|
| 1 AACU | 10 Feb 1937–24 May 1937; 16 Sep 1937–11 Apr 1938 | various |

**1939–1945**

| | | |
|---|---|---|
| 1 Sqn | Feb 1943–Mar 1943 | Typhoon |
| 3 Sqn | May 1939–Sep 1939 | Hurricane |
| 19 Sqn | Jul 1942; 10–16 Sep 1946 | Spitfire |
| 32 Sqn | Mar 1940–Aug 1940 | Hurricane |
| 41 Sqn | May 1943 | Spitfire |
| 64 Sqn | Oct 1940 | Spitfire |
| 66 Sqn | Nov 1940–Feb 1941 | Spitfire |
| 72 Sqn | Aug 1940–Oct 1940; Jul 1941–Oct 1941; Mar 1942–Jun 1942 | Spitfire |
| 74 Sqn | Oct 1940–Feb 1941 | Spitfire |
| 79 Sqn | Mar 1940–10 May 1940; 21 May 1940–8 Sep 1940+ | |
| 91 Sqn | Oct 1944 | Spitfire |
| 92 Sqn | Sep 1940–Sep 1941 | Spitfire |
| 124 Sqn | Nov 1941–May 1942 | Spitfire |
| 133 Sqn | May 1942–Sep 1942 | Spitfire |
| 141 Sqn | Sep 1940 | Beaufighter |
| 154 Sqn | 5 Nov 1944–1 Mar 1945 | Spitfire, Mustang |
| 213 Sqn | Jun 1940 | Hurricane |
| 222 Sqn | Aug 1942 | Spitfire |
| 229 Sqn det | Oct 1939–Jun 1940 | Blenheim, Hurricane |
| 242 Sqn | May 1940–Jun 1940 | Spitfire |
| 264 Sqn | Jan 1941–Apr 1941 | Defiant |
| 287 Sqn det | Nov 1941–Jul 1944 | various |
| 322 Sqn | Nov 1944–Jan 1945 | Spitfire |
| 340 Sqn | Sep 1942–Mar 1943 | Spitfire |
| 341 Sqn | Mar 1943–Oct 1943 | Spitfire |
| 345 Sqn | Oct 1944–Nov 1944 | Spitfire |
| 401 Sqn | Oct 1941–Mar 1942; Aug 1942–Sep 1942; Oct 1943–Apr 1944 | Spitfire |
| 411 Sqn | Oct 1943–Apr 1944 | Spitfire |
| 412 Sqn | Oct 1943–Mar 1944 | Spitfire |
| 485 Sqn | Jul 1943–Oct 1943 | Spitfire |
| 601 Sqn | Sep 1939–Dec 1939 | Blenheim |
| 602 Sqn | Aug 1942 | Spitfire |
| 609 Sqn | Feb 1941–Jul 1941; Sep 1941–Nov 1941; Sep 1942–Nov 1942 | Spitfire, Typhoon |
| 610 Sqn | May 1940–Sep 1940 | Spitfire |
| 611 Sqn | Sep 1942–Jul 1943 | Spitfire |
| 1421 Flt | 6–11 Nov 1940 | Hurricane, Spitfire |

**Post-1945**

| | | |
|---|---|---|
| 436 Sqn det | Dec 1945–Apr 1946 | Dakota |
| 600 Sqn | 10 May 1946–10 Mar 1957 | Spitfire, Meteor |
| 615 Sqn | 10 May 1946–10 Mar 1957 | Spitfire, Meteor |
| London UAS | Oct 1946–15 Dec 1947; 1 Apr 1957–8 Feb 1959 | |
| 61 Gp CF | 1 Mar 1958–15 Jan 1959 | |
| BBF | 21 Feb 1958–28 Feb 1958 | |
| 1 AEF | 8 Sep 1958–7 Feb 1959 | Chipmunk |

## MEMORIALS

St George's Chapel is a memorial to both Biggin Hill and the Battle of Britain; it is one of the most evocative memorials of this period and, as such, should be high on the 'must visit' list. The Spitfire and Hurricane gate-guards are plastic, but that does not detract from the overall setting and atmosphere. If you do go then take advantage of the knowledge and enthusiasm of the guides or you will miss many of the fascinating features that they can point out.

The memorial museum is still in the planning stage.

The Chapel, along with its plastic 'gate guards' (Hurricane and Spitfire) is a fitting memorial to this historic RAF airfield.

# BISTERNE

**UTM/Grid:** OS map 195–SU155030
**Lat/Long:** N50°49.00 W001°46.45
**Nearest Town:** Ringwood 2 miles to north

**County:** Hampshire

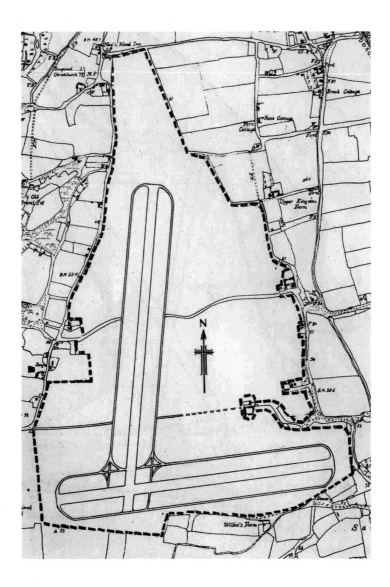

## HISTORY

Bisterne was completed as an Advanced Landing Ground in September 1943, the site having been chosen during the 1942 survey visit to this part of Hampshire. The land was reasonably flat and, with the closure of a couple of minor roads from the nearby village of Kingston and the usual ditch- and hedge-work, the airfield was provided with the standard two Sommerfeld Track runways. The runways were laid in a rough 'L'-shape and were given perimeter tracks, from which sprang the eighty dispersal points, also constructed of Sommerfeld Track. There was no immediate occupation of the site but, whilst animals continued to graze the fields, some construction work continued. By the time the

## AIRFIELD DATA DEC 1944

| | | | |
|---|---|---|---|
| Command: | RAF Fighter Command | Runway surface: | Sommerfeld Track |
| Function: | Advanced Landing Ground | Hangars: | 4 × Blister |
| Runways: | 020 deg 1,600yd | Dispersals: | 80 × Sommerfeld Track |
| | 080 deg | Personnel: | Other Ranks – Tented camp |

operational unit arrived, in spring 1944, the airfield was up to full ALG-standard and had four Blister hangars, although accommodation was still in tented camps.

The P-47s of the 371st Fighter Group moved in during early March, under the command of Colonel Bingham T Kleine. Bisterne was to be their main base in England, although they did have a spell at Ibsley in late-April when Bisterne's runways needed repair – most of the ALGs destined for use by P-47s had been give PSP reinforcement, but this does not appear to have been the case at Bisterne, hence the runway wear-and-tear problem. At some stage, an additional, larger hangar was erected on the west side of the airfield. The three squadrons of Thunderbolts commenced operations on 12 April 1944 and, over the next few months, were heavily engaged with both escort and fighter-bomber work, the latter dominating as D-Day approached. The 371st was one of the

first Groups to move to France, departing Bisterne on 17 June for Beuzeville. It was a few days before the final elements of the Group had gone but, with the American presence over, this airfield, which had on some days witnessed massed launches of up to fifty Thunderbolts, was no longer required. The runway mesh was taken up for possible re-use and hangars also vanished; by autumn the airfield had been officially de-requisitioned and was returned to farming.

## UNITS

### USAAF Units
**371st FBG**

| | |
|---|---|
| Squadrons: | 404th FBS, 405th FBS, 406th FBS |
| Aircraft: | P-47 |
| Dates | Mar 1944–Jun 1944 |
| First mission: | 12 Apr 1944 |
| Last mission: | May 1945? (from Frankfurt) |

A scene played out at many ALGs; a Thunderbolt being bombed-up – probably not at Bisterne, where the resident unit was the 371st FBG. (US National Archives)

# BOGNOR

**County:** West Sussex

**UTM/Grid:** OS map 197–SU915005
**Lat/Long:** N50°47.15 W00°42.30
**Nearest Town:** Bognor 2 miles to south-east

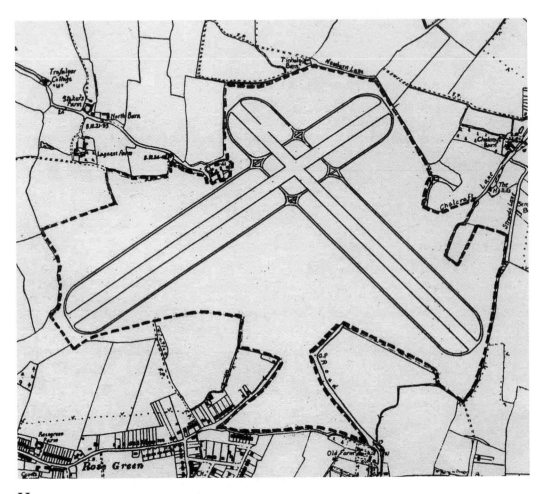

## HISTORY

After a survey undertaken in mid-1942, the site for Bognor Advanced Landing Ground was requisitioned in December and work commenced in early 1943. Situated on reasonably flat farmland to the north of Rose Green, construction was reasonably straightforward, other than the need to close a minor road from Lagness. Removal of hedges, filling of ditches and some other grading work provided a reasonable surface for the 'scissor-shaped' pair of runways, both of which were give Sommerfeld Track surfaces. Bognor was opened on 1 June 1943 and placed under the control of Tangmere (four miles to the north).

No.122 Airfield moved in immediately and its Spitfire squadrons conducted a mixture of ALG training and ground-attack training, whilst also flying a number of escorts and sweeps. This was a fairly typical routine for the squadrons operating from these ALGs, part of the aim being to give air and ground-crew experience in operating from airfields with few facilities. No significant problems were encountered and the three squadrons left in July. During the autumn the airfield was given various improvements, such as taxiways, hardstands and four Extra Over Blister (EOB) hangars, to prepare it for its

## Airfield Data Dec 1944

| | | | |
|---|---|---|---|
| Command: | RAF Fighter Command | Runway surface: | Sommerfeld Track |
| Function: | Advanced Landing Ground | Hangars: | 4 × Extra Over Blister |
| Runways: | 072 deg 1,600yd | Dispersals: | Temporary of Sommerfeld Track |
| | 151 deg 1,400yd | Personnel: | Other Ranks – Tented camp |

real operational use the following year. No.132 Airfield's Spitfire IXs duly arrived from North Weald in March 1944, as air assets were deployed to their forward locations. Whilst the Blister hangars provided cover for some of the aircraft, the majority of personnel had to manage with the tented camp that sprang up on the edge of the airfield, although a number of nearby buildings were also requisitioned. The Spitfire Wing stayed for three months, during which time it undertook escort, sweep and fighter-bomber operations. On D-Day its initial role was as part of the fighter umbrella but, before long, ground-attack had taken priority. The Wing moved to Tangmere on 22 June, but a few days later two new units arrived. No.83 Group Support Unit moved down from Redhill, bringing a large number of aircraft, primarily Spitfires, Mustangs and Typhoons, along with the reserve of pilots that would be used to 'top up' operational units in the Group. The second unit was the air-ambulance Ansons of No.1310 Flight, one of the virtually unknown units involved in the invasion of Europe but an important one, as it flew urgent medical supplies to the beachhead and returned with casualties. Both units stayed only a short while at Bognor and with the departure of the GSU in mid-

September there was no further need of this temporary airfield. By autumn, removal work was underway, as hangars and runway tracking were taken up for possible use elsewhere; however, the December 1944 survey still had Bognor on the books as an ALG with Fighter Command.

The site was handed back to its original owners in early 1945 and, like most such airfields, there is now little trace of Bognor ALG, although an experienced eye can still detect where it once was.

## Units

### HQ Units
### 1939–1945

| | | |
|---|---|---|
| 19 Sqn | 6 Jun 1943–2 Jul 1943 | Spitfire |
| 66 Sqn | 31 Mar 1944–22 Jun 1944+ | Spitfire |
| 122 Sqn | 1 Jun 1943–1 Jul 1943 | Spitfire |
| 331 Sqn | 31 Mar 1944–22 Jun 1944 | Spitfire |
| 332 Sqn | 31 Mar 1944–22 Jun 1944 | Spitfire |
| 602 Sqn | 1 Jun 1943–1 Jul 1943 | Spitfire |
| 1310 Flt | 25 Jun 1944–21 Jul 1944 | Anson |
| 83 Gp SU | 25 Jun 1944–25 Sep 1944 | Spitfire, Mustang, Typhoon |

A number of Spitfire squadrons used Bognor, initially for evaluation in 1943 and then as part of the D-Day air Order of Battle. This Spitfire XII is not a Bognor aircraft.

# BRENZETT (Ivychurch)

**County:** Kent

**UTM/Grid:** OS map 189–TR015280
**Lat/Long:** N51°01.00 E000°52.30
**Nearest Town:** New Romney 3 miles to south-east

## HISTORY

Laid out in the flat marshlands north of Dungeness, as were a number of other Advanced Landing Grounds, this site was selected during the summer 1942 survey and was requisitioned later in the year. Construction began in early 1943 and entailed the closing of minor roads to make room for the two Sommerfeld Track runways. The usual hedge removal and ditch filling, along with removal of other obstacles, presented few problems but, as with all these sudden appearances by construction parties, one wonders what the local population in this quiet part of Kent made of the whole thing. To the locals the airfield was known as Ivychurch, as it nestled closest to the small village of that name. Although the main accommodation for these temporary airfields was always intended to be tents, it was also standard practice to acquire suitable local barns and other buildings, if appropriate, and a number of

buildings were taken over on the east side of the airfield around Moat House.

The airfield was scheduled for completion by March 1943, but there is some confusion as to the date it was actually declared ready and, whilst it appears to have been used for 'tented camp' evaluation in spring 1943, it was not declared 'operational' until late-summer, by which time it had two Blister hangars (later increased to five). There was, apparently, no plan to test Brenzett's suitability by deploying a fighter Wing but, in August, the Spitfires of 122 Squadron used it as bolt-hole when their airfield at Kingsnorth, five miles to the north, needed some relief, although this appears to have lasted only a couple of days. Then, as with all of the ALGs, peace returned to the fields for a few months, although additional construction-work took place on the extra hangars and the provision of hardstands, in the

# AIRFIELD DATA DEC 1944

| Command: | RAF Fighter Command | Runway surface: | Sommerfeld Track |
|---|---|---|---|
| Function: | Advanced Landing Ground | Hangars: | 5 × Blister |
| Runways: | N/S 1,600yd | Dispersals: | 4 × Hardcore |
| | E/W 1,400yd | Personnel: | Other Ranks – Tented camp |
| | 270 deg 2,000 × 50yd | | |

case of Brenzett the latter comprised four hardcore-areas.

As D-Day approached no fighter Wing appeared at Brenzett; indeed, this clutch of airfields to the north of Dungeness – Brenzett, Lydd and New Romney – were not used for the invasion build-up. However, this phase of the war did not pass entirely without action and in early July the airfield became home to the three Mustang squadrons of No.133 Wing. They were not here to support the operations in Europe but had been sent to bolster the anti-V-1 defences; the Mustangs proved successful on these anti-*Diver* operations and the score of flying bombs soon mounted. Other offensive sorties were also flown but it was as part of the new air-defence network that Brenzett earned its laurels. The Mustangs eventually left in early October 1944 and there was no further need of this temporary airfield. Disposal was agreed in November but it still appears in the December 1944 survey as an ALG with Fighter Command. However, by early 1945, the clearance parties had done their job and no significant trace remained of the airfield.

There is now an excellent volunteer-run museum close to the old airfield site.

## UNITS

### HQ Units at Brenzett

| No.133 (Polish) | 9 Jul 1944–10 Oct 1944 | 129, 306, |
|---|---|---|
| (F) Wing | | 315 Sqn |

### 1939–1945

| 122 Sqn det | Aug 1943 | Spitfire |
|---|---|---|
| 129 Sqn | 8 Jul 1944–11 Oct 1944 | Mustang |
| 306 Sqn | 8 Jul 1944–10 Oct 1944 | Mustang |
| 315 Sqn | 10 Jul 1944–10 Oct 1944 | Mustang |

## MEMORIALS

Impressive brick memorial within the grounds of the Brenzett Aeronautical Museum, located on the edge of the ALG. Among the various plaques on the memorial is one inscribed: 'this memorial is dedicated to units of the Polish Air Force, RAF, RCAF, RNZAF and American 9th Air Force who served in Advanced Landing Grounds in Kent during 1943/44 and those who sacrificed their lives for our freedom. Their names liveth forever.'

Other plaques list the Kent ALGs and their units, whilst there is also a plaque to the Women's Land Army, appropriate as the museum is housed in a WLA building.

The Brenzett Aeronautical Museum is located on the edge of the old airfield site and includes a fine collection of memorabilia as well as an impressive memorial.

# BROOKLANDS
# (Weybridge)

County: Surrey

UTM/Grid: OS map176–TQ067620
Lat/Long: N51°21.05 W000°28.20
Nearest Town: South-west outskirts of Weybridge

## HISTORY

Now home to the excellent Brooklands museum, this is an airfield with a long history – stretching back to World War One – but with an equally rich heritage of motor racing, to which the site owed its origin. An almost 3-mile-long concrete race-track was opened in July 1907 on the land of The Honourable Hugh Locke-King, the same year that the first (unsuccessful) attempt at aviation was also made from Brooklands. The following year, A V Roe made a successful flight at Brooklands and, in many respects, this was the origin of British aviation. Despite a few months when aviation was effectively banished from the site, Roe and a number of other early pioneers soon established themselves and, by 1910, such great names as A V Roe, Martin and Handyside, and Shorts were in residence and Brooklands was very much in the aircraft-production business. A flying-training school was established in 1912 and it was in the training role that the airfield made its

contribution to the Royal Flying Corps in World War One – as well, of course, as supplying aircraft.

The flying field was the reasonably large and flat grass-area enclosed by the concrete race track, whilst around the perimeter the number of hangars (one 190 × 70ft and seven 170 × 70ft), sheds and buildings continued to increase, in a somewhat ad hoc fashion, to cater for the pupil pilots, a number of RFC squadrons that formed at Brooklands (none of which became resident squadrons) and the ever-increasing aircraft-production facilities, the latter being joined in 1915 by another of the great names – Sopwith. With this mixture the airfield must have been a fascinating and incredibly busy place by 1916; by the end of the war the various aircraft companies had produced over 4,600 aircraft at Brooklands and a large number of pilots had been trained. It was logical for an Aircraft Acceptance Park to be formed on-site to accept into service the aircraft being produced and

A frequent scenario at training establishments; a somewhat battered Shorthorn, July 1916.

Hawker Hardy under test in 1934.

Snipe B9966 at Brooklands 11 March 1918.

A sleek-looking Nautilus of 405 Flight. (Ray Sturtivant)

No.10 AAP duly formed here on 1 August 1917, to receive primarily the SE5a and Snipe, although a number of other types were also involved. This unit remained in residence until April 1920 when it was disbanded.

Brooklands survived the post-war debacle of British aviation, with Vickers turning its hand to civil types as the military market died and Hawker becoming the other major company at the site. It was private flying that was the saving grace of many manufacturers and, indeed, the whole ethos of flying in Britain and, in the late-1920s, clubs and small flying schools sprang up all over the country; by the early 1930s the Surrey airfield was home to the Brooklands Aero Club and the Brooklands School of Flying, joined the following year by the College of Aeronautical Engineering. The latter was ideally placed to take advantage of the expertise of Vickers and Hawker, both of whom continued to develop and flight-test new aircraft at Brooklands. When the RAF at last turned to expansion the two companies were ready to respond and one of the most significant

The Vickers works produced a number of military and civil types in the 1920s and 1930s; the Virginia was the RAF's standard heavy bomber in the late 1920s early 1930s.

events was the first flight on 15 June 1936 of the prototype Wellington. This twin-engined bomber became the mainstay of Bomber Command for the first three years of the war, as well as having a successful career with Coastal Command and as a training aircraft; the factory eventually built 2,515 of these aircraft in a number of variants. The previous October, Hawker's Kingston factory had delivered the prototype Hurricane to Brooklands and this had made its first flight on 6 November.

The factory complexes grew as production increased and, despite attempts to camouflage the site, it was well known to the Luftwaffe, although surprisingly only one significant attack was made on the airfield. This took place on 4 September and caused damage to the Vickers facilities and the death of eighty-three workers. Hawker decided to focus its production efforts at its other factories, leaving Vickers to continue to expand and in due course to take on a satellite field at Wisley in 1943. Wellingtons remained the major type under construction at the airfield, although a number of new designs, such as the Warwick, entered production and others, such as the four-engined Windsor bomber, had reached advanced stages of development.

The company acquired the airfield in 1948 and, despite a massive reduction in military orders, it continued to produce new designs for both the military and civil markets. In 1948 a long-desired concrete runway was laid across the centre of the site – not essential for the likes of the 1951 Viking but vital for types such as the BAC 1-11 and the VC-10. The latter aircraft was the last to be designed and built at Brooklands and the prototype first flew from here on 29 June 1962, by which time the constrained size and surroundings of the airfield had already made it somewhat unsuitable for modern aircraft. By the time the last of the fifty-four members of the VC-10 family had flown in February 1970, the decision had pretty much been taken to close the airfield. It is also worth noting that a great deal of work on the Concorde was carried out at Brooklands and, although the aircraft never flew from this airfield, the connection is a strong one – one of the museum's most recent acquisitions is an ex-British Airways Concorde.

Runway 01/19 remained in use for pre-booked visitors and was the scene of a number of air events, plus some live taxi-runs by museum aircraft. However, on 29 May 2004, Merchantman G-APEP made a taxi-run down the runway – the last ever aviation use of this 4,000ft concrete strip. It is not the end of flying, however, as a new 1,500ft grass strip is being built.

## DECOY SITES

| Q | Wisley | TQ075589 |

## UNITS

**Pre-1919**

| 1 Sqn | 1 May 1914–13 Nov 1914 | various |
| 8 Sqn | 1–6 Jan 1915 | BE2c |
| 9 Sqn | 1 Apr 1915–23 Jul 1915 | various |
| 10 Sqn | 8 Jan 1915–1 Apr 1915 | various |
| 46 Sqn | 19–20 Apr 1916 | various |
| 2 RS | 12 Nov 1914–31 Jan 1917 | various |
| W&O School | 24 Oct 1916–2 Oct 1917 | BE2, RE7 |
| Wireless School | Mar 1916–24 Oct 1916 | BE2, RE7 |
| Wireless TF/P | Oct 1916 | |

## MEMORIALS

1. The Brooklands Museum is a superb 'memorial' to the site's aviation and motor-racing heritage and, as far as the aviation side is concerned, has an excellent array of airframes and associated displays. Much of the focus is, not surprisingly, on Vickers products – from the amazing Loch Ness Wellington restoration to the Vickers Merchantman (www.brooklandsmuseum.com).

2. Brooklands memorial unveiled July 1957–bronze plaque with short history of the site.

3. Stone pillar and plaque inscribed:

A. V. ROE. From this area, on various dates in 1907–08, A. V. Roe made a series of towing flights and flight trials with an aircraft of his own design and construction, powered in the later trials by an 18/24HP Antoinette engine. These trials were made along the finishing straight of the motor-racing track on this site. A. V. Roe thus became the first of the long series of famous pioneers and pilots of many nations who made air history on this flying field of Brooklands. This tablet was placed here in June 1954 by Vickers-Armstrong Aircraft Division and was unveiled by Sir Alliott Verdon-Roe, then in his 78th year.

The most famous association of an aircraft type with Brooklands is the Wellington, some 2,515 of which were built in the factory.

# CALSHOT

**County:** Hampshire

**UTM/Grid:** OS map 196–SU480018
**Lat/Long:** N50°48.8 W001°19.2
**Nearest Town:** Southampton 6 miles to north-west

RAF Calsot under construction.

## HISTORY

Calshot Naval Air Station opened on 29 March 1913, under Lieutenant Spenser D Grey, as one of the first of the series of air stations established by the Admiralty. In addition to a coastal-defence function, Calshot's main role was as an experimental unit for all aspects of seaplane operations, including armament, for the RNAS and RFC. The station was provided with three aircraft-sheds, to hold up to twelve aircraft, along with a few other buildings and with accommodation in Coastguard cottages on the Spit and across the estuary at Warsash. In the few months before war broke out, Calshot, now under the command of one of the great RNAS airman, Squadron Commander A M Longmore, undertook numerous trials, including the first air-dropping of torpedoes. The tiny air-station was crammed with aircraft in mid-July 1918, as it was a concentration point for the Royal Review of the Fleet at Spithead – the 'massed' flypast involving seventeen machines from Calshot.

In addition to its trials role, Calshot was also involved in training seaplane-pilots and this continued into the war years, as did the experimental work.

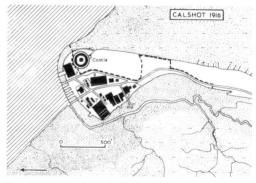

Plan of Calshot as it was in 1916.

The station was also called on to maintain coastal patrols for convoy protection and anti-submarine cover. By 1916, Calshot was operating two sub-stations at Bembridge and Portland, each of which was equipped with four seaplanes. The busy routine of Calshot and its sub-stations, which became the Portsmouth Group on 1 January 1917, continued

London of 201 Squadron; this unit spent 10 years at Calshot from 1929.

The Supermarine racer at Calshot in 1931, the year in which the RAF won the Schneider Trophy outright.

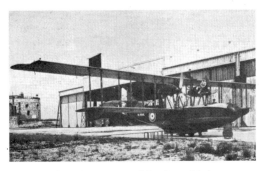

Felixstowe flying boat on one of the clips, with the distinctive feature of Calshot Castle in the background.

and, during the year, some 3,500 hours were flown on such patrols, albeit with only one submarine sunk (UB32 on 18 August) – and that by an aircraft operating from Cherbourg. This station, along with Newhaven and Polegate had joined the Portsmouth Group in early summer 1917.

The formation of the RAF on 1 April 1918 saw Portsmouth Group become No.10 Group, whose headquarters remained at Calshot. The RAF's re-organization of the RNAS assets saw the organization at Calshot become two flying-boat flights, Nos.345 and 346 Flights, and No.410 Flight with seaplanes; all three subsequently became part of 240 Squadron. Anti-submarine patrols remained the main role for the rest of the war, with thousands of hours being flown and a number of attacks being made.

In the post-war period, Calshot became the School of Naval Co-operation and Aerial Navigation, with its main role being the training of aircrew for flying boats and other maritime aircraft. This basic role was retained throughout the 1920s, with a variety of

name changes, and the station also became the centre for RAF Marine Craft development and training.

Perhaps the best known activity at Calshot was its involvement in the Schneider Trophy Races, the RAF's High Speed Flight spending a two-month period here in 1927 to prepare for the race. This was the first of a number of detachments by the Flight for Schneider work, culminating in the final victory of September 1931, and Air Speed Record attempts. Calshot was busy throughout the 1920s and 1930s and virtually every type of seaplane or flying boat in RAF service was here at one time or another; by the early 1930s the main training unit was split into three flights: 'A Flight' for floatplane training, 'B Flight' for flying boats and 'C Flight' to provide advanced night- and navigation-training. In March 1937 the latter Flight was used as the nucleus of 240 Squadron. The following year Calshot, like every other RAF station, was improving its defences, as war seemed increasingly likely; airfield-defence sites were built, subsequently boosted by balloons and anti-aircraft guns, and the Spit was finally bought from its owners, which meant that the bathing huts could be cleared away and civilians kept at a distance.

August 1939 saw the departure of the two operational squadrons to their war stations in Scotland and Calshot increased its intake of trainees. However, most of these trainees were not aircrew but were for marine craft. The station had also taken on an important role as a flying-boat maintenance and modification centre. Increased numbers meant more accommodation was needed and parts of Eaglehurst camp were used for huts. The move of the Marine Training School to Galloway in May 1942 brought most training to an end, but the maintenance and repair of marine craft continued to increase, as did the work on flying boats. A number of Air Sea Rescue units formed at Calshot during the war.

Lerwick of 209 Squadron, July 1939; the Squadron was never based at Calshot but aircraft were modified here.

Calshot 26 April 1932.

The two main roles continued into the immediate post-war period and flying returned when 201 and 230 Squadrons flew in. Training of aircrew also returned. No.235 (Flying Boat) OCU formed at Calshot in July 1947 from No.4 OTU, with an establishment of five Sunderland GR.5s. When it disbanded, in October 1953, aircraft and personnel went to Pembroke Dock to form a Flying Boat Training Squadron for the final days of the RAF's involvement with flying boats and Calshot also entered its final phase. The two operational squadrons had departed in early 1949, shortly after their return from intensive involvement in the Berlin Airlift; both squadrons moved to Pembroke Dock, destined to be the RAF's last operational flying-boat base. The OCU, along with a small detachment of the Air-Sea Warfare Development Unit, departed late-1953, when Calshot was transferred to Maintenance Command. As home to No.238 Maintenance Unit the task of marine-craft repair and maintenance continued for almost another ten years – but on 1 April 1961 the history of the airfield came to an end.

## UNITS

### HQ Units at Calshot

No.10 Gp      1 Apr 1918–Jun 1918
No.74 Wing   8 Aug 1918–15 May 1919

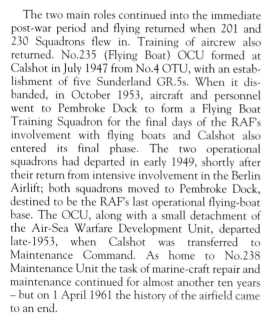

### Pre-1919

| | | |
|---|---|---|
| 345 Flt | May 1918–May 1919 | H12/12B, F.2a |
| 346 Flt | May 1918–May 1919 | H12/12B, F.2a |
| 410 Flt | 31 May 1918–May 1919 | Short 184, Campania |
| 210 TDS | Jun 1918–15 May 1919 | various |
| STF | Aug 1918–1919; Feb 1925–1 Oct 1931 | Fairey IIId, IIIf, Southampton |

### 1919–1938

| | | |
|---|---|---|
| 201 Sqn | 1 Jan 1929–Aug 1939 | |
| 240 Sqn | 31 Mar 1937–Aug 1939 | |
| SoAN | 13 Feb 1920–1 Apr 1920 | various |
| SoNCAN | 1 Apr 1920–5 Feb 1928 | F.5 |
| APF | 5 Feb 1923–Dec 1926 | Southampton, F.5 |
| HSF | Jul 1927–Oct 1931+ | various |
| STS | 1 Oct 1931–Sep 1939 | |
| FBTS | 2 Jan 1939–24 Jun 1940 | Singapore, Scapa, Stranraer, London |

### Post-1945

| | | |
|---|---|---|
| ASWDU det | Jan 1945–May 1948 | |
| 235 OCU | 31 Jul 1947–17 Oct 1953 | Sunderland |

# CHAILEY

**County:** East Sussex

**UTM/Grid:** OS map 198–TQ370192
**Lat/Long:** N50°57.15 W000°02.45
**Nearest Town:** Brighton 9 miles to south

## HISTORY

Another result of the mid-1942 airfield site-surveys, the land at Chailey was requisitioned in January 1943 and was eventually given the standard layout of Sommerfeld Track runways, hardstands and hangars. Construction was a little drawn-out, as power cables had to be buried and a public house, The Plough, demolished; as the east side of the site was wooded, there was a tree-felling programme to make room for the NW/SE runway. The village after which the airfield was named lay just to the north-east and, as usual with the mile-long runways, a number of roads had to be closed. According to RAF records, Chailey was the first ALG to be officially declared ready for use – 1 April 1943, but it was to be over a year before any aircraft used the airfield. In the meantime, further development took place and the airfield was provided with four Blister hangars and three dispersal-areas of 'hardcore and ash'. The runways were marked out with white strips on the corners and the touchdown point was indicated by a white chalk-mark.

The first, and only, unit arrived in April 1944 from Deanland, ten miles to the south-east. No.131 Airfield (Wing from May) brought their Spitfire IXs to Chailey and specialized in fighter-bomber operations over Europe as part of the pre-invasion bombing strategy. On D-Day the squadrons, in common with most Spitfire units, became part of the massive fighter-umbrella over and around the beaches, but they were soon back in the bombing role. The Wing moved to Appledram in late-June and, from a situation where almost fifty Spitfires could be seen dispersed around the airfield or roaring off down one of the strips, all was suddenly quiet.

Chailey appears in the December 1944 survey as an ALG with Fighter Command, but it had already been signed-off for disposal; by January 1945 it had been cleared and the cows were back.

## AIRFIELD DATA DEC 1944

| | | | |
|---|---|---|---|
| Command: | RAF Fighter Command | Runway surface: | Sommerfeld Track |
| Function: | Advanced Landing Ground | Hangars: | 4 × Blister |
| Runways: | NW/SE 1,200yd | Dispersals: | 3 × Hardcore and ash |
| | E/W 1,500yd | Personnel: | Other Ranks – Tented camp |
| | 270 deg 2,000 × 50yd | | |

Spitfire IX of 308 Squadron; this unit was at Chailey in May and June 1944 as part of No.131 (Polish) Wing.

## UNITS

### HQ Units at Chailey

No.131 Airfield/ 26 Apr 1944–28 Jun 1944   302,
  (Polish) (F) Wing                                        308, 317
                                                              Sqn

### 1939–1945

| | | |
|---|---|---|
| 302 Sqn | 26 Apr 1944–28 Jun 1944 | Spitfire |
| 308 Sqn | 26 Apr 1944–28 Jun 1944 | Spitfire |
| 317 Sqn | 26 Apr 1944–28 Jun 1944 | Spitfire |

# CHATTIS HILL

**County:** Hampshire

**UTM/Grid:** OS map 185–SU320356
**Lat/Long:** N51°07.05 W001°31.19
**Nearest Town:** Stockbridge 2 miles to east

## HISTORY

A 120-acre rectangular field atop the Houghton Downs, west of Stockbridge, was acquired in mid-1917 as a landing ground for the Royal Flying Corps and in mid-September two newly formed squadrons arrived, 91 Squadron from Spittlegate and 92 Squadron from London Colney, being joined a few weeks later by 93 Squadron from Croydon. All were intended as training units to prepare aircrew for operational squadrons and, as such, they operated a variety of types from the BE2c and RE8 to the Sopwith Pup. A tented camp grew up for the large number of RFC personnel, although billets were also acquired in Stockbridge, where the officers made use of the Grosvenor Arms; the aircraft were housed in Bessonneau hangars.

It was by no means an ideal site, being a windy hilltop but one that also had a habit of waterlogging. Nevertheless, despite some changing round of units, primarily the arrival of designated Training (Ex-Reserve) Squadrons, Chattis Hill retained its training role to the end of the war. Indeed, it was intended in 1918 that the station would be given permanent facilities and work commenced on six large aeroplane-sheds and a range of technical buildings. When the war ended this construction work was halted and Chattis Hill awaited its fate. Over the next few months the number of aircraft increased as the airfield was used as a storage and disposal centre but, by late-1919, it appears to have closed.

That might well have been the end of this site as an airfield, except for the fact that the highly effective Luftwaffe attacks on the Supermarine and other factories in Southampton started a hunt for dispersal sites. The field at Chattis Hill, which had for some years been used as a horse 'gallops', was chosen as a site for the assembly and flight testing (and eventual delivery) of Spitfires. A series of sheds were constructed in the nearby woods and Supermarine was in residence from late-1940, the first Spitfires flying from here by March 1941. This was the start of what would be an impressive total of aircraft to pass through this unprepossessing site to the end of the war. Supermarine did not give up the site until 31 May 1948, although flying had ceased in 1945.

## UNITS

### Pre-1919

| | | |
|---|---|---|
| 91 Sqn | 14 Sep 1917–15 Mar 1918 | various |
| 92 Sqn | 14 Sep 1917–17 Mar 1918 | Pup |
| 93 Sqn | 3 Oct 1917–19 Mar 1918 | various |
| 34 TS | 18 Mar 1918–15 Jul 1918 | various |
| 43 TS | 20 Mar 1918–15 Jul 1918 | various |
| 43 TDS | 15 Jul 1918–15 May 1919 | Avro 504, Camel, FK8 |
| W/T School | 16 Apr 1918–21 Nov 1918 | various |

Sopwith Pups were operated from Chattis Hill by 92 Squadron; this is not a Chattis Hill picture.

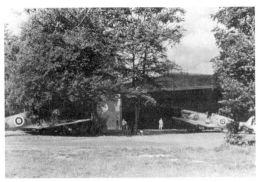

During World War Two the airfield was used a flight-test location for Spitfires produced in Southampton.

# CHILBOLTON

**County:** Hampshire

**UTM/Grid:** OS map 185–SU392383
**Lat/Long:** N51°08.38 W001°26.08
**Nearest Town:** Andover 4 miles to north-west

## HISTORY

Chilbolton is one of those airfields whose name is little known but whose importance is worthy of greater recognition, not necessarily because of its wartime record, although it certainly played its part, but because of the aircraft development and test work undertaken in the late-1940s and 1950s on such types as the Attacker, Gnat and Swift.

The airfield had its origins in 1939 with a decision to create a dispersal airfield for Middle Wallop's bombers, it being standard practice at this period to plan a dispersal (or satellite) within a short distance of an operational bomber-station. Chilbolton is five miles due east of Middle Wallop and was laid out on an area of relatively flat chalk-downs, just south of the village that donated its name. It was literally lit-

tle more than a cleared field in its early days and appears to have been ready for use by summer 1940. In September the Hurricanes of 238 Squadron moved in from Middle Wallop, the latter having become a Sector Airfield for the re-organized No.10 Group of Fighter Command. Chilbolton was, thus, involved in the latter stages of the Battle of Britain and its Hurricanes scored a number of successes.

When 238 Squadron departed in May 1941 they were replaced by the Spitfires of the Polish 308 Squadron; this, however, was a short detachment and the Poles moved out as 501 Squadron moved in. Indeed, the latter part of 1941 saw a number of fighter squadrons rotate through Chilbolton, primarily tasked with air defence but, with the arrival of 245 Squadron's Hurricane IICs, increasingly turning to

## AIRFIELD DATA DEC 1944

| Command: | Fighter | Runway surface: | Concrete, tar and wood-chips |
|---|---|---|---|
| Function: | Operational | Hangars: | 3 × Blister, 2 × T.2 |
| Runways: | 200 deg 1,800 × 50yd | Dispersals: | 48 × Loop |
| | 300 deg 1,600 × 50yd | Personnel: | Officers – 225 |
| | 250 deg 1,400 × 50yd | | Other Ranks – 2,575 |
| | | | (No WAAF accommodation) |

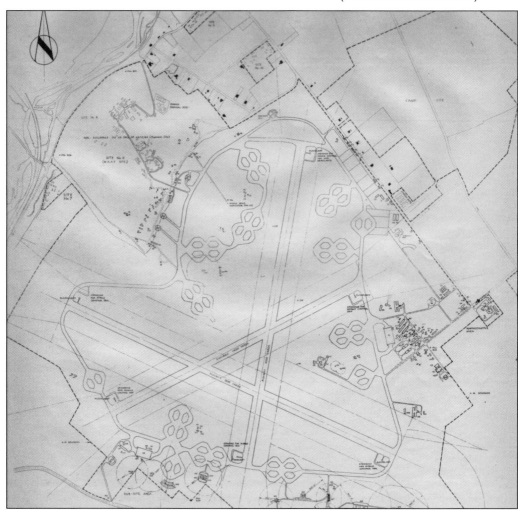

offensive operations. During early 1942, the airfield underwent an improvement programme that included a concrete perimeter-track defining the 'D'-shaped airfield area and a number of fighter revetments on the west and north sides of the airfield. Three Blister hangars were built, later supplemented by two T.2 hangars, and a technical site was laid out on the north-east corner. During this period the grass area was used as an RLG by 41 Operational Training Unit at Old Sarum and this unit continued to use Chilbolton even after it had been declared operational again with No.10 Group in April. No fighters appeared and in autumn the airfield was transferred to No.70 Group; the following month it was allocated as a satellite to Netheravon. In a complete change of role the airfield became home to the Glider

Supermarine Scimitar under flight trials at Chilbolton.

The 245 Squadron artist drew this impressive cartoon of one of the Squadron's airfields; the unit spent a few months at Chilbolton in late 1941.

Pilot Exercise Unit and, from January 1943, glider towing, mainly Horsas, became the normal sight at Chilbolton. Two Hurricane squadrons arrived for a brief stay in March 1943 as part of Exercise Spartan, the comprehensive Army Co-Operation exercise that involved much of southern England. However, this intense activity was soon followed by peace and quiet as, in May, the GPEU moved back to Netheravon and Chilbolton was allocated for use by the USAAF.

Construction work was required before the new tenants could move in and it was during this phase that Chilbolton was given its three hard-runways, along with forty-eight dispersals and the two T.2 hangars. However, it is interesting to note that, in the RAF's December 1944 airfield summary, Chilbolton is still shown as a grass airfield in the photograph but that three runways of 'concrete, tar and wood-chips' are detailed. The airfield was handed back to No.10 Group on 1 June 1943 but remained empty until finally transferred to the Americans at the end of the year. The 5th Tactical Air Depot moved in from Zeals and, in March 1944, this non-flying unit was joined by the three P-47s squadrons of the 368th Fighter-Bomber Group from Greenham Common. This unit had arrived in England in January and flew its first operation on 14 March, moving to Chilbolton the following day. As part of the IXth Air Force its major task was attacking enemy transportation targets, such as bridges and railway facilities, although it also attacked other military installations. The Group was heavily engaged on and around D-Day and their home base was the scene of frantic activity as high sorties rates were maintained. The 368th was one of the first IXth Air Force units to move to France, leaving Chilbolton for Cardonville on 20 June.

The airfield remained in American hands and was used as a casualty station, transport aircraft flying the wounded back from the battle area for transfer to the special hospital-complex at Stockbridge, just a few miles south of the airfield. Troop Carrier Command effectively took over the airfield and, in September, the 422nd TCG's three C-47 squadrons moved in and immediately flew supply missions to Normandy. This work continued for a number of days but the Group was soon training for the next big airborne-operation – the assault on Holland (Operation *Market-Garden*). The first major drop took place on 17 September with two waves, the Group contributing forty-five aircraft to each wave. For the remainder of September the Group used both Chilbolton and Greenham Common, but on 5 October it deployed to France.

By March 1945 the airfield had returned to RAF control and No.41 OTU re-appeared, complete with its diverse fleet of aircraft. This unit disbanded in June but the airfield had once more become associated with Middle Wallop, acting as a forward satellite, being used by 25 Squadron in late-May and 183 Squadron in mid-June, the latter having arrived to convert from Typhoons to Spitfire XIVs. In August one of the Spitfire units departed but in its place came 247 Squadron with their Tempest IIs, an aircraft type that was soon also in the hands of 183 Squadron. This two-squadron Tempest Wing, the first of its kind, had been earmarked for Tiger Force, the new air element destined to deploy to the Far East to help finish the war against Japan. However, this move never took place, as the war ended and the Wing remained at Chilbolton.

The immediate post-war future for the airfield was uncertain, although 247 Squadron received its first Vampire in March 1946, the Squadron having been designated as the first unit to receive the de Havilland jet. However, in June, both flying units

A number of buildings survive at the site but most of the airfield has gone.

The 368th FG was based at Chilbolton from March to June 1944; this P-47 of the Group's 397th FS is probably pictured after the Group had moved to France. (US National Archives)

departed and by November the airfield had been virtually abandoned. For the vast majority of wartime-build airfields that would have been the end but, in February 1947, Vickers-Supermarine moved their flight-test centre here from High Post. An assembly shed was put up alongside one of the existing T.2s and the runway at Chilbolton witnessed a good deal of trial work, including first flights, of a number of types, starting with the Attacker and Swift. Supermarine departed in 1957 but, since February 1953, Folland Aircraft had also been using Chilbolton, working on the Midge/Gnat. The Folland Flight Development Unit eventually moved to Dunsfold in 1961 and this Hampshire airfield fell silent. Part of the site was used for the Appleton Observatory, with its massive satellite dish, and other areas were sold off for various uses.

There is still a Chilbolton airfield, the present site (also known as Stonefield Park) being located on the western side of the old wartime field. The small grass strip is operated by the Chilbolton Flying Club.

| | | |
|---|---|---|
| 183 Sqn | 17 Jun 1945–8 Oct 1945; 15 Nov 1945 | Typhoon, Spitfire, Tempest |
| 184 Sqn | 1–11 Mar 1943 | Hurricane |
| 222 Sqn | 10–15 Sep 1945 | Tempest |
| 238 Sqn | 30 Sep 1940– 1 Apr 1941; 16 Apr 1941–20 May 1941 | Hurricane |
| 245 Sqn | 1 Sep 1941–19 Dec 1941 | Hurricane |
| 247 Sqn | 20 Aug 1945–7 Jan 1946; 16 Feb 1946– 27 Jun 1946 | Typhoon, Tempest, Vampire |
| 308 Sqn | 31 May 1941–24 Jun 1941 | Spitfire |
| 501 Sqn | 25 Jun 1941–5 Aug 1941 | Spitfire |
| 504 Sqn | 11–26 Aug 1941 | Hurricane |
| GPEU det | 18 Dec 1942–8 Jan 1943 | |
| GPEU | 8 Jan 1943–10 May 1943 | Tiger Moth, Hector, Hotspur |
| 41 OTU | 23 Mar 1945– 26 Apr 1945 | Hurricane, Spitfire, Master |

## UNITS

### HQ Units at Chilbolton

| | | |
|---|---|---|
| No.122 Airfield | 25 Feb 1943–13 Mar 1943 | 132, 174, 184 Sqn |
| No.124 (RP) Wing | Apr 1946 | no Sqn |

### 1939–1945

| | | |
|---|---|---|
| 26 Sqn | 23 May 1945–20 Aug 1945 | Spitfire |
| 54 Sqn | 15 Nov 1945–28 Jun 1946 | Tempest |
| 174 Sqn | 1–11 Mar 1943 | Hurricane |

### USAAF Units

#### 368th FBG

| | |
|---|---|
| Squadrons: | 395th FS, 396th FS, 397th FS |
| Aircraft: | P-47 |
| Dates: | 15 Mar 1944–20 Jun 1944 |
| First mission: | 14 Mar 1944 |

#### 422nd TCG

| | |
|---|---|
| Squadrons: | 303rd TCS, 304th TCS, 305th TCS |
| Aircraft: | C-47 |
| Dates: | 11 Sep 1944–5 Oct 1944 |

# CHRISTCHURCH

**County:** Dorset

**UTM/Grid:** OS map 195–SZ185932
**Lat/Long:** N50°44.03 W001°44.53
**Nearest Town:** Christchurch one mile to west

## HISTORY

From the mid-1920s, a series of fields on the west side of Christchurch were developed as a private airfield for flying club and even some commercial air service activity, although neither was particularly successful. The first flying from this area appears to have taken place from fields near Somerford Garage, the Hampshire Aero Club operating from 1928. During this period the site was known variously as Somerford, Fishers Field, Christchurch Airport and even Bournemouth Airport.

Like most such private airfields it was closed at the outbreak of war, but in April 1940 the site was allocated to the Special Duties Flight (SDF) for use in support of the Air Ministry Research Establishment at Swanage. This very special flight had been formed at Perth in November 1939 and was closely linked

with Martlesham Heath, from where its 'A Flight' operated from December 1940. The SDF subsequently became the Telecommunications Flying Unit (TFU), with its main base at Hurn but maintaining a flight of eight aircraft at Christchurch until May 1942. A single Bellman hangar erected during the first months of the airfield's use was later joined by three Extended Over Blisters and one Bessonneau, as facilities were gradually improved. One of the more unusual trials-units, but one that stayed only a matter of days, was No.420 Flight, whose aircraft were used for evaluating the practicalities of sowing an aerial minefield in the path of bomber formations!

Aircraft strength increased in October 1940 with the arrival of 'H Flight' of No.1 AACU, this unit primarily operating Battles. Further development of the

## AIRFIELD DATA DEC 1944

| | | | |
|---|---|---|---|
| Command: | Fighter | Runway surface: | 4 of BRC fabric, 1 of mesh (245 deg) |
| Function: | Operational satellite | Hangars: | 3 × Extended Over Blister, 1 × Bellman, |
| | | | 1 × Bessonneau |
| Runways: | 245 deg 1,650yd | Dispersals: | nil |
| | N/S 1,000yd | Personnel: | Officers – 4 |
| | NE/SW 1,000yd | | Other Ranks – 245 |
| | E/W 1,000yd | | |
| | NW/SE 950yd | | |

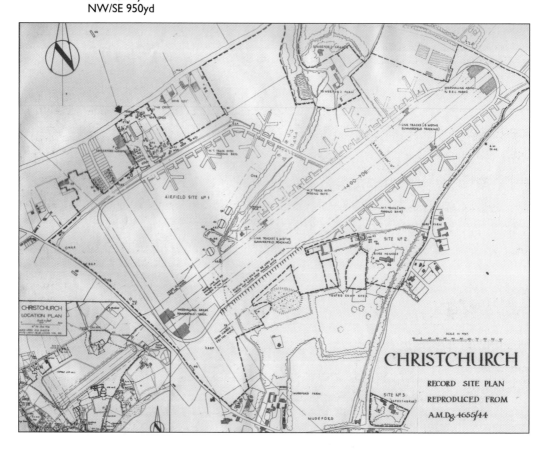

airfield was underway at the end of the year, as it had been decided to locate a shadow factory for Airpseed on the west side of the airfield for the construction of Oxfords. By summer 1941 the airfield and the factory were increasingly busy and the decision was taken to concentrate on aircraft production and move the other units away, although the TFU continued to maintain a presence. The airfield was officially transferred to No.10 Group of Fighter Command for use as a satellite for Hurn, but for the next three years its focus was on aircraft construction, which included

Horsa gliders; by 1943, Airspeed was also involved in converting Spitfires into Seafires.

The hunt for airfields in southern England that were suitable for fighter-bomber operations gave Christchurch its only involvement in operations when it was allocated for use by the 405th Fighter Group. Additional runways were laid using BRC fabric as the single wire-mesh runway was inadequate for the new users. The P-47s of the 405th arrived in early March and flew their first operations the following month. The three squadrons of Thunderbolts were

P-47 of the 405th FG; the three Thunderbolt squadrons of this Group operated from Christchurch during the D-Day period.

The 833rd Engineer Aviation Battalion laying PSP at Christchurch.

The prototype Airspeed Ambassador made its maiden flight from this airfield on 10 July 1947.

kept busy in the weeks leading up to D-Day and the residents of Christchurch must have wondered what this sudden noise and activity was all about. With news that the Allies had invaded Normandy, the reason for this frenetic activity would have become apparent, but within weeks of the landings the P-47s were moved to France, taking up residence at Picauville.

No.89 Gliding School had formed in March 1944 at Christchurch (Somerford) and flew Cadets, Sedbergh and Grunau Baby gliders to July 1963, having become No.622 VGS in September 1955. However, with the departure in June 1944 of the Americans, the airfield was pretty much left to Airspeed and they decided to expand their operation by moving staff and work across from Hurn. This situation was recognized in January 1946, when the airfield was transferred to the Ministry of Aircraft Production as a factory airfield. On 10 July 1947, Christchurch witnessed the first flight of Airspeed's new airliner, the Ambassador. Whilst this was a fine piece of engineering it was not a commercial success. Airspeed was also working on the DH Vampire and to enable flight testing of the trainer version a tarmac runway was laid in 1950 and over the next few years, with Airspeed having become part of de Havilland, Vampires, Venoms and Sea Vixens flew from Christchurch. Sadly, the contraction of the British aircraft industry brought production at this site to an end in 1962 and, despite some interest in resurrecting a private flying field, there was to be no more flying from Christchurch.

A number of the airfield buildings survive but the main airfield area has now vanished under housing, some road names on which preserve the aviation connection.

## UNITS

### 1939–1945

| | | |
|---|---|---|
| SDF | 27 Apr 1940–10 Nov 1941 | various |
| 420 Flt | 25–29 Sep 1940 | Harrow |
| 1 AACU | 11 Oct 1940–1 Jul 1941 | |
| TFU | 10 Nov 1941–May 1942 | |
| 89 GS | Mar 1944–Sep 1955 | Cadet, Sedbergh |

### Post 1945

| | | |
|---|---|---|
| 622 VGS | 1 Sep 1955–1 Jul 1963 | Cadet |

### USAAF Units
#### 405th FG

| | |
|---|---|
| Squadrons: | 509th FS, 510th FS, 511th FS |
| Aircraft: | P-47 |
| Dates: | 7 Mar 1944–22 Jun 1944 |
| First mission: | 11 Apr 1944 |
| Last mission: | 8 May 1945 (from Kitzingen) |

## MEMORIALS

1. Road names on the estate that now covers site reflect aspects of the airfield and its units.
2. The Stars and Stripes of the 405th FG hangs in the Priory, presented when the unit departed.

# COOLHAM

**County:** West Sussex

**UTM/Grid:** OS map 198–TQ125222
**Lat/Long:** N50°59.15 W000°23.45
**Nearest Town:** Horsham 6 miles to north-east

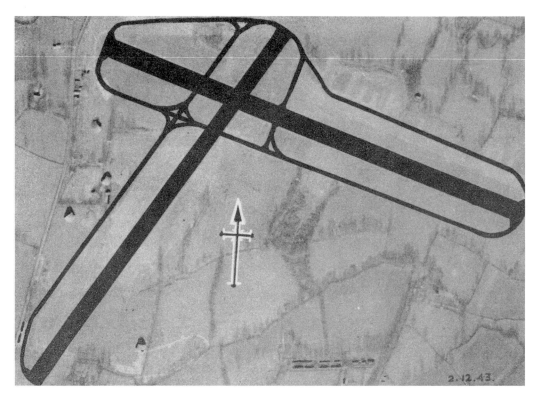

## HISTORY

The aerial photograph, albeit of poor quality, gives a good idea of the type of farmland on which most of these Advanced Landing Grounds were built. When the survey team carried out its investigations in 1942, it was looking for areas of reasonably flat land that could house two runways, each nearly a mile long, at roughly right-angles to each other. Coolham ALG was just south of the village from which it took its name and requisition of land was approved in autumn 1942. Construction of this ALG started in January 1943 and it opened on 1 April, by which time it had two Sommerfeld Track runways with connecting perimeter tracks, five Blister hangars and a comprehensive series of dispersals, mainly of Sommerfeld Track. With construction over, the ALG was left to wait the call for action and livestock moved back in to graze the fields.

No.133 Airfield took up residence in April 1944 with three squadrons, all of which had converted to

Mustangs or were in the process of doing so. Like all the ALGs the basic accommodation was in tents but, as usual, a number of local buildings were taken over for a variety of uses, in this case Sauceland Farmhouse and Farleys Farmhouse, both on the perimeter of the airfield.

Coolham mounted its first operational sorties on 26 April and from then on all three squadrons were heavily engaged with offensive *Ramrods*, *Rangers* and *Rhubarbs* over Europe. The Mustang proved an ideal aircraft for operations from this type of temporary airfield and, unlike the more delicate Spitfire, suffered less in the way of incidents, although Coolham did record a number of accidents, such as a bomb falling off a taxiing aircraft. On the 'great day', 6 June 1944, the Wing was tasked with escorting part of the massive airborne-operation by paratroops and gliders. One of the few aerial victories of the day was scored by 129 Squadron when they downed a Fw190.

# AIRFIELD DATA DEC 1944

| | | | |
|---|---|---|---|
| Command: | RAF Fighter Command | Runway surface: | Sommerfeld Track |
| Function: | Advanced Landing Ground | Hangars: | 5 × Blister |
| Runways: | 120 deg 1,500yd | Dispersals: | 50 × Sommerfeld Track, 5 × Hardcore |
| | 050 deg 1,200yd | Personnel: | Other Ranks – Tented camp |

Throughout the war there were a number of recorded instances of fighter pilots landing to rescue colleagues from downed aircraft; one such instance occurred when Squadron Leader Horbaczewski, CO of 315 Squadron, taxied back to dispersal at Coolham with a passenger, having picked up Warrant Officer Tamowicz after he was shot-down in France.

When the Mustang squadrons moved out in June they were replaced by the Spitfires of No.135 Wing – but for only five days. Coolham had been very busy for a few months in mid-1944, but its period of activity was soon over. Clearance work began in October, but one final piece of drama remained when a damaged B-24 landed here in January. It was repaired and flown out – no mean feat from one of these 'temporary' ALGs. That final episode over, the now cleared airfield was released back to agriculture and, as with most that we have mentioned, there is now little trace to be seen as you look over the Sussex fields.

Pilots of 306 Squadron relax by their 'luxury accommodation'.

The memorial at Coolham commemorates all the airfield's units, flying and ground.

## UNITS

### HQ Units at Coolham

| | | |
|---|---|---|
| No.133 Airfield/ | 1 Apr 1944–22 Jun 1944 | 129, 306, |
| (Polish) (F) Wing | | 315 Sqn |
| No.135 | 30 Jun 1944–4 Jul 1944 | 222, 349, |
| (F) Wing | | 485 Sqn |

### 1939–1945

| | | |
|---|---|---|
| 129 Sqn | 3 Apr 1944–22 Jun 1944 | Spitfire, Mustang |
| 222 Sqn | 30 Jun 1944–4 Jul 1944 | Spitfire |
| 306 Sqn | 1 Apr 1944–22 Jun 1944 | Spitfire, Mustang |
| 315 Sqn | 1 Apr 1944–22 Jun 1944 | Mustang |
| 349 Sqn | 30 Jun 1944–4 Jul 1944 | Spitfire |
| 485 Sqn | 30 Jun 1944–4 Jul 1944 | Spitfire |

## MEMORIALS

Stone memorial with inset plaques depicting unit badges and unit list; main inscription:

This memorial commemorates and honours the airmen of many nations who fought valiantly in defence of Britain whilst serving at Coolham Advanced Landing Ground Airfield during Operation Overlord in June 1944. Those who made the ultimate sacrifice and died far from their homeland will be remembered for evermore.

# CROYDON (Waddon)

**County:** Surrey

**UTM/Grid:** OS map 177–TQ306635
**Lat/Long:** N51°21.15 W000°07.30
**Nearest Town:** Croydon 2½ miles to north-east

Aerial view of Croydon in 1959.

## HISTORY

Originally known as Beddington Aerodrome, the airfield opened in 1916 and was used during World War One by the Royal Flying Corps for Home Defence. The site was acquired in 1915 and, in typical fashion for the period, a minimum amount of preparation work was carried out to provide a reasonable operating surface. In terms of structures, the aircraft were given Bessonneau hangars whilst personnel went into tents, although a number of buildings around New Barn Farm were also acquired. The first aircraft, two BE2c 'fighters', arrived in early January 1916 and effectively became part of London's Home Defence unit – 39 Squadron – when it formed in April. However, the main role for Croydon was as a training airfield and No.17 Training Squadron formed here on 15 December 1915 as part of No.14 (Training) Wing. This unit remained in residence to June 1917

and operated a diverse fleet, although the main types were the Avro 504, BE2c and RE8. A number of training units were based at Croydon up to June 1919 and the airfield certainly played a role in providing a steady supply of pilots to the RFC and RAF.

The training role decreased with the end of the war and the disbandment of squadrons, which arrived here without aircraft, and the closure of the final training unit, No.29 Training Squadron, must have made 1919 a sad year. Indeed, the RAF declared no further interest in Croydon and in spring 1920 the airfield was handed over for civil use. At this time there were, in fact, two separate airfields here – Beddington and Waddon – but these were merged to form Croydon Aerodrome.

The site had a complex history in the latter part of the war and first years of peace; No.1 National

## AIRFIELD DATA DEC 1944

| | | | |
|---|---|---|---|
| Command: | Dept of Civil Aviation | Runway surface: | Grass |
| Function: | Civil Airport | Hangars: | 4 × Extended Over Blister |
| Runways: | NW/SE 1,300yd | Dispersals: | 22 × twin-engine |
| | E/W 1,200yd | Personnel: | Officers – 88 (5 WAAF) |
| | NE/SW 1,100yd | | Other Ranks – 786 (210 WAAF) |

Aircraft Factory had opened in January 1918 with its test-flying ground at Waddon, but after less than a year it was closed, as the panic requirement for aircraft had ended. Waddon became the National Aircraft Depot and, instead of building aircraft, was responsible for disposing of them. In April 1920 the old National Aircraft Depot was sold to Handley Page. However, the main development was in commercial aviation when Croydon became London Airport and experienced a rapid expansion of commercial business, with numerous flights to and from Europe by British and European carriers. During the mid-1920s the expansion continued; all evidence of the two separate World War One airfields vanished and considerable building work took place. In 1924 Imperial Airways was formed by the merger of a number of British carriers and for the next few years the development of Croydon and Imperial were closely linked. The following year Parliament passed the Croydon Airport Act, authorizing development of a purpose-built international airport – the first in Britain. Commercial services continued to develop, as new buildings, including an impressive terminal, were erected, the bulk of this work being complete by the start of 1928.

Commercial activity continued to flourish during

The Croydon Plough Lane site.

May 1940 with Hurricanes of 17 Squadron dispersed on the edge of the airfield.

A typical site at Battle of Britain airfields – re-arming Hurricane guns for the next sortie; this is not a Croydon shot.

Hurricanes of 85 Squadron spent a few weeks at Croydon in late 1940.

the 1930s, but when war became imminent all civil aircraft dispersed to other airfields and RAF fighters began to take up residence, the Gladiators of 615 Squadron being first to arrive, although they were soon followed by the Hurricanes of 3 and 17 Squadrons.

In the months preceding the Battle of Britain, various squadrons and aircraft types came and went but, as the Battle commenced, the two operational units, both with Hurricanes, were 111 Squadron and 1 Squadron RCAF. Like most of No.11 Group's airfields, the station was singled out for attack during the August offensive by the Luftwaffe and on more than one occasion serious damage was inflicted, the first major raid taking place on 15 August. However, rapid repair-work meant that Croydon was open for operations in a short space of time, a routine that was followed after subsequent attacks in August. Fighter squadrons rotated through the airfield during the height of the Battle as they became fatigued or casualties grew too high for easy replacement. Once the Battle was over, the station, like the rest of Fighter Command, turned its attention to the offensive, as squadrons undertook bomber escort and fighter sweeps on Europe. The airfield was not ideally placed for this role and by late-1941 it was being used by Army Co-operation squadrons, although it was usual for only one squadron to be in residence. By 1943 Croydon was being used by support and transport units and it was the latter role that soon came to dominate. After D-Day, Transport Command used the airfield for flights to the Continent and it was also home to No.1 Aircraft Delivery Flight.

After the war Croydon was a Dakota base for Transport Command, but this fairly intensive period ended in late-summer 1946. By this time, commercial activity had re-commenced, the first 'new' operators being the oddly named Railway Air Services, although they were soon joined by the likes of Jersey Airways and Scottish Airways. However, none of the international carriers returned and it was apparent that Croydon had no future, as its grass runways were unsuitable for use by the modern generation of airliners – and a new airfield, Heathrow, had opened. The only flying at Croydon was by smaller regional operators and flying clubs and by the mid-1950s the decision had been taken to close the airfield. Today much of the site has vanished under housing and industrial developments, but there is still a large grass area where the runways once were, although landscaping of the site has disguised its wartime shape, and stretches of concrete can still be found. However, the terminal building and control tower have survived.

## UNITS

### HQ Units at Croydon

| | |
|---|---|
| No.1 Group | 29 Aug 1919–Dec 1919 |
| No.110 (T) Wing | 3 Jul 1944–15 Feb 1946 |

### Pre-1919

| | | |
|---|---|---|
| 39 Sqn det | 1916 | BE2c |
| 93 Sqn | 23 Sep 1917–3 Oct 1917 | various |
| 17 TS | 15 Dec 1915–1 Jun 1917 | various |
| 29 TS | 14 Dec 1918–30 Jun 1919 | various |
| 40 TS | 1 Ju 1917–14 Dec 1918 | various |
| 65 TS | 1–10 May 1917 | |

### 1919–1938

| | | |
|---|---|---|
| 10 Sqn | 15 Oct 1919–31 Dec 1919 | no aircraft |
| 22 Sqn | 20 Nov 1919–31 Dec 1919 | no aircraft |
| 32 Sqn | 8 Oct 1919–31 Dec 1919 | SE5a |
| 41 Sqn | 8 Oct 1919–31 Dec 1919 | SE5a |
| 83 Sqn | 15 Oct 1919–31 Dec 1919 | no aircraft |
| 84 Sqn | 8 Oct 1919–Jan 1920 | SE5a |
| 207 Sqn | 8 Oct 1919–10 Jan 1920 | HP 0/400 |
| ACIS | 25 Jun 1919–1 Feb 1920 | various |

### 1939–1945

| | | |
|---|---|---|
| 1 Sqn | 7 Apr 1941–1 May 1941 | Hurricane |
| 1 Sqn RCAF | 3 Jul 1940–16 Aug 1940 | Hurricane |
| 3 Sqn | 2 Sep 1939–12 Oct 1939; 13 Nov 1939–28 Jan 1940 | Hurricane |
| 17 Sqn | 2–9 Sep 1939; 26 Feb 1941–1 Apr 1941 | Hurricane |
| 72 Sqn | 1–12 Sep 1940 | Spitfire |
| 85 Sqn | 19 Aug 1940–3 Sep 1940 | Hurricane |
| 92 Sqn | 30 Dec 1939–9 May 1940 | Blenheim, Spitfire |
| 111 Sqn | 4 Jun 1940–19 Aug 1940, 3–8 Sep 1940 | Hurricane |
| 116 Sqn | 12 Dec 1943–2 Jul 1944 | various |
| 145 Sqn | 10 Oct 1939–9 May 1940 | Blenheim |
| 147 Sqn | 1 Sep 1944–15 Sep 1946 | Dakota, Anson |
| 285 Sqn det | Aug 1943–Nov 1944 | Defiant, Martinet |
| 287 Sqn | 19 Nov 1941–3 Jul 1944 | various |
| 302 Sqn | 30 Jun 1942–7 Jul 1942 | Spitfire |
| 317 Sqn | 30 Jun 1942–7 Jul 1942 | Spitfire |
| 414 Sqn | 12 Aug 1941–5 Dec 1942 | Lysander |
| 501 Sqn | 21 Jun 1940–4 Jul 1940 | Hurricane |
| 605 Sqn | 7 Sep 1940–25 Feb 1941 | Hurricane |
| 607 Sqn | 22 May 1940–4 Jun 1940 | Hurricane |
| 615 Sqn | 2 Sep 1939–15 Nov 1939 | Gladiator |
| 11 Gp AACF | 5 May 1941–19 Nov 1941 | Blenheim, Lysandser |
| 1 ADF | 23 Jan 1942–4 Jul 1944 | |

### Post-1945

| | | |
|---|---|---|
| 167 Sqn | Apr 1945–1 Feb 1946 | Dakota |
| 271 Sqn det | Feb 1945–Aug 1945 | Dakota |
| 435 Sqn det | Aug 1945–Mar 1946 | Dakota |
| 437 Sqn det | Nov 1945–Jun 1946 | Dakota |
| 143 GS | 1945–1946 | |

## MEMORIALS

1. Croydon has one of the most impressive of all RAF monuments, a large black obelisk decorated with the crests of fighter units and Fighter Command, along with various inscriptions. It primarily commemorates the Battle of Britain.

2. Croydon Airport Visitor Centre: the old terminal building (Airport House) contains a display of material relating to the history of the airfield (www.croydonairport.org.uk).

The Croydon memorial is an impressive obelisk; sadly there is little trace of the airfield itself.

# DEANLAND

**County:** East Sussex

**UTM/Grid:** OS map 199–TQ523118
**Lat/Long:** N50°53.00 E000°10.00
**Nearest Town:** Lewes 5 miles to west

## HISTORY

Deanland was laid in what the planners considered the ideal ALG arrangement, with its two runways being at right-angles and in the shape of a cross, whereas many of the ALGs had the runway pattern modified to suit the landscape features. Having been surveyed in 1942, plans for the airfield were approved towards the end of the year and work commenced in early 1943. Construction was reasonably straightforward: only one significant road was closed, part of Eleven Acre Wood was felled and a fair number of hedges grubbed out and ditches either filled or bridged. The Royal Engineers undertook much of the work, with No.16 Airfield Construction Group being involved in laying runways, perimeter track and dispersals. The latter consisted of four large concrete-rectangles and were unusual for this type of airfield, where dispersals were more frequently simply areas of tracking: on the 1944 plan they are recorded as 'Refuelling Concrete'. Although no accommodation was provided for personnel, there were four Over Blister hangars for aircraft.

Deanland was declared open on 1 April 1944, one of the final phase of such airfields, and received its operational Wing, the Polish No.131 Airfield, the same day. The Spitfires undertook training and familiarization in mobile operations – living and working in 'primitive' conditions required some getting used to but was essential for units earmarked to deploy to France. A number of operational sorties were flown but in late-April the Wing moved to Chailey, being replaced by No.141 Airfield, renamed 141 Wing the following month. This unit's Spitfires flew a variety of missions and on D-Day was part of the fighter umbrella – along with hundreds of other Spitfires, they were tasked with beach cover, although 234 Squadron flew escort to the airborne operation and undertook ground-attack. The Wing continued to operate in support of the invasion until it was decided

## AIRFIELD DATA DEC 1944

| | | | |
|---|---|---|---|
| Command: | RAF Fighter Command | Runway surface: | Sommerfeld Track |
| Function: | Advanced Landing Ground | Hangars: | 4 × Over Blister |
| Runways: | WSW/ENE 1,600yd | Dispersals: | 4 × 200 × 100ft Refuelling Concrete |
| | SSW/NNE 1,400yd | Personnel: | Other Ranks – Tented camp |
| | 270 deg 2,000 × 50yd | | |

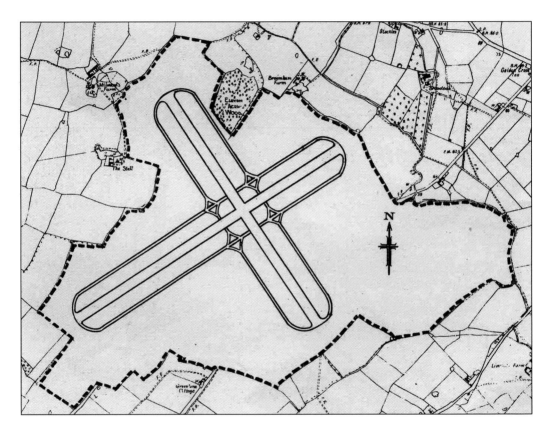

that the V-1 threat meant it was prudent to move, as the airfield was virtually under the flight path of these bombs. The Spitfires flew out in June but, within a few weeks, it was decided to base anti-*Diver* squadrons at Deanland. First in were the Spitfire XIVs of 91 and 322 Squadrons; both were soon in action. As far as the airfield was concerned, some repair work was necessary on the runways and a number of additional wooden buildings were erected, including messes and accommodation. A third Spitfire squadron arrived in mid-August and all three began to prepare for a move to the Continent. The squadrons finally left Deanland in early October – but only as far as Biggin Hill, although two of them did eventually deploy overseas.

This departure spelled the end for Deanland and a works party removed most of the airfield infrastructure, although some stretches of tracking were left.

There is still a flying field at this location, the private strip of Deanland (Lewes) was opened in 1963 and is now an active GA airfield, proud of its heritage. The short grass-strip plays host to a variety of based aircraft and welcomes flying visitors (prior permission).

Spitfire of 611 Squadron; the unit was at Deanland in early summer 1944 but this picture is undated and there is no location given.

## UNITS

### HQ Units at Deanland

| Unit | Date | Squadrons |
|------|------|-----------|
| No.131 Airfield | 1–26 Apr 1944 | 302, 308, 317 Sqn |
| No.149 Airfield/ (LRF) Wing | 4 Apr 1944–29 Jun 1944 | 64, 234, 611 Sqn |

### 1939–1945

| Sqn | Date | Aircraft |
|-----|------|----------|
| 64 Sqn | 29 Apr 1944–26 Jun 1944 | Spitfire |
| 91 Sqn | 21 Jul 1944–7 Oct 1944 | Spitfire |
| 234 Sqn | 29 Apr 1944–19 Jun 1944 | Spitfire |
| 302 Sqn | 1–26 Apr 1944 | Spitfire |
| 308 Sqn | 1–28 Apr 1944 | Spitfire |
| 317 Sqn | 1–26 Apr 1944 | Spitfire |
| 322 Sqn | 21 Jul 1944–10 Oct 1944 | Spitfire |
| 345 Sqn | 16 Aug 1944–10 Oct 1944 | Spitfire |
| 611 Sqn | 30 Apr 1944–24 Jun 1944 | Spitfire |

## MEMORIALS

Memorabilia held at the present Deanland Airfield and commemorative plaque and oak tree at West entrance; there is also a plaque in Ripe Church.

# DETLING

**County:** Kent

**UTM/Grid:** OS map 178–TQ812595
**Lat/Long:** N51°18.18 E000°36.03
**Nearest Town:** Maidstone 4 miles to south-west

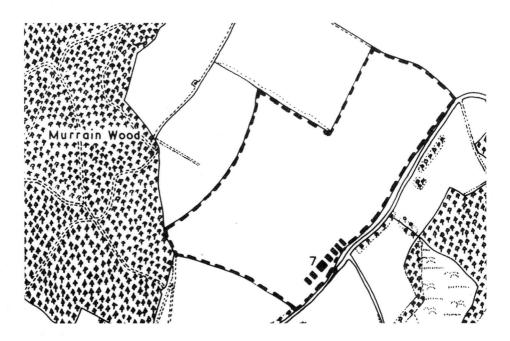

## HISTORY

The site at Detling played a part in the air defence of England during both World Wars, although the site is now the Kent County Showground and there is little evidence of its aviation heritage. Sitting on the pronounced wooded-ridge of the downland that runs east from Rochester, a landing-ground site was identified in 1915, when the RNAS was responsible for Home Defence. A roughly 100-acre area was levelled and the first aircraft arrived before work was complete. By February 1916 the based unit had become No.3 Wing, but a combination of unsuitable aircraft and some debate on the airfield's suitability – plus a greater demand for the aircraft elsewhere – led the RNAS to abandon the site in April and move to Manston. The site was reduced to Care and Maintenance but, with the RFC taking on responsibility for Home Defence, it was brought back into use by them in April 1917 and used by a detachment from 50 Squadron. Its BE2s and BE12s proved unsuccessful but, for a while, there was no alternative and it duly flew day- and night-patrols. On 25 July, the Squadron's 'B Flight' was used to form the core of a new unit, 112 Squadron, although this new formation moved out to Throwley a few days later. At last

the need for better Home Defence types was addressed and Camels were used to equip another new unit at Detling in February 1918, this unit then taking over the defence role at Detling, while 50 Squadron concentrated at Bekesbourne.

The airfield itself had also undergone some development, with additional hangars to supplement the Bessonneau hangars and a number of other buildings, as well as some improvement to the operating surface. The German daylight-raiders made a few more attacks on London in spring 1918 but the defences were now too strong and the bombers lost heavily, although the only success for a Detling pilot was that by Major Fred Sowrey on 18 May, a shared victory with a 141 Squadron crew from Biggin Hill. With the end of the war it was only a matter of time before the airfield went out of use; the Squadron, having re-equipped with Snipes in June 1919, disbanded in October, with the airfield closing in December.

When the RAF was looking for new airfield sites under the early 1930s Expansion Programme, one of its first sources was locations that had been used for landing grounds in World War One. The grass area to the north of the main road from Maidstone was once

Lysander V9587 of 4 Squadron at Detling in January 1942. (Andy Thomas)

more chosen and a roughly oval area was requisitioned for use as a bomber satellite. A number of hangars and other buildings were constructed on the north-east side of the airfield but at this stage it was still a fairly simple airfield, the longest take-off being roughly 1,300 yards oriented NE/SW. Detling opened on 14 September 1938 as part of Bomber Command's No.6 Group and the same month the Hinds of 500 Squadron arrived from Manston. In November, the airfield and its squadron were transferred to No.16 Group of Coastal Command. The Hind was unsuitable for the new general-reconnaissance role and the squadron duly received Ansons in early 1938; it was with the 'faithful Annie' that 500 Squadron went to war, flying coastal patrols and convoy escort.

The Phoney War ended in May 1940 and the squadron was soon taking on additional roles, whilst Detling became home to more units, including a Lysander detachment and various Fleet Air Arm squadrons. The location of Detling made it suitable for offensive operations over the Channel and, from May 1940, it was also in use by Blenheim fighter detachments, initially providing cover for the evacuation from Dunkirk. One noteworthy incident was the award of an Empire Gallantry Medal (later exchanged for a George Medal when the gallantry system changed) to Corporal Daphne Pearson for her actions on 31 May in helping rescue the crew of an Anson that crashed on the airfield. Detling retained its offensive role with Coastal Command and Fleet Air Arm units as the enemy opened its air offensive on England. Although it was not a fighter airfield it was very much on the Luftwaffe target list and was hit a number of times during the Battle of Britain, the single most devastating attack taking place on 13 August 1940. A force of Ju87s attacked in the early evening and, with virtually no opposition, the attack was accurate and effective, with hangars destroyed, messes hit and the operations room flattened, as well as twenty-two aircraft being destroyed. Casualties amounted to

sixty-seven killed and included the station commander. Despite the upheaval the airfield was soon back in operation and the Ansons, Swordfish and other types maintained their offensive. The airfield underwent a number of changes, in part brought on by the destruction wrought by the German attacks, which led to temporary buildings and Blister hangars taking the place of the permanent structures. Two areas of dispersals were developed, one to the north-east and one to the south-west, much of the latter being on the other side of the main road.

Various units came and went over the next few months; for example, the operational Fleet Air Arm units were joined by the Warwicks of 280 Squadron in the ASR role, whilst some arrived and stayed for slightly longer, such as 'D Flight' of No.2 Anti-Aircraft Co-operation Unit, with its mixture of aircraft for target-towing duties. However, by late-1942, most had departed and Detling had a period of comparative calm until it was transferred to Army Co-operation Command on 1 January 1943. For the next few months Detling was essentially a training base, as squadrons used the airfield for work-up with new aircraft or new roles and during this period Hurricanes, Mustangs and Austers rubbed shoulders. However, a return to operational status was indicated in October, with the arrival of No.125 Airfield, two of whose units (132 and 602 squadrons) had Spitfire IXs, whilst the third unit, 184 Squadron, had Hurricane IVs.

The Spitfires carried out escort missions whilst the Hurricanes focused on ground targets, although the pace of operations, especially for the latter, was limited. Changes came in early 1944, with the Hurricanes being replaced by Typhoons and the Spitfire squadrons rotating with two similarly equipped units. There was a bit more tweaking of units until No.125 Airfield moved to Ford on 18 April. A month later the three Spitfire squadrons of the Hornchurch Wing arrived,

The Operations Room of 2 Squadron at Detling, 1943.

## AIRFIELD DATA DEC 1944

| | | | |
|---|---|---|---|
| Command: | Fighter Command | Runway surface: | Grass |
| Function: | Forward Airfield, Biggin Hill sector | Hangars: | 14 × Blister, 1 × Bellman, 1 × Bessonneau |
| Runways: | NE/SW 1,400yd | Dispersals: | 41 × Spur, 23 × BRC fabric |
| | E/W 900yd | Personnel: | Officers – 41 |
| | N/S 900yd | | Other Ranks – 1,746 |
| | | | (281 WAAF) |

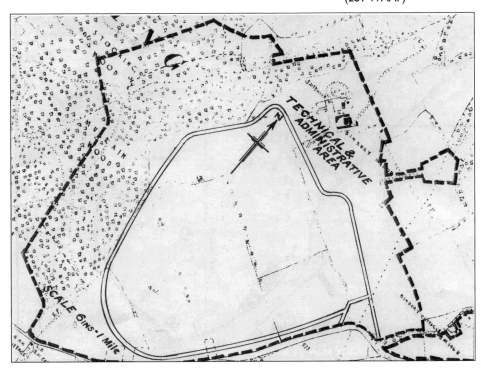

80, 229 and 274 Squadrons, all being highly experienced in the routine of fighter sweep and escort. The Wing operated as fighter cover during the D-Day period although, as with all the fighter squadrons, it also undertook both planned and ad hoc ground-attack missions. Detling was very much in 'V-1 alley', a situation that was aptly demonstrated when a flying bomb landed on the edge of the airfield on 21 June. The Spitfire Wing departed and two squadrons tasked with anti-*Diver* patrols arrived. These two units, 1 and 165 Squadrons, were equipped with Spitfire IXBs, a fighter with only marginal performance when it came to tackling the V-1s, although some success was scored. Both departed in late-July, but were back again a few weeks later; in the meantime, the airfield hosted three Spitfire squadrons for escort work. It had been an interesting but frustrating year for the airfield's units and quite suddenly Detling was considered surplus to immediate requirements.

All the flying units had gone by December and the airfield was reduced to Care and Maintenance on 1 January 1945.

All was not quiet on the ground at Detling, as the site was used by the RAF Regiment's No.1336 Wing as an Air Disarmament School for training personnel in how to deal with a variety of situations connected with taking over material and installations from the Luftwaffe. This role continued to late-summer 1945, but on 1 October the airfield was transferred to No.60 Group for No.75 Signals Wing, which formed here the following April. In terms of flying, Detling became home to gliders, firstly No.141 Gliding School and later No.168 GS and the Reserve Command Gliding Instructors' School. The final glider unit, 615 VGS (a renumbering of 168 GS) moved out to Kenley in the late-1950s. The 1950s had seen a number of other units, flying and non-flying, use Detling but none stayed long. Finally, on 1

April 1956, the airfield was reduced once more to Care and Maintenance. The final unit departed at the end of the year and the airfield was eventually put up for disposal on 1 October 1959, at which point Kent County Council acquired part of the site for a county showground.

## Decoy Sites

| | | |
|---|---|---|
| Q/K | Lenham | TQ920534 |

## Units

### HQ Units at Detling

| No.125 Airfield | 12 Oct 1943–4 May 1944 | 132, 184, 453, 602 Sqn |
|---|---|---|
| No.75 Wing | 1 Dec 1945–1 Nov 1946 | |

### Pre-1919

| 50 Sqn det | Apr 1917–Mar 1918 | BE2c, BE12 |
|---|---|---|
| 112 Sqn | 25–30 Jul 1917 | |
| 143 Sqn | 14 Feb 1918–31 Oct 1919 | Camel, SE5a, Snipe |

### 1939–1945

| 1 Sqn | 22 Jun 1944–11 Jul 1944; 10 Aug 1944–18 Dec 1944 | Spitfire |
|---|---|---|
| 4 Sqn det | May 1940 | Lysander |
| 13 Sqn det | Jul 1941–Aug 1942 | Lysander |
| 26 Sqn | 4–8 Aug 1941; 13 Jan 1943–1 Mar 1943; 22 Jun 1943–19 Jul 1943 | Lysander, Tomahawk, Mustang |
| 48 Sqn det | Aug 1939–Jul 1940 | Anson, Beaufort |
| 53 Sqn | 3 Jul 1940–Nov 1940 | Blenheim |
| 59 Sqn | Jul 1940–22 Jul 1941 | Blenheim |
| 80 Sqn | 19 May 1944–22 Jun 1944 | Spitfire |
| 118 Sqn | 20–23 Jan 1944; 12 Jul 1944–9 Aug 1944 | Spitfire |
| 124 Sqn | 26 Jul 1944–9 Aug 1944 | Spitfire |
| 132 Sqn | 12 Oct 1943–17 Jan 1944; 10 Mar 1944–18 Apr 1944 | Spitfire |
| 165 Sqn | 22 Jun 1944–12 Jul 1944; 10 Aug 1944–15 Dec 1944 | Spitfire |
| 184 Sqn | 12 Oct 1943–6 Mar 1944 | Spitfire |
| 229 Sqn | 19 May 1944–22 Jun 1944 | Spitfire |
| 235 Sqn | 26 May 1940–10 Jun 1940 | Blenheim |
| 239 Sqn | 19–31 May 1942 | Mustang |
| 274 Sqn | 19 May 1944–22 Jun 1944 | Spitfire |
| 280 Sqn | 10 Feb 1942–30 Jul 1942 | Anson |
| 318 Sqn | 20 Mar 1943–5 Aug 1943 | Hurricane |
| 453 Sqn | 19–21 Jan 1944; 4 Feb 1944–18 Apr 1944 | Spitfire |
| 500 Sqn | 28 Sep 1938–30 May 1941 | Hind, Anson |
| 504 Sqn | 12 Jul 1944–13 Aug 1944 | Spitfire |
| 567 Sqn | 1 Dec 1943–14 Nov 1944 | various |
| 602 Sqn | 12 Oct 1943–17 Jan 1944 | Spitfire |
| 655 Sqn | 7 Apr 1943–12 Aug 1943 | Auster |
| 1 CACF/U | 18 May 1940–11 Oct 1943 | Anson, Blenheim |
| 2 AACU | 11 Jun 1941–14 Feb 1943 | various |
| 1624 Flt | 14 Feb 1943–1 Dec 1943 | Defiant, Gladiator, Battle |
| 3 ADF | 23 Jul 1943–20 Sep 1943 | |
| 1493 Flt | 26 Jul 1943–18 Oct 1943 | Lysander, Master |
| 4 ADF | 21 Sep 1943–20 Oct 1943 | |

### Fleet Air Arm Units

| 801 Sqn | 31 May 1940–23 Jun 1940 | Skua |
|---|---|---|
| 806 Sqn det | May 1940 | Skua |
| 812 Sqn det | Aug 1940; 10 Apr 1941–16 May 1941 | Swordfish |
| 816X Flt det | 12 Mar 1941–16 Apr 1941 | Swordfish |
| 821 Sqn | 1–14 Jul 1941 | Swordfish |
| 825 Sqn | May 1940; Jul 1940 | Swordfish |
| 826 Sqn | 31 May 1940–1 Jun 1940 | Albacore |

### Post-1945

| 651 Sqn | Nov 1955–Apr 1957 | Auster |
|---|---|---|
| 657 Sqn | Sep 1951–Nov 1955 | Sycamore |
| 1903 Flt | 14 Feb 1955–30 Jan 1956 | Auster |
| 615 VGS | late-1950s | various |

## Memorials

Memorial stone on the airfield with plaque inscribed:

Detling Airfield. This stone was erected by the Kent County Agricultural Society as a tribute to the men and women who served on this site during the Second World War and to commemorate the 60th anniversary of the Battle of Britain. It was unveiled by Air Chief Marshal Sir Andrew Wilson KCB AFC 15th July 2000.

A small plaque on a memorial stone marks the RAF's wartime role at what is now the Kent County Showground.

# DUNSFOLD

**County:** Surrey

**UTM/Grid:** OS map 186–TQ027361
**Lat/Long:** N51°06.52 W000°31.50
**Nearest Town:** Guildford 8½ miles to north-west

Mitchells of 98 Squadron attack a target in France, April 1944, as part of the D-Day bombing campaign.

## HISTORY

Until recently an active airfield with British Aerospace, Dunsfold had its origins in 1942 when land was requisitioned for an Army Co-operation airfield, although it had also been under consideration as an Advanced Landing Ground. The land was requisitioned in April 1942 and work commenced almost immediately to construct a standard three-runway airfield in this quiet part of Surrey, the nearest other airfield being Farnborough some fifteen miles to the north-west. Most of the construction work was carried out by the Royal Canadian Engineers, one of the very few airfields this organiza-

tion built in England. The area was fairly flat but the usual problems of road closure, hedge removal and ditch filling had to be tackled; the three runways were standard dimensions, the longest being 2,000 yards and the other two 1,400 yards. Dispersal areas, which were square concrete pads, were clustered off the south and east perimeter-tracks, whilst the T.2 hangars and main technical-area were set off the northern perimeter-track. The engineers handed the airfield over on 16 October, but it did not officially open until December.

The Canadian involvement continued with the

98 Squadron at Dunsfold December 1943.

B-25s line-up ready to get airborne on another bombing mission.

B-25 Mitchell FW189 at Dunsfold, 1944.

The Supreme Commander, General Eisenhower, visited the airfield to brief crews.

arrival of No.39 (RCAF) Wing, two Mustang squadrons moving in the same month, whilst a third Mustang unit, 430 Squadron, arrived on 8 January 1943, having formed at Hartford Bridge on the first of the month. Training was the order of the day and the squadrons were frequently deployed for short periods to other airfields, as well as being involved in numerous exercises with the army. However, one of the most interesting exercises took place at Dunsfold and involved the Canadian Engineers. With thoughts turning to the invasion of Europe, a great many experiments were taking place in rapid airfield and runway construction and the Canadians had come up with a new system based on bitumen-impregnated Hessian (known as PBS – Prefabricated Bituminous Strip). A strip 1,000 yards long and 50 yards wide was laid on the airfield and, in June, intensive flying trials were conducted involving a variety of aircraft and conditions, including deliberate damage and repair. The results were assessed as excellent and PBS became one of the standard techniques for rapid

runway construction, although it is less well known than the various types of metal tracking.

When Army Co-operation Command disbanded in June 1943, the airfield was allocated to the new Tactical Air Force and two of the Mustang units moved to Gatwick, leaving 400 Squadron behind as the first unit for the new No.128 Airfield. The planned build-up of units was cancelled and the formation moved to Woodchurch, leaving Dunsfold for new occupants and a new role. On 18 August two Mitchell squadrons flew in and it was these units, 98 and 180 Squadrons, later joined by 320 Squadron, that saw the bulk of operational activity from Dunsfold and with which the airfield is most associated. The Mitchells went into action on 23 August and over the next fifteen months (as No.139 Wing) they took part in a large number of bombing missions over Europe, attacking a wide variety of targets and establishing a reputation for highly accurate attacks. The pace of operations increased as D-Day approached and the Mitchells attacked rail targets as

## AIRFIELD DATA DEC 1944

| | | | |
|---|---|---|---|
| Command: | RAF Fighter Command | Runway surface: | Concrete and wood-chippings |
| Function: | Forward Airfield | Hangars: | 12 × Blister, 2 × T.2 |
| Runways: | 257 deg 2,000 × 50yd | Dispersals: | 38 × 100ft square Frying Pan |
| | 210 deg 1,400 × 50yd | Personnel: | Officers – 108 (6 WAAF) |
| | 306 deg 1,400 × 50yd | | Other Ranks – 1,133 (205) |

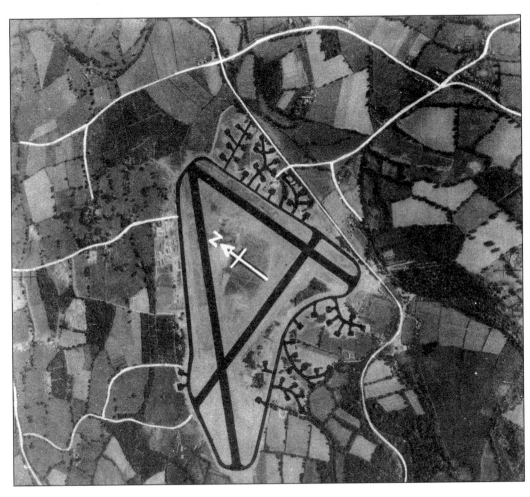

well as defence sites, airfields and gun emplacements. In May the airfield had been transferred to Air Defence of Great Britain (the new name – albeit temporary – for Fighter Command) but the Mitchell Wing remained the major operational residents until they finally departed for the Continent in October. The December 1944 survey showed Dunsfold as a forward airfield with the Tangmere Sector; it also noted that, whilst all three runways could be extended, it would entail some demolition.

For a few months the airfield was in Care and Maintenance, but in early February the No.83 Group Support Unit arrived from Tangmere, Dunsfold becoming a satellite for Odiham. With the end of the war, Dunsfold was one of a number of airfields used for receiving returning PoWs and a large number of transport flights took place in May and June. It was not only people that arrived for demob, the airfield became a Disbandment Centre for squadrons and at least three units met their fate at Dunsfold. February

1946 saw Dunsfold back in Care and Maintenance; in August it was transferred to Technical Training Command, but they had no use for the site, and the following month it was leased to Skyways Ltd and became their main operating-base. However, in March 1950, Skyways, like many civil-operation start-ups at this period, went into liquidation, although a rump company was created and operated for a time.

The main future for Dunsfold now lay with aircraft production and Hawker Aircraft arrived on site in May 1950, taking over the T.2 hangars for final-assembly work and flight testing. Over the next fifty years the airfield saw many classic types, starting with the Sea Hawk and Hunter, progressing via the Gnat and culminating in the Harrier. Dunsfold is synonymous with the Harrier and, whilst the company name went through various changes, ending up as British Aerospace, this fantastic British aircraft is, in itself, reason enough for Dunsfold to have a place in aviation history. The company announced in 1999 that the airfield was to close and it finally withdrew from the site the following year.

## UNITS

### HQ Units at Dunsfold

| | | |
|---|---|---|
| No.39 (RCAF) Wing | 3 Dec 1942–1 Aug 1943 | 168, 400, 414, 430 Sqn |
| No.139 (Bomber) Wing | 12 May 1944–16 Oct 1944 | 98, 180, 320 Sqn |

### 1939–1945

| | | |
|---|---|---|
| 21 Sqn det | Apr 1944–Jun 1944 | Mosquito |
| 98 Sqn | 18 Aug 1943–27 Mar 1944; 10 Apr 1944–18 Oct 1944 | Mitchell |
| 180 Sqn | 18 Aug 1943–16 Oct 1944 | Mitchell |
| 231 Sqn | 7–28 Jul 1943 | Mustang |
| 276 Sqn | 6–14 Nov 1945 | Spitfire |
| 320 Sqn | 18 Feb 1944–18 Oct 1944 | Mitchell |
| 400 Sqn | 4–28 Dec 1942; 14 Jan 1943–28 Jul 1943 | Spitfire |
| 402 Sqn | 10–24 Jul 1945 | Spitfire |
| 414 Sqn | 5 Dec 1942–9 Apr 1943; 19 Jun 1943–5 Jul 1943 | Spitfire |
| 430 Sqn | 11 Jan 1943–5 Jul 1943 | Mustang |
| 486 Sqn | 18 Sep 1945–12 Oct 1945 | Tempest |
| 1 FPTU | Jul 1945–? | Anson, Proctor |
| 83 Gp SU | 22 Feb 1945–1 Aug 1945 | |

## MEMORIALS

1. By control tower a plinth inscribed: 'This aerodrome was built by the Royal Canadian Engineers assisted by Canadian Forestry Corps, Royal Canadian Army Service Corps and Ordnance Corps 1942. It was handed over for the use of the RCAF 16 October 1942.'

2. Plaque in Dunsfold church along with 320 Sqn colours.

3. Plaque on Rose Cottage, Dunsfold. Inscription: 'From its wartime headquarters in this cottage in 1944 No.98 Squadron, RAF, was launched into the invasion of Europe led by Wg Cdr G J C Paul.'

# EASTCHURCH
# (HMS *Pembroke II*)

**County:** Kent

**UTM/Grid:** OS map 178–TQ985695
**Lat/Long:** N51°23.28 E000°51.12
**Nearest Town:** Sheerness 4½ miles to north-west

## HISTORY

Eastchurch holds a prominent place in the story of naval aviation, as it was here that the Admiralty, with a degree of reticence, authorized the first involvement of naval personnel with aeroplanes. An airfield was laid out on a 400-acre site by Francis McClean in 1910 for use by the Royal Aero Club and it was his offer of free flying-instruction to naval officers that led to this early interest in aviation, although it was an interest generated by the officers involved rather than by the Admiralty. What helped was that two of the initial four officer pilots who began training in March 1911 were resourceful and determined – Lieutenant C R Samson and Lieutenant A M Longmore, names that would become well known in military aviation circles. Eastchurch was primarily involved with private flying, still very much the preserve of the wealthy, but Francis McClean was keen to expand activities and he invited Short Brothers to move their aircraft works from Leysdown, which they promptly did. The company expanded rapidly and built more hangars, as

types such as the S27 went into production. With the death of Horace Short in April 1917, the facilities were acquired by the government and aircraft production continued.

The Admiralty had been persuaded of the need to train pilots and with Eastchurch established as the first naval air station, although not called such, it became home to training – by the end of 1911 referred to as the Naval Training Wing. Expansion of facilities was authorized in early 1912, with Eastchurch becoming Naval Wing HQ in April with the Royal Warrant that established the Royal Flying Corps, although it was still a civil airfield and the military were paying-lodgers. Charles Samson took command of the Wing in summer 1912 and, under his leadership, both Eastchurch and naval aviation underwent rapid expansion; it was very much a case of the right man in the right place. The Wing undertook trials work, including bombing, in addition to training pilots, and continued to expand by acquisition or construction of buildings. In recognition of

Fawns of 100 Squadron.

small bomb-loads – it was the latter problem that the new bomber-types were meant to address. By this time Eastchurch had been on the receiving end of a bombing attack when airship L10 dropped a stick of bombs over the airfield (in mistake for London!) on 8 August 1915.

One of the major tasks of the RNAS at this period was Home Defence and inadequate aircraft flew from a number of air stations and landing grounds in a usually vain effort to find, never mind destroy, the raiders. As far as Eastchurch was concerned, this was yet another duty for the War Flight. The latter disbanded in February 1917, by which time the airfield itself had grown into an impressive facility. The AIR 1 plan for 1916 shows a roughly rectangular area some 3,000 yards long at its maximum dimension, with a run of hangars, mainly Bessonneau type, down the centre and a clutch of administrative and technical buildings to the left of centre in what would appear to be an arrangement that limited the take-off and landing runs. Development of the airfield had been almost continuous throughout the war and a survey in 1918 showed no fewer than twenty-nine hangars of various shapes and sizes.

the dominance of the military at the airfield, it acquired the name HMS *Pembroke II* (the other *Pembroke* being its parent station at Chatham). On 1 July 1914 naval aviation was split from the RFC, with the creation of the Royal Naval Air Service (RNAS), and the decision was taken to concentrate the navy's landplanes at Eastchurch, thus making it an operational as well as a training station.

The first operational unit on site was 4 Squadron of the Royal Flying Corps, which flew its BE2 variants from here for a few weeks in summer 1914 on coastal patrols, although Eastchurch was also operating what it called a 'War Flight' on similar patrols. In August the Eastchurch (Mobile) Squadron was formed, although it spent little time at its home airfield and by September was at St Pol as 3 Squadron RNAS. A number of other units either formed at or used the airfield over the next few months, but it was the training school that remained the most active resident. The Wing had not given up its trials work and amongst the types to be tested was the Handley Page 0/100 strategic bomber, designed to attack targets in Germany. The RNAS had been at the forefront of promoting strategic bombing of military and industrial targets and a number of significant attacks had been made, albeit with little damage because of

Various training units were based here during the war, including the Gunnery Schools Flight (GSF), Observers School Flight (OSF) and Design Flight (DF); Eastchurch must have been a truly fascinating place in World War One. The RAF took over the airfield on 1 April 1918 but, other than a change of overall name to No.58 Wing and some movement of units, little changed. The Naval Flying School became No.204 Training Depot Station on the same day and the RFC retained the airfield in the post-war period as home to a variety of training units, which underwent various changes of name.

For much of the next decade the airfield was dominated by the Armament and Gunnery School (AGS), but it also housed a number of operational

FK3 at Eastchurch, 1917.

TB8 at Eastchurch March 1918, with naval personnel relaxing on the grass. (Peter Green)

## AIRFIELD DATA DEC 1944

| | | | |
|---|---|---|---|
| Command: | RAF Flying Training | Runway surface: | Grass |
| Function: | Aircrew Reselection Centre | Hangars: | 3 × Bellman |
| Runways: | SE/NW 1,600yd | Dispersals: | 51 × Sommerfeld Track, rectangular |
| | N/S 1,200yd | Personnel: | Officers – 134 (16 WAAF) |
| | E/W 1,200yd | | Other Ranks – 2,194 (294 WAAF) |

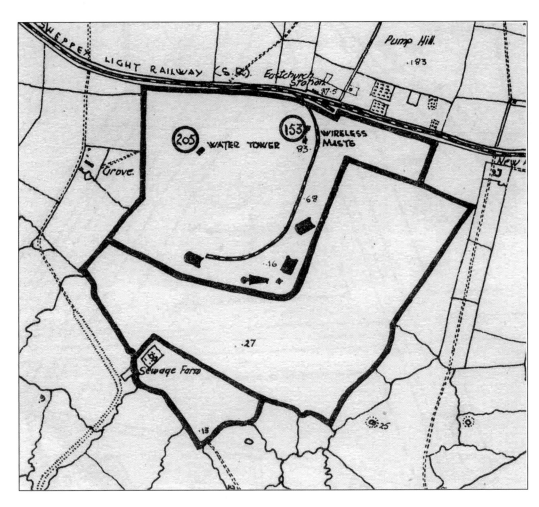

squadrons, longest serving of which was 207 Squadron, which took up residence in October 1923 and remained until November 1929, its DH9As giving way to Fairey IIIFs in December 1927. Other units came and went but training remained dominant, yet another change of nomenclature creating the Air Armament School (AAS). The only other significant flying-unit during the 1920s was the Coastal Defence Co-operation Flight, in residence from 1924 to 1932. The AAS was a significant unit and, during its time at Eastchurch, it continued to grow and develop its role, one of the reasons for its presence here being the nearness of a series of ranges for both trials and training; the Isle of Sheppey was also a reasonable, remote location for such activities. This situation continued into the late-1930s until, in 1938, operational units returned to the airfield as the RAF prepared for war. The arrival of 21 Squadron in

August 1938 and 48 Squadron the following month did not, however, signify an operational capability, as both were concerned with either re-equipment or training. The Station was allocated to No.16 Group of Coastal Command, but this organization did not position any of its limited operational resources; instead, by summer 1939, the resident unit departed and the airfield was reduced to Care and Maintenance (13 September) whilst consideration was given to its wartime role. Initial use, from December, was a Polish Training Centre tasked with orientation and then posting of Polish Air Force personnel who had escaped to Britain. This Centre moved to safer havens in May 1940 and at the end of that month Eastchurch joined the war when a detachment of 59 Squadron Blenheims flew anti-shipping sorties from here. For the remainder of 1940 a number of squadrons spent short periods detached here, performing a variety of roles, including the Spitfires of 19 Squadron from July to September.

Eastchurch was in a vulnerable location but, given enough warning, fighters based here were also well placed to intercept aircraft approaching London. The airfield was itself attacked on 13 August, when Do17s of KG2 caused damage to hangars and other buildings, with sixteen people killed. The attack also destroyed a number of aircraft as, on this particular day, Eastchurch had five squadrons in residence, the Spitfires of 266 Squadron having arrived the previous day and the Blenheims of 53 Squadron also being present once more, as were Battles of 12 and 142 Squadrons. Its vulnerability was confirmed by a number of other attacks in subsequent weeks, each of which caused further damage and casualties. The decision was taken that the airfield was untenable and the flying units quickly moved out; Eastchurch saw little further use until the main threat of attack was over in spring 1941.

In June 1941, the airfield was transferred to Technical Training Command and became home to ground-based units, such as the RAF Artillery School, which was joined in September by No.1 Parachute and Cable Establishment, the RAF persevering with this unusual airfield-defence system. From mid-1942 the airfield was once more hosting flying units, although this invariably involved squadrons being deployed here for specific operations, the Dieppe operation of August 1942, for example, when Eastchurch housed two Spitfire squadrons. It was a similar story for the rest of the war and no unit stayed here for more than a few weeks, although early 1944 was a particularly hectic period with Typhoon units. However, by that time the airfield had undergone two more changes of ownership, having transferred to No.72 Group of Army Co-operation Command in October 1942 and to No.54

Officers of 39 Squadron at Eastchurch, 1923.

Group of Flying Training Command in May 1943.

Eastchurch was one of many airfields used for evaluating the three-squadron mobile Airfield concept that had been introduced as part of the preparations for the invasion of Europe. No.122 Airfield formed at Eastchurch on 1 April 1943 and its Spitfire squadrons practised mobile operations as well as air gunnery, for which they were supported by No.1493 Target Towing Flight. During its time at Eastchurch, the Airfield swapped squadrons with other units but maintained its three-squadron strength. However, this burst of activity was soon over and an Aircrew Re-selection Centre was opened (and stayed here until August 1946); it was, perhaps, unfortunate that such a unit, whose task it was to find new trades for aircrew no longer fit for their original flying duty, was soon co-located with a busy flying-unit – No.18 Armament Practice Camp (APC) forming here in October. A number of new hangars (Bellman type) were erected and a series of track dispersals laid out – fifty-one of these rectangular Sommerfeld Track dispersals being listed in the December 1944 survey. This was the reason for all the Typhoon 'dets' in early 1944, as squadrons rotated through the airfield to work with the APC, although in the case of the Typhoons this also included rocket-projectile work. The APC moved to Fairwood Common in August 1944, but the airfield retained some flying for the final months of the war with 567 Anti-Aircraft Co-operation Squadron; this unit was associated with 765 Squadron of the Fleet Air Arm and it seems likely that the latter also appeared at Eastchurch, although their allocated base was at Manston.

By mid-1946 everyone had gone and on 1 September the airfield was reduced once more to Care and Maintenance, being declared inactive the following April. Most of the site reverted to agriculture but one area was acquired by the Home Office and, like so many wartime airfields, became the site of a prison.

Blenheim of 21 Squadron after a landing accident in 1938.

# UNITS

## HQ Units at Eastchurch

| | | |
|---|---|---|
| Naval Wing HQ | 1912–? | |
| No.122 Airfield | 4 Apr 1943–1 Jun 1943 | 122, 132, 174, 181, 185, 602 Sqn |

## Pre-1919

| | | |
|---|---|---|
| 4 Sqn | 21 Jul 1914–13 Aug 1914 | BE2, BE2a, BE2c |
| 204 TDS | 1 Apr 1918–Mar 1919 | various |
| 1 OS | Jul 1918–28 Dec 1918 | DH9 |
| 2 MOS | 28 Dec 1918–Jun 1919 | various |

## RNAS/FAA Units

| | | |
|---|---|---|
| Naval Training Wing | 1911–1 Apr 1918 | |
| War Flight | ?–Feb 1917 | |
| Eastchurch Sqn | Aug 1914–Sep 1914 | various |
| 2 Sqn RNAS | 10–16 Sep 1914; 17 Oct 1914–21 Jun 1915 | |
| 2 Wg RNAS | 21 Jun 1915–Aug 1915 | |
| 4 Sqn RNAS | 3 Aug 1915–Oct 1915 | |
| 4 Wg RNAS | Oct 1915–Apr 1916 | |
| GSF | 1 May 1916–25 Apr 1917 | |
| OSF | 25 Dec 1916–? | |
| Design Flt | 14 Aug 1916–17 Mar 1917 | |

## 1919–1938

| | | |
|---|---|---|
| 21 Sqn | 15 Aug 1938–2 Mar 1939 | Hind, Blenheim |
| 33 Sqn | 14 Sep 1929–5 Nov 1930 | Horsley |
| 48 Sqn | 1–28 Sep 1938; 10 Oct 1938–25 Aug 1939 | Anson |
| 100 Sqn | May 1924–Jul 1924 | Vimy |
| 207 Sqn | 3 Oct 1923–9 Nov 1929 | DH9a, Fairey IIIF |
| AGS | 1 Apr 1922–1 Jan 1932 | |
| CDCF | 1 Dec 1924–23 May 1933 | |
| AMMF | 1 Nov 1924–9 Jan 1925 | Snipe |
| AAS | 1 Jan 1932–1 Nov 1937 | Various |
| 1 AAS | 1 Nov 1937–15 Aug 1938 | Various |
| 2 AAS | 1 Jul 1938–2 Sep 1939 | Wallace |

## 1939–1945

| | | |
|---|---|---|
| 19 Sqn det | Jul 1940–Sep 1940 | Spitfire |
| 53 Sqn | 1–13 Jun 1940 | Blenheim |
| 59 Sqn | 31 May 1940–6 Jun 1940 | Blenheim |
| 65 Sqn | 14–20 Aug 1942 | Spitfire |
| 122 Sqn | 18 May 1943–1 Jun 1943 | Spitfire |
| 124 Sqn | 30 Jun 1942–5 Jul 1942 | Spitfire |
| 132 Sqn | 5 Apr 1943–18 May 1943 | Spitfire |
| 142 Sqn | 12 Aug 1940–6 Sep 1940 | Battle |
| 165 Sqn | 15–20 Aug 1942 | Spitfire |
| 174 Sqn | 21 Jan 1944–4 Feb 1944 | Typhoon |
| 175 Sqn | 24 Feb 1944–8 Mar 1944 | Typhoon |
| 181 Sqn | 6–21 Feb 1944 | Typhoon |
| 182 Sqn | 5–23 Jan 1944 | Typhoon |
| 183 Sqn | 14–25 Jul 1944 | Typhoon |
| 184 Sqn | 5 Apr 1943–31 May 1943; 11 Mar 1944–3 Apr 1944 | Hurricane, Typhoon |
| 245 Sqn | 25–30 Apr 1944; 12–22 May 1944 | Typhoon |
| 247 Sqn | 1–24 Apr 1944 | Typhoon |
| 263 Sqn | 23 Jul 1944–6 Aug 1944 | Typhoon |
| 266 Sqn | 12–14 Aug 1940; 29 Jun 1944–13 Jul 1944 | Spitfire, Typhoon |
| 291 Sqn det | Dec 1943–Jun 1945 | various |
| 401 Sqn | 3–28 Jul 1942 | Spitfire |
| 567 Sqn det | Dec 1943–Jun 1946 | various |
| 1493 Flt | 14 Apr 1943–26 Jul 1943 | Lysander, Master |
| 18 APC | 26 Dec 1943–8 Aug 1944 | |

# MEMORIALS

Impressive wall plaque near church, inscribed:

> This memorial commemorates the first home of British aviation 1909. Near this spot at Leysdown, Eastchurch (Mussel Manor) (Stonepits Farm) flights and experiments were made by members of the Aero Club (later Royal) of Great Britain. Also the establishment of the first aircraft factory in Great Britain by Short Brothers 1909 and the formation of the first Royal Naval Air Service Station 1911.

# EASTLEIGH (Southampton) (HMS *Raven*)

**County:** Hampshire

**UTM/Grid:** OS map 196–SU454170
**Lat/Long:** N50°57.0 W001°21.3
**Nearest Town:** On the north-east outskirts of Southampton

Spitfire prototype K5054; the connection of Eastleigh with the Spitfire is enough to assure the airfield's place in RAF history.

## HISTORY

Although this site to the north-east of Southampton had a few minor flirtations with aviation as early as 1910, it was not until the Royal Flying Corps set their sights on creating an airfield here that we have the true origins of Eastleigh. An area of North Stoneham Farm was acquired for use as an Aircraft Acceptance Park and a number of hangars and storage sheds were erected. However, the plan appears to have changed and, before construction was complete, the airfield was allocated to the new American bomber-force. On 23 July 1918 the airfield was duly commissioned as Naval Air Station Eastleigh – the title reflecting that this was US Navy – and was one of very few purely American airfields in England during this period. Crated DH9As arrived and were assembled, tested and sent across to France for the operational squadrons of 10th Bombing Group. The airfield continued to expand as more assembly sheds and workshops were added, with repair and overhaul being added to the basic-assembly task. To the Americans the airfield was known as Base B and it was, without

doubt, a success, the first period of aircraft construction at an airfield that would become famous for this activity. However, the end of the war brought a rapid run-down and, over a period of a few months, the Americans went home, finally abandoning Eastleigh on 10 April 1919. Later in the year a number of RAF squadrons passed through the airfield, but it was a sad association, as they had no aircraft and had come to disband. By early 1920 this phase was over and the station closed in May.

Some civil flying took place from Eastleigh during the 1920s, but it seemed unlikely that it would ever again be a busy airfield. However, in 1929, the local authority acquired part of the site for a municipal airport, although plans progressed only slowly and it was November 1932 before the airfield was officially open. Initial users were the Hampshire Aero Club but, over the next couple of years, two commercial operators, Jersey Airways and Railway Air Services, were operating from Eastleigh. Of more significance was the interest shown in using the airfield for flight

Shark of 821 Squadron releasing a torpedo; the Squadron operated Sharks and Swordfish from Eastleigh. (Ray Sturtivant)

testing and, in September 1932, Supermarine took over part of the airfield, leasing two hangars; a variety of Supermarine and Vickers products appeared at Eastleigh, although it was a few more years before that most famous product, the Spitfire, appeared. The mid- to late-1930s was also a time when a number of RAF and FAA squadrons spent brief periods here, the latter acquiring a small area of the site and erecting its own Bessonneau hangars. This naval facility was later given a dummy deck, marked on the runway and including lighting for night flying. In typical fashion for naval squadrons, it was a question of periods ashore and periods embarked, hence the dates given below are not continuous periods at the airfield.

One of the most notable events in British military aviation took place at Eastleigh on 5 March 1936, when the prototype Spitfire made its first flight from the airfield; Spitfire variants played a major part in much of the RAF's air war and, to many people, was the aircraft that won the Battle of Britain. For this reason alone, the name of Eastleigh is assured a place in aviation annals.

The airfield became RAF Southampton on 1 August 1936 but, despite this official naming, it was still more commonly referred to as Eastleigh or, at best, as Southampton-Eastleigh. The following year was notable for three events: the arrival of part of Air Service Training's flying school from Hamble in February; an impressive collection of FAA aircraft using Eastleigh for the Navy Review at Spithead in May; and the Supermarine display (not open to the public) in June. As the inevitability of war loomed, a

number of RAF and FAA squadrons came and went, Supermarine attempted to increase Spitfire production to meet increased orders and a new manufacturer, Cunliffe-Owen Aircraft Ltd, opened a facility on the south side of the airfield at Swaythling, their OA-1 making its first flight on 12 January 1939.

The Fleet Air Arm had come to dominate the military presence and, to reflect this, the airfield became HMS *Raven* on 1 July 1939. Its initial role was as a training school, with Sharks and Ospreys of 780 Squadron used as a conversion-course unit to bring civilian-trained pilots up to naval standards. With a diverse fleet of aircraft, the unit undertook this task until moved to Lee-on-Solent in October 1940. It was a similar pattern for the other training unit, 759 Squadron, formed on 26 May to train Telegraphist Air Gunners (TAGs), but it was renumbered 758 squadron on 1 July and it was as the latter unit that it acquired a diverse fleet, including the Osprey, Shark, Skua and Roc, for this task. This squadron moved to Arbroath in October 1940, leaving behind some of its aircraft. Other squadrons formed at or passed through Southampton and the Fleet Air Arm remained the major military user of the airfield throughout the war, although for much of this time its main function was ground training for the likes of the Safety Equipment School, the School of Air Medicine and a fire training establishment.

The Germans were well aware of the aircraft factories at Southampton and, despite attempts to camouflage buildings, it was not a difficult target to find. The first air-raid took place on 24 August but caused little damage; a return on 11 September was more

Spitfire EN199 at Eastleigh. (Peter Green)

effective, the bombers hitting the Cunliffe-Owen works, causing severe damage. By the time the Luftwaffe came back again on 8 October, the naval flying-training units had departed for safer havens. Although a few more raids took place they did not cause much damage, the serious disruption to Spitfire production having been caused by attacks on Supermarine's other facilities in the area, notably the Woolston and Itchen factories. Both of the airfield's aircraft production facilities played an important part throughout the war and a great many types passed through Eastleigh, the Cunliffe-Owen works in particular proving adept at turning its hand to production or modification of a variety of types; it is often not appreciated that Eastleigh was far more than 'just' Spitfires.

With the end of the war it was all change for the airfield, as the navy ran down its presence eventually relinquishing HMS *Raven* in April 1946. The airfield was taken over by the Ministry of Civil Aviation the following month, although the first civil operator, Channel Island Airways, had started services the previous December. The Hampshire Aero Club was soon up and running and there was a military presence from October 1946, albeit short-lived, with Southampton University Air Squadron. The once famous aircraft-production side of the airfield was soon in terminal decline and, although Cierva used the Cunliffe-Owen facilities to produce types such as the Air Horse, an impressive but ultimately unsuccessful helicopter, there appeared to be little future, Supermarine having already departed. However, in January 1951, Saunders-Roe took over facilities at Southampton and also pressed ahead with the Skeeter helicopter acquired from Cierva. This was followed by work on the Scout but in 1959 the Company was acquired by Westland, who moved production to Hayes the following year.

It was also a gloomy period for the commercial operation of the airport, with the Ministry unwilling

to invest and pessimistic about the future. However, in May 1961, the local authority re-acquired the airport and, with the support of carriers such as Silver City and, later, British United, persevered. More importantly they invested, the major capital expense being the construction of a 5,653ft runway plus a parking apron and updated terminal, all of which opened in 1966. The next twenty years were not easy and there were times when Southampton Airport's future looked bleak (again), but it managed to survive the hard times and, with the boom in regional airports in since the early 1990s and helped by significant private investment, survived and even flourished. The airfield is now in the hands of BAA (British Airport Authority) and its single asphalt-runway has witnessed steadily growing traffic numbers.

## UNITS

### 1919–1938

| | | |
|---|---|---|
| 7 Sqn | 27 Oct 1919–19 Nov 1919 | no aircraft |
| 28 Sqn | 20 Oct 1919–20 Jan 1920 | no aircraft |
| 42 Sqn det | Mar 1938–Sep 1938 | Vildebeeste |
| 45 Sqn | 15 Oct 1919–31 Dec 1919 | no aircraft |
| 101 Sqn | 11 Oct 1919–31 Dec 1919 | no aircraft |
| 201 Sqn | 2 Sep 1919–31 Dec 1919 | no aircraft |
| 224 Sqn | 17 Jan 1938–26 Mar 1938 | Anson |
| 269 Sqn | 17 Jan 1938–24 Mar 1938 | Anson |
| 800 Sqn | 29 Feb 1936–7 Jun 1938+ | Nimrod, Osprey |
| 801 Sqn | 23 Nov 1935–29 Jan 1938+ | Nimrod, Osprey |
| 802 Sqn | 5 May 1937–23 Jun 1937 | Nimrod, Osprey |

### 1939–1945

**FAA Units**

| | | |
|---|---|---|
| 758 Sqn | 1 Jul 1939–14 Oct 1940 | various |
| 759 Sqn | 26 May 1939–1 Jul 1939 | no aircraft |
| 760 Sqn | 1 Apr 1940–16 Sep 1940 | Skua, Roc, Sea Gladiator |
| 780 Sqn | 2 Oct 1939–7 Oct 1940 | various |
| 811 Sqn | 15 May 1939–12 Aug 1939 | Swordfish |
| 814 Sqn | 1 Dec 1938–11 Jan 1939; 24 Mar 1939–2 Jun 1939 | Swordfish |
| 821 Sqn | 4 Nov 1936–29 Jul 1939+ | Shark, Swordfish |
| 822 Sqn | 21 May 1936–28 Sep 1936; 15 May 1939–12 Aug 1939 | Shark, Swordfish |

### Post-1945

| | | |
|---|---|---|
| Southampton UAS | 18 Oct 1946–1 Oct 1947 | Tiger Moth |

# FAIROAKS

**County:** Surrey

**UTM/Grid:** OS map 176–TQ005623
**Lat/Long:** N51°21.1 W000°33.2
**Nearest Town:** Woking 2 miles to south

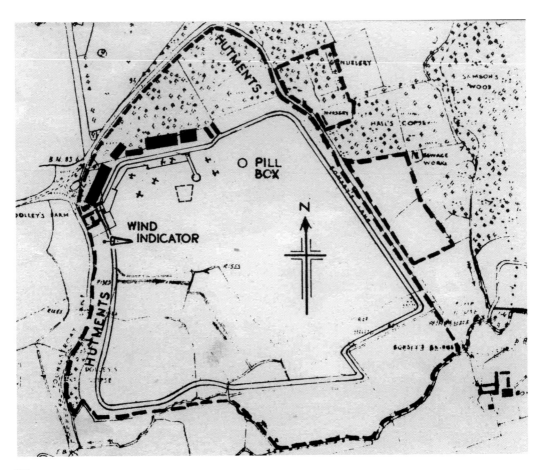

## HISTORY

Although Fairoaks was an Expansion Period airfield, it was not arranged in the standard pattern and was designated for training-unit use, opening in the late-1930s for No.18 E&RFTS (Elementary and Refresher Flying School). The airfield was also known as Dolley's Farm and may have had some private use before the RAF arrived. The E&RFTS was operated by Universal Flying Services and was mainly equipped with Tiger Moths. This basic-training role continued throughout the war, the based unit having been renamed 18 EFTS at the outbreak of war. The original series of hangars and other buildings in the north-west corner of the airfield steadily grew, the main addition being nine Blister hangars of various

types, although the Ministry of Aircraft Production also erected a number of hangars on the other side of the A319. The grass surface was ideal for the Tiger Moths and their pilot training and Fairoaks was a busy airfield; by mid-1941 it was a Class A school with an allocation of thirty aircraft.

By 1944 Fairoaks had three RLGs allocated to it: Bray, Smiths Lawn and Winkfield. The training role continued into the post-war period as Tiger Moths gave way to Chipmunks and even Ansons; there was also a change of name to more accurately reflect the training being carried out – No.18 Reserve Flying School. The RAF's interest in the airfield came to an end in July 1953, the end of the Korean War bringing

## AIRFIELD DATA DEC 1944

| | | | |
|---|---|---|---|
| Command: | RAF Flying Training | Runway surface: | Grass |
| Function: | EFTS (Parent) | Hangars: | RAF: 5 × Blister, 2 × Double Blister, 1 × Extended Over Blister, 1 × Civil, 1 × Double Extended Over Blister. MAP: 1 × Civil (80ft × 80ft), 1 × Civil (350ft × 90ft), 1 × Civil (110ft × 100ft), R-type (240ft × 114ft) |
| Runways: | NE/SW 950yd | Dispersals: | nil |
| | NW/SE 950yd | Personnel: | Other Ranks – 175 |
| | N/S 850yd | | |
| | E/W 880yd | | |

an end to the main period of reservist flying. For the final three years of the 1940s, the London University Air Squadron had also been resident, moving to Booker in October 1950.

It was not until 1967, however, that the MoD relinquished the airfield, at which point it was acquired by Doug Arnold and became Fairoaks Airport. The Fairoaks School of Flying was soon followed by private owners – but perhaps the greatest interest became Arnold's collection of historic aircraft. Over the past almost forty years as a private airfield Fairoaks has undergone a number of changes of owner and resident aircraft.

Today Fairoaks Airport (EGTF) operates a single asphalt-runway (06/24) of 2,400ft and is used by a number of private operators and clubs, such as the London Transport Flying Club, as well as being the HQ for the Alan Mann Group. There are various buildings that relate to its wartime period and it is a pleasant place to while away a few hours in the Prop Coffee Shop (www.fairoaks-airport.co.uk).

## UNITS

**1919–1938**

| | | |
|---|---|---|
| 18 E&RFTS | 1 Oct 1937–3 Sep 1939 | Tiger Moth |

**1939–1945**

| | | |
|---|---|---|
| 18 EFTS | 3 Sep 1939–14 May 1947 | Tiger Moth |

**Post-1945**

| | | |
|---|---|---|
| 167 GS | 1945–1948 | Cadet |
| 18 RFS | 14 May 1947–31 Jul 1953 | Tiger Moth, Chipmunk, Anson |
| LUAS | 15 Dec 1947–6 Oct 1950 | Chipmunk, Anson |

# FARNBOROUGH

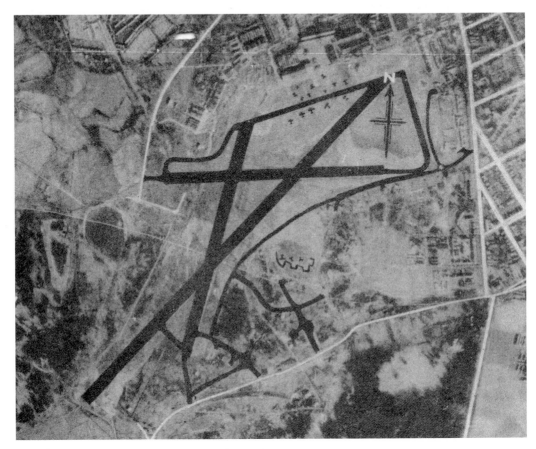

## HISTORY

Farnborough is best known for its role over the last fifty years as home to the exhibition of the latest and best in aviation – the Society of British Aircraft Constructors' (SBAC) show. However, this is a much-skewed view of what has been one of the most important, albeit not operational, airfields in the UK. Farnborough's role in the early development of military aviation and its subsequent involvement with testing and evaluation have secured its place in British aviation heritage and it is good to see that a Trust has been established to preserve at least some elements of this heritage.

The British Army had been involved with balloons since the late-nineteenth century and the Balloon Factory had been established at Aldershot, a

major garrison town, whilst the Royal Engineers re-organized the military employment of balloons. By early summer 1905, the balloon establishment was in need of a new location for the dirigible types then being developed and an area on Farnborough Common was chosen, as it had plenty of space and was close to the existing facilities at Aldershot.

The first building erected was an impressive balloon-shed and this was soon followed by other structures, including gas holders and various workshops; the site was expanded further with the creation of the Balloon School and the growing importance of the Balloon Factory. On 16 October 1908, Samuel Cody flew his Wright-type aeroplane from the common, achieving the first sustained flight in England. This

Atmospheric shot of a line-up of Maurice Farmans.

activity, the aircraft having been built in the airship shed, was met with mixed official reaction, as the military was still in favour of airships. It was not until 1911 that this official view was changed and, in April that year, the Farnborough site became the Army Aircraft Factory, concerning itself with airships and aeroplanes. The Air Battalion of the Royal Engineers had formed in February and two months later established its No.1 (Airship) Company at South Farnborough. It was this unit that became 1 Squadron Royal Flying Corps the following May, the justification used by 1 Squadron for being the RAF's oldest squadron – although 2 Squadron counterclaims that it was the first aeroplane squadron (it formed at Farnborough with BE types the same day, 13 May 1912).

Farnborough remained at the heart of this initial build-up of RFC strength, with other squadrons forming or passing through the airfield. Facilities were expanded, with a variety of hangars, workshops and other buildings being erected, although there was still a fair amount of tentage at the airfield. Various unit-changes took place as the nascent RFC prepared for and then departed to World War One, with the now extensive site of Farnborough still being involved with airships and aeroplanes, having acquired a development and training role for both. By late-1914 the operational work-up of squadrons was temporarily complete and the airfield became more of a training establishment (as home to No.1 Reserve Squadron) and repair depot, eventually becoming an Aircraft Park. The diverse nature of Farnborough's roles continued throughout the war, with a number of squadrons forming and equipping before moving on, with aircrew training with the Reserve Squadron (until it left in 1916) and with specialist training-units such as the School for Wireless Operators. However, it was, perhaps, the Aircraft Repair Depot and the general role of the Royal Aircraft Factory in the design, test and construction of aircraft that were more significant – there were even a number of wind

tunnels on site. It was a complex and busy airfield and, at almost 300 acres and with over 5,000 personnel, was one of the largest military airfields.

The formation of the RAF in April 1918 brought a change of name, from the Farnborough organization to Royal Aircraft Establishment (RAE), and, whilst aircraft production ceased with the end of the war, the Establishment continued to play a key role in aircraft development. The RAE absorbed a number of other units over the next few years, as the RAF settled into a post-war organization, whilst the Repair Depot took on a storage and disposal role. A brief return to operational flying took place in the early 1920s with the presence of 4 Squadron, one of the units that had originally formed at Farnborough, but although this unit was in residence, on and off until the late-1930s, the airfield's main rationale remained that of development and trials. During the 1930s the RAE undertook a wide range of trials on aircraft and equipment; new facilities were constantly being added, including water tanks and wind tunnels.

With the outbreak of war the RAE remained in residence and soon acquired German aircraft and equipment for evaluation, the first being a Bf109. The role of the RAE and its scientists and specialists in analysing and assessing enemy equipment was highly important and is all too often passed over. Throughout the war the Establishment performed this vital role and a peek inside its hangars would have been fascinating, as there was very little enemy equipment it didn't obtain. However, it was also concerned with developing material for the RAF and its work on instruments, weapons and a host of other subjects was crucial. The Luftwaffe only managed one effective raid on Farnborough, when a small force of Ju88s dropped bombs on the airfield, causing some damage to RAE installations.

The airfield underwent a number of improvements during the war, including three runways, the longest of which was over 6,000ft, whilst buildings were mod-

A number of RFC squadrons were formed at Farnborough and BE-types were a common site, such as this BE12.

# AIRFIELD DATA DEC 1944

| | | | |
|---|---|---|---|
| Command: | RAF Technical Training | Runway surface: | Concrete |
| Function: | Experimental Station | Hangars: | 4 × Permanent, various Blisters and others |
| Runways: | 251 deg 2,050yd | Dispersals: | 10 × Diamond, 7 × Circular |
| | 223 deg 1,360yd | Personnel: | Officers – 201 (16 WAAF) |
| | 183 deg 1,000yd | | Other Ranks – 1,596 (557 WAAF) |
| | 300 deg 1,000yd | | |

The RAE evaluated a number of enemy aircraft types, such as this Heinkel 111 in September 1940.

ified or added to. The Establishment remained after the war and photographs taken in 1946 show the marvellous collection of German aircraft that it had managed to acquire. Although workload and size reduced as peacetime conditions returned, the RAE remained at the forefront of military aviation and, in 1947, it was joined at Farnborough by the Empire Test Pilots School (ETPS). The airfield was also home to a variety of other units, including the Institute of Aviation Medicine and the Met Research Flight, which, in its latter years, operated the very distinctive Hercules W.2 with its long nose-probe. The SBAC held their first show here in 1948 and since then Farnborough has been the showcase, at first annually and then bi-annually, of new products from British, and later worldwide, aircraft and equipment manufacturers. The show now takes place in alternate years in July (2004, 2006 and so on) and, despite the fact that very few new aircraft are produced, it is still a showcase for both military and civil aviation.

With the departure of much of RAE's flying to Bedford and the move of ETPS to Boscombe Down in 1968, the based flying at Farnborough was greatly reduced; whilst the latest extension of the runway to 7,814ft made it suitable for most aircraft, the approaches and environmental issues, as housing encroached on the airfield, put pressure on military flying operations. The latter years of the airfield's military career – and it is worth noting that, since 1948, it had been a Ministry and not RAF airfield – included a number of flying units, with the MRF,

elements of the RAE's Experimental Flying Department and the Army Air Corps. By the early 1980s flying strength had reduced again and it was decided that Ministry of Defence (Procurement Executive) – MoD(PE), the operators of the airfield – could not justify keeping all of its flying stations; it was announced in 1981 that Farnborough would close in 1985. The decision was challenged, in part because of the perceived national value of the SBAC show and lack of an alternate venue, and the airfield was reprieved, although with a change to its operational structure. Part of the airfield was leased for general aviation, primarily business aviation, purposes but it soon became apparent that there was no official future for the airfield and an alternative use had to be found. By the early 1990s an aerospace park had been established and, whilst the GA element did not exactly flourish, it did survive.

The closure arguments took place again and it was finally agreed to sell (actually a 99-year lease) the airfield to a commercial operation, whilst retaining rights to hold the SBAC show on the site in alternate years (July 2006 is the next show after this book's publication). By 1997, TAG Aviation had been declared the successful bidders and, following an multi-million pound investment in developing the airfield, new control tower and other buildings, as well as 'civilizing' the runway, the 'new' airfield

Sea Hornet PX214 on the test catapult January 1946. (Aldon Ferguson)

Formation of Devons over the threshold of Runway 36 sometime in 1955. (Aldon Ferguson)

duly opened. The airfield (EGLF) now has a single paved-runway of 8,000ft and has established itself as a successful business-aviation airfield.

## UNITS

### HQ Units at Farnborough
RFC Administrative Wing

| | | |
|---|---|---|
| No.22 Gp | 12 Apr 1926–1 Dec 1940 | |
| No.70 Gp | 25 Nov 1940–17 Jul 1945 | |
| AC Command | 1 Dec 1940–31 May 1945 | |

### Pre-1919

| | | |
|---|---|---|
| 1 Sqn | 13 May 1912–1 May 1914 | airships |
| 2 Sqn | 13 May 1912–26 Feb 1913 | various |
| 4 Sqn | 16 Sep 1912–14 Jun 1913 | various |
| 5 Sqn | 26 Jul 1913–28 May 1914 | various |
| 6 Sqn | 31 Jan 1914–21 Sep 1914; 4–7 Oct 1914 | various |
| 7 Sqn | 1 May 1914–8 Aug 1914; 29 Sep 1914–24 Oct 1914; 19 Nov 1919–31 Dec 1919 | various |
| 10 Sqn | 1–8 Jan 1915 | various |
| 15 Sqn | 1 Mar 1915–13 Apr 1915 | various |
| 31 Sqn | 11 Oct 1915–Nov 1915 | BE2c |
| 53 Sqn | 11–26 Dec 1916 | various |
| 70 Sqn | 22 Apr 1916–Dec 1916 | 1½ Strutter |
| 100 Sqn | 23 Feb 1917–21 Mar 1917 | BE2c |
| 101 Sqn | 12 Jul 1917–7 Aug 1917 | BE2b, BE12 |
| 1 RS | Aug 1914–7 Apr 1916 | various |
| 4 RS | 29 Jan 1915–1 Mar 1915 | various |
| SWO | 24 Aug 1916–18 Oct 1917 | |
| WS | 1915–Aug 1916; 18 Oct 1917–8 Nov 1917 | |
| 1 (T) WS | 8 Nov 1917–9 Nov 1918 | |
| RAE | 1 Apr 1918–23 Mar 1994 | various |

### 1919–1938

| | | |
|---|---|---|
| 4 Sqn | 30 Apr 1920–Sep 1922; 18 Sep 1923–16 Feb 1937 | F2b, Atlas, Audax |
| 53 Sqn | 28 Jun 1937–8 Apr 1938 | Hector |
| 108 Sqn | 18 Feb 1937–7 Jul 1937 | Hind |
| SoP | 23 Dec 1919–6 Jan 1948 | various |
| 1 GCF | 1 Apr 1934–13 Jun 1935 | Queen Bee |
| 1 AACU | 11 Apr 1938–1 Oct 1942 | Henley, Queen Bee |

### 1939–1945

| | | |
|---|---|---|
| 16 Sqn det | Oct 1941–Nov 1941 | Lysander |
| 285 Sqn det | Nov 1944–Jun 1945 | Hurricane, Mustang |
| 287 Sqn det | Jul 1944–Aug 1944 | Spitfire |
| 290 Sqn det | Aug 1944–Feb 1945 | Hurricane, Martinet, Oxford |
| 653 Sqn | 8 Jul 1942–7 Sep 1942 | Tiger Moth |
| 22 Gp CF | 6 Oct 1939–1 Dec 1940 | |
| 70 Gp CF | 1 Dec 1940–17 Jul 1945 | |
| 7 AACU | Jun 1942–Nov 1943 | various |
| AFEE | Dec 1943 | various |

### Post-1945

| | | |
|---|---|---|
| 664 Sqn | Oct 1969–Mar 1978 | Sioux, Scout |
| 656 Sqn | Mar 1978–Mar 1982 | Scout, Gazelle |
| MRF | 1 Sep 1946–18 Dec 1950, Dec 1952–1994 | various |
| ETPS | 12 Jul 1947–29 Jan 1968 | various |

## MEMORIALS

Various plaques and memorials are located at Farnborough, plus the new FAST (Farnborough Air Sciences Trust) museum. The latter is situated in the Old Balloon School and, in addition to various airframes, is attempting to preserve and display some of the many and often wondrous items of testing equipment used at Farnborough during its long history (www.apbe54.dsl.pipex.com).

The SBAC shows at Farnborough have been central to the British Aerospace industry for over 50 years; the Scottish Aviation Twin Pioneer puts on a display.

# FORD
## (HMS *Peregrine*)

**County:** West Sussex

**UTM/Grid:** OS map 181–SU995029
**Lat/Long:** N50°49.0 W000°35.3
**Nearest Town:** Littlehampton 2¼ miles to south-east

Aerial view of Ford in September 2002 showing the well-preserved runway layout.

## History

Ford was, perhaps, one of the most important airfields in Sussex during World War Two, not so much for the size of its operation but because of the role that one of its units, the Fighter Interception Unit (FIU), played in the development of night-fighter tactics. Changing hands between the Fleet Air Arm and the RAF on a regular basis, Ford was home to many units, both operational and training, during its career. The airfield's origins were as a training station, whose construction was approved in late-1917. Work commenced on an 85-acre site early the following year under the name Ford Junction, the nearest rail station, although the site was also known as Yapton after a nearby village. In addition to some grading work on the grass surfaces, the major work entailed construction of facilities for a Training Depot Station, the major element of which was a series of hangars, more accurately 'General Service Sheds' and a variety of wooden buildings. Before the airfield was

Ford was allocated to the United States Army Air Service in the latter part of World War One as a number training station; this is not a Ford picture.

complete, it had been decided to allocate it to the US Army Air Service and the Americans duly arrived at Ford Junction in August 1918, the intention at this

On the eve of war the FAA was still operating a large number of biplanes, such as this Shark of 750 Squadron. (Ray Sturtivant)

During the RAF's wartime tenure a large number of Spitfire units rotated through Ford.

Both the RAF and FAA operated Mosquitoes from Ford. (Ray Sturtivant)

Oxford PH188 of 778 Squadron at Ford in 1946.

stage being to train and operate on Handley Page 0/400s. Before this, however, the RFC had made limited use of the airfield, when 148 Squadron moved in on 1 March and two days later had part of its strength taken away to form 149 Squadron, both operating FE2bs in the night-bomber role: after a few weeks of training both left for operations in France.

Three operational American squadrons passed through the airfield between September and November, two actually forming here, but it was the formation on 15 September of the Night Bombardment Training School that signified the true purpose of the airfield. The unit's first HP 0/400 strategic bomber was assembled on-site but it is doubtful if it ever flew from here; indeed, the end of the war brought a sudden stop to all activity, with the Aero squadrons moving to Tangmere. The RAF took control of the – probably incomplete – airfield and used it for the sad purpose of disbanding squadrons, most of which were cadre-only by the time they arrived at Ford Junction. There is some evidence to suggest that No.50 Training Squadron used the airfield for a short period in 1919, but this is by no

means certain; what is certain is that in January 1920 the airfield was closed.

Ten years later the site was opened as the Sussex Aero Club, whose founders J E Doran-Webb and Dudley Watt were also trying to develop and market aircraft, their first products being the DW.1 and DW.2, the former being a variant of the wartime SE5a fighter! Various commercial activities took place over the next few years, including the import and marketing of the Ford Trimotor but, whilst there were fascinating episodes and interesting tenants, such as Alan Cobham, there was only one truly noteworthy development – and one that proved to be ahead of its time – the development of aerial refuelling by Cobham's Flight Refuelling.

Military interest was resurrected in the late-1930s and on 1 November 1937 the Air Ministry acquired the airfield, although Flight Refuelling did not vacate its hangars on the western side of the airfield until May 1940. The airfield 're-opened' a year later, in December 1938, as a School of Naval Co-operation within No.17 Group of Coastal Command. However, on 24 May 1939, the airfield was transferred from

## AIRFIELD DATA DEC 1944

| | | | |
|---|---|---|---|
| Command: | RAF Fighter Command | Runway surface: | Tarmac and wood-chips |
| Function: | Night Fighter Forward Airfield | Hangars: | 16 × Extended Over Blisters, 5 × Bellman, 4 × Over Blisters, 1 × General Purpose |
| Runways: | 248 deg 2,000 × 50yd | Dispersals: | 27 |
| | 337 deg 1,600 × 50yd | Personnel: | Officers – 227 |
| | | | Other Ranks – 2,614 (299 WAAF) |

No.17 Group to the Admiralty and became HMS *Peregrine* for the three squadrons (750, 751, 752) of the No.1 Observer School, whilst also housing an Immediate Use Reserve Pool, storing primarily Albacores and Swordfish. During the first part of 1940 a significant number of naval squadrons passed through Ford (the Junction having been dropped when it re-opened). Ford was on the Luftwaffe target list and was attacked on 18 August as part of the series of raids on RAF 'fighter' airfields; the airfield was convincingly plastered by Ju87s. Plans had already been laid to move the training units to safer airfields and these were now accelerated.

The School moved out in 1940, although one of

the squadrons and a number of other units, such as the School of Naval Photography, remained as lodger units when Ford was handed to No.11 Group of RAF Fighter Command. HMS *Peregrine* was paid off on 30 September, after the Blenheim night-fighters of 23 Squadron had moved in a few days earlier. Ford was attacked a number of times in October, but without any serious effect, although a number of the buildings damaged in the series of raids from August were replaced rather than repaired. It was not long before Ford was developing effective tools with which to strike back. The arrival of the Fighter Interception Unit, along with the growing expertise of 23 Squadron, who in addition to the night-fighting role

Avenger of 703 Squadron, probably early 1950s.
(Ray Sturtivant

A number of Ford-based units operated the Firebrand, this
particular one belonged to 827 Squadron.

Firefly T2 with its strange cockpit arrangement.
(Ray Sturtivant)

703 Squadron was a diverse unit and operated a variety of
types; this bombed-up Sea Fury is being admired during an
Open Day. (Ra Sturtivant)

pioneered night-intruder work, put the airfield cen-
tre-stage in night tactical-development.

Tarmac runways and other facilities were built, the
first runways being laid in 1941, and, over the next
few years, various squadrons spent periods at Ford.
The biggest change came in April 1944, when the
FIU gave way to three fighter-bomber squadrons of
No.122 Airfield. Over the next few weeks the units
rotated, with No.125 Airfield taking over in May and
being joined by No.144 Wing, giving Ford a total of
six squadrons – albeit for a very short period as, post-
D-Day, it was not long before all had gone.
Squadrons based at Ford had been involved with
offensive operations since the early intruder work by
23 Squadron and medium bombers, such as the
Bostons of 88 Squadron, had operated on *Circus*
operations by day, whilst the night-intruder
Beaufighters and later Mosquitoes had prowled the
night skies over Europe.

With the Allies firmly ashore in Europe the tactical air effort moved to the Continent and, in October
1944, Ford became home to the Night Fighter
Development Wing, two of whose main components
were the FIU and the Fleet Air Arm's 746 Squadron.
The December 1944 survey listed Ford as a night-
fighter forward airfield in the Tangmere Sector and
considered that its two runways could each be

extended to around 3,000 yards, the major constraint
being the need to divert the main road. A total of
twenty-six hangars were listed, the majority of these
being Blister variants but, other than that, facilities
were still limited and all accommodation was in 'temporary buildings except for a limited number of married quarters'.

The Fleet Air Arm re-acquired the airfield on 1
August 1946 and HMS *Peregrine* was re-commis-
sioned in the middle of the month. Over the next
two years a large number of FAA squadrons used the
airfield, many reforming or re-equipping and then
quickly moving on, whilst it was also used as a shore
base. Alan Cobham was also back, Flight Refuelling
having taken over hangars at the Yapton site. The
airfield was paid off once more on 30 June 1948, but
remained open as a satellite to Lee-on-Solent,
although this was only a temporary closure whilst
major rebuilding work took place, including extending runway 06/24 to 3,000 yards. The airfield had one
more spell as HMS *Peregrine* from 1 February 1950 to
13 November 1958, maintaining its mixed roles of
trials, by 703 and 771 squadrons, and operational flying. In August 1951 the airfield was home to the
navy's first operational jet unit, 800 Squadron
equipped with Supermarine Attackers. A few years
later the Sea Hawk underwent evaluation and entry

Firefly of 1840 Squadron operating from Ford in the early 1950s. (Ray Sturtivant)

to service at Ford, 700X Flight forming for the purpose in August 1957. Ford must have been a truly wondrous place in the 1950s – as a glance at the unit listing will show – with an amazing array of units and types; Sea Fury, Sea Venom, Attacker, Wyvern and Sea Hawk were just a few of the types that used the airfield. However, on 13 November 1958, HMS *Peregrine* was paid off for the last time and one of the FAA's most fascinating and heritage-rich air stations came to an end.

The airfield site had a mixed fate, part being taken over as a prison but the major part being used as an industrial park; while many of the buildings have gone, the outline of the airfield is still evident and, from the air, Ford's unusual twin-runway layout is still distinctive, albeit partly hidden by buildings.

## UNITS

### HQ Units at Ford

| | | |
|---|---|---|
| No.18 (TR) Wing | 7 Aug 1919–1 Oct 1919 | |
| No.122 Airfield | 15–19 Apr 1944 | |
| No.125 Airfield/ (F) Wing | 4 May 1944–17 Jun 1944 | 132, 453, 602 Sqn |
| No.133 (Polish) (F) Wing | 26 Jun 1944–9 Jul 1944 | 129, 306, 315 Sqn |
| No.144 (RCAF) (F) Wing | May 1944–Jun 1944 | 441, 442, 443 Sqn |

### Pre-1919
### USAS

| | | |
|---|---|---|
| 92nd Aero | Sep 1918–15 Nov 1918 | F.40 |
| 140th Aero | Sep 1918–15 Nov 1918 | BE2c |
| 326th Aero | Sep 1918–15 Nov 1918 | DH4 |
| NBTS | 15 Sep 1918–Nov 1918 | various |

### 1919–1938

| | | |
|---|---|---|
| 10 Sqn | 17 Feb 1919–31 Dec 1919 | cadre only |
| 22 Sqn | 1 Sep 1919–31 Dec 1919 | F2b |
| 97 Sqn | 4 Mar 1919–19 Jul 1919 | DH10? |
| 115 Sqn | 4 Mar 1919–18 Oct 1919 | cadre only |
| 144 Sqn | 14 Dec 1918–4 Feb 1919 | cadre only |
| 148 Sqn | 1 Mar 1918–25 Apr 1918 | FE2b, FE2d |
| 149 Sqn | 3 Mar 1918–2 Jun 1918 | FE2b |
| 215 Sqn | 2 Feb 1919–18 Oct 1919 | cadre only |
| SNC | 29 Dec 1937–24 May 1939 | various |

### 1939–1945

| | | |
|---|---|---|
| 16 Sqn | 26 Feb 1943–13 Mar 1943 | Tomahawk, Spitfire |
| 19 Sqn | 15 Apr 1944–12 May 1944; 15–25 Jun 1944 | Mustang |
| 23 Sqn | 12 Sep 1940–6 Aug 1942 | Blenheim, Havoc, Boston |
| 29 Sqn | 3 Sep 1943–1 Mar 1944 | Mosquito |
| 65 Sqn | 15 Apr 1944–14 May 1944; 15–25 Jun 1944 | Mustang |
| 66 Sqn | 12–20 Aug 1944 | Spitfire |
| 88 Sqn det | Sep 1942–Mar 1943 | Boston |
| 96 Sqn | Oct 1942–Aug 1943; Jun 1944–Sep 1944 | Beaufighter, Mosquito |
| 107 Sqn det | May 1941–Jan 1942 | Boston |
| 122 Sqn | 15 Apr 1944–14 May 1944; 15–26 Jun 1944 | Mustang |
| 127 Sqn | 12–20 Aug 1944 | Spitfire |
| 132 Sqn | 18 Apr 1944–25 Jun 1944 | Spitfire |
| 141 Sqn | 10 Aug 1942–18 Feb 1943 | Beaufighter |
| 170 Sqn | 28 Feb 1943–13 Mar 1943 | Mustang |
| 174 Sqn det | Mar 1942–Jul 1942 | Hurricane |
| 256 Sqn | 24 Apr 1943–25 Aug 1943 | Beaufighter, Mosquito |
| 287 Sqn det | Nov 1941–Jul 1944 | various |
| 288 Sqn det | Jan 1944–Nov 1944 | various |
| 302 Sqn | 16 Jul 1944–4 Aug 1944 | Spitfire |
| 306 Sqn | 27 Jun 1944–8 Jul 1944 | Mustang |
| 308 Sqn | 16 Jul 1944–4 Aug 1944 | Spitfire |
| 315 Sqn | 25 Jun 1944–10 Jul 1944 | Mustang |
| 317 Sqn | 16 Jul 1944–4 Aug 1944 | Spitfire |
| 331 Sqn | 13–30 Aug 1944 | Spitfire |
| 332 Sqn | 12–20 Aug 1944 | Spitfire |
| 418 Sqn | 15 Mar 1943–8 Apr 1944 | Boston, Mosquito |
| 441 Sqn | 13 May 1944–15 Jun 1944 | Spitfire |
| 442 Sqn | 15 May 1944–15 Jun 1944 | Spitfire |
| 443 Sqn | 15 May 1944–15 Jun 1944 | Spitfire |
| 453 Sqn | 18 Apr 1944–25 Jun 1944 | Spitfire |
| 456 Sqn | 29 Feb 1944–31 Dec 1944 | Mosquito |
| 602 Sqn | 18 Apr 1944–25 Jun 1944 | Spitfire |
| 604 Sqn | 18 Feb 1943–24 Apr 1943 | Beaufighter |
| 605 Sqn | 7 Jun 1942–15 Mar 1943 | Havoc, Boston |
| 611 Sqn | 19–22 Nov 1943 | Spitfire |

| Unit | Dates | Aircraft |
|---|---|---|
| 11 Gp TTF | Oct 1941 | Lysander |
| FIU | 26 Jan 1941–1 Oct 1944 | Blenheim, Beaufighter |
| NFDW | 16 Oct 1944–15 Jul 1945 | Mosquito, Beaufighter |
| FIDU | 1 Oct 1944–? | |

**FAA Units**

| Unit | Dates | Aircraft |
|---|---|---|
| 746 Sqn | 1 Dec 1942–3 Apr 1944; 1 Oct 1944–23 Aug 1945 | Fulmar, Firefly |
| 750 Sqn | 24 May 1939–May 1940 | Osprey, Shark |
| 751 Sqn | 24 May 1939–May 1940 | Walrus |
| 752 Sqn | 24 May 1939–May 1940 | Proctor, Vega Gull |
| 782 Sqn | 23 Oct 1939–10 Nov 1939 | no aircraft |
| 793 Sqn | 25 Oct 1939–1 Oct 1940 | Roc |
| 812 Sqn | 24 Apr 1940–19 Jun 1940+ | Swordfish |
| 815 Sqn | 16 May 1940–6 Jun 1940+ | Swordfish |
| 816 Sqn | 31 May 1940–14 Jun 1940+ | Swordfish |
| 819 Sqn | 15 Jan 1940–27 May 1940+ | Swordfish |
| 820 Sqn | 1–20 Mar 1940 | Swordfish |
| 826 Sqn | 15 Mar 1940–7 May 1940 | Albacore |
| 829 Sqn | 15 Jun 1940–23 Aug 1940 | Albacore |

**Post-1945**

| Unit | Dates | Aircraft |
|---|---|---|
| 161 GS | 1946 | |

**FAA Units**

| Unit | Dates | Aircraft |
|---|---|---|
| 700 Sqn | 18 Aug 1955–19 Sep 1958 | various |
| 700X Flt | 27 Aug 1957– | Scimitar |
| 702 Sqn | 17 Oct 1957–11 Aug 1958 | various |
| 703 Sqn | 15 Apr 1950–17 Aug 1955 | various |
| 703A Flt | 17–22 Feb 1954; 30 Jun 1954–4 Jul 1954 | Firefly |
| 703X Flt | 15 Mar 1954–21 Dec 1954 | Gannet |
| 703W Flt | 4 Oct 1954–1 Nov 1954 | Wyvern |
| 720 Sqn | 1 Aug 1945–27 May 1948+ | Anson, Oxford |
| 745 Sqn | 20 Aug 1957–22 Sep 1957 | Avenger |
| 762 Sqn | 15 Jan 1946–1 May 1948 | various |
| 764 Sqn | 1 Feb 1955–21 Jun 1957 | Sea Hawk |
| 767 Sqn | 1 Mar 1956–1 Apr 1957; 20 Sep 1956–20 Feb 1957 | Sea Hawk |
| 771 Sqn det | 20 Sep 1945–17 Aug 1955 | various |
| 778 Sqn | 3 Jan 1946–18 Jul 1947 | Mosquito, Anson |
| 779 Sqn | | |
| 781 Sqn det | 24 May 1950–17 Aug 1955 | various |
| 787 Sqn det | 29 Apr 1945–4 Jun 1945 | Firefly |
| 800 Sqn | 21 Aug 1951–11 Jun 1954; 6 Mar 1957–16 Apr 1957 | Attacker; Sea Hawk |
| 801 Sqn | 1 Jul 1947–19 Nov 1947+; 27 Jul 1954–31 Jan 1955+; 23–28 May 1955 | Sea Hornet; Sea Fury; Sea Hawk |
| 802 Sqn | 9–11 Dec 1950; 17 May 1955–7 Jun 1955; 25 Jun 1958–18 Jul 1958 | Sea Fury; Sea Hawk |
| 803 Sqn | 26 Nov 1951–3 Feb 1954; 6 Jun 1955–31 Aug 1955 | Attacker; Sea Hawk |
| 804 Sqn | 20 Dec 1947–25 May 1948+; 12–19 Jun 1954; 8 May 1958–29 Jul 1958+ | Seafire; Sea Hawk |
| 806 Sqn | 12–16 Jun 1953; 27 May 1955–31 Aug 1955 | Sea Hawk |
| 807 Sqn | 15 Jun 1950–18 Aug 1950 | Sea Fury |
| 809 Sqn | 1–22 Feb 1955 | Sea Venom |
| 810 Sqn | 15 Jun 1950–15 Aug 1950 | Firefly |
| 811 Sqn | 15 Sep 1945–6 Dec 1946; 20 May 1955–8 Jun 1955; 1 Sep 1955–14 Oct 1955 | Mosquito; Sea Hawk |
| 812 Sqn | 20 Dec 1947–26 May 1948+ | Firefly |
| 813 Sqn | 1 Sep 1945–30 Sep 1946; 1 May 1947–14 Oct 1947+; 18 Feb 1953–24 Sep 1954; 31 Mar 1955–4 Jun 1955; 17–21 Nov 1955; 26 Nov 1956–20 Mar 1957; 30 Sep 1957–22 Aug 1958 | Firebrand; Wyvern |
| 814 Sqn | 8–14 May 1952 | Firefly |
| 815 Sqn | 20–23 Jun 1952; 3 Jun 1954–8 Nov 1954+ | Barracuda; Avenger |
| 820 Sqn | 28 Mar 1957–28 Aug 1957+; 4 Nov 1957–2 Dec 1957 | Gannet |
| 821 Sqn | 20–23 Jun 1952 | Firefly |
| 824 Sqn | 9–13 Jul 1954; 5–17 Apr 1956 | Avenger; Gannet |
| 825 Sqn | 23 Aug 1957–9 Sep 1957 | Gannet |
| 826 Sqn | 15 May 1951–17 Jan 1952+ | Firefly |
| 827 Sqn | 15 Nov 1950–4 Mar 1952+; 1 Nov 1954–10 May 1955; 19 Nov 1955 | Firefly, Wyvern; Firebrand |
| 830 Sqn | 21 Nov 1955–16 Apr 1956 | Wyvern |
| 831 Sqn | 21 Nov 1955–10 Dec 1957 | Wyvern |
| 890 Sqn | 30 Jan 1952–27 Oct 1952 | Attacker |
| 895 Sqn | 1–3 Aug 1957 | Sea Hawk |
| 1840 Sqn | 30 Jun 1951–11 Jun 1954 | various |
| 1840A Sqn | 1 Oct 1952–28 Mar 1953 | |
| 1842 Sqn | 28 Mar 1953–10 Mar 1957 | |

## MEMORIALS

1. Memorial in Climping Church to those who died in the August 1940 air attack.
2. Garden of Remembrance on the airfield site, dedicated May 1989.

# FRISTON

**County:** East Sussex

**UTM/Grid:** OS map 199–TV534982
**Lat/Long:** N50°45.38 E000°10.18
**Nearest Town:** Eastbourne 5 miles to north-east

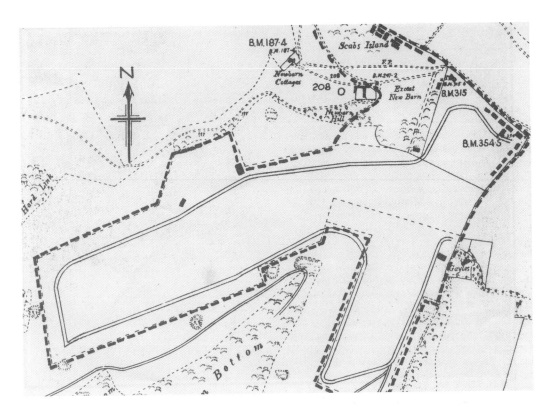

## HISTORY

This pre-war private field was taken on by Fighter Command in the summer of 1940 as an Emergency Landing Ground (ELG), although the first RAF presence had taken place a few years earlier, when two Army Co-operation units, 2 Squadron and 4 Squadron, spent a few weeks here in summer 1936. This type of detachment often receives scant mention in squadron records, but the 2 Squadron record does show a summer detachment to Fridays Wood – was this the same place? The private airstrip was known as Gayles (after a farm on the east side of the site) and sometimes East Dean; after this brief military appearance for an army exercise there appears to have been no further involvement by the RAF, although some historians mention its possible use for Auxiliary Air Force camps.

The airfield was located close to the coast, indeed virtually on the cliff top, on an area of gently undulating grassland and, as the plan shows, it was a some-

what unusual shape. In May 1941 it was upgraded to be a forward satellite for Kenley, but its main use remained that of an emergency field, although it also housed an ASR detachment with Lysanders from Shoreham. Further work was carried out in the winter of 1941–42, with a number of buildings being erected on the north-east corner of the airfield, and Friston re-opened on 15 May 1942; by the end of the month it had received its first Hurricane squadron, 253 Squadron from Hibaldstow. They were joined a few weeks later by 32 Squadron. At around the same time, contractors arrived to carry out further development of the airfield, including some grading work and the erection of Blister hangars, one of which was damaged in a hit-and-run attack by a pair of Bf109s on 9 July. The Hurricane squadron had left shortly before and the airfield reverted to short-term detachments, primarily Spitfires to counter hit-and-run German raiders. These detachments were provided

## AIRFIELD DATA DEC 1944

| | | | |
|---|---|---|---|
| Command: | RAF Fighter Command | Runway surface: | Grass |
| Function: | Operational | Hangars: | 2 × Over Blister |
| Runways: | NE/SW 1,675yd | Dispersals: | nil |
| | N/S 950yd | Personnel: | Officers – 99 (3 WAAF) |
| | 270 deg 2,000 × 50yd | | Other Ranks – 1,301 (152 WAAF) |

by the Kenley Wing, but the most significant action came in August, when two squadrons moved in to participate in the Dieppe operation. In addition to its offensive role during Operation *Jubilee*, Friston also played host to a number of damaged aircraft and, for these few days in August, the airfield was very much part of the war. After this burst of excitement the routine of detachments against hit-and-run raiders was resumed, but with only occasional success.

The airfield surfaces were not ideal in wet weather but 349 Squadron did over-winter here in 1943–44, suffering from both rain and snow. There were continued attempts to improve the airfield and a number of buildings were erected but, with a shortage of local buildings to requisition, much of the accommodation remained under canvas. By spring 1944 the airfield's Spitfire squadrons were playing a part in the growing offensive over Europe, flying *Ramrods* and *Rhubarbs*, and this pace of activity increased as the invasion approached. On D-Day itself, the airfield's units, like most Spitfire squadrons, were tasked with beachhead fighter-cover. Within days they were also back in the fighter-bomber game. The airfield's location, once again, made it a magnet for aircraft in trouble and, despite its often unsuitable nature, it was used as a safe haven by a number of damaged aircraft. With the V-1 threat at its height, Friston was given detachments of Spitfire XIIs and XIVs, as these had more chance of catching the flying bombs. Both squadrons, 41 and 610, were soon scoring successes and the airfield's tally steadily mounted, although the Mustang-equipped 316 Squadron soon replaced 41 Squadron.

By autumn 1944 the operational squadrons had gone and Friston had reverted to the role of an ELG, although receiving far less traffic than previously. A number of other units used the airfield in 1944 and 1945, including the Austers of 666 Squadron, but the hectic period of 1944 was over. By 25 May 1945, Friston was in Care and Maintenance and, by early June, was being administered by Dunsfold. The airfield was officially derequisitioned on 8 April 1946.

A few years later the site was being used by the South Downs Gliding Club, a relationship that lasted some ten years. However, there is now little trace of this once important and oft-visited airfield.

41 Squadron was one of a number of units to operate Spitfires out of Friston.

## UNITS

### 1919–1938

| | | |
|---|---|---|
| 2 Sqn | Jul–Aug 1936 | Audax |
| 4 Sqn | Jul–Aug 1936 | Audax |

### 1939–1945

| | | |
|---|---|---|
| 32 Sqn | 14 Jun 1942–7 Jul 1942; 14–20 Aug 1942 | Hurricane |
| 41 Sqn | 28 May 1943–21 Jun 1943; 3–11 Jul 1944 | Spitfire |
| 64 Sqn | 6–19 Aug 1943 | Spitfire |
| 131 Sqn | 28 Aug 1944–Nov 1944 | Spitfire |
| 253 Sqn | 14 Jun 1942–7 Jul 1942; 16–20 Aug 1942 | Hurricane |
| 306 Sqn | 19 Aug 1943–22 Sep 1943 | Spitfire |
| 308 Sqn | 7–13 Sep 1943 | Spitfire |
| 316 Sqn | 11 Jul 1944–27 Aug 1944 | Mustang |
| 349 Sqn | 22–26 Oct 1943; 10 Nov 1943–11 Mar 1944 | Spitfire |
| 350 Sqn | 25 Apr 1944–3 Jul 1944 | Spitfire |
| 411 Sqn | 1–9 May 1943 | Spitfire |
| 412 Sqn | 21 Jun 1943–14 Jul 1943 | Spitfire |
| 501 Sqn | 30 Apr 1944–2 Jul 1944 | Spitfire |
| 610 Sqn | 2 Jul 1944–12 Sep 1944 | Spitfire |
| 666 Sqn | 18 Apr 1945–28 May 1945 | Auster |
| ASRF | May 1941–15 Oct 1941 | Lysander |

# FROST HILL FARM

**County:** Hampshire

**UTM/Grid:** OS map 185–SU517525
**Lat/Long:** N51°16.2 W001°15.6
**Nearest Town:** Overton 1½ miles to south

## HISTORY

The site at Frost Hill farm first appears in the records as a scatter field for use by Odiham in 1940 and, as such, was nothing more than a large, reasonably clear field to which aircraft could deploy in an emergency. This allocation was made in early 1940 but there was no recorded use of the field, although it seems likely that at least a few trial landings were made. Indeed, the field was so promising as a landing ground that it was spiked with poles to prevent unwelcome visitors during the invasion scare of late-1940.

The first confirmed use of the field was in late-1940, by training types of the Franco-Belgian School at Odiham, but, again, records are indeterminate. The school formed at Odiham in October and was primarily equipped with Magisters, for training refugee-pilots prior to their being accepted into the RAF. This utilization appears to have continued into 1941. The following year the site was surveyed for upgrade into one of the new Advanced Landing Grounds and it was included on the list of suitable locations but with a low priority for development. At some time in 1943 the airfield was given two Sommerfeld Track runways, one of 1,600yd (NW/SE) and the other 1,000yd (E/W) but it was not given the other, usual, ALG facilities.

Despite this effort the airfield was not used, or at least no units are recorded as being based here. Unlike other ALGs it was abandoned after the invasion but was kept on the RAF books until the end of the war – the impression one gets is that everyone forgot it even existed – after which the metal tracking was lifted and the site returned to agriculture.

## UNITS

**1939–1945**

| | |
|---|---|
| Franco-Belgian School | Nov 1940–Jun 1941 |

# FUNTINGDON

**County:** West Sussex

**UTM/Grid:** OS map 197–SU790085
**Lat/Long:** N50°52.05 W000°52.36
**Nearest Town:** Chichester 5 miles to east

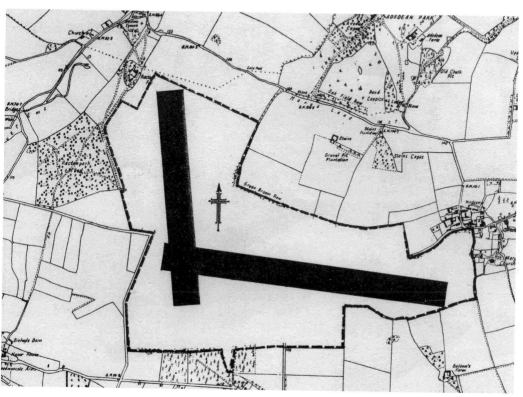

## HISTORY

Funtingdon was one of a series of Advanced Landing Grounds around Chichester and was only a few miles north of the major airfield at Thorney Island. A glance at the unit list shows how busy this airfield was during 1944, with Spitfire, Mustang and Typhoon Wings taking turns to use this Sussex field. The site was surveyed during 1942 and, by the end of the year, it had been decided that construction would commence early the following year. The village of Funtingdon was located on the east edge of the airfield, one of the runways passing close to the village, and the 'L'-shaped site required little major construction work, other than the usual field clearing (hedges and ditches) plus a bit of tree felling and only one minor road to close.

Funtingdon ALG officially opened on 15 September 1943, when two Mustang squadrons (4 and 268) moved in from Odiham. The squadrons were here to evaluate both themselves and the air-

field and there were no major problems during the three-week deployment. The airfield's two Sommerfeld Track runways, of standard length, had proved acceptable. With the departure of the Mustangs construction commenced again to full ALG standard, with the addition of hangars (Extra Over Blister type) and dispersals.

When the airfield re-opened in early 1944 it was allocated to 2nd Tactical Air Force (TAF) and, at the beginning of April, No.143 Airfield moved in. The three Typhoon squadrons flew *Noball* operations against V-1 sites but left at the end of the month, following which a succession of Wings came and went, none staying for very long. In rotation these were 144 Airfield, 122 Wing, 123 Wing, 136 Wing, 145 Wing, 135 Wing and 132 Wing – the most complex set of movements of any of the ALGs and one that is hard to explain!

The airfield was de-requisitioned in December

# AIRFIELD DATA DEC 1944

| | | | |
|---|---|---|---|
| Command: | RAF Fighter Command | Runway surface: | Sommerfeld Track |
| Function: | Advanced Landing Ground | Hangars: | 4 × Extra Over Blister |
| Runways: | 089 deg 1,600yd | Dispersals: | Sommerfeld Track, temporary |
| | 343 deg 1,200yd | Personnel: | Other Ranks – Tented camp |

Typhoon pilots of 440 Squadron pose with an inscribed bomb; this Canadian unit was at Funtingdon for three weeks in April 1944 – this picture is probably not taken during that period.

1944 and it did not take long for the few structures and the runway tracking to be removed. As with most of the Sussex ALGs, this is now a difficult site to see, but driving along the road west from Funtingdon village you can, with the eye of faith, notice where hedges and ditches are not quite back to their pre-1943 state.

## UNITS

### HQ Units at Funtingdon

| | | |
|---|---|---|
| No.143 (RCAF) Airfield | 2–20 Apr 1944 | 438, 439, 440 Sqn |
| No.144 (RCAF) Airfield/(F) Wing | 21 Apr 1944–May 1944 | 441, 442, 443 Sqn |
| No.122 (RP) Wing | 13 May 1944–18 Jun 1944 | 19, 65, 122 Sqn |
| No.123 (RP) Wing | 17 Jun 1944–1 Jul 1944 | 198, 609 Sqn |

| | | |
|---|---|---|
| No.136 (F) Wing | 17–22 Jun 1944 | 164, 183 Sqn |
| No.145 (French) (F) Wing | 22 Jun 1944–1 Jul 1944 | 329, 340, 341 Sqn |
| No.135 (F) Wing | 4 Jul 1944–6 Aug 1944 | 33, 222, 349, 485 Sqn |
| No.132 (Norwegian) (F) Wing Sqn | 6–13 Aug 1944 | 66, 127, 331, 332 |

### 1939–1945

| | | |
|---|---|---|
| 4 Sqn | 15 Sep 1943–6 Oct 1943 | Mustang |
| 19 Sqn | 20 May 1944–15 Jun 1944 | Mustang |
| 33 Sqn | 17 Jul 1944–6 Aug 1944 | Spitfire |
| 65 Sqn | 14–28 May 1944; | Mustang |
| | 4–15 Jun 1944 | |
| 66 Sqn | 6–12 Aug 1944 | Spitfire |
| 122 Sqn | 14 May 1944–15 Jun 1944 | Mustang |
| 127 Sqn | 6–12 Aug 1944 | Spitfire |
| 164 Sqn | 18–22 Jun 1944 | Typhoon |
| 183 Sqn | 18 Jun 1944–1 Jul 1944 | Typhoon |
| 198 Sqn | 18–22 Jun 1944 | Typhoon |
| 222 Sqn | 4 Jul 1944–6 Aug 1944 | Spitfire |
| 268 Sqn | 15 Sep 1943–9 Oct 1943 | Mustang |
| 329 Sqn | 22 Jun 1944–1 Jul 1944 | Spitfire |
| 331 Sqn | 6–13 Aug 1944 | Spitfire |
| 332 Sqn | 6–12 Aug 1944 | Spitfire |
| 340 Sqn | 22 Jun 1944–1 Jul 1944 | Spitfire |
| 341 Sqn | 22 Jun 1944–1 Jul 1944 | Spitfire |
| 349 Sqn | 4 Jul 1944–6 Aug 1944 | Spitfire |
| 438 Sqn | 3–19 Apr 1944 | Typhoon |
| 439 Sqn | 2–19 Apr 1944 | Typhoon |
| 440 Sqn | 3–20 Apr 1944 | Typhoon |
| 441 Sqn | 23 Apr 1944–13 May 1944 | Spitfire |
| 442 Sqn | 23–25 Apr 1944; | Spitfire |
| | 1–15 May 1944 | |
| 443 Sqn | 22 Apr 1944–15 May 1944 | Spitfire |
| 485 Sqn | 3 Jul 1944–7 Aug 1944 | Spitfire |
| 609 Sqn | 18 Jun–1 Jul 1944 | Typhoon |

# GATWICK

**County:** Surrey

**UTM/Grid:** OS map 187–TQ270404
**Lat/Long:** N51°09.00 W000°10.05
**Nearest Town:** Reigate 6 miles to north-west

Aerial view of Gatwick 1940.

## HISTORY

Now the busiest single-runway commercial airport in the world, Gatwick's claim to fame in World War Two was its involvement in the development of the Army Co-operation role; along with Old Sarum, it holds an important place in the history of this aspect of air power. The strange shape of the airfield is explained by its origins as a landing ground within the racecourse and it was first licensed as an airfield

in August – by Home Counties Aircraft Services Ltd. The Surrey Aero Club formed the same year and proved somewhat more stable than the commercial owners of the airfield. Ownership changed hands a number of times during the 1930s but development of facilities continued and, by 1936, the airfield included a terminal building, a number of hangars and other buildings. This was also the year that

## AIRFIELD DATA DEC 1944

| | | | |
|---|---|---|---|
| Command: | RAF Fighter Command | Runway surface: | 238 and 277 Army Track, NW/SE Grass |
| Function: | Forward Airfield | Hangars: | 6 × Blister, 1 × Bellman |
| Runways: | 238 deg 1,400yd | Dispersals: | 17 × Frying Pan (100ft), 12 × Blenheim, |
| | | | 3 × Frying Pan (50ft) |
| | 277 deg 1,200yd | Personnel: | Officers – 85 (6 WAAF) |
| | NW/SE 1,000yd | | Other Ranks – 1,037 (206 WAAF) |

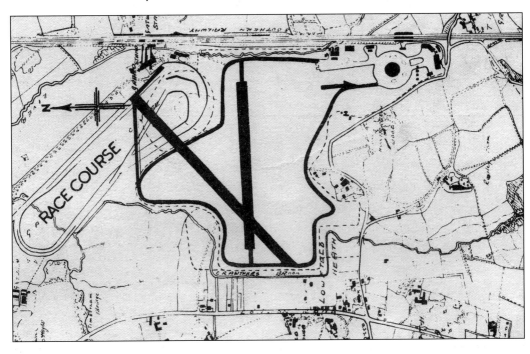

British Airways arrived, although they moved on within months because of waterlogging of the grass airfield, a problem that re-occurred over the next few years. The future remained uncertain, but the RAF found it an ideal location at which to operate a flying school and No.19 E&RFTS formed on 1 October 1937, the Tiger Moths being operated by Airports Ltd, owners of Gatwick. The following year, strength was increased with the addition of sixteen Magisters for training direct-entry officer-pilots and Gatwick became a very busy training base. In addition to the two main training types, the school had a number of other aircraft, such as Battles and Harts. June 1938 witnessed the first public event at Gatwick, when the *Daily Express* Air Display was held here, for which a number of RAF operational types paid a visit for static and flying displays.

The outbreak of war brought a halt to training activities, aircraft and instructors moving elsewhere,

and for a few months Gatwick was without a based flying unit, although the engineering side of Airports Ltd had already taken on modification work for Whitleys. A number of airlines were interested in acquiring rights to use the airfield but, despite early discussions, it was decided to retain the airfield for RAF use. The first such use was by a detachment of 92 Squadron on an ad hoc basis from February 1940, whilst the Squadron was converting to Spitfires, but it was the arrival of No.70 Wing in June 1940 that signalled real RAF interest in the airfield; a few days after arrival the Wing became Station HQ of RAF Gatwick. For the remainder of 1940 a variety of aircraft and squadrons used the airfield, but it was the arrival in September of 26 Squadron's Lysanders from West Malling that opened Gatwick's army co-operation career. In recognition of this, the airfield was transferred to No.71 Group of Army Co-operation Command in January. With various command

Lysander smoke canister trial on the edge of the airfield.

changes and new aircraft, such as the Tomahawk and Mustang, 26 Squadron was one of the units involved in developing and evaluating the army co-operation role. It had been joined at Gatwick in early 1941 by 239 Squadron, initially for anti-aircraft calibration work, but soon broadening its involvement to a wider AC role.

Waterlogging had continued to plague Gatwick and by autumn 1941 two Army Track runways had been laid in an attempt to ease the problem, although much of the airfield remained a quagmire after heavy rain. The Mustang became the main operational type for the resident units and Gatwick also played host to visiting units, including a number of AC squadrons deployed to work with the experienced based-squadrons. This routine continued into 1943, by which time the mobile concept of operations was firmly established, with Wings of two or three squadrons operating from limited facilities and living in tents. No.123 Airfield used Gatwick in this fashion from April 1943 and its stay of a few weeks was followed by similar such detachments. During this period the airfield itself changed little, other than continued attempts to improve drainage and, at some point, the erection of six Blister hangars. By spring 1944 it was usual for Gatwick to have three squadrons in residence and, during the D-Day period, the airfield played a major role in photographic reconnaissance, although two of the Mustang squadrons were temporarily attached to the Air Spotting Pool for naval bombardment on D-Day itself. In late-June 1944, No.35 Wing was replaced by the Spitfire-equipped No.36 Wing, but they stayed only a few weeks before moving to West Malling, primarily because of conflict with the balloon barrage that was being extended as part of the anti-flying-bomb defences. The airfield was out of use until late-August and, indeed, it was never again used by operational squadrons. For the latter months of 1944 Gatwick was used by support squadrons for calibration and co-operation duties, but in January it was handed over to a disarmament unit, becoming No.103 Air Disarmament Wing in June 1945. Prior to its final release from RAF service on 31 August 1946, the airfield played host to a number of flying and non-flying units, all in the support role.

Gatwick was handed to the Ministry of Civil Aviation, but over the next ten years it saw little use, as its facilities were very limited; however, it was selected for development as London's second airport (after Heathrow) and in March 1956 was closed for redevelopment. The most important elements were the 7,000ft runway and concrete parking-area, although a new terminal building and support facilities were also provided, including a revamped railway station. London Gatwick Airport opened on 9 June 1958 but it was a not an immediate success – it took the formation of British United Airways in 1960 and the growth of the holiday-charter market to give Gatwick the boost it needed. Despite the odd blip in its development over the past forty-five years, usually caused by the collapse of a major carrier, Gatwick has gone from strength to strength. It has remained primarily a holiday-charter airport despite the best efforts of some carriers, especially British Airways, to change this image. The airport's infrastructure has also continued to evolve, including growth of the runway to over 10,000ft and a conglomeration of hangars, terminals (North and South Terminal) and associated support buildings.

The Government has recently announced its backing for a second runway at Gatwick 'at some time in the future'; this has yet to pass the tortuous planning process, but without such a development the future growth of the airport is limited.

## DECOY SITES

| | | |
|---|---|---|
| Q | Lower Beeding | TQ236299 |

Lysander of 26 Squadron, 1941.

# Units

## HQ Units at Gatwick

| | | |
|---|---|---|
| No.70 Wing | 28 Jun 1940–1 Jul 1940 | |
| No.123 Airfield | 7 Apr 1943–23 Jun 1943 | 26, 183, 239 Sqn |
| No.129 Airfield | 4 Jul 1943–13 Aug 1943; 15 Oct 1943–2 Apr 1944 | 414, 430 Sqn |

## 1919–1938

| | | |
|---|---|---|
| 19 ERFTS | 1 Oct 1937–3 Sep 1939 | Tiger Moth, Magister |

## 1939–1945

| | | |
|---|---|---|
| 2 Sqn | Dec 1941–Jan 1943; 4 Apr 1944–27 Jun 1944 | Tomahawk, Mustang |
| 4 Sqn | 4 Apr 1944–27 Jun 1944 | Spitfire |
| 18 Sqn | 26 May 1940–12 Jun 1940 | Blenheim |
| 19 Sqn | 15–24 Oct 1943 | Spitfire |
| 26 Sqn | 3 Sep 1940–13 Jan 1943+ | Lysander, Tomahawk, Mustang |
| 53 Sqn | 13 Jun 1940–3 Jul 1940 | Blenheim |
| 57 Sqn | 29 May 1940–11 Jun 1940 | Blenheim |
| 63 Sqn | 15 Jun 1942–16 Jul 1942 | Mustang |
| 65 Sqn | 15–24 Oct 1943 | Spitfire |
| 80 Sqn | 27 Jun 1944–5 Jul 1944 | Spitfire |
| 92 Sqn det | Feb 1940–May 1940 | |
| 98 Sqn | 15 Jun 1940–31 Jul 1940 | Battle |
| 116 Sqn | 27 Aug 1944–7 Sep 1944 | various |
| 141 Sqn | 15 Oct 1940–3 Nov 1940 | Defiant |
| 168 Sqn | 6–31 Mar 1944 | Mustang |
| 171 Sqn | 25 Aug 1942–7 Dec 1942 | Tomahawk, Gatwick |
| 175 Sqn | 9 Dec 1942–14 Jan 1943 | Hurricane |
| 183 Sqn | 8 Apr 1943–3 May 1943 | Typhoon |
| 229 Sqn | 28 Jun 1944–1 Jul 1944 | Spitfire |
| 239 Sqn | Sep 1940–Oct 1942+ | Lysander, Tomahawk, Hurricane, Mustang |
| 268 Sqn | 8 Apr 1944–27 Jun 1944 | Mustang |
| 274 Sqn | 28 Jun 1944–5 Jul 1944 | Spitfire |
| 287 Sqn | Jul 1944–Jan 1945 | various |
| 400 Sqn | Jun 1941–Jun 1942 | Lysander, Tomahawk, Mustang |
| 414 Sqn | 5–31 Jul 1943; 10–13 Aug 1943; 3 Nov 1943–5 Feb 1944; 11 Mar 1944–1 Apr 1944 | |
| 430 Sqn | 5 Jul 1943–13 Aug 1943; 15 Oct 1943–4 Jan 1944; 27 Feb 1944–1 Apr 1944 | Mustang |
| 655 Sqn | 22 Mar 1943–7 Apr 1943 | Auster |
| 1 AACF | 27 Dec 1940–25 Jan 1941 | Lysander, Wallace |
| 84 Gp CS | 29 Aug 1943–1 Mar 1944 | various |
| 1 ADF | 27 Aug 1944–12 Oct 1944 | |

## Post-1945

| | | |
|---|---|---|
| 162 GS | late-1946 | Cadet |

Pilots of 2 Squadron share a joke; note the D-Day stripes on the Spitfire wing.

Typhoon of 183 Squadron, Gatwick April 1943.

# GOSPORT (HMS *Siskin*)

**County:** Hampshire

July 1925 Jubilee display at Gosport.

## HISTORY

Records sometimes refer to Gosport (Fort Grange) and Gosport (Fort Rowner) but, in aviation terms, this is somewhat misleading, as the airfield was actually laid out on the large grass-area between these two mid-nineteenth century artillery forts and the escarpment that dropped down to the River Alver. It was a logical place to construct an aerodrome for the Royal Flying Corps and the area was cleared and levelled in early 1914, with aircraft of 5 Squadron arriving on 6 July; they and their aircraft lived in tents for a few weeks until they moved to France. Fort Grange was also used for accommodation and workshops. The Royal Naval Air Service arrived next, forming 1 Squadron RNAS at Gosport in October but moving to Dover in January 1915, leaving the airfield – still little developed – for the next RFC squadron. Within a matter of days, three squadrons had moved in to form 5th Wing and the squadrons were given a training task in addition to their own work-up, although, in August, 8 Squadron moved to France.

Gosport continued to expand, with further devel-opment of the airfield and the take-over of Fort Rowner as more squadrons formed, trained and departed. Indeed, Gosport had become a major RFC Station and an interesting variety of aircraft types made use of this large field with its impressive back-drop of the two forts. By spring 1916 the RFC's ad hoc training system was settling down, with squadrons taking on their true operational role and specialist training-squadrons being formed; for Gosport this meant the departure of the resident units and the arrival/formation of dedicated reserve squadrons. No.1 RS moved in from Farnborough in April and No.27 RS formed the following month, both being equipped with the usual diverse array of aircraft types. One of the most influential aviators of the period – Major R Smith-Barry – arrived on 24 December 1916 to take command of No.1 RS and it was not long before he and his staff had developed new training concepts; the Gosport System was later adopted by other RFC training schools. The airfield had undergone a number of changes, the main one

An unorthodox 'landing' in the trees at Gosport/Fort Grange.

being the construction of new aircraft-sheds and workshops; Smith-Barry now re-organized the Squadron into three Flights and introduced a syllabus of training that relied on dual instruction followed by consolidation, a concept that has been used in every flying course since. Furthermore, he attempted to address the limitations of some of the equipment, not least being the inter-communication between the instructor and his pupil – the outcome of this was the Gosport Tube. Accommodation was also improved, with some officers occupying a rented mansion, Alverbank, although this was later given back and the staff moved back to the Forts.

Smith-Barry's views carried weight and he was given authority to form his Special School of Flying to train instructors; this was achieved through the amalgamation of three Training Squadrons (1, 25 and 55) to form the new school with its six Flights. The School remained in residence to the end of the war and, via a number of name changes, became the South-West Area Flying Instructors' School – an accurate if not very emotive name. Operational units had also been present during the latter months of the war and, with the addition of even more specialist units in late 1918, the airfield had become both crowded and very interesting. To control this amalgam of units, HQ Gosport was formed on 28 October 1918 but, with the end of the war the following month, the run-down of units began and this HQ was disbanded in May 1919.

It had been decided, however, to keep Gosport as an active station and part of the trials work it had adopted the previous summer now bore fruit when the Development Flight became responsible for torpedo development. Over the next few years a variety of torpedo bombers were evaluated at Gosport and experimental work on the weapons themselves conducted. In addition to this trials work the unit also trained pilots in the art of torpedo dropping.

A number of operational and other units came and

went during the 1920s but Gosport remained primarily a trials unit, a role that increased in 1930 with the formation of the Base Training Squadron, with four main Flights: A – Army and Navy Co-operation, B – TAG training, C – Deck Landing, D – Torpedo training. Within a few years the main emphasis was once more on torpedo work and the Flight structure had changed to reflect this, eventually becoming the Torpedo Development Unit. Throughout the 1930s various other units used Gosport, some for operational work and others for training and development, the latter including the Coast Defence Development Unit, a logical move as the airfield had been (and was to be) home to a variety of Coastal Flights. With the outbreak of war, some of the ancillary units departed and the Air TDU expanded, as did the airfield when the two hard-runways were replaced by four grass-strips – an unusual move but one that saw an additional two grass-strips added later. More hangars were added and a number of new buildings were also erected, partly to suit the needs of the Fleet Air Arm Maintenance Unit that, in April 1940, took over most of the workshop area. Torpedo development and the training of specialist personnel – and from time to time torpedo squadrons – were the rationale for Gosport but its location inevitably made it a target for the Luftwaffe and, in common with most major airfields in southern England, it was attacked a number of times in August 1940.

Every torpedo-dropping type used by the RAF and FAA was evaluated at Gosport but it was the work on the weapons themselves, including trials on the most effective employment, that made the ATDU a crucial part of the maritime war – air-dropped torpedoes were amongst the most potent anti-ship weapons. Squadrons still appeared to undertake torpedo training, for example a number of the Beaufighter units destined for the Coastal Command Strike Wings, and the airfield also housed specialist flights connected with the ranges along the coast. Naval involvement increased from early 1944 with the arrival of 764 Squadron, as part of the ATDU to

This April 1918 shot clearly shows one of the old forts in the background.

## AIRFIELD DATA DEC 1944

| | | | |
|---|---|---|---|
| Command: | RAF Coastal Command | Runway surface: | First two tarmac, rest grass |
| Function: | Aircraft Torpedo Development Unit | Hangars: | 5 × Extended Over Blister, 4 × A-type, 2 × Bellman, 1 × C, 1 × Bessonneau |
| Runways: | NNW/SSE 533yd | Dispersals: | 23 × BRC Fabric |
| | NE/SW 600yd | Personnel: | Officers – 147 (16 WAAF) |
| | N/S 1,550yd | | Other Ranks – 3,100 (714) |
| | NE/SW 1,500yd | | |
| | NW/SE 1,250yd | | |
| | E/W 850yd | | |

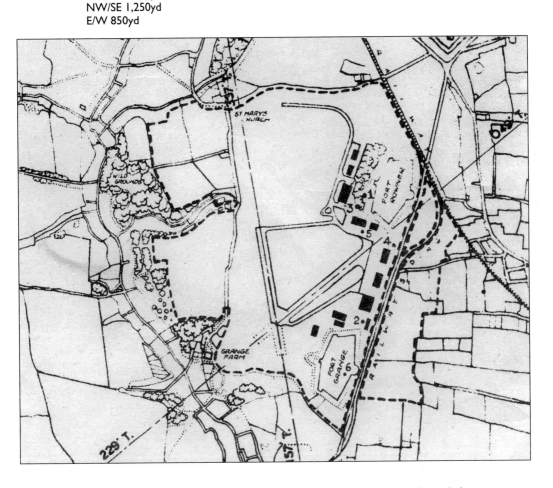

evaluate the Barracuda in the torpedo role. Indeed, this was a precursor to the handover of the station in the post-war period to the Fleet Air Arm. Although the December 1944 survey showed that Gosport had six runways, it also noted that the two tarmac-runways 'are not normally used and the airfield is treated as wholly grass'. Although Gosport had seen very little actual operational service in World War Two, it

played a very important role and deserves greater recognition that it usually receives – but this was ever the fate of such trials units.

On 1 August 1945 the airfield was handed over to the navy, becoming HMS *Siskin* (the name HMS *Woodpecker* had been proposed but rejected) but with a number of RAF units, including the ATDU remaining as lodger units. In typical FAA fashion an

A captured German Albatros under test at Gosport. (Peter Green)

Cuckoo of 210 Squadron dropping torpedo; the Squadron spent three years here from 1920.

almost bewildering array of units came and went over the next few years, including 705 Squadron, the Fleet Air Arm's helicopter developmental unit. It was not long before helicopters were the station's main occupation and this remained true until naval flying all but ceased here in November 1955. Early the following year, the long-serving ATDU departed to Culdrose and the airfield was paid off on 31 May 1956, although it was used as an RLG for a number of months. Parts of the site remained in military use and helicopters have used it from time to time but its career as a dedicated flying field was over.

## UNITS

### HQ Units at Gosport

| | | |
|---|---|---|
| 5th Wing | 29 Nov 1914–Nov 1915 | |
| 7th Wing | 8 Nov 1915–May 1916 | |
| 17th Wing | 9 Aug 1916–2 Aug 1917 | |
| No.17 Gp | Feb 1939–Feb 1942 | |

### Pre-1919

| | | |
|---|---|---|
| 5 Sqn | 6 Jul 1914–14 Aug 1914 | various |
| 8 Sqn | 6 Jan 1915–15 Apr 1915 | BE2a, BE2b, BE2c |
| 13 Sqn | 10 Jan 1915–19 Oct 1915 | BE2c, Scout |
| 14 Sqn | 5 Aug 1915–7 Nov 1915 | BE2c, Caudron G.III |
| 17 Sqn | 1 Feb 1915–5 Aug 1915 | BE2c |
| 22 Sqn | 1 Sep 1915–1 Apr 1916 | various |
| 23 Sqn | 1 Sep 1915–15 Mar 1916 | various |
| 28 Sqn | 7 Nov 1915–23 Jul 1917 | various |
| 29 Sqn | 7 Nov 1915–25 Mar 1916 | various |
| 31 Sqn | 18 Jan 1916–Jul 1916+ | BE2c |
| 40 Sqn | 26 Feb 1916–10 Aug 1916 | BE2c, Avro 504, FE8 |
| 41 Sqn | 15 Apr 1916–22 May 1916; 14 Jul 1916–15 Oct 1916 | FB5, DH2, |
| 45 Sqn | 1 Mar 1916–3 May 1916 | various |
| 56 Sqn | 8 Jun 1916–14 Jul 1916 | various |

| | | |
|---|---|---|
| 60 Sqn | 15–28 May 1916 | Morane H |
| 78 Sqn det | Dec 1916–Sep 1917 | various |
| 79 Sqn | 1–8 Aug 1917 | various |
| 81 Sqn | 7–15 Jan 1917 | various |
| 88 Sqn | 24 Jul 1917–2 Aug 1917 | various |
| 1 Sqn RNAS | Oct 1914–Jan 1915 | |
| 1 RAS | 7 Apr 1916–2 Aug 1917 | various |
| 27 RS | 22 May 1916–2 Aug 1917 | various |
| 55 RS | 23 Jul 1917–2 Aug 1917 | various |
| SoSF | 2 Aug 1917–1 Jul 1918 | various |
| SWA FIS | 1 Jul 1918–? | various |
| SoACCA | 31 Jan 1918–Sep 1918 | BE2e, BE12 |
| SEF | May 1918–1919 | various |
| DS | 17 Aug 1918–Feb 1920 | |
| AASDF | Oct 1918–Dec 1918 | Camel |
| EF | Oct 1918–? | |
| 10 RS | 25 Jun 1918–24 Feb 1919 | various |

### 1919–1938

| | | |
|---|---|---|
| 3 Sqn | 8 Nov 1922–1 Apr 1923 | Walrus, FE8 |
| 42 Sqn det | Mar 1938–Sep 1938 | Vildebeeste |
| 100 Sqn | Jun 1932–Jul 1932 | Vildebeeste |
| 186 Sqn | 17 Feb 1919–1 Feb 1920 | Cuckoo |
| 210 Sqn | 1 Feb 1920–1 Apr 1923 | Cuckoo |
| 224 Sqn det | Jan 1938–Mar 1938 | Anson |
| 813 Sqn FAA | 18 Jan 1937–23 Feb 1937 | Swordfish |
| CBCS/F | Sep 1919–Sep 1921 | DH9a |
| AASDF | Oct 1919–Dec 1918 | Camel |
| TTS | Oct 1919–Feb 1920 | Cuckoo |
| TDF/S | 1920–1930s | various |
| SoNC | Apr 1923–Dec 1937 | various |
| DF | May 1925–Apr 1940 | Wellesley |
| (1)CDTF | 23 May 1932–1 Aug 1933 | |
| 2 CDTF | 23 May 1932–Apr 1935? | Vildebeest |
| 3 CDTF | 1 Aug 1933–Apr 1935 | Hart |
| CDDU | 1 Apr 1935–14 Dec 1936 | |
| 1 CACF/U | 14 Dec 1936–15 Sep 1939 | |
| 17 Gp CF | Jul 1938–Jan 1942 | various |

Deck-landing trials using a Ripon and a marked-out area of grass, 1935.

Shark L2336 at Gosport in 1939; the unusual 6-wheeled vehicle in the background is intriguing. (Ray Sturtivant)

## 1939–1945

| | | |
|---|---|---|
| 48 Sqn | 30 Nov 1942–23 Dec 1942 | Hudson |
| 86 Sqn | 6 Dec 1940–2 Feb 1941 | Blenheim |
| 248 Sqn | 16 Apr 1940–22 May 1940 | Blenheim |
| 608 Sqn | 27 Aug 1942–9 Nov 1942 | Hudson |
| 667 Sqn | 1 Dec 1943–20 Dec 1945 | various |
| 708 Sqn FAA | 15 Jan 1945–6 Sep 1945 | Firebrand, Seafire |
| 764 Sqn FAA | 19 Feb 1944–1 Jul 1944 | Barracuda |
| 848 Sqn FAA | Dec 1943–Jan 1944 | Avenger |
| 2 AACU | 5 May 1939–? | |
| 1 AACU | 25 Sep 1939–11 Oct 1940 | Battle |
| 8 AACU | 1941 | |
| 1622 Flt | 14 Feb 1943–1 Dec 1943 | Defiant, Hurricane, Gladiator |
| CCFC | 15 Mar 1944–? | |
| TDU | Sep 1939–11 Nov 1943 | various |
| ATDU | 11 Nov 1943–18 May 1956 | various |

## Post-1945

| | | |
|---|---|---|
| 163 GS | 19 Sep 1946–Jul 1948 | Cadet |

## FAA Units

| | | |
|---|---|---|
| 705 Sqn | 7 May 1947–1 Nov 1955 | various |
| 706 Sqn | 7 Sep 1953–30 Oct 1953; 1–15 Mar 1954 | Whirlwind |
| 707 Sqn | 14 Aug 1945–1 Oct 1945 | Swordfish, Barracuda |
| 720 Sqn | 27 May 1948–5 Jan 1950 | Oxford |
| 771 Sqn | 12–14 Sep 1945 | |
| 778 Sqn | 15 Aug 1944–9 Aug 1945 | various |
| 845 Sqn det | 21 Nov 1955–10 Jan 1956 | Whirlwind |

## MEMORIALS

Pillar surmounted by globe and eagle.

September 1948 and a Tiger Moth of 727 Squadron ends up on its nose.

# GRAVESEND (Chalk)

**County:** Kent

**UTM/Grid:** OS map 178–TQ665720
**Lat/Long:** N51°25.03 E000°23.50
**Nearest Town:** Now within Gravesend town area

## HISTORY

Gravesend Airport opened on 12 October 1932 on a 148-acre site just south of Chalk village, hence the alternate name that is sometimes used, although the area had first been used by Edgar Percival as a landing ground a few years before. The Gravesend School of Flying was one of the first occupants and the airport had a grass surface, two hangars, control tower and clubhouse – but few aeroplanes. It had been hoped that commercial operators would use the airport, as it was reasonably well placed for London; however, this hope remained unrealized, other than for weather diversion when Croydon was unusable. At one stage it was even called London East/Gravesend in an attempt to encourage traffic, a marketing ploy used today by virtually every airport within 100 miles of London! Private aviation and the flying school flourished in the early 1930s – the heyday of light aviation in the UK – but commercial activity remained stagnant, despite continued attempts to attract carriers such as KLM. In 1932, Percival Aircraft set up a factory on the airfield and a number of Gulls and Mew Gulls were built here before the company moved to larger premises at Luton in October 1936. Essex Aero arrived shortly afterwards

Pilots of 66 Squadron in their crewroom at Gravesend, 1940.

and, although never a large concern, the company became involved in aircraft modification and support, this role expanding during the war to manufacture of specialist products, such as self-sealing fuel-tanks.

The airport was acquired by Gatwick's owner, Airports Ltd, in 1937 but they, too, were unable to make a success of the venture; however, as at their main airport, they were able to acquire an RAF train-

# AIRFIELD DATA DEC 1944

Command: RAF Fighter Command
Function: Operational Station (Biggin Hill Sector)
Runways: ENE/WSW 1,480yd

W/S 1,420yd
270 deg 2,000 × 50yd

Runway surface: Grass
Hangars: 8 × Blister, one × T.1
Dispersals: 30 × Frying Pan (65ft),
6 × Blenheim
Personnel: Officers – 48 (6 WAAF)
Other Ranks – 1,480 (212 WAAF)

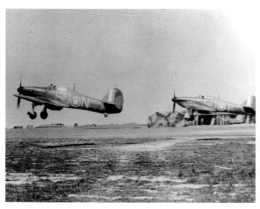

Hurricanes of 501 Squadron scramble 15 August 1940.

The CO of 66 Squadron, Sqn Ldr Leigh, prepares to climb aboard his Spitfire, Gravesend 1940.

ing contract: No.20 ERFTS duly formed on 1 October 1937 and, in addition to training RAF pilots, it acquired a contract for FAA pilots. Operated by Airports Ltd, the school had a mix of aircraft, including Tiger Moths, Hinds, Audax and Battles. As with most such training units, the outbreak of war led to dispersion to safer airfields and Gravesend became a satellite for Biggin Hill – its career as a fighter station was about to start. Although some use was made of the airfield in the latter part of 1939, it was the arrival of 32 Squadron's Hurricanes in January 1940 that gave Gravesend its first resident fighter-unit. The Squadron stayed to late-March and was replaced by 56 Squadron, a pattern of rotating units becoming the standard scenario for this Kent airfield. As the unit list shows, Gravesend hosted a large number of fighter squadrons over the next four years, the norm being for a single squadron at any one time. The airfield played a role in the Battle of Britain but despite, being in the Luftwaffe target list, it was not subject to any significant attack. Day- and night-fighter units continued to use the airfield to 1944 (with an increasing emphasis on offensive operations) and, with improvements in facilities, the airfield was able to handle three fighter squadrons.

Improvements to the landing ground included re-grading of the runways and lengthening of the runs,

some records suggest the use of Sommerfeld Track surfaces but the December 1944 survey states that both were of grass. By 1944 hangarage comprised eight Blister and one T.1, whilst thirty-six hardstands had been provided, these being distributed around the perimeter track. Mustangs, Spitfires, Typhoons, Mosquitoes and Lysanders (for Air Sea Rescue) used the airfield while the RAF employed its air power over Europe as a precursor to D-Day. The invasion period saw Gravesend at it busiest but, within weeks, it had all come to a halt – the German flying-bomb campaign against London caused the RAF to abandon a number of airfields as being untenable: Gravesend was one such airfield. Balloons formed a major part of the inner defence-line against the new threat and from Gravesend a veritable forest of balloons was visible; during this final period the airfield acted as a control centre for aircraft that had to penetrate the barrage.

After the war its future looked bleak as it went into Care and Maintenance: only Essex Aero had remained throughout the war and it managed to survive to March 1956. A few months later the Air Ministry relinquished control of the airfield and it was almost immediately seized on as a suitable location for a major housing estate for the rapidly-growing town. There is no trace of the airfield – other than the memorial (if you can find it).

## DECOY SITES

| Q | Cliffe Marshes | TQ727778 |
|---|---|---|
| Q | Luddesdown | TQ688662 |

## UNITS

### HQ Units at Gravesend

| No.122 Airfield | 20 Oct 1943–15 Apr 1944 | 19, 65, 122 Sqn |
|---|---|---|
| No.125 Airfield | 24 Jun 1943–2 Jul 1943 | 19, 132 Sqn |
| No.122 (RP) Wing | 12–13 May 1944 | 19, 65, 122 Sqn |
| No.140 (B) Wing | 12 May 1944–18 Jun 1944 | 21, 464, 487 Sqn |

### 1920–1938

| 20 ERFTS | 1 Oct 1937–3 Sep 1939 | |
|---|---|---|

### 1939–1945

| 2 Sqn | 16 Jul 1943–7 Aug 1943 | Mustang |
|---|---|---|
| 4 Sqn | 16 Jul 1943–7 Aug 1943 | Mustang |
| 19 Sqn | Jun 1943; 24 Oct 1943–15 Apr 1944 | Spitfire |
| 21 Sqn | 17 Apr 1944–18 Jun 1944 | Mosquito |
| 32 Sqn | 3 Jan 1940–27 Mar 1940 | Hurricane |
| 64 Sqn | 19 Aug 1943–6 Sep 1943 | Mustang |
| 65 Sqn | 29 Jul 1942–14 Aug 1942; 24 Oct 1943–15 Apr 1944 | Spitfire |
| 66 Sqn | 10 Sep 1940–30 Oct 1940 | Spitfire |
| 71 Sqn | 14–20 Aug 1942 | Spitfire |
| 72 Sqn | 8–26 Jul 1941; 20 Oct 1941–22 Mar 1942 | Spitfire |
| 74 Sqn | 30 May 1941–9 Jul 1941 | Spitfire |
| 85 Sqn | 23 Nov 1940–1 Jan 1941 | Hurricane |
| 92 Sqn | 24 Sep 1941–20 Oct 1941 | Spitfire |
| 111 Sqn | 30 Jun 1942–7 Jul 1942 | Spitfire |
| 122 Sqn | 3 Nov 1943–15 Apr 1944 | Spitfire, Mustang |
| 124 Sqn | 3 May 1942–1 Aug 1942 | Spitfire |
| 132 Sqn | 20 Jun 1943–3 Jul 1943 | Spitfire |
| 133 Sqn | 31 Jul 1942–17 Aug 1942 | Spitfire |
| 141 Sqn | 3 Nov 1940–29 Apr 1941 | Defiant |
| 165 Sqn | 20 Aug 1942–2 Nov 1942 | Spitfire |
| 174 Sqn | 5 Apr 1943–12 Jun 1943 | Typhoon |
| 181 Sqn | 24 Mar 1943–5 Apr 1943 | Typhoon |
| 193 Sqn | 17 Aug 1943–18 Sep 1943 | Typhoon |
| 232 Sqn | 14–20 Aug 1942 | Spitfire |
| 245 Sqn | 30 Mar 1943–28 May 1943 | Typhoon |
| 247 Sqn | 29 May 1943–4 Jun 1943 | Typhoon |
| 257 Sqn | 12 Aug 1943–17 Sep 1943 | Typhoon |
| 264 Sqn | 1–11 Jan 1941 | Defiant |
| 266 Sqn | 7–10 Sep 1943 | Spitfire |
| 277 Sqn | 7 Dec 1942–15 Apr 1944 | various |
| 284 Sqn | 7–17 May 1943 | no aircraft |

| 306 Sqn | 11–19 Aug 1943 | Spitfire |
|---|---|---|
| 350 Sqn | 30 Jun 1942–7 Jul 1942 | Spitfire |
| 401 Sqn | 19 Mar 1942–3 Jul 1942 | Spitfire |
| 464 Sqn | 17 Apr 1944–8 Jun 1944 | Mosquito |
| 487 Sqn | 18 Apr 1944–18 Jun 1944 | Mosquito |
| 501 Sqn | 25 Jul 1940–10 Sep 1940 | Hurricane |
| 604 Sqn | 3–27 Jul 1940 | Gladiator |
| 609 Sqn | 28 Jul 1941–24 Sep 1941 | Spitfire |
| 610 Sqn | 27 May 1940–8 Jul 1940 | Spitfire |
| 1421 Flt | 8–31 Oct 1940 | Hurricane |
| 18 APC | 18 Oct 1943–26 Dec 1943 | Martinet |

## MEMORIALS

1. Plaque in Thong Lane Sports Centre.
2. Brick memorial with marble plaque dedicated 2 March 2003, inscribed:

> RAF Gravesend 1939–1944. This memorial commemorates the site of the former Royal Air Force Station which served a crucial role in the defence of the United Kingdom during World War II. The original airport called Gravesend London East covered the whole of the Riverview Park Estate. The airfield was extended on the East of Thong lane in 1942/43. It originally served as a civilian airport and flying school. At the outbreak of the war the RAF requisitioned the airfield to strengthen Fighter Command requirements. In the summer of 1940 the skies above Kent witnessed the greatest aerial battle ever fought and seen by the British public. The 'Battle of Britain' took place between 10th July and 31st October and RAF Gravesend played a major role as one of the most active fighter stations with 501 Squadron (Hurricanes) and 66 (F) Squadron (Spitfires) flying almost non-stop to repel and eventually defeat the Luftwaffe.

The memorial at Gravesend was unveiled in March 2003.

# HAMBLE

**County:** Hampshire

**UTM/Grid:** OS map 196–SU477071
**Lat/Long:** N50°51.50 W001°19.10
**Nearest Town:** Southampton 4 miles to north-west

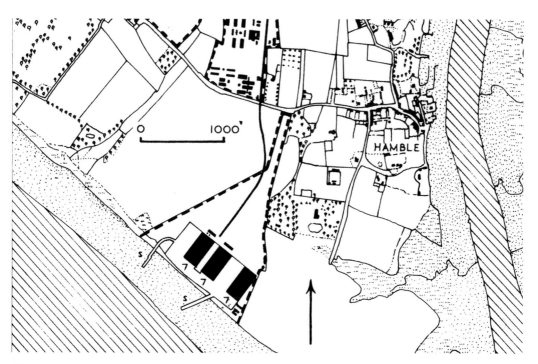

## HISTORY

Southampton Water and the land around it has been associated with aviation since the early days of this new technology, but the area – and even a famous name such as Hamble – is all too often forgotten in a list of notable aviation sites. The first definite landing ground here was a small private field known as Browns, from about 1913, located on the other side of the estuary from the seaplane station at Calshot. Little is known about the private flying from this field, but it did receive some military visitors. At about the same time, and as interest in development of aircraft spread, two companies based here combined to produce the HL1 floatplane (the HL coming from Hamble River Engineering and Luke & Co), for which they constructed sheds and a slipway at Hamble Point. The venture came to nothing, but the sheds were requisitioned by the Admiralty in December 1914 for possible military use. A year later they were allocated to Fairey Aviation for seaplane development and production. The company moved in and, having made some improvements to the site, began work on licence-building Short 827s, the test

flights taking place from Southampton Water. Fairey's works at Hamble assembled and test-flew a large number of floatplanes, of various types, during the war but they were not the only aviation company in the area.

A second aircraft manufacturer, A V Roe, also found the area attractive and acquired a 100-acre site with river frontage for a brand new factory-airfield. In what was a first for the UK, this was laid out as a 'garden factory' complete with workers' housing and facilities, as well as an impressive production-shed. The site was subject to government acquisition partway through the construction phase but remained an Avro establishment, although not developed in quite the way A V Roe had intended. By September 1916 a design team was in place and, although the first new type had already flown from Hamble, the pace of work now increased. The Admiralty, however, needed a new air-station to act as an acceptance park for the increasing number of new floatplanes and it, too, chose Southampton Water as an ideal site. The new site, also called Hamble and designated as No.1

Gnats under production in the Folland works at Hamble.

(Southern) Marine Acceptance Depot, was constructed between the two existing manufacturing works and comprised a series of aircraft sheds and two slipways. Construction did not commence until late-1917 or early 1918 and progress was slow, such that, by the end of the war, it was still far from complete – and was promptly demolished.

Somewhat surprisingly, both aircraft manufacturers survived, although the 1920s were a difficult time for both. By the mid-1920s, Avro was forced to invest in a new airfield, referred to as Hamble (North), as the existing field was too small for the aircraft now being developed; the old airfield was retained but saw limited flying use, the most significant aspect of which was testing of Cierva autogyros. In 1928 the two locations were sold, the larger airfield being acquired by Armstrong-Whitworth; the true significance of this was the creation of a flying school for military reserve-officers and for civilian pilots. The famous Air Service Training school was formed here in 1931 and was formally opened on 25 June. The Reserve School became No.3 Elementary and Reserve Flying School (dropping the Reserve in 1939) and Hamble was soon firmly established as an important flying-training establishment. The school operated a variety of training types, with new aircraft entering service throughout the 1930s, this list including the Atlas, Avian, Cadet, Cutty Sark, Hart, Hind, Siskin and Tutor.

Aircraft manufacture returned to the area in 1936, when the already confusing sequence of Hamble airfields saw another created, just west of Hamble (North), by British Marine Aircraft for construction of the Sikorsky S-42 flying boats. The works was in operation by late-1937 and, the following year, became Folland Aircraft Ltd, the major work at this time being maintenance contracts for Imperial

Airways flying boats. At around the same time, Hamble (South) was given a new lease of life when Armstrong-Whitworth refitted the factory for the AW Ensign airliner, the prototype of which first flew on 23 January 1938. Production was only just gearing up when the war started and the lines were converted to produce the Albemarle, with a first flight being made on 20 March 1940.

Meanwhile the training routine had changed, with the formation of No.11 AONS in November 1939; however, by the following July both training units had departed. The Southampton area had become a major centre of aircraft manufacture, including significant production of Spitfires, and a section of the Ferry Pilot Pool (FPP) was established at Hamble in summer 1940, this subsequently becoming No.15 FPP. The men and women, soon mainly the latter, of the FPP were kept very busy ferrying aircraft from Hamble and surrounding airfields. The various manufacturers played a vital role in the war effort, producing not only new aircraft but also components and undertaking a large amount of repair and modification work.

With the end of the war Hamble returned to a training role, the military element being Southampton University Air Squadron and the civil element being Air Service Training, although from 1947 the latter also ran No.14 Reserve Flying School. AST also maintained its involvement in aircraft repair, modification and overhaul for both military and civil contracts. Likewise, Fairey and Folland continued to be active into the 1950s, the Gnat being one of the distinctive products from the latter company; neither, however, carried out flight testing from their Hamble locations.

As can be seen from the list of units, a number of other training units operated from Hamble in the later 1940s and 1950s, but the most significant development occurred in 1960, when AST's parent, Hawker Siddeley, disposed of the school, which then became the Government-run College of Air Training. A two-year course on singles (Chipmunks) and twins (Apaches) was designed to take *ab initio* students and turn them into airline pilots. Over the next ten years this course proved a great success; aircraft types changed during the period and, in 1970, the twin-engine flying element of the course was moved to Hurn. Fortunes changed with the fortunes of the airline industry, or rather the two State customers (BEA and BOAC), and, despite an RAF contract in the mid-1970s, it was increasingly difficult to maintain the facility due to lack of students. When British Airways withdrew its support in 1982 it signalled the end. A successor company, Specialist Flying Training, attempted to make a go of it with a reduced training-fleet and an involvement in the development of new aircraft, such as the Firecracker.

The Supermarine 510 (Swift) on test out of Hamble – the airfield can be seen in the background.

However, when they moved out to Carlisle in 1983 the airfield had little hope of securing an aviation future and it closed its doors in mid-1984.

Like so many airfields, Hamble has vanished under housing and there is now little evidence of what was once an important part of the British aviation story.

## UNITS

### 1939–1945

| | | |
|---|---|---|
| 3 ERFTS | 1 Apr 1931–3 Sep 1939 | |
| 3 EFTS | 3 Sep 1939–20 Jul 1940 | Tiger Moth |
| 11 AONS | 20 Nov 1939–20 Jul 1940 | various |
| 3 FPP | Jun 1940–Jul 1941 | Anson, Argus |
| 15 FPP | Jul 1941–Sep 1945 | Anson, Argus |

### Post-1945

| | | |
|---|---|---|
| Southampton UAS | 1 Oct 1947–11 Dec 1978 | Tiger Moth, Chipmunk |
| 14 RFS | 15 Aug 1947–15 Aug 1953 | Tiger Moth |
| 1 BANS | 1 Feb 1951–30 Jun 1953 | Anson |
| 2 AEF | 8 Sep 1958–11 Dec 1978 | Chipmunk |

## MEMORIALS

The industrial park on the site is called Ensign Park – poor recognition of the part played by this former airfield!

# HAMMERWOOD
## (East Grinstead)

**County:** East Sussex

**UTM/Grid:** OS map 188–TQ440391
**Lat/Long:** N51°08.0 E000°03.4
**Nearest Town:** East Grinstead 3 miles to west

## HISTORY

Hammerwood House became HQ to the Auster-equipped 660 Squadron in November 1943, when this Air Observation Post squadron arrived at what was little more than a grass field surrounded by trees. Two strips had been laid out on fields belonging to Bower Farm and the intention was for the squadron to familiarize itself with mobile operations from strips with no facilities (except the house) and work with army units in the area as part of the preparation for the invasion of France.

It is always a problem looking at AOP strips as they could, in effect, be set up almost anywhere – this was the nature of their task and there were hundreds of 'strips' (such as a stretch of beach or area of grass near a HQ unit) that could be called AOP strips simply because an Auster or other AOP aircraft landed there! It is sometimes difficult, therefore, to know which 'airfields' to include and which to omit, the choice usually falling on squadron records and which locations they chose to record as 'bases'. Two Auster squadrons used Hammerwood, or East Grinstead as it also appears in the records – 660 Squadron from November 1943 and 659 Squadron from April 1944. The pace of activity increased as D-Day approached and everyone realized the importance of 'army air-power'. Within days of the Allied forces going ashore the AOP squadrons were on the move to the Continent, 659 Squadron going to Cully on 14 June. After D-Day the 'airfield' went out of use almost immediately.

## UNITS

**1939–1945**

| | | |
|---|---|---|
| 659 Sqn | 23 Apr 1944–9 Jun 1944 | Auster |
| 660 Sqn | 1 Nov 1943–22 Apr 1944 | Auster |

# HARTFORD BRIDGE
# (Blackbushe)

**UTM/Grid:** OS map 187–SU805595
**Lat/Long:** N51°19.30 W000°50.30
**Nearest Town:** Reading 10 miles to North-West

**County:** Hampshire

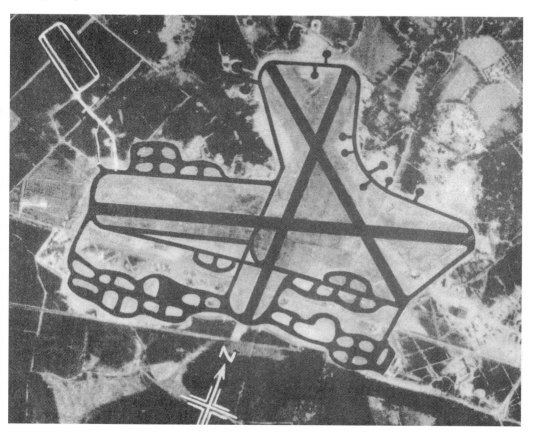

## History

This is one of those airfields where name confusion is rife. It started its RAF life as Hartford Bridge and is referred to as such in many official documents; however, the name was later changed to Blackbushe and, by late-1944, this name had been adopted in RAF records – indeed, it is as Blackbushe that the airfield is best known, primarily because of its post-war use.

The site was requisitioned in October 1941 for a bomber airfield and the main contractor, McAlpines, started work immediately on a standard three-runway layout. Work progressed with few problems and Hartford Bridge opened on 1 November 1942; the Royal Aircraft Establishment, which had already been making some use of the airfield during the construction phase, became the major occupant. The Tomahawks and Mustangs of 171 Squadron had been

in residence during December, forming at Hartford Bridge on the first of the month. The next operational unit in residence was 140 Squadron, whose Venturas and Spitfires arrived from Mount Farm in March 1943. This was one of the RAF's unsung squadrons, in that it and its predecessor Flight had been responsible for much of the development of photographic reconnaissance when based at Benson. They were joined in June by the Spitfire-equipped 16 Squadron and together formed No.34 (PR) Wing. Meanwhile, the RAE was also active at the airfield, the most important work concerning glider towing, primarily on the Horsa and Hamilcar.

The operational pace of the airfield was increased in summer 1943 with the arrival of light-bomber units of No.2 Group, comprising two Boston squadrons and a Ventura squadron, although the latter was replaced

## AIRFIELD DATA DEC 1944

| | | | |
|---|---|---|---|
| Command: | RAF Fighter Command | Runway surface: | Concrete and wood-chippings |
| Function: | Forward Airfield, Night Fighter | Hangars: | 6 × Blister, 3 × T.2, 2 × Bessonneau |
| Runways: | 262 deg 2,000 × 50yd | Dispersals: | 50 × Special Loop, 18 × Frying Pan (100ft) |
| | 317 deg 1,400 × 50yd | Personnel: | Officers – 189 (6 WAAF) |
| | 011 deg 1,400 × 50yd | | Other Ranks – 2,791 (407 WAAF) |

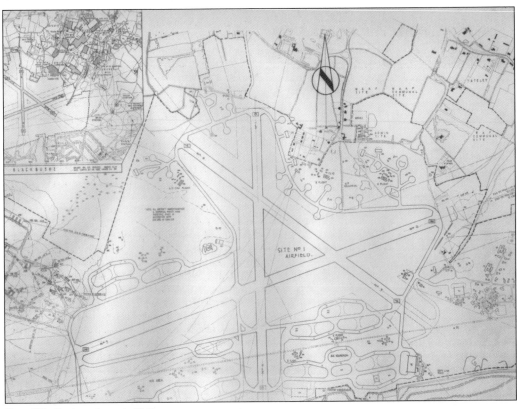

Plan of Blackbushe as it was in 1945.

by another Boston unit a few weeks later. This gave Hartford Bridge a Wing of three Boston squadrons, all of which were engaged with hazardous low-level attacks on pinpoint targets. In December, as part of the continuing re-organization of tactical air-power for the forthcoming invasion, the squadrons officially became No.137 Airfield. The airfield was thus incredibly busy, with two operational Wings in residence.

The PR Wing left in April – to Northolt – but the Spitfires of 322 Squadron arrived the same month for day-fighter cover, being joined in May by the Mosquito-equipped 264 Squadron. These two squadrons were placed under No.141 Airfield and

Hartford Bridge was back to a two-Wing Station. Whilst the fighters were kept busy they met with little success, although a number of night claims were made; however, for the bombers the pace of operations increased as the pre-invasion target list was methodically attacked. When D-Day dawned the Bostons were given a special task, for which they had been fitted with special tanks in their bomb bays; as the amphibious force moved towards the enemy shore the Bostons laid a smoke screen and this was assessed as successful – for the loss of two aircraft. On 20 June the fighter Wing was disbanded, with the departure of 322 Squadron to West Malling. The Mosquitoes departed the following month but the

140 Squadron Gladiator and pilots at Hartford Bridge.

Boston of 342 Squadron; the Squadron was at Hartford for over a year, including the D-Day period.

Fine airborne study of a Boston of 107 Squadron.

bombers continued to fly support missions over the Continent, although the nomenclature had changed to No.137 Wing. The Bostons finally moved out in October as part of the move of 2nd TAF units to the Continent, the Hartford Bridge Wing going to Vitry-en-Artois (airfield B50). The Mosquito-equipped No.138 Wing operated from Hartford for a few weeks but it, too, moved to the Continent in

mid-November. Within days another Mosquito Wing formed at Hartford; No.136 Wing, comprising 418 and 605 Squadrons, arriving to convert from pure night-fighting to a more tactical role.

In December the name of the airfield was officially changed to Blackbushe, although the confusion is still evident in the December 1944 airfield summary, as the entry is headed Blackbushe but the location map still lists the airfield as Hartford Bridge. The December 1944 survey suggested that the main runway could be extended to 3,000 yards, both the other runways could have small extensions and that a fourth runway of 4,300 yards could be laid but that this work would 'entail diversion of the main London to Southampton road and the demolition of two cottages'. One of the most unusual features of the airfield plan is the arrangement of dispersals, the bulk of which were located on the south side of the A30 road.

No.136 Wing returned to operations in late-December and it played a full part in the offensive against German lines of communication and other tactical targets until it moved overseas, to Coxyde (airfield B71), on 15 March 1945.

Blackbushe was handed to Transport Command and, in late March, the first Warwick unit, 167 Squadron, moved in from Holmsley South. They were joined in April by the Polish 301 Squadron, also with Warwicks. Both units flew cargo and passenger routes to and from Europe, including casualty evacuation, until the Poles departed in July. Although Blackbushe now housed a single squadron it was a diverse one, as it acquired additional types, including Ansons and Dakotas, to reflect an increasing requirement and diversity of transport tasks.

The pace of operations increased in the immediate post-war period and, in July, a second unit, 162 Squadron with Mosquitoes and tasked with 'express delivery', arrived from Bourn, one of many bomber squadrons to adopt a transport role during this period. At some stage the airfield was provided with a FIDO system to reflect the important part it was playing within Transport Command. In February 1946 British European Airways took over some of the transport work and 167 Squadron disbanded. Other changes in the early months of 1946 included use of Blackbushe as a terminal for the Air Despatch Letter Service, as well as for 24 Squadron's route from Prestwick, although the latter squadron was not actually based at Blackbushe. A number of other units, military and civil, made some use of the airfield during this period but, in many cases, this was ad hoc and the disbandment in July of 162 Squadron removed the last based RAF squadron from Blackbushe. The airfield had been operating as No.160 Staging Post for a few months but, on 15

Not a wartime shot but a fine view of one of the historic aircraft that graced Blackbushe as part of the Doug Arnold collection in 1980.

November 1946, it was officially closed after what had been an intense operational period and a hectic few months as a transport base.

An RAF Care and Maintenance party remained on site until the airfield was transferred to the Ministry of Civil Aviation on 15 February 1947 to become Blackbushe Airport. A number of commercial operators used the airport and there was a particularly busy period during the 1948 Berlin Airlift, famous names such as Silver City and Airwork being seen at Blackbushe. The RAF returned in November 1950, when the Auxiliary Air Force's only transport unit, 622 Squadron, formed here and was equipped primarily with Valettas; however, the unit only survived three years. That was pretty much it in military terms, although a US Navy handling-unit was present in the mid-1950s to look after transit traffic. They constructed a hangar on the NE side of the airfield to create their own little enclave, although, sadly, this unique hangar has now been demolished.

However, Blackbushe was very much a civil airport but, like many, it – or rather its occupants – met with mixed success. The major blow fell in 1960, when the Ministry of Civil Aviation announced that the airport was to close. Major operators such as Eagle Airways moved out but the airfield, or at least a part of it, survived for use by business and light aviation.

There have been various owners and various problems in the last forty years but Blackbushe is once more a thriving airfield, with a large number of privately owned light-aircraft and a number of flying schools on site.

## UNITS

### HQ Units at Hartford Bridge

| | | |
|---|---|---|
| No.137 Airfield/ (B) Wing | 14 Nov 1943–17 Oct 1944 | 88, 107, 342 Sqn |
| No.141 (F) Wing | 12 May 1944–21 Jul 1944 | 264, 322 Sqn |

### 1939–1945

| | | |
|---|---|---|
| 16 Sqn | 29 Jun 1943–16 Apr 1944 | Spitfire |
| 21 Sqn | 19 Aug 1943–27 Sep 1943 | Ventura |
| 88 Sqn | 19 Aug 1943–16 Oct 1944 | Boston |
| 107 Sqn | 20 Aug 1943–1 Feb 1944; 23 Oct 1944–19 Nov 1944 | Boston, Mosquito |
| 140 Sqn | 16 Mar 1943–7 Apr 1944 | Ventura, Spitfire, Mosquito |
| 162 Sqn | 10 Jul 1945–14 Jul 1946 | Mosquito |
| 167 Sqn | 30 Mar 1945–Feb 1946 | Warwick, Anson, Dakota |
| 171 Sqn | 7 Dec 1942–1 Feb 1943 | Mustang |
| 226 Sqn | 13 Feb 1944–17 Oct 1944 | Mitchell |
| 264 Sqn | 7 May 1944–26 Jul 1944 | Mosquito |
| 301 Sqn | 4 Apr 1945–2 Jul 1945 | Warwick |
| 305 Sqn | 23 Oct 1944–19 Nov 1944 | Mosquito |
| 322 Sqn | 24 Apr 1944–20 Jun 1944 | Spitfire |
| 342 Sqn | 6 Sep 1943–17 Oct 1944 | Boston |
| 418 Sqn | 21 Nov 1944–15 Mar 1945 | Mosquito |
| 430 Sqn | 1–8 Jan 1943 | Tomahawk |
| 605 Sqn | 21 Nov 1944–15 Mar 1945 | Mosquito |
| 613 Sqn | 23 Oct 1944–20 Nov 1944 | Mosquito |
| 34 Wing SU | 16 Oct 1944–11 Dec 1945 | various |

### Post-1945

| | | |
|---|---|---|
| 128 Sqn det | Oct 1945–Mar 1946 | Mosquito |
| 167 Sqn | 30 Mar 1945–Feb 1946 | Warwick, Anson, Dakota |
| 622 Sqn | 1 Nov 1950–30 Sep 1953 | Valetta |
| ADLS det | 15 Jan 1946–? | |

## MEMORIALS

There is some memorabilia in the airport terminal.

# HAWKINGE

**County:** Kent

**UTM/Grid:** OS map 189–TR213395
**Lat/Long:** N51°06.7 E001°09.6
**Nearest Town:** Folkestone 2 miles to south

Hawkinge vanishing under housing in summer 2003.

## HISTORY

Initially known as Folkestone – and only two miles from that coastal town – when it was first used by the Royal Flying Corps as a landing ground during World War One, the airfield eventually took the name Hawkinge in January 1917. Acquisition was approved in 1914 of a 166-acre site made up of farmland from Lord Radnor's estate and a site known as Megone field (from which W H Megone is said to have made a number of short hops in 1912 in an aircraft he built in his shed). One of the main reasons for the selection of this site was for use as a staging post for aircraft travelling to the operational squadrons in France and, whilst there is some uncertainty as to when the first aircraft passed through, it was certainly used for this purpose from early 1915. By autumn that year, the airfield had been provided with at least three Bessonneau hangars – and a fascinating navigation-aid to help pilots point towards

the French end of the route at St Omer: it is reported that two circles were laid out at Folkestone airfield that, when lined up, pointed straight at France. Whilst this would have allowed a pilot to very roughly set his compass, it would not have been of that much use.

The number of aircraft passing though Hawkinge's Aeroplane Despatch Centre continued to increase and it thus played an important role in the build-up of British air strength in France. The airfield's facilities continued to grow to meet the demand and it soon sprouted a fair collection of General Service sheds (nine by late-1917) and other buildings, whilst its two strips, one of 2,400ft (east/west) and the other 2,000ft (north/south) were an impressive length for the period. As No.12 Aircraft Acceptance Park (SE Area), Hawkinge took on the entire AAP responsibility for this area but, by the end of the war, the

Hector of 2 Squadron; this unit was here in the late 1930s.

Hawkinge from the air, 1936 – a typical grass airfield with permanent structures on one side.

Hurricanes of 32 Squadron, 31 July 1940. (Andy Thomas)

Pilots of 32 Squadron enjoy a peaceful few minutes in July 1940.

planned final expansion of the site had not been completed. Traffic was now reversed and a number of squadrons came back to Hawkinge from France in early 1919, sadly only to become part of the wholesale disbandment of the Royal Air Force.

The airfield facilities and its locations meant that the airfield itself survived the disbandment process and, in April 1920, it became a fighter station when 25 Squadron re-formed here with Snipes. The squadron departed at the end of 1923 to take part in the 'Chanak Crisis' but returned a year later. During its absence the Snipes of 56 Squadron moved in and, for two years in the mid-1920s, another Snipe unit, 17 Squadron, was also based at Hawkinge. However, with 25 Squadron back in residence Hawkinge witnessed that regular changing of fighter types that was typical of UK-based units in the late-1920s and 1930s, a wonderful array of biplanes that was brought to an end in December 1938 when the squadron was re-equipped with the Blenheim If fighter – no doubt much to the annoyance of single-seat fighter pilots who thus lost their highly agile (but outdated) biplanes. The airfield was also in use from 1930 as the Wessex Area Storage Unit, the large number of hangars providing suitable storage-space for aircraft prior to their being issued to squadrons. Also, from 1930 onwards, Hawkinge was home to the routine of summer camps for auxiliary and reserve squadrons,

this essential part of the yearly training for part-time pilots that gave them the opportunity for a period of concentrated flying and ground study. (Note: These summer camps are not listed in the unit table.)

Hawkinge was a delightful station, with its grass landing-area, line of sturdy GS-sheds and well-established facilities; with the RAF Expansion Plans of the early 1930s onwards, it was one of the airfields at which further construction took place, most of which, in this case, were less to do with operational enhancements and more to do with domestic and administration improvements, such as Officers' and Sergeants' Mess buildings. An Army Co-operation unit, 2 Squadron, had arrived in November 1935 to give Hawkinge the standard complement of two squadrons, but both moved out of the airfield shortly

## AIRFIELD DATA DEC 1944

| | | | |
|---|---|---|---|
| Command: | RAF Fighter Command | Runway surface: | Grass |
| Function: | Forward Airfield | Hangars: | 4 × General Service, 4 × Extra Over Blister, 2 × Over Blister |
| Runways: | NE/SW 1,100yd | Dispersals: | 9 × Twin-engine |
| | E/W 1,100yd | Personnel: | Officers – 102 |
| | N/S 900yd | | Other Ranks – 1,393 (202 WAAF) |

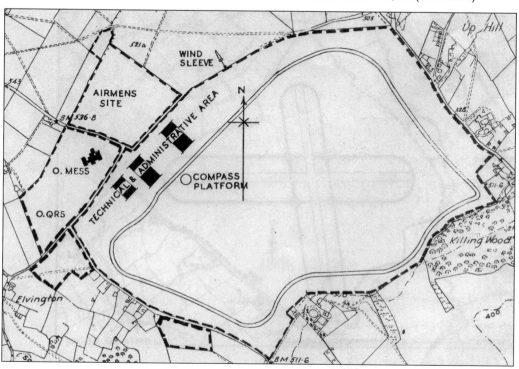

after the outbreak of war.

In December 1939 a detachment of Hurricanes of 3 Squadron arrived from Croydon and Hawkinge entered the phase for which it is best remembered – a front-line fighter base. Fighter Command took control of the airfield in January 1940 and used it as a satellite station, although in this early part of the Phoney War non-fighter units also used the airfield. Fighter deployments were soon the main order of business, Hurricanes and Blenheims using the airfield, although in May it was also the base of the only operational sorties flown by Hawker Hectors. With the crisis in France, all manner of air assets were thrown into the battle and, between 27 and 29 May, the Hectors of 613 Squadron made a number of low-level attacks on gun batteries in the Calais area, with the final day seeing the Hectors, supported by Lysanders, making a supply drop to the garrison.

Hawkinge was now being prepared for the coming battle: the camouflage that had been applied to buildings the previous year was checked and improved, more slit trenches were dug, protective pens were built for the fighters and anti-aircraft defences were brought in – including a PAC device. By July, Hawkinge's squadrons were involved in the first phase of what was to become the Battle of Britain, the war over the Channel. It was not long before the Luftwaffe turned its attention to Fighter Command's airfields and Hawkinge, being so far 'forward', was a vulnerable target. The first in a series of effective attacks took place on 12 August 1940, causing severe damage and a number of casualties. Over the next few days and weeks the airfield was hit a number of times and it is a tribute to the resilience and effectiveness of the station's personnel that it was seldom out of action for more than a few hours. The

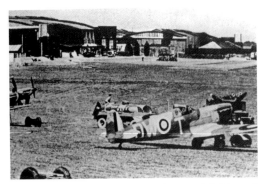

The Battle of Britain scenario at Hawkinge with Spitfires of 610 Squadron.

scale of daylight German attacks over England was drastically reduced from late-October, as the German High Command paused to consider its next tactic, having failed to win air superiority. For airfields such as Hawkinge it was a valuable breathing space in which to repair damage and put into place lessons learnt. One such move was the creation in November 1940 of No.421 Flight, equipped with Spitfires, to carry out spotting missions to look for incoming German aircraft and to monitor shipping movements in the Channel. This proved highly effective and the Flight became 91 Squadron in February 1941.

The Channel had claimed many RAF pilots during the Battle and it was a logical step to provide airfields such as Hawkinge with a Search and Rescue flight, this task initially being performed by a detachment from 4 Squadron, a daily detachment from their base at Manston, but with an ASR Flight being formed in June, which grew to become 277 Squadron. By summer 1941 Fighter Command was on the offensive and the resident fighter-squadrons began offensive fighter-sweeps across the Channel. This was to be the airfield's primary function for the rest of the war, various units and aircraft types operating from Hawkinge over the next three years. Hit-and-run fighter-bomber raids by Bf109s and Fw190s on coastal towns and installations proved a major problem over this same period and were very difficult to counter, although Hawkinge's fighters were often scrambled in an attempt to intercept or flew standing patrols over likely areas.

As with other airfields along this stretch of coast, Hawkinge's location made it an obvious port of call for aircraft in difficulties; it received a regular stream of RAF and, from 1942, USAAF aircraft, many of the latter being bombers. Partly in response to this and partly because of the likely increase in based aircraft, the airfield's main runway was extended and additional facilities provided, including nine large hardstands and three Blister hangars. The first

increase in striking power came with the arrival of No.157 Wing of Coastal Command on 14 May, its two constituent units, the Fleet Air Arm's 854 and 855 Squadrons, both equipped with Avengers, arriving a few days later. They were here as part of the D-Day build-up and were tasked with anti-submarine and anti-shipping patrols; both squadrons moved to Thorney Island in early August. RAF fighter units took up residence once more and, in addition to offensive operations over Europe, were involved in the anti-*Diver* operations against the V-1.

Fighter ops continued to the end of the war and Hawkinge could be proud of its record as a front-line fighter station. The airfield was reduced to Care and Maintenance on 7 November 1945.

The WAAF Technical Training Unit moved in during June 1946, the airfield having been transferred to No.22 Group within Technical Training Command and re-opened on 1 June. The WRAF, which it had become on 1 February 1949, remained at Hawkinge with various training and administrative functions until December 1961. The only consistent flying that took place during this period was the gliding activities of the Home Command Gliding Centre, which moved in during December 1955 and, renamed as No.1 Gliding Centre, remained to December 1961. The airfield was once more placed in Care and Maintenance, although the technical site was disposed of in 1963. The Battle of Britain returned to Hawkinge in 1968, as this was one of the locations used for the superb film of that name. Filming over, the airfield was abandoned once more and for over thirty years returned to peaceful grassland. However, in recent years it has almost completely vanished under a housing development, although some of the original buildings remain. The Kent Battle of Britain Museum, set up in the old operations-building in 1971, continues to record and display the heritage of this historic RAF airfield and is well worth a visit.

## DECOY SITES

Q                    Wootten                    TR238481

Line-up of Spitfires of 91 Squadron.

# Units

## HQ Units at Hawkinge

| | |
|---|---|
| Rear HQ BEF Air Component | May 1940–Jun 1940 |
| No.157 (GR) Wing | 17 May 1944–8 Aug 1944 |

## 1919–1938

| | | |
|---|---|---|
| 38 Sqn | 14 Feb 1919–4 Jul 1919 | as cadre |
| 83 Sqn | 14 Feb 1919–Sep 1919 | as cadre |
| 120 Sqn | 20 Feb 1919–17 Jul 1919 | DH9 |
| 56 Sqn | 1 Nov 1922–7 May 1923 | Snipe |
| 17 Sqn | 1 Apr 1924–14 Oct 1926; | Snipe, |
| | 2–22 May 1940 | Hurricane |
| 2 Sqn | 30 Nov 1935–29 Sep 1939 | Audax, |
| | | Hector, |
| | | Lysander |
| 25 Sqn | 26 Apr 1920–28 Sep 1922; | Snipe, |
| | 3 Oct 1923–22 Aug 1939+ | Gladiator |

## 1939–1945

| | | |
|---|---|---|
| 1 Sqn det | Jun 1940–Jul 1940 | Hurricane |
| 3 Sqn det | Dec 1939–Feb 1940 | Hurricane |
| 16 Sqn | 17 Feb 1940–13 Apr 1940 | Lysander |
| 25 Sqn | 10–12 May 1940 | Blenheim |
| 26 Sqn | 6–11 Oct 1944 | Spitfire |
| 41 Sqn | 30 Jun 1942–8 Jul 1942; | Spitfire |
| | 12 Apr 1943–21 May 1943 | |
| 65 Sqn | 30 Jun 1942–7 Jul 1942 | Spitfire |
| 66 Sqn | 8–9 Oct 1942 | Spitfire |
| 79 Sqn | 1–11 Jul 1940 | Hurricane |
| 91 Sqn | 9 Jan 1941–23 Nov 1942; | Spitfire |
| | 11 Jan 1943–20 Apr 1943; | |
| | 21 May 1943–28 Jun 1943 | |
| 124 Sqn | 7–10 Apr 1945 | Spitfire |
| 132 Sqn | 29 Sep 1944–14 Dec 1944 | Spitfire |
| 234 Sqn | 27 Aug 1945–21 Sep 1945 | Mustang |
| 245 Sqn det | May 1940–Jul 1940 | Hurricane |
| 277 Sqn det | Dec 1941–Oct 1944 | various |
| 278 Sqn det | Feb 1945–Oct 1945 | various |
| 313 Sqn | 21 Aug 1943–18 Sep 1943 | Spitfire |
| 322 Sqn | 31 Dec 1943–25 Feb 1944 | Spitfire |
| 350 Sqn | 1 Oct 1943–30 Dec 1943; | Spitfire |
| | 10–14 Mar 1944; | |
| | 8 Aug 1944–29 Sep 1944 | |
| 402 Sqn | 8 Aug 1944–30 Sep 1944 | Spitfire |
| 416 Sqn | 14–20 Aug 1942 | Spitfire |
| 441 Sqn | 1 Sep 1944–30 Dec 1944; | Spitfire |
| | 3–29 Apr 1945 | |
| 451 Sqn | 2 Dec 1944–11 Feb 1945; | Spitfire |
| | 3–17 May 1945 | |
| 453 Sqn | 2 May 1945–14 Jun 1945 | Spitfire |
| 501 Sqn | 8–10 Oct 1942; | Spitfire |
| | 21 Jun 1943–30 Apr 1944 | |
| 504 Sqn | 25 Feb 1945–28 Mar 1945 | Spitfire |
| 567 Sqn | Nov 1944–21 Aug 1945 | various |
| 605 Sqn | 21–28 May 1940 | Hurricane |
| 611 Sqn | 31 Dec 1944–3 Mar 1945 | Mustang |
| 616 Sqn | 14–20 Aug 1942 | Spitfire |
| 658 Sqn | 2–6 Jul 1945 | Auster |
| PAS | 15–29 Feb 1940 | Queen Bee |
| 1416 Flt | 1 Mar 1940–31 Mar 1940 | Lysander |
| 421/1421 Flt | 15 Nov 1940–11 Jan 1941 | |
| ASRF | Jun 1941–22 Dec 1941; | Lysander, |
| | 17 Apr 1940–26 May 1940 | Walrus |

## FAA Units

| | | |
|---|---|---|
| 854 Sqn | 23 May 1944–7 Aug 1944 | Avenger |
| 855 Sqn | 31 May 1944–3 Aug 1944 | Avenger |

## Post-1945

| | | |
|---|---|---|
| 3 APS | 10 Aug 1945–1 Nov 1945 | |
| 1 ADF | Sep 1945 | |
| HCGC | 1 Dec 1955–30 Mar 1959 | Cadet |
| 1 GC | 31 Mar 1959–8 Dec 1961 | Cadet, |
| | | Sedbergh |

# Memorials

1. Stone and metal (the compass-swinging circle) monument to all who served at Hawkinge, dedicated 29 April 1978.

2. Kent Battle of Britain Museum with replica fighters outside and a fine collection of artefacts and memorabilia on the Battle in general and Hawkinge in particular. (www.kbobm.org)

# HEADCORN

**County:** Kent

**UTM/Grid:** OS map 189–TQ880460
**Lat/Long:** N51°10.9 E000°41.3
**Nearest Town:** Ashford 8 miles to east

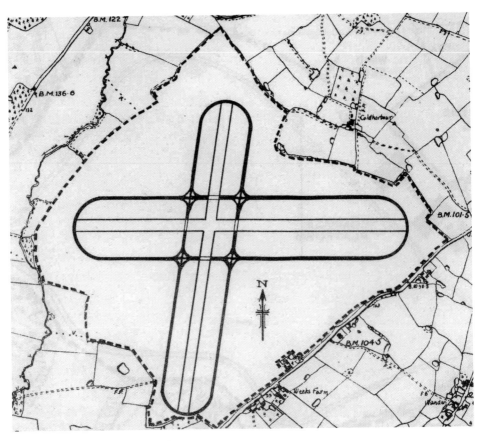

## HISTORY

There is invariably confusion between Lashenden and Headcorn – not helped by the fact that the present GA airfield calls itself Lashenden (Headcorn) whilst it is, in fact, located on the former site! The two landing grounds are very close together but little trace now remains of Headcorn – when you manage to find the memorial and lean over the adjacent fence to look across the fields there is nothing to show that Spitfires and P-47s once operated from here.

The site was selected for ALG development and then rejected, as it was considered that development work would be too involved, only to be re-selected a few months later. Construction commenced in early 1943 and two Sommerfeld Track runways were laid out in a skewed-cross pattern, connected by taxiways

and with the usual minimum of facilities – a few tents in the first instance. The airfield opened on 20 August 1943, when two Canadian Spitfire squadrons arrived from nearby Lashenden in one of the shortest airfield moves ever. Although these were the first aircraft to arrive, the airfield had been in use as the HQ of No.17 (RCAF) Wing with control of No.126 and No.127 Airfields, the latter comprising Headcorn's two squadrons. The airfield was also home to No.405 Repair and Salvage Unit; which, all in all, made this Kent ALG one of the busiest of its type. The Spitfires were here to learn how to operate in field conditions and continued their offensive operations over Europe, a pattern that carried on until they returned to Kenley on 14 October, the ALGs not being designed for winter operations.

# AIRFIELD DATA DEC 1944

| | | | |
|---|---|---|---|
| Command: | Fighter Command | Runway surface: | Grass |
| Function: | Advanced Landing Ground | Hangars: | Nil |
| Runways: | 090 deg 1,600yd | Dispersals: | 70 × Sommerfeld Track |
| | 180 deg 1,300yd | Personnel: | Other Ranks – Tented camp |

The 362nd FG was obviously not impressed with the move to Headcorn. (363nd FG)

Headcorn had proved its suitability – and had even coped with fourteen 'visiting' bombers, including twelve B-17s, on 6 September, an unplanned arrival and one that put great strain on the runway tracking! As with all the ALGs, the winter period was used to repair the runway tracking and improve facilities. The runways were strengthened using steel planking, as the airfield had been allocated to the USAAF and designated for a P-47 Group. Taxiways were extended and additional hardstands built, as well as a Butler hangar. The Thunderbolts of the 362nd Fighter Group arrived from Wormingford on 15 April 1944, its three squadrons having been operational since early February. Having arrived at Headcorn, this IXth Air Force Group gave up much of its former escort duties and took on the fighter-bomber role. It was an intensive few weeks and the Group was heavily involved during the D-Day period. With Allied forces firmly ashore, it was only a matter of time before the tactical groups moved to Europe; the 362nd's fighters moved to Lignerolles (airfield A12) on July 2 and the Group abandoned Headcorn a few days later.

Work on removing the runways commenced immediately and by autumn there was little trace of the airfield other than the scars it had left, but these soon healed as agriculture returned. The airfield appears to have had two other names during its life,

with some references to Coldharbour in 1943 and local usage of the name Egerton.

## UNITS

### HQ Units at Headcorn
No.17 (RCAF) Wing  4 Jul 1943–May 1944
No.127 Airfield        20 Aug 1943–14 Oct 1943  403, 421 Sqn

### 1939–1945
| | | |
|---|---|---|
| 403 Sqn | 20 Aug 1943–14 Oct 1943 | Spitfire |
| 421 Sqn | 20 Aug 1943–14 Oct 1943 | Spitfire |

### USAAF Units
| | |
|---|---|
| 362nd FG | |
| Squadrons: | 377th FS, 378th FS, 379th FS |
| Aircraft: | P-47 |
| Dates: | 15 Apr 1944–7 Jul 1944 |
| First mission: | 8 Feb 1944 (from Wormingford) |
| Last mission: | 1 May 1945 |

## MEMORIAL

A brick memorial overlooks one of the fields that was part of Headcorn ALG. The plinth includes an airfield plan and the various plaques record the units.

A brick memorial overlooks one of the fields that was part of Headcorn ALG. The plinth includes an airfield plan and the various plaques record the units.

# HIGH HALDEN

**County:** Kent

**UTM/Grid:** OS map 189–TQ890397
**Lat/Long:** N51°07.19 E000°42.15

**Nearest Town:** Ashford 6½ miles to east

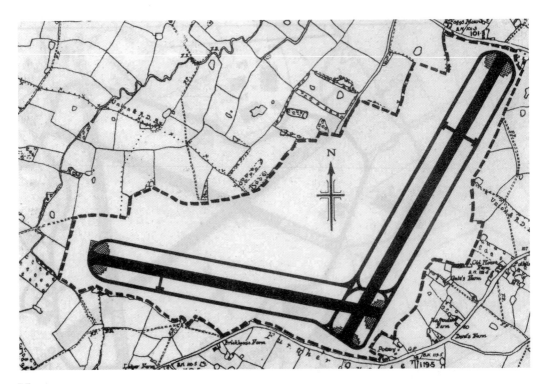

## HISTORY

High Halden was yet another of the Advanced Landing Grounds constructed in the area west and south of Ashford in Kent, an area that housed eleven airfields within a 10-mile arc of Ashford. Although selected for development in mid-1942, and finally approved late in the year, it was not an ideal site and required a fair amount of preparation, including ground work and the usual hedge, ditch and tree work. The plan shows the unusual runway-layout – and the additional tracking that had to be laid at the end of each runway – and the way that the runways appear squeezed between two roads. At this stage it was laid out as a standard ALG with Sommerfeld Track runways, limited taxiways and hardstands, and two Blister hangars; it was then put on standby and not evaluated by the basing of squadrons.

Over the winter period the site was upgraded and, as it had been allocated to the IXth Air Force, it was given appropriate facilities for use by the Americans, including longer runways with steel-plating surfaces. The taxiways used Sommerfeld Track, as did the

seventy hardstands. Work was completed on schedule in early April and the P-47s of the 358th Fighter Group arrived from Raydon on 13 April. This Group had been operational since December 1943 with the 8th Air Force but, on 1 February 1944, it transferred to the IXth Air Force. Having arrived at High Halden, its major role was that of fighter-bomber, attacking a variety of targets around the planned invasion area and, like most of the Thunderbolt groups, specializing in the destruction of transport targets, especially bridges. This routine was continued either side of D-Day, although on 6 June itself the Group acted as escort to part of the airborne assault. It was always planned that the fighter-bombers would move to France as soon as possible and the 358th departed High Halden for Cretteville (airfield A14) on 3 July.

It was normal practise for these ALGs to be dismantled almost as soon as the last aircraft had left, but it appears that High Halden was adopted as a possible forward operating strip by the RAF's first

## AIRFIELD DATA DEC 1944

| | | | |
|---|---|---|---|
| Command: | RAF Fighter Command | Runway surface: | US Steel-Planking |
| Function: | Advanced Landing Ground | Hangars: | nil |
| Runways: | 040 deg 1,800yd | Dispersals: | 70 × Sommerfeld |
| | 110 deg 1,400yd | Personnel: | Other Ranks – Tented camp |

358th FG Thunderbolt at High Halden.

The typical current view of an ALG – a stretch of fields with the only evidence of their former use being breaks in hedge-lines and ditches; High Halden March 2004.

jet-fighter unit, 616 Squadron, then based at Manston with Meteors. The Squadron was tasked with anti-*Diver* patrols; as Ashford was a frequent hunting-ground, it was certainly sensible to have a bolt hole in this area and High Halden had better runways, as it had been built to withstand the P-47. The only recorded use (or attempted use) by a Meteor was 14 August, when Sergeant Gregg crashed just short of the airfield; having become low on fuel he had made for High Halden. The following month the airfield was declared surplus and authority was given for its dismantling, although in the December survey it was still listed as an ALG with Fighter Command.

By January 1945 work had started on removing the airfield tracking; before long the fields had been returned to their original owners and High Halden was little more than a rapidly-fading memory.

## UNITS

### 1939–1945
### USAAF Units
#### 358th FG

| | |
|---|---|
| Squadrons: | 365th FS, 366th FS, 367th FS |
| Aircraft: | P-47 |
| Dates: | 13 Apr 1944–3 Jul 1944 |
| First mission: | 20 Dec 1943 (with 8th Air Force from Leiston) |
| Last mission: | May 1945 (from Mannheim) |

# HOLMSLEY SOUTH (Station 455)

**County:** Hampshire

**UTM/Grid:** OS map 195–SZ215995
**Lat/Long:** N50°47.7 W001°41.8
**Nearest Town:** Christchurch 6 miles to south-west

## HISTORY

Originally intended for use by Coastal Command, the airfield at Holmsley South was constructed in 1941–1942 to the, by then, standard pattern of three hard runways and perimeter track, but with limited facilities in terms of hangars and buildings. The latter comprised two Bellman hangars, one of which was positioned in the southern part of the airfield, along with a group of temporary huts and structures as an 'administrative and technical area'. Although far from complete, the airfield was opened on 1 September 1942, as Coastal Command was desperate for airfields. In the event, it was a few more weeks before any aircraft arrived, first-in being a detachment of Wellingtons from 547 Squadron, although they were soon joined by B-24s of the USAAF's 330th Bombardment Squadron, part of the 93rd Bomb Group. The Liberators had been loaned to No.19 Group, Coastal Command for anti-

submarine work during the period of Operation *Torch*, the invasion of North Africa.

Work on the airfield infrastructure continued and by the time the Americans left at the end of November it was just about ready to receive its permanent establishment of two Coastal Command squadrons. The following month 58 Squadron arrived with Whitleys, but promptly set about converting to the far more effective Halifax GR.II, being joined in March 1943 by 502 Squadron. These two units remained operational from Holmsley throughout 1943, playing a part in the intensive, and often costly, war against the U-boats in the Bay of Biscay. When the Halifax units departed at the end of the year the airfield was transferred to No.10 Group of Fighter Command and, after a few weeks with little activity, it became home, albeit briefly, to the three

## AIRFIELD DATA DEC 1944

| | | | |
|---|---|---|---|
| Command: | RAF Transport Command | Runway surface: | Tarmac |
| Function: | Parent Station (No.116 Wing) | Hangars: | 2 × Bellman |
| Runways: | 247 deg 1,970yd | Dispersals: | 38 × Concrete |
| | 302 deg 1,400yd | Personnel: | Officers – 187 (10 WAAF) |
| | 58 deg 1,370yd | | Other Ranks – 2,776 (328 WAAF) |

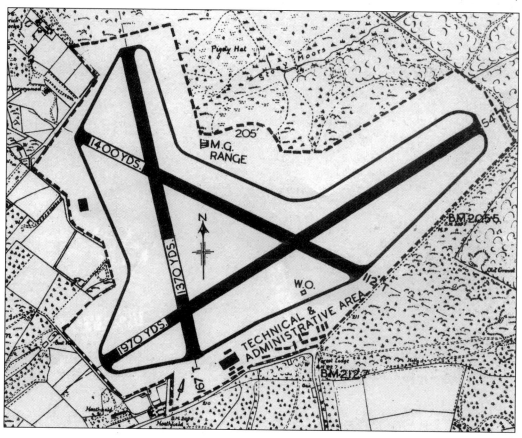

Canadian Spitfire squadrons of No.144 Airfield. After two weeks of work-up training they departed to Westhampnett, changing places with No.121 Wing. The latter comprised three Typhoon squadrons, whose aircraft were soon heavily occupied in attacking targets in and around Normandy. They were joined in April by the Mosquitoes of 418 Squadron, an intruder squadron that remained here until July, by which time No.121 Wing, having moved to France, had been replaced by the Mustang-equipped No.133 Wing from Coolham. Although operational, the Wing stayed less than a week and Holmsley was handed to the Americans, to become Station 455.

The Marauders of the 394th Bomb Group – the

'Bridge Busters' – moved into Holmsley from Boreham on 24 July 1944, their advance party of ground personnel having arrived the previous week. This move was made to put the bombers closer to their targets in France as the Allies continued to advance and whilst waiting for suitable airfields to become available on the Continent. The four B-26 squadrons continued to attack a variety of tactical targets in support of the ground forces.

The Group's stay at Holmsley South was short-lived and the anticipated move to France came on 20 August, when the aircraft flew to Tour-en-Bessin. The airfield had another few months when it was empty and it was not until October that the new

Typhoon of No.121 Airfield/(RP) Wing; the three squadrons of this organisation were at Holmsley from April to August 1944. (Peter Green)

'owners', No.116 Wing, a Transport Command unit, took control. Equipped with Warwicks, 167 Squadron reformed at Holmsley and, in the latter weeks of the year, commenced transport services to Europe. They were joined in December by 246 Squadron; this unit operated long-range transport flights with Halifaxes, Liberators and Yorks, although from April 1945 it started to receive C-54 Skymasters. Transport operations continued from the airfield to October 1946, after which it was placed under Care and Maintenance for a short period before final closure.

The area is under Forestry Commission control and is essentially a park and well worth a visit today – not only because of the fine memorial erected in 2002 but because, wandering around the old airfield-site, you can still find stretches of runway and dispersal areas.

## DECOY SITES

| Q | Ridley Plain | SU210072 |
|---|---|---|

## UNITS

### HQ Units at Holmsley South

| No.144 Airfield | 14 Mar 1944–<br>1 Apr 1944 | 441, 442,<br>443 Sqn |
|---|---|---|
| No.121 Airfield/<br>(RP) Wing | 1 Apr 1944–<br>28 Aug 1944 | 174, 175,<br>245 Sqn |
| No.133 Wing | 22–26 Jun 1944 | 129, 306,<br>315 Sqn |

### 1939–1945

| 58 Sqn | 2 Dec 1942–31 Mar 1943;<br>29 Jun 1943–6 Dec 1943 | Whitley,<br>Halifax |
|---|---|---|
| 129 Sqn | 22–24 Jun 1944 | Mustang |
| 167 Sqn | 1 Oct 1944–30 Mar 1945 | Warwick |
| 174 Sqn | 1 Apr 1944–17 Jun 1944 | Typhoon |
| 182 Sqn | 22 Jun 1944–3 Jul 1944 | Typhoon |
| 184 Sqn | 14–20 May 1944;<br>17–27 Jun 1944 | Typhoon |
| 245 Sqn | 1 Apr 1944–27 Jun 1944 | Typhoon |
| 246 Sqn | 1 Dec 1944–16 Oct 1946 | various |
| 295 Sqn | 1 May 1943–30 Jun 1943 | Whitley,<br>Halifax |
| 306 Sqn | 22–27 Jun 1944 | Mustang |
| 315 Sqn | 22–25 Jun 1944 | Mustang |
| 418 Sqn | 8 Apr 1944–14 Jul 1944 | Mosquito |
| 441 Sqn | 18 Mar 1944–1 Apr 1944 | Spitfire |
| 442 Sqn | 18 Mar 1944–1 Apr 1944 | Spitfire |
| 443 Sqn | 18–27 Mar 1944 | Spitfire |
| 502 Sqn | 2 Mar 1943–10 Dec 1943 | Whitley,<br>Halifax |
| 547 Sqn | 22 Oct 1942–10 Dec 1942 | Wellington |
| 1320 Flt | 8 May 1944–22 May 1944 | Typhoon |
| HDF | 15 Nov 1944–Mar 1945 | Halifax |
| 1552 Flt | 8 Dec 1945–5 Feb 1946 | Oxford,<br>Anson |

### USAAF Units

**394th BG**

| Squadrons: | 584th BS, 585th BS, 586th BS, 587th BS |
|---|---|
| Aircraft: | B-26 |
| Dates: | 24 Jul 1944–25 Aug 1944 |
| First mission: | Mar 1944 (from Boreham) |
| Last mission: | May 1945 (from Venlo) |

**330th BS**

| Oct 1942–28 Nov 1942 | B-24D |
|---|---|

## MEMORIALS

The Friends of New Forest Airfields dedicated an impressive memorial at Holmsley South on 16 Aug 2002; the concrete pillar bears a three-bladed propeller, along with plaques naming the airfields within the New Forest area. A smaller plinth carries a map of the area showing the positions of the airfields.

The impressive memorial erected by the Friends of New Forest Airfields; it commemorates all the airfields in the area but is located at Holmsley South.

# HORNE

**County:** Surrey

**UTM/Grid:** OS map 187–TQ332435
**Lat/Long:** N51°10.23 W000°04.38
**Nearest Town:** Redhill 6½ miles to north-west

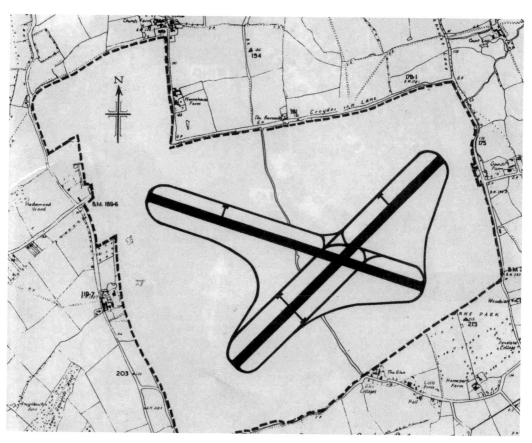

## HISTORY

Horne was the only ALG in Surrey and was the most northerly of all the ALGs prepared as part of the air build-up for D-Day. The site was selected in 1942 and construction took place the following year, with an 'X'-shape of two Sommerfeld Track runways being laid out on farmland to the south of the small village after which the airfield was named. A number of minor roads were closed and the usual hedge removal and culverting of ditches produced a reasonably efficient temporary airfield. The new airfield was not tested in 1943 and during the following winter was given additional facilities, including four Blister hangars and thirty-two tracking dispersals. The grazing animals were removed in spring 1944, when the three squadrons of No.142 Airfield arrived from

Scorton. The squadrons were operational immediately, flying their first mission on 2 May and, over the next few weeks, undertaking the full gamut of operations from escort to fighter sweep, the pace of ops increasing just before and after D-Day. With the need to place tactical air-power as close as possible to the battlefield in Normandy, the airfield at Horne was one of the first to be abandoned, as it was too far to the north. By late-June 1944 the Wing had departed and Horne was de-requisitioned later in the year, its tracking being ripped up and the fields being returned to agriculture.

As is invariably the case with these ALGs, there is little trace left at Horne of its six weeks of hectic activity in 1944.

# Airfield Data Dec 1944

| | | | |
|---|---|---|---|
| Command: | RAF Fighter Command | Runway surface: | Sommerfeld Track |
| Function: | Advanced Landing Ground | Hangars: | 4 × Blister |
| Runways: | NE/SW 1,600yd | Dispersals: | 32 × Sommerfeld Track |
| | NW/SE 1,600yd | Personnel: | Other Ranks – Tented camp |

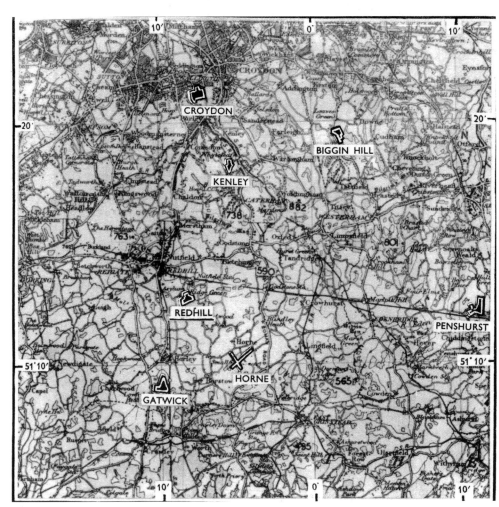

Area map showing Horne and its relationship nearby airfields such as Gatwick and Redhill; Horne was the most northerly of the ALG fields.

## Units

### HQ Units at Horne
No.142 Airfield/    28 Apr 1944–25 Jun 1944    130, 303,
  (F)Wing                                          402 Sqn

### 1939–1945
| | | |
|---|---|---|
| 130 Sqn | 30 Apr 1944–19 Jun 1944 | Spitfire |
| 303 Sqn | 30 Apr 1944–19 Jun 1944 | Spitfire |
| 402 Sqn | 30 Apr 1944–19 Jun 1944 | Spitfire |

## Memorials

Paintings in Clubhouse of Golf Course adjacent to old airfield site.

# HURN

**County:** Hampshire

**UTM/Grid:** OS map 195–SZ115980
**Lat/Long:** N50°46.9 W001°50.3
**Nearest Town:** south-west outskirts of Bournemouth

## HISTORY

A site on the outskirts of Bournemouth was chosen in 1940 for development into a standard three-runway airfield and opened in July 1941 as a satellite for Ibsley, by which time most of its facilities were complete. However, for its first few months of existence it saw little use. From November 1941 the Special Duties Flight at Christchurch became the Research Section of the Telecommunications Flying Unit (TFU) and moved to Hurn, although a flying detachment also remained at Christchurch. Their work was part of the Telecommunications Research Establishment, an important organization in the development of equipment. This unit moved out the following May and Hurn was ready for a new role as an airborne-forces base with No.38 Wing. Within a couple of months two Whitley

squadrons, 296 and 297, were in residence and, although they flew a number of leaflet-dropping sorties over France, their main task, for which they later re-equipped with Albemarles, was glider-towing. Their work-up proceeded well and, in August 1943, aircraft went to North Africa to participate in the airborne assault on Sicily. By the time the aircraft returned to Hurn, a third unit, 570 Squadron, had formed.

No.2 Overseas Aircraft Despatch Unit formed here in September 1943 and was responsible for a variety of aircraft types, such as Halifaxes, Wellingtons, Liberators and Dakotas, as well as Albemarles destined for Russia. Airborne-force operations remained the main rationale of the airfield into 1944 but, as the date of the invasion approached, the airfield under-

Pensive-looking pilot of 440 Squadron, summer 1944.
(Peter Green)

Two Typhoon Wings used Hurn in 1944.

Preparing an Air Sea Rescue kit for a 277 Squadron
Lysander.

B-26 Marauders of the 397th BG operated from Hurn for
a few weeks in 1944. (US National Archives)

went a major change, with the departure of the resident units to clear the way for fighter operations. Hurn was one of the busiest airfields in the period leading up to D-Day, with some 200 aircraft in two Typhoon Wings, each of three squadrons, plus two Mosquito units. It was also home to No.403 Repair and Salvage Unit during the period April to June, this unit being primarily responsible for Typhoons.

The night-fighter squadrons were also busy, as the Luftwaffe remained active at night with intruder operations, and there was a particular need to protect the invasion concentration-areas and beachheads – with 604 Squadron having a number of successful nights. By August this hectic period of day- and night-operations was over, although a brief occupation by B-26s of the 397th Bomb Group kept Hurn busy for a few more weeks. The airfield was back in RAF control in October, but it was taken over by BOAC and soon became their main airfield, with flights increasing as 'civil' routes increased towards the end of the war. Hurn was transferred to the Ministry of Civil Aviation and other commercial carriers joined BOAC, the number of flights increasing dramatically in the immediate post-war period. However, the opening of London

Airport in 1946 saw a run-down of services as carriers moved to the new airport. Within a short period of time the airfield was virtually deserted, although the BOAC Development Flight remained into the 1950s and Vickers-Armstrongs undertook some test flying from here, having taken over one of the BOAC hangars. Vickers-Armstrongs increased in importance, with the company expanding its facility and developing a production line for the Varsity and Viscount.

Military types re-appeared when Airwork Services formed a Fleet Requirements Unit (FRU) to work with the navy, types ranging from the Mosquito to the Canberra, the name of the unit and its role changing during its period at Hurn. This fascinating unit eventually moved out to Yeovilton in the 1970s, by which time Hurn was also struggling in respect to commercial operators.

The situation remained unstable for a number of years: the airport was taken over by Bournemouth and Dorset Councils and attempts were made to attract new operators. Private owners and flying clubs have been an important part of the airport's activities since the 1960s. Private owners have also included warbird owners and, in the late-1990s, the airport was

home to a 'squadron' of Vampires and Venoms owned and operated by Source Classic Aircraft. Flight Refuelling Ltd moved in from Tarrant Rushton in 1980 and, over the years, have continued to play a role in the airport's development.

Commercial operations have once again become a major factor for Bournemouth International Airport.

## UNITS

### HQ Units at Hurn

| | | |
|---|---|---|
| No.143 Airfield/ (RCAF) (F) Wing | 18 Mar 1944–1 Sep 1944 | 438, 439, 440 Sqn |
| No.16 Wing | 1–20 Apr 1944 | |
| No.22 Wing | 16 Apr 1944–12 May 1944 | |
| No.22 Sector | 12 May 1944–6 Jun 1944 | |
| No.136 (F) Wing | 22 Jun 1944–20 Jul 1944 | 164, 183, 266 Sqn |

### 1939–1945

| | | |
|---|---|---|
| 88 Sqn | Sep 1942–Mar 1943 | Boston |
| 125 Sqn | 25 Mar 1944–31 Jul 1944 | Mosquito |
| 164 Sqn | 22 Jun 1944–17 Jul 1944 | Typhoon |
| 170 Sqn | 17 Jun 1942–10 Oct 1942 | Mustang |
| 181 Sqn | 1 Apr 1944–20 Jun 1944 | Typhoon |
| 182 Sqn | 1 Apr 1944–24 Jun 1944 | Typhoon |
| 183 Sqn | 1–14 Jul 1944 | Typhoon |
| 193 Sqn | 3–11 Jul 1944 | Typhoon |
| 197 Sqn | 3-20 Jul 1944 | Typhoon |
| 198 Sqn | 22 Jun 1944–8 Jul 1944 | Typhoon |
| 239 Sqn | 6 Dec 1942–25 Jan 1943 | Mustang |
| 247 Sqn | 24 Apr 1944–26 Jun 1944 | Typhoon |
| 257 Sqn | 2–8 Jul 1944 | Typhoon |
| 263 Sqn | 10–23 Jul 1944 | Typhoon |
| 266 Sqn | 13–20 Jul 1944 | Typhoon |
| 277 Sqn det | Apr 1944–Oct 1944 | various |
| 295 Sqn | 30 Jun 1943–15 Mar 1944 | Halifax, Albemarle |
| 296 Sqn | 25 Jul 1942–3 Jun 1943+ | Whitley, Albemarle |
| 297 Sqn | 5 Jun 1942–24 Oct 1942 | Whitley |
| 412 Sqn | 1–6 Mar 1943 | Spitfire |
| 418 Sqn | 14–29 Jul 1944 | Mosquito |
| 438 Sqn | 18 Mar 1944–27 Jun 1944 | Typhoon |
| 439 Sqn | 18 Mar 1944–27 Jun 1944 | Typhoon |
| 440 Sqn | 18 Mar 1944–27 Jun 1944 | Typhoon |
| 570 Sqn | 15 Nov 1943–14 Mar 1944 | Albemarle |
| 604 Sqn | 3 May 1944–13 Jul 1944 | Mosquito |
| 609 Sqn det | Jul 1944 | Typhoon |
| 620 Sqn det | Nov 1943–Mar 1944 | Stirling |
| TFU | 10 Nov 1941–May 1942 | |
| 1498 Flt | Dec 1942–14 Aug 1943 | Lysander, Martinet |
| 3 OADU | 9 Jan 1943–25 Jul 1944 | |

### Post-1945

| | | |
|---|---|---|
| 2 AEF | 11 Dec 1978–? | Chipmunk |
| SUAS | 11 Dec 1978–1986 | Chipmunk, Bulldog |

# IBSLEY

**County:** Hampshire

**UTM/Grid:** OS map 195–SU155090
**Lat/Long:** N50°52.30 W001°46.53
**Nearest Town:** Ringwood 2 miles to south

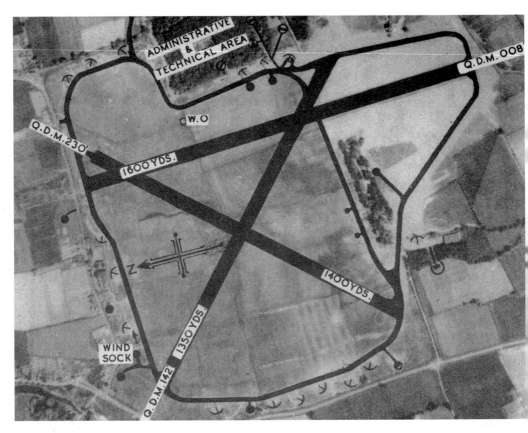

## HISTORY

One of the series of airfields constructed in the New Forest, Ibsley was opened on 15 February 1941 as a fighter satellite for Middle Wallop and the following day the Hurricanes of 32 Squadron arrived from the parent station. Ibsley was far from complete and it took a few more months before all the basic facilities and infrastructure were in place – by which time the resident unit was 118 Squadron with Spitfires, being joined by 501 Squadron in August. The Spitfires' primary task was escorting medium-bombers on *Circus* missions, although they also flew their own offensive sorties. By late-1941 the airfield was virtually complete, with runways, perimeter track, dispersals and Blister hangars, and was considered ready for a Wing of three squadrons, 234 Squadron arriving in November to complete the trio of Spitfire units. The Ibsley Wing was soon in the thick of the action and making a name for itself and, other than the changeover of

one of the squadrons in April 1942, it established a routine that proved, in some respects, a model for other fighter Wings. Following the posting of its charismatic and experienced leader – Ian 'Widge' Gleed – the Wing was disbanded in mid-summer 1942, as the RAF abandoned Ibsley ready for its new American occupants.

The P-38 Lightnings of the 1st Fighter Group moved from Goxhill, their training base, to Ibsley in late-August 1942, flying their first combat mission on 2 August. Under the command of Lieutenant Colonel John N Stone, the Group flew from this Hampshire airfield until November, by which time its ground echelon had already departed, as the Group had been assigned to the XIIth Air Force for operations in North Africa. The station returned to No.10 Group, two of its old squadrons came back and the routine of Fighter Command operations was

## AIRFIELD DATA DEC 1944

| Command: | Fighter | Runway surface: | Tarmac |
|---|---|---|---|
| Function: | Forward Airfield | Hangars: | 12 × Blister, 2 × Bellman |
| Runways: | 010 deg 1,600yd | Dispersals: | 36 × Circular and Pen, Tarmac |
| | 320 deg 1,400yd | Personnel: | Officers – 177 (7 WAAF) |
| | 050 deg 1,350yd | | Other Ranks – 2,122 (381 WAAF) |

resumed. There was some changing of units over the next few months but, for most of the time, Ibsley was back with three fighter-squadrons. By September 1943 the resident units were the three Spitfire V squadrons of the Czech Wing, although they were joined the same month by 263 Squadron.

The airfield was once more in American hands in spring 1944 with the arrival of the 48th Fighter-Bomber Group (FBG), a unit that converted to P-47s on its arrival in the UK and became operational on the type in late-April. Like most of these Groups, it dropped the 'Bomber' part of its title in May, although the fighter-bomber role remained its primary mission. Under the command of Colonel George L Wertenbaker Jr, the three squadrons of the 48th were kept busy as D-Day approached, attacking a wide vari-

ety of ground targets, a routine that continued once the Allies had landed in Normandy. With rapidly prepared tactical strips available in the bridgehead, the Group moved across the Channel to Deux Jumeaux on 18 June. However, a few weeks later, Ibsley became the temporary home to the P-38s of the 367th Fighter Group, the three squadrons arriving from Stoney Cross on 6 July and leaving on 22 July.

That pretty much brought Ibsley's operational career to an end; later in the year it was used as an RLG by the Oxfords of No.7 FIS, based at Upavon, and in March 1945 it was transferred to Transport Command's No.46 Group to act as a satellite for Stoney Cross. The main user during this period was the Glider Pilot Pick-Up Training Flight and they stayed until October. There was no post-war future for Ibsley and it was not long

P-38 of the 367th FG; the unit spent two weeks here in July 1944. This picture is dated October 1944 and the location is not given.

The control tower (in poor condition) is one of the few surviving buildings.

before buildings were being dismantled or sold and in 1947 the airfield was officially de-activated.

Virtually the entire airfield has now vanished and the area, having been used for gravel extraction, is a park, in which the only significant wartime-building is the (very dilapidated) control tower.

## DECOY SITES

| Q | Verwood | SU100066 |
|---|---------|----------|
| Q | Woodgreen | SU185162 |

## UNITS

### HQ Units at Ibsley
| 100th FW | 13 Jan 1944–15 Apr 1944 |
|----------|-------------------------|
| 70th FW | 17 Apr 1944–9 Jun 1944 |

### 1939–1945
| 32 Sqn | 16 Feb 1941–17 Apr 1941 | Hurricane |
|--------|-------------------------|-----------|
| 66 Sqn | 27 Apr 1942–24 Aug 1942; 23 Dec 1942–9 Feb 1943 | Spitfire |
| 118 Sqn | 18 Apr 1941–16 Aug 1942+; 23 Dec 1942–3 Jan 1943 | Spitfire |
| 124 Sqn det | Mar 1943–Jul 1943 | Spitfire |
| 129 Sqn | 13–28 Feb 1943; 13 Mar 1943–28 Jun 1943 | Spitfire |
| 165 Sqn | 30 Jun 1943–30 Jul 1943 | Spitfire |
| 234 Sqn | 5 Nov 1941–27 Apr 1942+ | Spitfire |
| 263 Sqn | 5 Dec 1943–5 Jan 1944 | Typhoon |
| 268 Sqn det | Dec 1941–May 1942 | Tomahawk, Mustang |
| 310 Sqn | 19 Sep 1943–19 Feb 1944 | Spitfire |
| 312 Sqn | 21 Sep 1943–19 Feb 1944 | Spitfire |
| 313 Sqn | 18 Sep 1943–20 Feb 1944+ | Spitfire |
| 421 Sqn | 16–22 Aug 1942 | Spitfire |
| 453 Sqn | 28 Jun 1943–20 Aug 1943 | Spitfire |
| 501 Sqn | 5 Aug 1941–24 Aug 1942 | Spitfire |
| 504 Sqn | 30 Dec 1942–30 Jun 1943 | Spitfire |
| 616 Sqn | 2 Jan 1943–17 Sep 1943 | Spitfire |

| 7 FIS | | | |
|-------|--|--|--|
| GP-UTF | 19 Mar 1945–29 Oct 1945 | Dakota, Hadrian |

### USAAF Units
**1st FG**
| Squadrons: | 71st FS, 94th FS |
|------------|------------------|
| Aircraft: | P-38 |
| Dates: | 24 Aug 1942–13 Nov 1942 |

**48th FGB**
| Squadrons: | 492nd FS, 493rd FS, 494th FS, 495th FS |
|------------|------------------------------------------|
| Aircraft: | P-47 |
| Dates: | 29 Mar 1944–18 Jun 1944 |
| First mission: | 20 Apr 1944 |
| Last mission: | May 1945 (from Illesheim) |

**367th FG**
| Squadrons: | 392nd FS, 393rd FS, 394th FS |
|------------|------------------------------|
| Aircraft: | P-38 |
| Dates: | 6–22 Jul 1944 |

## MEMORIALS

Stone pillar surmounted by airfield plan and area map, plus list of units that used Ibsley, unveiled 24 April 2000.

The memorial was dedicated in April 2000 and includes an excellent plan of the airfield.

# KENLEY

**County:** Surrey

Kenley from the air in June 2003.

## HISTORY

Kenley is one of the best known of Fighter Command's front-line airfields in the Battle of Britain; it has a long history as an operational base, stretching back to the latter months of World War One. Kenley had its origins in mid-1917, when it was established as No.7 Aircraft Acceptance Park to take on new aircraft from local manufacturers and prepare them for issue to operational units, the main types being Camel, DH9, Dolphin, RE8, Salamander and SE5a. This was an important role and the airfield was provided with no less than fourteen large hangars, each 170ft × 80ft, although the flying surface itself was an area of fairly rough grass. In the latter months of the war Kenley was home to a number of operational squadrons, most of which formed here to work up for deployment to the Front, including 116 Squadron with its HP 0/400s.

By mid-1919 both the AAP and the squadrons had gone and the row of hangars was left virtually empty.

However, the Communications Squadron became 24 Squadron in February 1920 and it was not long before more units took up residence, as Kenley had been declared a permanent station for the small post-war RAF. During the 1920s a number of squadrons and aircraft types used Kenley and this was its first period as a fighter station, with the likes of 32 Squadron and its Sopwith Snipes. This same pattern continued into the early 1930s and, whilst there were no dramatic developments, the facilities at the airfield were improved during this period – although many of the old hangars were also demolished. The first major development came in 1939, when two concrete runways were laid, which also entailed demolishing more of the old hangars. The runways were linked with a concrete perimeter-track and twelve aircraft-pens, each large enough for three fighters, were built around the perimeter. Most of the construction work

## AIRFIELD DATA DEC 1944

| | | | |
|---|---|---|---|
| Command: | Fighter Command | Runway surface: | Concrete |
| Function: | Forward Airfield, Biggin Hill sector | Hangars: | 4 × Over Blister, 4 × Extra Over Blister, 1 × Belfast Truss (2-bay) |
| Runways: | 212 deg 1,200 × 50yd | Dispersals: | 18 × Single-engine |
| | 312 deg 1,000 × 50yd | Personnel: | Officers – 142 |
| | | | Other Ranks – 605 (125) |

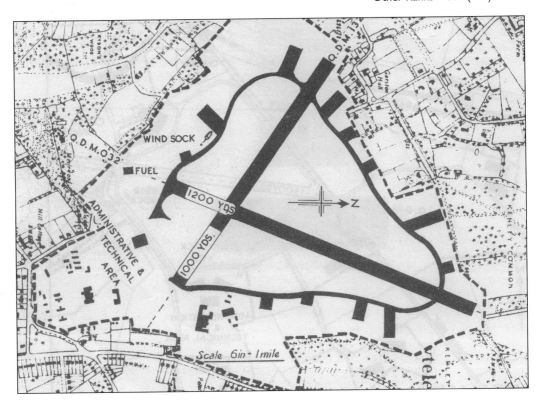

was carried out by Constable, Hart & Co and it was early 1940 before the airfield was ready for its permanent squadrons. When the new aircraft arrived they were not the delightful but antiquated biplanes, but the more purposeful Hurricanes. Kenley was then very much in the fighter business – and just in time. From then on it was usual for the airfield to house two or three fighter-squadrons; it was also a Sector Station ('B' Sector) and, as such, was to play a key role in the defensive network established by No.11 Group. Such was the importance of Kenley that it ended up with four decoy sites. Among the station's defences was a PAC (Parachute and Cable) system, a device that many viewed with suspicion but which succeeded in bringing down a Do17 on 18 August 1940. This first air attack on Kenley was also the most effective and caused damage to buildings and aircraft, although fortunately only nine people were killed. It caused barely a blip in the station's operational readiness and Kenley and its squadrons remained heavily engaged. As usual for airfields in this area, the fighter squadrons rotated as they became tired and depleted. From 1941, as the RAF moved to offensive operations, this rotation of fighter squadrons continued, including a number of Canadian units; indeed, during the first half of 1943, the entire Kenley Wing was made up of Canadian Spitfire squadrons. The Americans also made a brief appearance, two Spitfire-equipped units being present for a few weeks each in mid-1942.

Gauntlet of 17 Squadron; the unit operated Bulldogs and then Gauntlets from Kenley in the late 1930s.

Early two-bladed Hurricanes of 3 Squadron, Kenley, May 1938.

Hurricanes of 615 Squadron, August 1940. (Andy Thomas)

Spitfires of 616 Squadron at dispersal.

Fighter activity ceased in April 1944, the final operation having been flown on 13 March, when the Canadians moved out to Tangmere and the station was temporarily closed during the V-weapons blitz on the London area following D-Day. For the remainder of the war it was essentially in Care and Maintenance.

On 1 July 1945 the airfield passed to Transport Command and then, in 1946, to Reserve Command, which used it to store captured enemy-hardware – including the V-1 and V-2. Limited flying continued into the early 1950s by a number of units, including two Auster-equipped Auxiliary Air Force AOP Flights, which were part of 661 Squadron, and the London University Air Squadron. Kenley reprised its wartime role in 1951, when it was the location for the film *Angels One Five*, starring again a few years later, when *Reach for the Sky* was filmed here.

RAF Kenley finally closed in May 1959 – although the airfield was not actually abandoned by the RAF or the Ministry of Defence: in the early 1960s it was used by a number of Reserve Flights and by the Air Cadets Gliding School. After it was reduced to Care and Maintenance on 21 February 1966 it remained in military hands, the army taking over part of the site and the RAF gliders continuing to operate. This is pretty much the situation today, although it is also now 'Kenley Common' and public access is permitted to the airfield area (but dodge the gliders). The airfield is also used by the Surrey Hills Gliding Club. As with many such airfields, its future has been in doubt but, in 2002, the local MP stated that:

Kenley Airfield is a valuable resource for the people of Croydon and beyond. For the last twenty years it has provided the only gliding centre in Greater London with some 10,000 glider flights each year. It is a unique leisure facility for people of all ages and sexes.

A cynic might say that this was a sure indication that the airfield would be closing!

## DECOY SITES

| Q | Farleigh | TQ375610 |
| Q | South Godstone | TQ336476 |

| Q | Walton Heath | TQ229538 |
|---|---|---|
| Q | Woldingham | TQ388560 |

## UNITS

### HQ Units at Kenley

| | | |
|---|---|---|
| No.1 Gp | Dec 1919–19 May 1924 | |
| No.6 Gp | 1 May 1924–20 May 1926 | |
| Fighting Area | 20 May 1926–7 Jul 1926 | |
| No.127 Airfield | 4 Jul 1943–6 Aug 1943; | 403, 421 |
| | 14 Oct 1943–17 Apr 1944 | Sqn |
| No.17 Sector | 12 May 1944–6 Jun 1944 | 122, 126, |
| | | 127 Wing |
| No.61 Gp | 1 Aug 1946–31 Mar 1959 | |

### Pre-1919

| | | |
|---|---|---|
| 88 Sqn | 2–16 Apr 1918 | Bristol F2b |
| 91 Sqn | 27 Aug 1918–7 Mar 1919 | Dolphin |
| 95 Sqn | 1 Oct 1918–20 Nov 1918 | no aircraft |
| 108 Sqn | 14 Jun 1918–22 Jul 1918 | DH9 |
| 110 Sqn | 15 Jun 1918–1 Sep 1918 | DH9a |
| 116 Sqn | 27 Jul 1918–28 Sep 1918 | HP 0/400 |

### 1919–1938

| | | |
|---|---|---|
| 13 Sqn | 1 Apr 1924–30 May 1924 | Bristol F2b |
| 17 Sqn | 10 May 1934–23May 1939 | Bulldog, |
| | | Gauntlet |
| 23 Sqn | 6 Feb 1927–17 Sep 1932 | Snipe, |
| | | Gamecock, |
| | | Bulldog, |
| | | Demon |
| 24 Sqn | 1 Feb 1920–15 Jan 1927 | Bristol F2b, |
| | | DH9a |
| 32 Sqn | 1 Apr 1923–21 Sep 1932 | Snipe, |
| | | Grebe, |
| | | Gamecock, |
| | | Siskin, |
| | | Bulldog |
| 39 Sqn | 12 Apr 1920–12 Mar 1921 | Snipe |
| 46 Sqn | 3 Sep 1936–15 Nov 1937 | Gauntlet |
| 80 Sqn | 8–15 Mar 1937 | Gauntlet |
| 84 Sqn | Jan 1920 | SE5a |
| 600 Sqn | Oct 1938 | Demon |
| 615 Sqn | 1 Jun 1937–2 Sep 1939 | Audax, |
| | | Hector, |
| | | Gauntlet |
| (1)CS | 13 Apr 1919–1 Feb 1920 | |
| SCF | 15 Dec 1922–1 Apr 1924 | F2b |

### 1939–1945

| | | |
|---|---|---|
| 1 Sqn | 5 Jan 1941–7 Apr 1941, | Hurricane |
| | 1–14 Jun 1941 | |
| 3 Sqn | 28 Jan 1940–30 May 1940 | Hurricane |
| 17 Sqn | 25 May 1940–8 Jun 1940 | Hurricane |
| 64 Sqn | 16 May 1940–19 Aug 1940 | Spitfire |
| 66 Sqn | 3–10 Sep 1940; | Spitfire |
| | 13 Aug 1943–17 Sep 1943 | |
| 111 Sqn | 28 Jul 1942–21 Sep 1942 | Spitfire |
| 165 Sqn | 8 Aug 1943–17 Sep 1943 | Spitfire |

| | | |
|---|---|---|
| 253 Sqn | 8–24 May 1940; | Hurricane |
| | 29 Sep 1940–3 Jan 1941 | |
| 258 Sqn | 22 Apr 1941–10 Jul 1941+ | Hurricane |
| 302 Sqn | 7 Apr 1941–29 May 1941 | Hurricane |
| 312 Sqn | 29 May 1941–20 Jul 1941 | Hurricane |
| 350 Sqn | 16–31 Jul 1942 | Spitfire |
| 401 Sqn | 24 Sep 1942–23 Jan 1943 | Spitfire |
| 402 Sqn | 14–31 May 1942; | Spitfire |
| | 13 Aug 1942–21 Mar 1943 | |
| 403 Sqn | 23 Jan 1943–7 Aug 1943; | Spitfire |
| | 14 Oct 1943–24 Apr 1944 | |
| 411 Sqn | 22 Mar 1943–8 Apr 1943 | Spitfire |
| 412 Sqn | 2 Nov 1942–29 Jan 1943 | Spitfire |
| 416 Sqn | 1 Feb 1943–29 May 1943 | Spitfire |
| 421 Sqn | 6–11 Oct 1942; | Spitfire |
| | 29 Jan 1943–23 Mar 1943; | |
| | 17 May 1943–6 Aug 1943; | |
| | 14 Oct 1943–18 Apr 1944+ | |
| 452 Sqn | 21 Jul 1941–21 Oct 1941; | Spitfire |
| | 14 Jan 1942–23 Mar 1942 | |
| 485 Sqn | 21 Oct 1941–8 Jul 1942 | Spitfire |
| 501 Sqn | 10 Sep 1940–17 Dec 1940 | Hurricane |
| 602 Sqn | 10 Jul 1941–14 Jan 1942; | Spitfire |
| | 4 Mar 1942–17 Jul 1942+ | |
| 611 Sqn | 3 Jun 1942–13 Jul 1942 | Spitfire |
| 615 Sqn | 22 May 1940–29 Aug 1940; | Hurricane |
| | 16 Dec 1940–21 Apr 1941 | |
| 616 Sqn | 19 Aug 1940–3 Sep 1940; | Spitfire |
| | 8–29 Jul 1942 | |
| 56 ERFTS | 24 Aug 1939–3 Sep 1939 | Tiger Moth, |
| | | Hart |

### USAAF Units

| | | |
|---|---|---|
| 4 FS/52 FG | 25 Aug 1942–13 Sep 1942 | Spitfire |
| 308 FS | Aug 1942 | Spitfire |

### Post-1945

| | | |
|---|---|---|
| 61 Gp CF | 10 Sep 1946–1 Mar 1958 | various |
| 143 GS | 1948–Sep 1955 | various |
| 1957 Flt | 1 Feb 1949–10 Mar 1957 | Auster |
| 1960 Flt | 1 May 1949–10 Mar 1957 | Auster |
| 615 VGS | 1 Sep 1955–current | various |
| London UAS | 12 Jan 1956–? | Chipmunk, |
| | | Bulldog |

## MEMORIALS

Impressive stone memorial with carved figures, positioned on the edge of a taxiway on an old dispersal, inscribed:

> RAF Kenley tribute in honour of all personnel who served here 1917–1959. 'Never in the field of human conflict was so much owed by so many to so few.' Sir Winston Churchill 1940. Unveiled by ACM Sir Anthony Bagnall KCB OBE ADC AFRAeS RAF 19th August 2000.

The side panels list Kenley's units.

# KINGSNORTH

**County:** Kent

**UTM/Grid:** OS map 189–TR025380
**Lat/Long:** N51°06.12 E000°53.30
**Nearest Town:** Ashford 2 miles to north

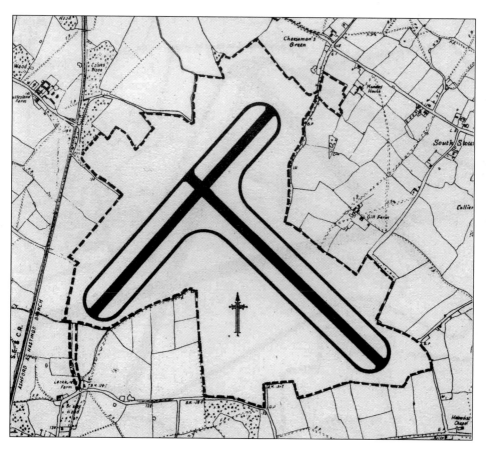

## HISTORY

Not to be confused with the World War One Kingsnorth airship station – also in Kent but in a different part of the county – this Kingsnorth was an Advanced Landing Ground used by the RAF and USAAF. The airfield was named after a village to the north-west: the village was actually nearer the Ashford ALG, but there was often little logic in airfield naming. Kingsnorth was laid out adjacent to the main railway-line from Ashford to Rye, the site having been chosen during the early 1942 survey of this area. Accepted for development, work commenced in January 1943 and, although the site was reasonably level, there were numerous hedges and ditches to cut or bridge before the two runways could be laid in

their 'T'-shaped pattern, the longest being oriented NW/SE.

Having been chosen as a training airfield, Kingsnorth was one of the first series of ALGs to open, work being complete by late-June and the airfield receiving its first occupants on 1 July 1943. The three Spitfire squadrons of No.122 Airfield arrived from Bognor and Selsey to test how well they could cope with mobile operations from a primitive airfield – and to see how well the airfield itself coped. Over the next few weeks the squadrons flew their usual routine of escorts and sweeps, there being some changeover of units within the Airfield, and few problems were forthcoming, although the

# AIRFIELD DATA DEC 1944

| | | | |
|---|---|---|---|
| Command: | RAF Fighter Command | Runway surface: | Pierced Planking and Sommerfeld Track |
| Function: | Advanced Landing Ground | Hangars: | nil |
| Runways: | 040 deg 1,575yd | Dispersals: | 70 × Sommerfeld |
| | | Personnel: | Other Ranks – Tented camp |

P-47s of the 36th FG taxy out.

Sommerfeld Track runways required some repair work – one of the problems with this type of tracking was its tendency to lift and produce not only a very uneven surface but also sharp areas of metal that caused problems for aircraft tyres. All aircraft had left by early October and construction personnel moved back in to upgrade the airfield and repair any damage; the major upgrade consisted of additional surfaced-dispersals and, for Kingsnorth, a new runway-surface of pierced steel-planking, when the decision was taken in early 1944 to allocate the airfield to an American fighter-bomber Group. This was also one of the limited number of airfields to be given a Butler hangar.

The 36th Fighter Group had arrived in England in late-March and, by 5 April, had arrived at Kingsnorth with three squadrons of P-47s. After a few weeks familiarization and training, the Thunderbolts joined the offensive to soften up the German defences around Normandy, the Group's main role being that of fighter-bombing, although it did fly a number of escort sorties. The intensity of operations increased around D-Day itself and the Group was kept busy, as close air-support was vital to expanding the Allied beachheads.

In common with all of TAC's Groups, the 36th moved to France in early July, going initially to Brucheville (airfield A16). Kingsnorth was quickly abandoned, closing on 20 July, and the runway surfaces were removed by late-summer, as was the Butler hangar. The December 1944 survey showed Kingsnorth as an ALG with Fighter Command, but with the comment that it had been de-requisitioned. There is some confusion in this record, as there is for many of the ALGs, as the survey states the runway surfaces were 'Pierced Planking and Sommerfeld', implying that the surfaces were still in place, whereas other records suggest that they had been lifted in late-summer. Either way, Kingsnorth was, to all intents and purposes, a 'dead' airfield and, by early 1945, the area had been returned to its original owners and there is now no trace of this wartime field.

## UNITS

### HQ Units at Kingsnorth

| | |
|---|---|
| No.122 Airfield | 1 Jul 1943–20 Oct 1943 |

### 1939–1945

| | | |
|---|---|---|
| 19 Sqn | 18 Aug 1943–29 Sep 1943 | Spitfire |
| 65 Sqn | 1 Jul 1943–5 Oct 1943 | Spitfire |
| 122 Sqn | 1 Jul 1943–5 Oct 1943 | Spitfire |
| 184 Sqn | 14–18 Aug 1943 | Hurricane |
| 602 Sqn | 1 Jul 1943–13 Aug 1943 | Spitfire |

### USAAF Units
**36th FG**

| | |
|---|---|
| Squadrons: | 22nd FS, 23rd FS, 53rd FS |
| Aircraft: | P-47 |
| Dates: | 5 Apr 1944–7 Jul 1944 |
| First mission: | 8 May 1944 |
| Last mission: | May 1945 (from Kassel) |

# LASHAM

**County:** Hampshire

**UTM/Grid:** OS map 185–SU677435
**Lat/Long:** N51°11.00 W001°01.45
**Nearest Town:** Basingstoke 5 miles to north

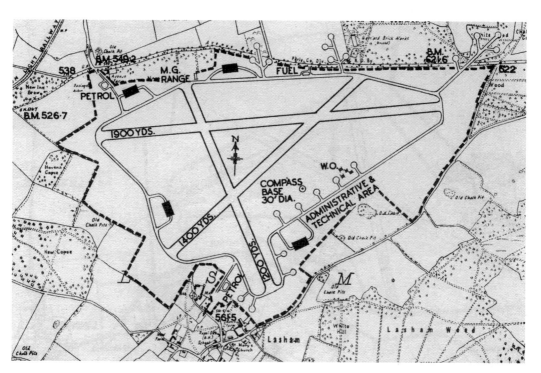

## HISTORY

A site five miles south of Basingstoke was selected in summer 1941 for development as a satellite for the bomber airfield under construction at Aldermaston and authority to requisition the land was given in September. The site, just north of the village from which it takes its name, was reasonably flat but quite wooded and the constructors, McAlpines, were tasked to produce a standard three-runway airfield, complete with linking perimeter-track and support facilities, including four T.2 hangars and an admin/technical area. Although originally intended to support an Operational Training Unit at Aldermaston, the overall plan for airfields in this region had changed by the time Lasham neared completion in late-1942. It had been decided to concentrate airborne forces in this area and, as part of the army build-up, there was also an increased requirement for Army Co-operation units; to help meet this need Lasham was allocated to Army Co-operation Command on 9 November, but it was a few months before any operational squadrons took up residence.

First arrivals were the Spitfires of 412 Squadron who, along with 175 Squadron, formed one of a number of experimental 'Airfields' for Exercise *Spartan*, the Command's first major army co-operation exercise and one that determined many of the tactics that would be employed for the rest of the war. The initial mix of aircraft types was not ideal and No.124 Airfield, which had formed at Lasham on 1 April 1943, settled down to the standard arrangement of three squadrons, each with the same aircraft type. With its three Typhoon squadrons the Airfield moved to Appledram on 2 June. The arrival of 320 Squadron with Mitchells gave Lasham its introduction to operations, as this established medium-bomber unit was tasked with attacks on a variety of targets in northern France and Holland. In the meantime, the airfield had become part of the new Tactical Air Force and, over the next few months, it acquired new units that gradually re-equipped in order to provide Lasham with an operational Wing (No.138 Airfield) of Mosquito squadrons. The Wing

General Aircraft used Lasham during the late 1940s for Mosquito modifications, including the TT.39 – although this prototype shot is probably not at Lasham.

was not fully operational until mid-March 1944 but, from that date until it left in October, it was fully engaged on ops, from daylight attacks on a variety of targets, including V-weapon launch sites (*Crossbow/Noball*), to night-intruder work. No.417 Repair and Salvage Unit was in residence from March to September 1944, the unit's main 'customers' being Mosquitoes. The Lasham Wing was soon making a name for itself with precision daylight attacks on special targets, such as headquarter buildings or rest-and-recreation centres, although perhaps the most notable was that of 11 April on a Gestapo records office in The Hague.

By the time of the December 1944 survey, the airfield was allocated to No.11 Group of Fighter Command for use as a forward airfield by the Tangmere Sector. The survey's report on the extensibility of the runways showed only one realistic option – extending runway 06 from 1,400 to 2,300 yards. There was no further operational use of Lasham and the airfield had a very quiet 1945 until it was selected for one final task. The immediate post-war period was a sad one for Lasham, as it housed the Disbandment Centres for No.83 and No.84 Groups, the latter having been formed out of the Group Support Unit. More units arrived and Lasham once more became fairly busy; No.49 Maintenance Unit moved in on 13 February 1946 and remained until May 1948, when it transferred to Colerne. The airfield was also home to No.411 (Polish) Repair and Salvage Unit from 17 December 1946, although this was short-lived and

the unit disbanded the following February.

Perhaps of more lasting interest, in view of the airfield's current occupation as a major gliding-centre, was the use from late-1945 of one of the hangars by General Aircraft for Mosquito overhaul and modification – but also for experimental work with tailless gliders. The airfield was closed for RAF operations on 26 October 1948 but it was retained on the books. However, during the 1950s, gliding had become a popular pastime and Lasham seemed to attract gliding clubs; such was its involvement that the 1955 National Gliding Championships were held here; since then the Lasham Gliding Centre has been a major force in gliding in the UK, as evidenced by the fact that on a good gliding-day dozens of gliders take to the air over this part of Hampshire.

The airfield had been transferred from the RAF to the Ministry of Civil Aviation on 15 July 1961 and, in addition to gliding, Lasham became home to Dan Air Engineering, part of the Dan Air airline. The demise of the airline did not mean the end to this engineering element and under a variety of names it has survived and over the years has undertaken modification, painting and scrapping of a variety of civil aircraft.

Present day Lasham (EGHL) is run by the Lasham Gliding Society and has a single asphalt-runway (09/27) of 1,800 yards, although light aircraft are also cleared to use the grass on either side of the runway.

# Airfield Data Dec 1944

| | | | |
|---|---|---|---|
| Command: | RAF Fighter Command | Runway surface: | Concrete and wood-chippings |
| Function: | Forward Airfield | Hangars: | 4 × T.2 |
| Runways: | 095 deg 1,900 × 50yd | Dispersals: | 52 × Frying Pan (125ft) |
| | 063 deg 1,400 × 50yd | Personnel: | Officers – 152 (10 WAAF) |
| | 175 deg 1,200 × 50yd | | Other Ranks – 2,122 (410 WAAF) |

Rear view of a Typhoon being serviced, a scene that was played out at numerous airfields in Southern England in the latter part of the war. Lasham played host to a number of 'Tiffie' units but this shot is not credited to Lasham.

## Units

### HQ Units at Lasham

| | | |
|---|---|---|
| No.124 Airfield | 1 Apr 1943–2 Jun 1943 | 175, 181, 182, 412 Sqn |
| No.138 Airfield/ (B) Wing | 10 Nov 1943–30 Oct 1944 | 107, 305, 613 Sqn |

### 1939–1945

| | | |
|---|---|---|
| 107 Sqn | 3 Feb 1944–30 Oct 1944 | Mosquito |
| 175 Sqn | 11–13 Mar 1943; 24 May 1943–2 Jun 1943 | Hurricane, Typhoon |
| 181 Sqn | 5 Apr 1943–2 Jun 1943 | Typhoon |
| 182 Sqn | 29 Apr 1943–2 Jun 1943 | Typhoon |
| 183 Sqn | 3–30 May 1943 | Typhoon |
| 305 Sqn | 18 Nov 1943–30 Oct 1944 | Mosquito |
| 320 Sqn | 30 Aug 1943–18 Feb 1944 | Mitchell |
| 412 Sqn | 7 Mar 1943–8 Apr 1943 | Spitfire |
| 451 Sqn | 12 Jun 1945–13 Sep 1945 | Spitfire |
| 453 Sqn | 14 Jun 1945–14 Sep 1945 | Spitfire |
| 602 Sqn | 14–29 Apr 1943 | Spitfire |
| 609 Sqn | 2–4 Jun 1945 | Typhoon |
| 613 Sqn | 12 Oct 1943–11 Apr 1944; 29 Apr 1944–30 Oct 1944 | Mosquito |
| 84 Gp SU | 21 Nov 1944–1 Aug 1945 | |
| 83 Gp DC | 26 Oct 1945–28 Oct 1945 | |
| 84 Gp DC | 1 Aug 1945–31 Dec 1945 | |

## Memorials

The Second World War Aircraft Preservation Society runs a small museum at the airfield and, although the aircraft collection is of Cold War vintage, the museum building, an old dispersal hut, includes memorabilia and details of the airfield's history.

# LASHENDEN

**County:** Kent

**UTM/Grid:** OS map 188–TQ855425
**Lat/Long:** N51°09.15 E000°39.00
**Nearest Town:** Maidstone 9 miles to north-west

July 2002 view of Lashenden with its active GA operations.

## HISTORY

There is invariably confusion between Lashenden and Headcorn, not helped by the fact that the present General Aviation airfield calls itself by the dual name of Lashenden (Headcorn) although it is, in fact, located on the former site! The two landing grounds are very close together (2 miles) and both about the same distance from the village of Headcorn. The site at Lashenden was selected during the early 1942 airfield survey and was approved in December as a second-line ALG, although this was subsequently

changed and Lashenden became one of the first series to be constructed. An area of flat-land south of the river was designated for requisition and for the construction of a standard ALG with two Sommerfeld Track runways, the longest one parallel to the river and the second one almost at right angles to it. As usual, few other buildings were provided, although a number of farm buildings were earmarked for acquisition. Construction commenced in early 1943 and was reasonably straightforward, although one significant

# AIRFIELD DATA DEC 1944

| Command: | RAF Fighter Command | Runway surface: | Sommerfeld Track |
|---|---|---|---|
| Function: | Advanced Landing Ground | Hangars: | nil |
| Runways: | 010 deg 1,600yd | Dispersals: | 70 × Sommerfeld Track |
| | 110 deg 1,400yd | Personnel: | Other Ranks – Tented camp |
| | 270 deg 2,000 × 50yd | | |

road had to be closed and the usual problems of hedges, ditches and power lines dealt with.

Lashenden opened on 6 August 1943 with the arrival of No.127 Wing, a Canadian formation with two Spitfire squadrons. Having moved from Kenley, the squadrons were at Lashenden for only two weeks, barely time to test either themselves or the airfield. The Spitfires hopped over the hedge to Headcorn on 20 August to continue living in tents, whilst Lashenden went back into construction. All the Advanced Landing Grounds had a second period of construction work in the autumn/winter of 1943–44 that equipped them with improved taxiways, more hardstands and, in some cases, one or two Blister hangars. The airfield was allocated to the XIXth Tactical Air Command, a spin-off formation from IXth Air Force and in April 1944 the HQ unit of the 100th Fighter Wing arrived, taking up accommoda-

tion (tents) on the airfield as well as a number of neighbouring buildings, including Shenley Hall. The Wing controlled four fighter-groups and one of these, the 354th FG, moved in to Lashenden from Boxted on 17 April. The Group's three P-51 squadrons had been in action since December 1943, having been the first P-51B unit. By the time that it arrived at its new Kent base, its major task was that of fighter-bomber attacks on targets in and around Normandy, although it still flew escort missions from time to time; indeed, like many of the units of IXth and XIXth TAC, it flew escort, for a glider mission, on D-Day itself, although immediately reverting to ground-attack as Allied tactical air-power became the key to expanding the bridgeheads. The move to France came on 17 June, one of the first Groups to make the move, the destination being Criqueville (airfield A2). Within days the final elements of the Group had departed and by

Spitfires line up in formation at Lashenden, September 1943. (Peter Green)

Fitting a drop-tank to a 354th FG Mustang.

autumn it had been agreed to release the site back to agriculture. As usual, the runways and other tracking were removed, as were most of the buildings, such as they were. By early 1945 the airfield was no more and it may have stayed that way except that, in the 1970s, part of the airfield site was acquired for use as a light-aircraft airfield. Despite the occasional problem since then it is still very much an active airfield.

The current airfield at Lashenden (EGKH) is operated by Shenley Farms and has two grass runways: runway 11 is on the same alignment as the original ALG runway but the secondary runway has been reoriented to 04/22 – neither is as long as their wartime counterparts. The airfield retains a number of wartime buildings and the view across the grass strip to the north must be similar to that of sixty years ago, making this an atmospheric site for anyone with an interest in wartime ALGs.

## UNITS

### HQ Units at Lashenden

| | | |
|---|---|---|
| 100th FW | 15 Apr 1944–Jun 1944 | |
| No.127 (RCAF) Airfield | 6–20 Aug 1943 | 403, 421 Sqn |

### 1939–1945

| | | |
|---|---|---|
| 403 Sqn | 7–20 Aug 1943 | Spitfire |
| 421 Sqn | 6–20 Aug 1943 | Spitfire |

### USAAF Units
#### 354th FG

| | |
|---|---|
| Squadrons: | 353rd FS, 355th FS, 356th FS |
| Aircraft: | P-51 |
| Dates: | 17 Apr 1944–17 Jun 1944 |
| First mission: | 5 Dec 1943 (from Boxted) |
| Last mission: | May 1945 (from Herzogenaurach) |

## MEMORIALS

A plaque on the wall of the Lashenden Air Warfare Museum carries the inscription: 'To the memory of all who served from this airfield 1943–1944. They raced the eagles, mounting high above the unforgiven lands, they wrote their names across the sky, with fiery hearts and burning hands. Leonard Taylor 1965.' The plaque lists the five squadrons to have used the airfield, three under a set of USAAF wings and two under a set of RAF wings.

# LEE-ON-SOLENT
## (HMS *Daedalus*, HMS *Ariel*)

**County:** Hampshire

**UTM/Grid:** OS map 196–SU560020
**Lat/Long:** N50°48.35 W001°12.25
**Nearest Town:** Gosport 3 miles to east

September 2002 aerial view of Lee-on-Solent.

## HISTORY

After a career spanning almost eighty years, the Royal Naval Air Station at Lee-on-Solent closed its doors to military aviation in 1996 – not bad for a site originally intended as an emergency expedient. The site for this airfield was chosen by the commanding officer of the seaplane training-unit at Calshot, when he was tasked in 1917 to increase the output of aircrew from the school. With a good beach-profile and suitable adjacent fields for hangars and buildings, this area near Gosport was duly acquired and the Naval Seaplane Training School opened on 30 July 1917, with courses commencing the following month using Short 827 seaplanes. Fixtures and fittings comprised an array of Bessonneau hangars plus various sheds and a tented camp, along with a number of requisitioned buildings. By November 1917 the decision had been taken to turn this temporary station into something more permanent, as a planned new location at Holy Island in Northumberland had been abandoned. The major expansion work comprised installation of a single slipway and the erection of proper aircraft-sheds.

The creation of the Royal Air Force on 1 April 1918 meant that the Lee unit became No.209 Training Depot Station within No.10 Group, RAF. Seaplane training remained the order of the day and the TDS had an impressive fleet of aircraft; by early 1919 this had settled down to three main types, the Short 184, NT2b and FBA, with a total of over seventy aircraft. On 15 May 1919 the TDS was disbanded, becoming the RAF and Naval Co-operation School. Lee-on-Solent thus survived the post-war

Fairey IIId of No.443 Flight at Lee. (Ray Sturtivant)

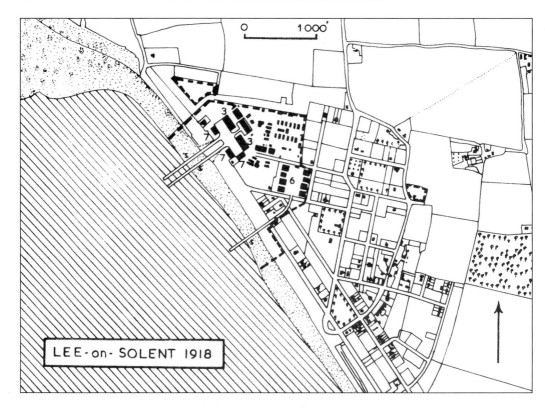

closures, although it was reduced to Care and Maintenance between December 1919 and 1 June 1920. The name of the main based-unit underwent various changes, in an attempt to reflect the nature of its role at any particular time, but for much of the 1920s and 1930s it was the School of Naval Co-operation. In addition to the training task for pilots and observers, the school undertook various experimental trials and evaluation work. New aircraft types entered service, including some of the wonderful series of Fairey products, such as the Flycatcher and the Fairey IIId.

By the early 1930s it had been decided to add a landplane element to Lee and an area was acquired for development of an airfield, this work being completed by October 1934. The airfield was now also home to a headquarters unit, HQ Coastal Area having moved in during January 1932, confirming the importance of Lee-on-Solent in the sphere of naval aviation. Expansion continued during the 1930s, with more building work, a re-organization of the School and an increase in the training task. Coastal Command was formed in May 1936, taking over from Coastal Area, and two of its new Groups were formed at Lee, initially at Wykeham Hall on 1 December that year, both of which stayed for a number of years.

The 26 Squadron cricket team pose with the Lee-on-Solent cricket Trophy, 1944.

As can be seen from the table of HQ units, Lee-on-Solent, and Wykeham Hall, was a popular location with command organizations throughout the 1930s. The airfield had become home to a diverse collection of flights and specialist units, some connected with the school and others being independent. It must truly have been a fascinating place, with both seaplane and landplane activity, playing host to virtually every type of naval aircraft.

The departure of the School of Naval Co-operation to Ford at the end of December 1937 gave Lee a more operational commitment for, in addition to the existing units, such as the AACU, it was now the shore base for the Fleet Air Arm's Catapult Flight and also hosted a variety of operational squadrons. To meet the new requirements, further building work took place over the next few years, involving dispersal points, a perimeter track and at least four Bellman and one C-type hangars. When the airfield was transferred to the Admiralty on 24 May 1939 it became HMS *Daedalus*; the RAF Group HQs departed and the navy formed HQ Flag Officer Air (Home) at Wykeham Hall – Coastal Command HQ left in August. In typical fashion for a Naval Air Station, Lee-on-Solent had a rapid changeover of units and a seemingly impressive array of units, although some were quite small. Most of the station's training role came to an abrupt end in August 1940, when the plan to remove such units to 'rear' areas was accelerated following the 8 August attack on the airfield.

The subsequent role of the station was primarily the commissioning of new flying squadrons or their conversion to new aircraft, although trials and evaluation work also continued, as did some training: for example, the Night Fighter School opened here in June 1942. This pattern is evident from a glance at the units table and virtually all front-line types passed through Lee, including rarities such as the Chesapeake dive-bomber, which equipped 811 Squadron in July 1941. With such heavy usage the grass surfaces were unable to cope and, in summer 1942, two runways were built: 06/24 of 3,000ft and 13/31 of 2,400ft, both having asphalt surfaces. This, too, proved inadequate and by mid-1943 the airfield had three runways to the pattern shown on the plan, the longest being 06/24, which had been extended to 4,500ft. During both construction phases new buildings and facilities had been added, including blast pens, dispersals and hangars. The 1955 airfield survey provides an interesting summary of the hangars: 12 × Mains, 8 × Fromson, 3 × Bellman, one × Type A, one × ARS: 'in addition there are five old seaplane hangars near the slipway now used as workshops. Only half Type-A hangar is in use, the remaining half awaiting repair of war damage. There is also a Type-C hangar at present under repair from war damage'.

Despite any construction work it was a hectic period for the station, with large numbers of aircraft in residence or passing through, and this pace of activity increased as D-Day approached.

During the D-Day period Lee-on-Solent was home to one of the most interesting groupings of units – the Air Spotting Pool, whose task it was to spot for naval bombardment fall of shot and to call corrections. The Pool comprised a number of FAA squadrons supported by two RAF squadrons and VCS-7 from the US Navy, the latter equipping with Spitfires for the purpose. The units had assembled from April

Seafox of 716 Flight. (Ray Sturtivant)

onwards and, by early June, had over 100 Spitfires/ Seafires on strength; this already impressive array was boosted by the Typhoons of No.1320 Flight and three RAF Mustang-units, although the latter were only involved for part of 6 June before being returned to their reconnaissance role. The Pool continued to operate into late-June but, as the opportunities for naval bombardment lessened, so the strength of the Pool was reduced and new tasks were added. By autumn 1944 most of Lee's fighter activity was over, the main operational type being the Barracuda.

With the end of the war the Station returned to its dual role of training and shore base for embarked squadrons and for the next ten years it was home to a diverse collection of squadrons, although training became the dominant feature and, as such, the airfield housed a wide range of aircraft types, including the unusual ASH-equipped Ansons for radar training. Although jets had arrived in the late-1940s, it was the arrival of helicopters in November 1955 that signified the true future of Lee-on-Solent. With a diverse fleet of helicopters, 705 Squadron moved in from Gosport and 845 Squadron reformed with Whirlwinds; Lee was now involved with helicopter-aircrew training and with trials and development of such techniques as helicopter ASW. Helicopters, in various guises and with various units, dominated the scene at Lee for the next forty years and, whilst a large number were based here at any one time, the airfield was not as hectic as it had once been. It was, of course, still open to fixed-wing flying; 781 Squadron, for example, operated a mixed fleet for its VIP and communications role. For a brief period (October 1959 to November 1965) the station became HMS *Ariel*, as one of its major units was the Air Electrical School, although Naval Air Command at Wykeham Hall retained the previous title.

Lee remained a fascinating airfield and there always appeared to be something unusual going one; for example, the slipway was re-opened in 1962 for use by the Inter-Service Hovercraft Trials Unit. This unit undertook trials and later training for all hovercraft operations, eventually becoming the Naval

July 1973 with Sea Devons of 781 Squadron and a fine view across to the wartime blister hangars. (Ray Surtivant)

Shark of 753 Squadron at Lee in 1939. (Ray Sturtivant)

Swordfish f 820 Squadron embarked on HMS Ark Royal, 1939. Lee-on-Solent was used as a shore-base by a large number of FAA squadrons.

The Control Tower and adjacent hangars following a Luftwaffe attack.

Hovercraft Trials Unit. With helicopter training, trials and squadron work-ups, plus the more public-relations face of Search and Rescue, taken over in February 1973 from the RAF along this stretch of coast, Lee's last twenty years were as busy if, perhaps, not as interesting as the rest of its career.

The military moved out of Lee in 1996 but the airfield remains active, with a variety of civil users, including the Hampshire Police Air Support Unit, the Coastguard SAR Flight (operated by Bristow Helicopters) and naval gliding and flying clubs. The airfield also houses a number of private aircraft.

## UNITS

### HQ Units at Lee-on-Solent

| | |
|---|---|
| Coastal Area | Jan 1932–1 May 1936 |
| Coastal Command | 1 May 1936–8 Aug 1939 |
| No.10 Gp | 12 Jul 1920–18 Jan 1932 |
| No.16 Gp | 1 Dec 1936–8 Nov 1938 |
| No.17 Gp | 1 Dec 1936–24 Feb 1939+ |
| No.18 Gp | 1 Sep 1938–21 Oct 1938+ |
| No.15 Gp | 15 Mar 1939–7 Jun 1939 |

| | | |
|---|---|---|
| Flag Officer Air (Home) | Jul 1939– ? | |
| Flag Officer Ground Training | 1950s | |
| Naval Air Command | ?–1970 | |

**1918–1919**

| | | |
|---|---|---|
| 209 TDS | 1 Apr 1918–15 May 1919 | various |

1919-1939:

| | | |
|---|---|---|
| RAF & NCS | 15 May 1919–14 Jul 1919 | various |
| SoNC | 23 Dec 1919–1 Apr 1920, 19 Apr 1923–29 Dec 1937 | |
| STS | 21 Apr 1921–19 Apr 1923 | Short 184, Fairey IIId Fairey IIIf |
| 443A Flt | 1930–1936+ | |
| 444 Flt | Jan 1925–Jul 1936+ | various |
| 1 GCF | 13 Jun 1935–4 Jan 1936, 27 Apr 1936–15 Feb 1937 | |
| 2 AACU | 15 Feb 1937–5 May 1939 | various |
| FTF | Apr 1938–24 May 1939 | Shark, Swordfish, Walrus |
| FRU | 11 Aug 1938–24 May 1939 | Swordfish |
| Rota EF | 17 Jun 1939–? | Rota |

Barracuda of 783 Squadron. (Ray Sturtivant)

## 1939–1945

| | | |
|---|---|---|
| 16 Sqn det | Jun 1941–Sep 1941 | Lysander |
| 26 Sqn | 28 Apr 1944–6 Oct 1944 | Spitfire, Hurricane |
| 42 Sqn det | Mar 1938–Sep 1938 | Vildebeeste |
| 63 Sqn | 28 May 1944–3 Jul 1944; 30 Aug 1944–19 Sep 1944 | Spitfire |
| 1320 Flt | 22 May 1944–14 Jun 1944 | Typhoon |

### FAA units:

| | | |
|---|---|---|
| 702 Sqn | 1 Jan 1938–21 Jan 1940; 27 Dec 1940–Jul 1943 | Seal, Swordfish |
| 703 Sqn | 3 Jun 1942–1 May 1944 | Kingfisher, Seafox, Swordfish |
| 710 Sqn | Aug 1939, Oct 1943 | Walrus |
| 739 Sqn | 15 Dec 1942–Jun 1943 | Swordfish |
| 753 Sqn | 24 May 1939–23 Aug 1940 | Shark, Nimrod |
| 754 Sqn | 24 May 1939–7 Sep 1940 | Seafox, Walrus |
| 763 Sqn | 31 May 1940–4 Jul 1940 | Albacore |
| 764 Sqn | 8 Apr 1940–3 Jul 1940 1 Jul 1944–1 Oct 1944 | Swordfish Avenger |
| 765 Sqn | 24 May 193–26 Aug 1940 18 Mar 1944–6 Oct 1945 | Swordfish Wellington |
| 771 Sqn | 29 Jun 1939–29 Jul 1939 | Swordfish |
| 778 Sqn | 28 Sep 1939–6 Jul 1940 | various |
| 780 Sqn | 28 Nov 1944–2 Jan 1945 | various |
| 781 Sqn | 20 Mar 1940–Jul 1945? | Various |
| 800 Sqn | Apr 1941–Oct 1942+ | varuous |
| 807 Sqn | 23 Jun 1942–12 Jul 1942 | Seafire |
| 808 Sqn | 25 Feb 1944–4 Aug 1944+ | Spitfire, Seafire |
| 810 Sqn | 2 Jun 1939–1 Mar 1940+, 21 Dec 1941–25 Feb 1942, 4 Apr 1943–21 May 1943 | Swordfish |
| 811 Sqn | 11 Jan 1938–29 Mar 1938 15 Jul 1941–1 Nov 1941 | Swordfish Hurricane |

| | | |
|---|---|---|
| 813 Sqn | 28 Oct 1941– 6 Dec 1941 | Swordfish |
| 826 Sqn | 1 Dec 1943–3 Feb 1944 | Barracuda |
| 827 Sqn | 23 Sep 1942–24 Apr 1943 | Albacore |
| 886 Sqn | 25 Feb 1944–19 Jul 1944+ | Spitfire, Seafire |
| 897 Sqn | 22 Mar 1943–5 May 1943; 26 Feb 1944–15 Jul 1944+ | Spitfire, Seafire |
| 1791 Sqn | 15 Mar 1945–19 Apr 1945 | Firefly |
| 1792 Sqn | 15 May 1945–15 Jun 1945 | Firefly |

### Post 1945:

| | | |
|---|---|---|
| 202 Sqn det | Mar–May 1988 | Sea King |
| Southampton UAS | Jul 1991–2 Apr 1993 | Bulldog |

### FAA units:

| | | |
|---|---|---|
| 700 Sqn | 18 Mar 1957–26 Sep 1957 | Whirlwind |
| 701 Sqn | 31 Oct 1957–20 Sep 1958 | Whirlwind |
| 702 Sqn | 30 Sep 1957–11 Oct 1957 | |
| 705 Sqn | 1 Nov 1955–10 Jul 1971 | Dragonfly, HT.1, HT.2, Whirlwind, Wasp |
| 770 Sqn | 7 Nov 1939–1 May 1940+ | various |
| 771 Sqn | 9 Mar 1947–Aug 1953+ | various |
| 772 Sqn det | 14 Feb 1983–Sep 1995 | Wessex, Sea King |
| 778 Sqn | 28 May 1948–16 Aug 1948 | various |
| 781 Sqn | 27 Jun 1946–Mar 1981? | various |
| 783 Sqn | 15 May 1947–18 Nov 1949 | Barracuda |
| 799 Sqn | 30 Jul 1945–28 Aug 1946+ | various |
| 807 Sqn | 18 May 1946–12 Mar 1947 | Seafire |
| 811 Sqn | 13 Dec 1954–16 Mar 1955 | Sea Hawk |
| 813 Sqn | 25 Mar 1949–18 Feb 1953+ | Firebrand |
| 826 Sqn | 14 May 1952–22 Nov 1955+ 14 Mar 1979–Jul 1979 | Firefly Sea King |
| 827 Sqn | 22 Jul 1946–17 Sep 1946+ | Firefly |
| 845 Sqn | 3 Oct 1955–4 Nov 1958+ | Whirlwind |
| 897 Sqn | 1–5 Jan 1957 | Sea Hawk |

## MEMORIALS

1. Fleet Air Arm memorial with inscription: 'These officers and men of the Fleet Air Arm died in the service of their country and have no grave but the sea 1939–1945.'

2. Plaque in St Michael's church, inscribed: 'In pious and perpetual memory of Lieutenant Commander Eugene Esmonde, RN VC DSO and all the faithful of the Fleet Air Arm who laid down their lives in the Great War.'

# LYDD

**County:** Kent

**UTM/Grid:** OS map 189–TR015230
**Lat/Long:** N50°58.17 E000°51.53
**Nearest Town:** Dungeness 5½ miles to south-east

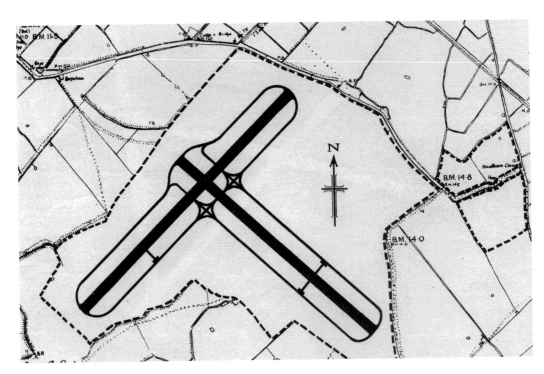

## HISTORY

The area around Lydd has had military connections for hundreds of years as part of the defences for the South Coast and, since the late-nineteenth century, the coastal area and its marshy hinterland have been used for military training ranges. It was this latter connection that first brought aviation to the area, with the Royal Engineers undertaking balloon trials as part of various army exercises. The first aviation location was part of the barracks at Lydd Camp and, by 1914, a detachment of aircraft had moved in for gunnery trials and training using the ranges. Aviation departed again shortly afterwards and balloons made a re-appearance in 1916, with the formation of No.2 Balloon School on a site slightly to the west of the World War Two airfield; indeed, one of the problems with a 'Lydd airfield' is that various aviation locations in and around the town carried the name Lydd. In the same year, a 60-acre site at Dering Farm was acquired for use as a Landing Ground and, with minimal development, it was soon home to a small Artillery Co-operation Flight, formed to work with

the guns exercising in the ranges. By August 1917 it had been raised to a Class 3 Landing Ground. The Artillery Co-operation School (ACS) was formed on 13 January 1917 and the Artillery Co-operation Flight became 'B Flight' of the new unit, although nothing changed in respect of its role. It was also allocated for use as a night ELG by the Home Defence unit in this area, 112 Squadron. This situation remained to the end of the war, although the Balloon School actually closed in September. Lydd was closed by early 1919 and returned to agriculture.

Some twenty years later, a site not far from the original LG was chosen as a decoy airfield; Midley being developed in 1940, but it is not clear what it was a decoy for, as the usual practise was to create a decoy close to an operational airfield. However, two years later the survey team looking for Advanced Landing Ground sites decided that the Walland Marsh to the west of Lydd was highly suitable and by the end of the year approval had been given for its development. Lydd was one of the first series to be

# AIRFIELD DATA DEC 1944

| | | | |
|---|---|---|---|
| Command: | RAF Fighter Command | Runway surface: | Sommerfeld Track |
| Function: | Advanced Landing Ground | Hangars: | 5 × Blister |
| Runways: | SE/NW 1,600 × 50yd | Dispersals: | 3 × Hardcore |
| | SW/NE 1,400 × 50yd | Personnel: | Other Ranks – Tented camp |

Aircrew of 245 Squadron pose at Lydd in September 1943.

built and opened on 25 June 1943, having been given the standard two Sommerfeld Track runways in a 'T'-shape with connecting perimeter-tracks. As usual, few buildings were provided and, as a base for mobile operations, tents were the order of the day. The three Typhoon squadrons of No.121 Airfield arrived on 1 July and operations over France gave the squadrons and the airfield a thorough evaluation. There were no significant problems with Lydd as an ALG, although it did record the unusual event of being bombed – a hit-and-run raider attacking on 15 September but causing no damage. The Typhoons moved out in early October and the airfield entered a second phase of construction, with repairs to the runway, provision of better dispersals and the erection of five Blister hangars. It was decided, however, that Lydd would be a reserve ALG and it did not receive an operational Wing during the D-Day period, although its near neighbours Brenzett and New Romney were both active. There was some support activity, including the RAF Regiment, at Lydd during this period and it is believed that one or two aircraft landed here, but it saw no dedicated flying. Although Lydd appears in the December 1944 airfield survey as a Fighter Command ALG, it was listed as de-requisitioned and work had already commenced on removing the Sommerfeld Track and other facilities.

The present Lydd airfield (EGMD) – or London Ashford Airport as it prefers to be called – is situated just east of Lydd on the Romney Marsh and has no connection with the wartime airfield. It opened in 1954 and is home to a number of private aircraft, flying schools and scheduled services across the Channel.

## DECOY SITES

| | | |
|---|---|---|
| Q | Midley | TQ982208 |

## UNITS

### HQ Units at Lydd
| | | |
|---|---|---|
| No.121 Airfield | 1 Jul 1943–7 Aug 1943 | 174, 175, 245 Sqn |

### Pre-1919
| | | |
|---|---|---|
| ACS | Jan 1917–29 Oct 1919 | various |

### 1939–1945
| | | |
|---|---|---|
| 174 Sqn | 1 Jul 1943–10 Oct 1943 | Typhoon |
| 175 Sqn | 1 Jul 1943–9 Oct 1943 | Typhoon |
| 245 Sqn | 1 Jul 1943–10 Oct 1943 | Typhoon |

# LYMINGTON (Station 551)

**UTM/Grid:** OS Map 196–SZ352953
**Lat/Long:** N50°45.40 W001°30.15

**County:** Hampshire

**Nearest Town:** Lymington 1 mile to west

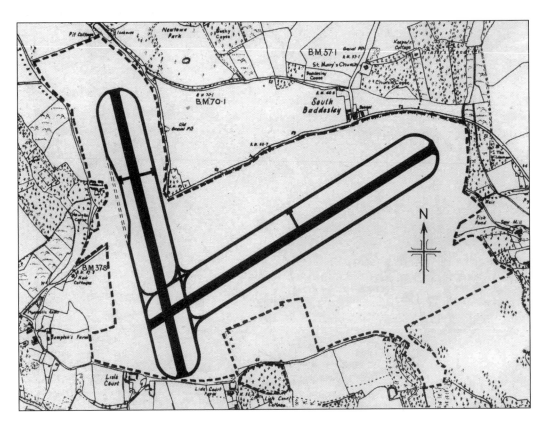

## HISTORY

The site at Lymington was chosen in 1942 for construction of an Advanced Landing Ground and work commenced early the following year. Much of the site was taken from the Pylewell House estate. A standard ALG was laid out, with two runways in a 'V'-shape, along with perimeter tracks and dispersals; by the time the first occupants arrived the airfield also had four Blister hangars and at least one of the runways had been strengthened with American pierced steel-planking. The reason for this is that it had been allocated to the USAAF (as Station 551) and it was standard for airfields operating the heavy P-47 to have strengthened matting. As with all the ALGs, accommodation was in tented camps but a number of requisitioned buildings were also used; for example, a group of farm buildings in Lisle Court Lane were used as ration stores and a stone barn was used for pilot debriefing.

The 50th Fighter Group's three squadrons of P-47s started to arrive in the UK in March 1944 and by early April were established at Lymington; after a few weeks of settling in, under the command of Colonel William D Greenfield, the Group flew its first offensive mission, a sweep over the French coast on 1 May. Fighter-bomber and escort missions kept the 50th busy over the next few weeks, building to a crescendo around D-Day. This mission profile continued into late-June, when the Group was one of the first to move across the Channel, the squadrons deploying to Carentan on 25 June.

With the Americans gone there was no further need of the airfield and by autumn it had been de-requisitioned and largely dismantled, although there is some suggestion that it might have been used by the Admiralty for storage to 1946. There is little to see now, although at least one Blister hangar has survived.

# AIRFIELD DATA DEC 1944

| | | | |
|---|---|---|---|
| Command: | RAF Fighter Command | Runway surface: | Matting |
| Function: | Advanced Landing Ground | Hangars: | 4 × Blister |
| Runways: | E/W 1,600yd | Dispersals: | 75 × Sommerfeld |
| | S/N 1,400yd | Personnel: | Other Ranks – Tented camp |

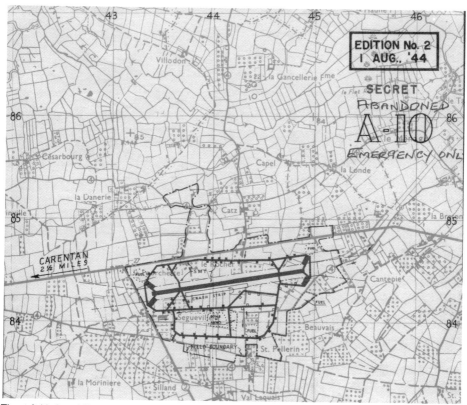

The airfield plan of Carentan in France, the airfield to which the Group moved when it left Lymington; this plan is used to illustrate the similarities between – and thus the value of operating from – the UK ALGs.

## UNITS

**1939–1945**
**USAAF Units**
**50th FG**
Squadrons: 10th FS, 81st FS, 313th FS

Aircraft: P-47
Dates: 5 Apr 1944–25 Jun 1944
First mission: 1 May 1944
Last mission: May 1945 (from Giebelstadt)

# LYMPNE
(HMS *Buzzard*,
HMS *Daedalus II*)

**County:** Kent

**UTM/Grid:** OS map 189–TR115355
**Lat/Long:** N51°04.42 E001°01.08
**Nearest Town:** Hythe 2 miles to east

Traces of the airfield can still be seen from the air, as in this summer 2003 shot.

## HISTORY

Lympne airfield opened in 1916 as a night Emergency Landing Ground north-west of Lympne village; it was not, however, the first airfield site chosen at Lympne. In autumn 1915 work had started on a Landing Ground near Folks Wood, but it was soon discovered that waterlogging was a major problem and construction was abandoned in favour of a new site. Aircraft from the Advanced Air Gunnery School based at Hythe were being detached here from early 1917, a number of Bessonneau hangars being provided, along with various huts. Further development took place when No.8 Aircraft Acceptance Park was set up at Lympne, the main work involving construction of six General Service sheds, the impressive brick structures that were typical of 'permanent' RFC airfields.

The main task of the AAP was delivering new aircraft to frontline units and, as such, Lympne saw an interesting variety of aircraft use its grass surface, including the Handley Page 0/100 and 0/400 bombers. A secondary task involved carrying out modifications on a range of aircraft, often in response to feedback from the front-line units. The airfield received one visit from the enemy when, on 25 May 1917, several Gothas bombed Folkestone and a number of bombs fell on Lympne. Various operational squadrons also used the airfield but, once World War One ended, Lympne's future became uncertain, its final task being the disbanding of squadrons returning from France. Hawkinge airfield was only a few miles away and the Air Ministry could not really jus-

Handley Page 0/400 of 115 Squadron at Lympne in 1918.

98 Squadron was at Lympne with DH9s for a month in spring 1918.

The Hind-equipped 21 Squadron spent two years here in the mid 1930s.

tify two airfields so close together – and Hawkinge won.

The solution for Lympne was to allow civilian operations from the site and, during the 1920s, various organizations made use of the airfield for both passenger and cargo operations; in 1924, Short Brothers used it for flight testing of new aircraft. The RAF showed little further interest in the site, although it was used by Biggin Hill's Night Flying Flight for various tests and exercises during the mid-1920s and, a little later, as a site for Auxiliary Air Force summer camps. However, in October 1936, Lympne was activated for use as a bomber base within No.1 (Bomber) Group. Two Hind squadrons duly moved in and for the next two years Lympne was a bomber station; various improvements were made to some of the old World War One buildings, although work was limited as it was still seen as a temporary station. This changed with the Munich Crisis of 1938 and a need for as many airfields as possible, leading to debate on how to use Lympne. The next eighteen months were confusing: the first unit to arrive, after a period when the station was in Care and Maintenance from October 1938, was a Training Command administration school, but in May 1939 the airfield was transferred to Fighter Command,

although initially the Fleet Air Arm used it as an outstation to Lee-on-Solent's Air Mechanics School. Between July and September the airfield was known as HMS *Buzzard*, but it then changed to HMS *Daedalus II* to reflect the connection with Lee.

Following the fall of France in June 1940, RAF activity increased and, in addition to fleetingly housing squadrons returning from France, the station was involved with the *Back Violet* flights, carried out by Lysanders of 16 and 26 Squadrons, supporting the last British troops. Shortly afterwards the airfield became a satellite for the Biggin Hill Sector and fighter detachments moved in for daylight standby. In mid-August, the airfield came under repeated attack by the Luftwaffe, suffering heavy damage that put it out of action for a short period. Having played some part in the Battle of Britain, Lympne became something of a backwater, with only spasmodic action during 1941. However, during 1941, facilities at the airfield were upgraded, with additional dispersals and fighter pens and the erection of three Blister hangars. Further expansion took place in late-1942 to bring the airfield to a state where it could sustain operations by two fighter squadrons. In part, this decision was due to the use of the airfield for intensive operations in August 1942 during Operation *Jubilee*, the assault on Dieppe, with Lympne being used by 401 Squadron and 133 (Eagle) Squadron. Over the next two years a number of operational units used Lympne, with some, like 1 Squadron, managing a fairly lengthy stay, whilst others came and went in a matter of weeks. By March 1943, the main operations from the airfield were *Ramrods* and *Rhubarbs* by Typhoons, although from just prior to D-Day the airfield housed a Spitfire Wing. The three squadrons of Spitfires of the North Weald Wing arrived in May and flew fighter sweeps and fighter-bomber ops, whilst one of its units, 74 Squadron, also participated in anti-*Diver* operations. When this Wing departed it

## AIRFIELD DATA DEC 1944

| | | | |
|---|---|---|---|
| Command: | RAF Fighter Command | Runway surface: | Grass |
| Function: | Operational Satellite | Hangars: | 4 × Blister |
| Runways: | NW/SE 1,400yd | Dispersals: | One × Single-engine |
| | NNE/SSW 900yd | Personnel: | Officers – 73 (3 WAAF) |
| | NNW/SSE 1,000yd | | Other Ranks – 1,060 (90 WAAF) |

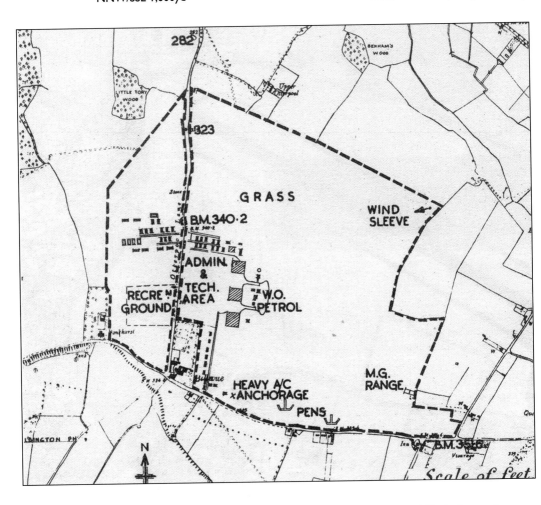

was replaced by three Czech Spitfire squadrons (310, 311 and 313 squadrons), although they soon departed to be replaced by another similarly-equipped Wing; this, too, soon gave way to a Wing equipped with Spitfire XIVs. The Lympne Wing finally departed in December 1944 to become part of No.83 Group's growing strength on the Continent; thus all the operational units had left by December 1944 and the airfield reverted to the status of an Emergency Landing Ground (ELG). The December 1944 survey sug-

gested that four runways could be laid out at Lympne, the longest being 2,000 yards, but that such work would 'entail serious demolitions and also road diversions'. It is also worth noting that, during this period of 1943–44, Lympne became a safe haven for damaged American heavy-bombers as, along with other coastal locations it was one of the first airfields pilots reached on the 'home' side of the Channel.

There was a final burst of activity by two Spitfire squadrons in April 1945 but, essentially, Lympne's

Typhoon EK176 of 1 Squadron, July 1943. (Andy Thomas)

last few months of war were quiet. The military lost interest with the end of the war and, on 1 January 1946, Lympne was transferred to the Ministry of Civil Aviation. Over the next few years a variety of civil operators used the airfield, including airlines, cargo carriers and private operators. A number of famous names, such as Silver City Airways, which used Bristol Freighters to ferry cars across the Channel to France, and Skyways, with a limited number of routes such as London–Lympne–Beauvais–Paris (partly by coach), tried to make a commercial success of operations from this remote Kent airfield. In 1967 a 4,400ft concrete runway was laid and the airfield became Ashford Airport the following year but, despite attempts to provide suitable facilities and create a market, it was always a difficult financial situation and by early 1970s the commercial operators had gone.

The runway was removed some years ago, although its outline can still be seen from the air, and, whilst the area of the airfield is still evident, it is bounded by houses on one side and an industrial park on the other. One Blister hangar and some wartime evidence still remains, but traces of Lympne are vanishing fast.

## UNITS

### HQ Units at Lympne

| | | |
|---|---|---|
| No.51 (AC) Wing | 23 May 1940–8 Jun 1940 | 2, 26 Sqn |
| No.134 (Czech) (F) Wing | 3 Jul 1944–27 Aug 1944 | 310, 312, 313 Sqn |

### Pre-1919

| | | |
|---|---|---|
| 69 Sqn | 24 Aug 1917–9 Sep 1917 | RE8 |
| 83 Sqn | Sep 1919–15 Oct 1919 | no aircraft |
| 98 Sqn | 1 Mar 1918–1 Apr 1918 | DH9 |

| | | |
|---|---|---|
| 102 Sqn | 26 Mar 1919–3 Jul 1919 | cadre only |
| 108 Sqn | 16 Feb 1919–3 Jul 1919 | cadre only |
| 120 Sqn | 17 Jul 1919–21 Oct 1919 | DH9 |
| 1 ASoAG | Jan 1917–Feb 1917 | various |

### 1919–1938

| | | |
|---|---|---|
| 21 Sqn | 3 Nov 1936–15 Aug 1938 | Hind |
| 34 Sqn | 3 Nov 1936–12 Jul 1938 | Hind |

### 1939–1945

| | | |
|---|---|---|
| 1 Sqn | 15 Mar 1943–15 Feb 1944; 11 Jul 1944–10 Aug 1944 | Typhoon, Spitfire |
| 2 Sqn | May 1940 | Lysander |
| 16 Sqn | 19 May 1940–3 Jun 1940 | Lysander |
| 18 Sqn | 19–21 May 1940 | Blenheim |
| 26 Sqn | 22 May 1940–8 Jun 1940 | Lysander |
| 33 Sqn | 7–10 Sep 1944 | Spitfire |
| 41 Sqn | 11 Jul 1944–5 Dec 1944 | Spitfire |
| 53 Sqn | 20–21 May 1940 | Blenheim |
| 59 Sqn | 20–21 May 1940 | Blenheim |
| 65 Sqn | 2–11 Oct 1942 | Spitfire |
| 72 Sqn | 30 Jun 1942–7 Jul 1942 | Spitfire |
| 74 Sqn | 15 May 1944–3 Jul 1944 | Spitfire |
| 91 Sqn | Mar 1941–11 Jan 1943 | Spitfire |
| 127 Sqn | 16 May 1944–4 Jul 1944 | Spitfire |
| 130 Sqn | 5–30 Apr 1944; 11 Aug 1944–30 Sep 1944 | Spitfire |
| 133 Sqn | 30 Jun 1942–12 Jul 1942; 17–22 Aug 1942 | Spitfire |
| 137 Sqn | 14 Dec 1943–2 Apr 1944+ | Hurricane, Typhoon |
| 165 Sqn | 12 Jul 1944–10 Aug 1944 | Spitfire |
| 186 Sqn | 1 Mar 1944–5 Apr 1944 | Spitfire |
| 245 Sqn det | Mar 1943–May 1943 | Typhoon |
| 310 Sqn | 1–11 Jul 1944 | Spitfire |
| 312 Sqn | 4–11 Jul 1944 | Spitfire |
| 313 Sqn | 4–11 Jul 1944 | Spitfire |
| 350 Sqn | 29 Sep 1944–3 Dec 1944 | Spitfire |
| 401 Sqn | 14–21 Aug 1942 | Spitfire |
| 451 Sqn | 6 Apr 1945–3 May 1945 | Spitfire |
| 453 Sqn | 6 Apr 1945–2 May 1945 | Spitfire |
| 504 Sqn | 11–12 Jul 1944 | Spitfire |
| 567 Sqn det | Nov 1944–Jun 1945 | various |
| 598 Sqn det | Mar 1945–Apr 1945 | various |
| 609 Sqn | 18 Aug 1943–14 Dec 1943 | Typhoon |
| 610 Sqn | 12 Sep 1944–4 Dec 1944 | Spitfire |
| 659 Sqn | | |

# MANSTON

**County:** Kent

**UTM/Grid:** OS map 179–TR333662
**Lat/Long:** N51°20.43 E001°21.00
**Nearest Town:** Ramsgate 3 miles to south-east

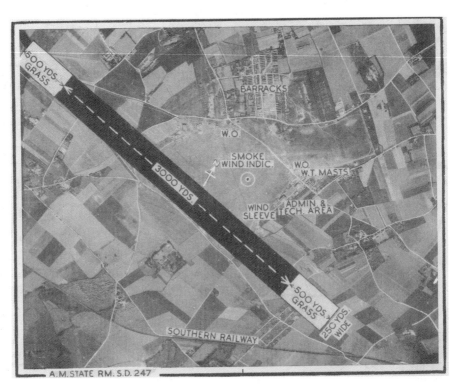

## HISTORY

Manston joined the select ranks of Victoria Cross airfields when this highest gallantry award was made to the leader of a courageous attack on the German battle-cruisers *Gneisenau* and *Scharnhorst*; Lieutenant Commander Eugene Esmonde gallantly led six Swordfish of 825 Squadron in a daylight torpedo-drop on 12 February 1942 – all were shot down and only five aircrew survived. The Swordfish had deployed to Manston because of its location as an ideal forward airfield from which to mount attacks on the enemy. It was this geographic situation that made Manston a fascinating airfield in World War Two, not only because of the large number of squadrons to make use of the airfield, but also because of its role as one of the emergency landing strips – a massive strip of concrete 3,000 yards long and 250 yards wide.

It was also appropriate that the VC was made to a member of the Fleet Air Arm, as Manston's early history was very much connected with naval aviation. In the early years of World War One the Admiralty

held responsibility for Home Defence and the Royal Naval Air Service established a number of Landing Grounds covering the approaches to London and other targets in southern England. Manstone (with an 'e' at this time) was probably in use from late-1915, as little more than a grass field for use as a night Emergency Landing Ground; however, the following year it was provided with one hangar and a number of other buildings and officially opened in spring 1916 as a sub-station to Westgate. In May, the nucleus of No.3 Wing moved in and Manston had its first based aircraft, primarily for training. Over the next two years the airfield housed a number of diverse units and its roles included modification of aircraft before despatch to operational units in France, trials and evaluation (for example, the Handley Page Training Flight with 0/100s) and an operational element – the aptly named War Flight. Training of Air Mechanics was added to the task in 1917 and the airfield facilities continued to expand, with hangars, wooden huts

'Wonga Bonga' of the Manston War Flight, the aircraft was named after the noise the enemy aircraft made! (Peter Green)

The rugged but ugly Atlas was a good Army Co-operation machine; 2 Squadron operated the type from Manston.

and a variety of other structures springing up; by 1918 the roughly square airfield was 2,000yd × 2,000yd with a clutch of hangars and huts on the east side and the major concentration of hangars and buildings on the west side.

Creation of the RAF in April 1918 brought a change of units, or at least a change of nomenclature and organization, with Manston becoming No.203 Training Depot Station to train day-bomber squadrons. The TDS was renumbered No.55 in July 1918 and the airfield also housed three numbered Flights, all of which were eventually absorbed into squadrons. With one or two other changes, this was pretty much the situation at the end of the war, with building work still going on, as the decision had been taken some months before that Manston would become a permanent station.

Although the end of the war brought a major reduction in strength at Manston – gone were the days when the airfield housed more than 100 aircraft – the airfield continued in the training role with the School of Technical Training and, from May 1921, No.6 Flying Training School. The primary role of the latter was refresher flying for pilots posted to units overseas, where the RAF maintained much of its strength during the 1920s on colonial policing. A number of operational squadrons were stationed at Manston in the 1920s and 1930s, the longest serving being 2 Squadron, who were here from March 1924 to November 1935 (other than an interlude in China for a few months in 1927). On 31 March 1931 a new bomber squadron was formed here – 500 (County of Kent), one of the new series of Special Reserve squadrons with a mix of regular and part-time volunteer personnel.

The 1930s saw a number of changes, with the School of Technical Training expanding and becoming No.3 SoTT (Men) and the arrival in 1936 of the School of Air Navigation. Both training establishments became increasingly busy as the RAF's expansion plans accelerated and additional facilities, mainly classrooms and barracks, had to be built. The station's grass runways were still home to a number of Squadrons and also housed occasional detachments, including Auxiliary Air Force summer camps. No.616 Squadron was on one such camp in summer 1939 when mobilization was ordered – the part-timers were instantly part of the 'real' Air Force. With the outbreak of war the training units moved out and Manston was used for detachments of operational squadrons, RAF and FAA, the airfield being transferred to Fighter Command on 15 November 1939. The station's fighters were soon in action. In addition to the fighters, Manston housed an unusual unit, the GRU (General Reconnaissance Unit), which operated DWI Wellingtons equipped with a large magnetic ring to explode mines, this role being maintained to April 1940. Meanwhile, the fighters were kept busy and were soon involved in operations over and around the Dunkirk area.

As can be seen from the unit list, Manston was home to a large number of squadrons from 1940 to 1944, many of which were only in residence for a short period. Throughout the Battle of Britain, Manston was very much in the front line and it was usual for up to three squadrons to deploy to the airfield from their home bases each day. Its location also meant that it was bound to be attacked. The first of the expected attacks took place on 12 August and the airfield was left badly damaged but not mortally wounded. The airfield was hit hard a number of times in the month and it was almost impossible to repair the damage between each attack although, thanks to good defence positions (slit trenches for air raid shelters), casualties were reasonably light. By the end of August the airfield was verging on being untenable but the switch of Luftwaffe attention away from Fighter Command's airfields gave Manston a much-needed respite; although it still received occasional unwelcome visits it was never

## AIRFIELD DATA DEC 1944

| | | | |
|---|---|---|---|
| Command: | RAF Fighter Command | Runway surface: | Concrete/tarmac |
| Function: | Forward Airfield | Hangars: | 7 × Extended Over Blister, 2 × Old Type (1916), 1 × Portable Callender |
| Runways: | 245 deg 3,000 × 250yd | Dispersals: | 26 × Single-engined |
| | | Personnel: | Officers – 157 (7 WAAF) |
| | | | Other Ranks – 3,829 (420 WAAF) |

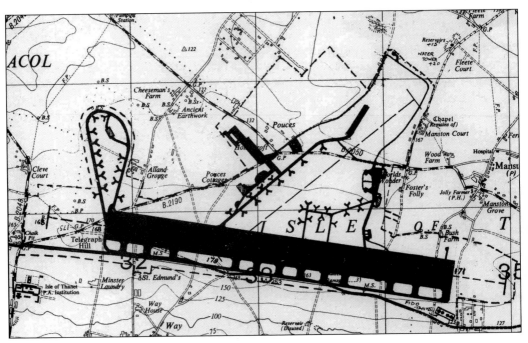

Manston plan dated early 1950s but the wartime layout is still dominant.

again in dire trouble and the damage of August 1940 was gradually repaired.

It was now time for Manston to go on to the offensive and its location, whilst still providing a degree of vulnerability to hit-and-run attacks, was ideal for launching sweeps over the Channel and Occupied Europe. The coming and going of units continued and just about every Allied fighter type appeared at Manston at some time, including both Whirlwind squadrons. By 1941 the airfield had two grass strips, both having been extended – to 5,700ft (NE/SW) and 4,800ft (N/S) – and other facilities had also been improved. The mix of fighter escort, anti-shipping sorties, offensive sweeps and fighter-bomber activities continued through 1942 and into 1943, with the Typhoon becoming one of Manston's regulars. Diversions of crippled aircraft were on the increase as the bomber offensive grew and the daylight operations of the 8th Air Force produced plenty of

damaged aircraft in search of the nearest safe haven – Manston looked very attractive despite its relatively short grass-strips. Manston was not the only coastal airfield with this problem and the decision was taken to build three emergency landing strips – massive stretches of concrete that would be ideal for damaged four-engined bombers. Manston was selected as one of the sites and a contract was issued in spring 1943 to John Laing & Son for this major construction project. Laying this vast expanse of concrete and its associated taxiways and dispersals took 600 men almost eleven months to complete; operational flying continued while this work was underway and Manston retained its position as one of the most important 'forward airfields', being used by the RAF, FAA and USAAF (as Station 137, even though they had no ownership of the airfield). The new runway opened in April 1944 and, in its first three weeks, witnessed fifty-six emergency landings, the start of

Tutors of 616 Squadron during the August 1939 Summer Camp at Manston.

Virginia of 500 Squadron; the unit spent most of the 1920s at this airfield.

February 1940 and a wheel-up landing for a 235 Squadron Blenheim; this was a frequent occurrence with the early Blenheim squadrons.

Mid 1940 and a fine shot of a 600 Squadron Blenheim. (Andy Thomas)

what was a major contribution to saving Allied aircrew and aircraft.

Manston's units also played a part in the D-Day air-campaign, with anti-shipping (especially E-boat hunting) and night-intruder sorties by Mosquitoes being two of the roles undertaken. The V-1 flying-bomb assault put the airfield in the front-line once more and its fighters undertook anti-*Diver* missions, the Tempests of 501 Squadron proving particularly effective. It was also home to the RAF's most secret aircraft, as 616 Squadron, the RAF's first jet-fighter squadron, had arrived in July. Manston's units recorded claims for 161 V-1s, an impressive tally; meanwhile, the offensive commitment seldom slackened and Spitfire Wings rotated through the airfield.

The run-down of units began even before the end of the war and, whilst Manston was maintained as an operational station post-1945, it was with Transport Command from July 1946 and became home to the Dakotas of 46 Squadron from October. Civil operations were authorized from mid-1946, when Manston became an RAF and Civil Customs Aerodrome; its main RAF function was as No.91 Staging Post, to

which the Overseas Ferry Unit was attached from May 1948 to July 1950.

The OFU moved out to make way for another major change in the airfield's fortunes, when it was allocated to Strategic Air Command for fighter deployments, part of the new reality of the Cold War and the Korean War. The American 7512nd Air Base Group arrived on 11 July 1950 and the first fighter-detachment was at Manston within days, the F-84s of the 20th Fighter Bomber Wing being the first of a number of USAF units to undertake deployments here. This routine was maintained to 1958, when the RAF took control once more – and on 1 August reduced it to Care and Maintenance. Re-opened in March 1959, the airfield was never again a base for operational squadrons, although it retained its Master Diversion status and its amazing runway, complete with a facility for foam-laying, ensured that it was an important facility. The RAF based a Search and Rescue helicopter Flight from 22 Squadron at Manston but, other than regular visitors and minor units such as an Air Experience Flight and gliding activities, it was a relative backwater, in terms of flying,

Blenheim crews of 235 Squadron brave the snow.

Spitfires of 92 Squadron on a rough and snow-covered Manston during winter 1941.

for its final forty years of RAF life. A number of ground units took up residence, the most significant being the Fire Service Central Training Establishment. A number of commercial operators have used the airfield since the late-1940s and it was the potential for further growth of civilian aviation that gave the airfield a future when the RAF finally departed in April 1999.

Manston – or Kent International Airport Manston, as it now is – has been home to a number of private operators and flying schools for some time, but it was a decision to develop the airfield as a cargo airport that appears to have secured its future. A recent £8 million investment saw the creation of a massive aircraft-apron and further development is planned. Large parts of RAF Manston still survive and its military heritage is well represented by the two local museums.

## DECOY SITES

| Q | Ash Level | TR299621 |
| Q | Monkton | TR280650 |

## UNITS

### HQ Units at Manston
| No.57 (TR) Wing | ?–3 Jul 1918 |
| No.50 (AC) Wing | 22–28 May 1940 |
| No.155 (GR) Wing | 22 Apr 1944–19 Sep 1944 |

### Pre-1919
| HP TF | 4 Jan 1916–19 Jan 1918 | HP 0/100 |
| War School | 11 Sep 1917–Apr 1918 | |
| Pilots Pool | Apr 1918–? | |
| 203 TDS | 1 Apr 1918–15 Jul 1918 | |
| 55 TDS | 15 Jul 1918–1 Sep 1918 | |
| 470 Flt | 27 May 1918–Nov 1918 | Camel |
| 555 Flt | 26 Jun 1918–Jul 1918 | DH9 |
| 556 Flt | 26 Jun 1918–Jul 1918 | DH9 |
| 2 OS | 14 Sep 1918–Sep 1919 | DH4, Avro 504 |

### 1919–1938
| 2 Sqn | 31 Mar 1924–20 Apr 1927; 27 Oct 1927–30 Nov 1935 | F2b, Atlas, Audax |
| 9 Sqn | 30 Sep 1924–26 Nov 1930 | Virginia |
| 48 Sqn | 16 Dec 1935–1 Sep 1938 | Cloud, Anson |
| 206 Sqn | 15 Jun 1936–1 Aug 1936 | Anson |
| 224 Sqn | 1–15 Feb 1937 | Anson |
| 500 Sqn | 16 Mar 1931–28 Sep 1938 | Virginia, Hart, Hind |
| 6 FTS | 21 Sep 1920–1 Apr 1922 | Avro 504 |
| 1 SoAN | 10 Jul 1936–2 Sep 1939 | |

### 1939–1945
| 1 Sqn | 18 Dec 1944–8 Apr 1945 | Spitfire |
| 3 Sqn | 10–17 Sep 1939; 12 Oct 1939–13 Nov 1939; 11 Jun 1943–28 Dec 1943 | Hurricane, Typhoon |
| 18 Sqn det | Jul 1941–Oct 1941 | Blenheim |
| 21 Sqn det | Oct 1940–Dec 1941 | Blenheim |
| 23 Sqn | 6 Aug 1942–14 Oct 1942 | Mosquito |
| 26 Sqn | 12 Oct 1941–30 Nov 1941; 1–4 Nov 1944 | Lysander, Spitfire |
| 32 Sqn | 8–22 Mar 1940; 7 Nov 1941–5 May 1942 | Hurricane |
| 56 Sqn | 29 May 1942–1 Jun 1942; 2 Jul 1943–23 Aug 1943+ | Typhoon |
| 59 Sqn det | 1941 | Blenheim |
| 63 Sqn | 1–4 Nov 1944 | Spitfire |
| 74 Sqn | 20 Feb 1941–30 Apr 1941 | Spitfire |
| 79 Sqn | 12 Nov 1939–10 May 1940 | Hurricane |
| 80 Sqn | 29 Aug 1944–20 Sep 1944 | Spitfire |
| 91 Sqn | 29 Oct 1944–8 Apr 1945 | Spitfire |
| 92 Sqn | 9 Jan 1941–20 Feb 1941 | Spitfire |
| 110 Sqn det | Jun 1939–Mar 1942 | Blenheim |
| 118 Sqn | 25 Sep 1944–15 Dec 1944 | Spitfire |
| 119 Sqn | 19 Jul 1944–9 Aug 1944 | Albacore |
| 124 Sqn | 25 Sep 1944–10 Feb 1945 | Spitfire |
| 137 Sqn | 17 Sep 1942–12 Jun 1943; 8 Aug 1943–14 Dec 1943; 1 Apr 1944–14 Aug 1944 | Hurricane, Whirlwind |

Various Typhoon units used this forward airfield; 609 Squadron taxy-out.

| 601 Sqn | 1 May 1941–30 Jun 1941 | Hurricane |
|---|---|---|
| 604 Sqn | 15 May 1940–20 Jun 1940 | Blenheim |
| 605 Sqn | 7 Apr 1944–21 Nov 1944 | Mosquito |
| 607 Sqn | 10 Oct 1941–20 Mar 1942 | Hurricane |
| 609 Sqn | 2 Nov 1942–22 Jul 1943; | Spitfire, |
| | 14 Dec 1943–16 Mar 1944+ | Typhoon |
| 615 Sqn | 22 May 1940–Aug 1940; | Gladiator, |
| | 11 Sep 1941–27 Nov 1941 | Spitfire |
| 616 Sqn | 21 Jul 1944–17 Jan 1945 | Meteor |
| 1 GRU | 19 Dec 1939–18 May 1940 | Wellington |
| 3 GRU | 24 Apr 1940–24 May 1940 | Wellington |
| 1401 Flt | 1 Apr 1943–25 Aug 1943; | Hudson, |
| | Sep 1943–14 Jan 1945 | Spitfire, |
| | | Hampden |

## Post-1945

| 3 Sqn | 2–12 Jun 1946; | Typhoon |
|---|---|---|
| | 5–19 Sep 1946 | |
| 22 Sqn det | Mar 1961–? | |
| 29 Sqn | 6–29 Oct 1945 | Mosquito |
| 46 Sqn | 11 Oct 1946–24 Nov 1947 | Dakota |
| 62 Sqn | 8–10 Dec 1947 | Dakota |
| 77 Sqn | 17 Dec 1946–10 Dec 1947 | Dakota |
| 130 Sqn | 27 Jan 1946–17 Jun 1946 | Spitfire |
| 567 Sqn | 21 Aug 1945–26 Apr 1946 | Spitfire |
| OFU | May 1948–Jul 1950 | |
| 618 VGS | 1 Mar 1963–9 Jan 1965 | |
| 617 VGS | Sep 1969–? | |

| 139 Sqn det | Jul 1941–Sep 1941 | Blenheim |
|---|---|---|
| 143 Sqn | 12 Feb 1944–9 Sep 1944 | Beaufighter |
| 151 Sqn | 18 May 1940–29 Aug 1940 | Hurricane |
| 164 Sqn | 6 Aug 1943–22 Sep 1943 | Hurricane |
| 174 Sqn | 3 Mar 1942–6 Dec 1942+ | Hurricane |
| 175 Sqn | 11–16 Jun 1945 | Typhoon |
| 183 Sqn | 15 Mar 1944–1 Apr 1944 | Typhoon |
| 184 Sqn | 12 Jun 1943–14 Aug 1943 | Hurricane |
| 193 Sqn | 8–12 Sep 1944 | Typhoon |
| 197 Sqn | 15 Mar 1944–1 Apr 1944; | Typhoon |
| | 3–11 Sep 1944 | |
| 198 Sqn | 24 Mar 1943–15 May 1943; | Typhoon |
| | 22 Aug 1943–16 Mar 1944 | |
| 222 Sqn | 1–19 Jul 1941; | Spitfire |
| | 1 May 1942–7 Jul 1942 | |
| 229 Sqn | 25 Sep 1944–22 Oct 1944 | Spitfire |
| 235 Sqn | 30 Oct 1939–27 Feb 1940 | Battle, |
| | | Blenheim |
| 242 Sqn | 19 Jul 1941–16 Sep 1941; | Hurricane, |
| | 14–20 Aug 1942 | Spitfire |
| 253 Sqn | 30 Oct 1939–14 Feb 1940 | Hurricane |
| 263 Sqn | 7–10 Sep 1943; | Whirlwind, |
| | 6–11 Sep 1944; | Typhoon, |
| | 1–25 Sep 1946 | Meteor |
| 266 Sqn | 10–11 Sep 1944 | Typhoon |
| 274 Sqn | 17 Aug 1944–20 Sep 1944 | Tempest |
| 310 Sqn | 27 Feb 1945–7 Aug 1945 | Spitfire |
| 312 Sqn | 27 Feb 1945–7 Aug 1945 | Spitfire |
| 313 Sqn | 27 Feb 1945–7 Aug 1945 | Spitfire |
| 331 Sqn | 30 Jun 1942–20 Aug 1942+; | Spitfire |
| | 2–9 Oct 1942 | |
| 332 Sqn | 14–20 Aug 1942 | Spitfire |
| 403 Sqn | 1–8 Jul 1942 | Spitfire |
| 406 Sqn | 27 Nov 1944–14 Jun 1945 | Mosquito |
| 415 Sqn det | Nov 1943–Jul 1944 | Wellington, |
| | | Halifax |
| 451 Sqn | 11–23 Feb 1945 | Spitfire |
| 501 Sqn | 2 Aug 1944–22 Sep 1944 | Tempest |
| 504 Sqn | 20–21 May 1940; | Hurricane, |
| | 13 Aug 1944–25 Feb 1945 | Spitfire |
| 600 Sqn | 20 Oct 1939–14 May 1940; | Blenheim |
| | 20 Jun 1940–24 Aug 1940 | |

## MEMORIALS

1. Museums: RAF Manston History Museum (www.rafmanston.co.uk) has a collection of post-war aircraft but exhibits also cover the airfield's history. Hurricane and Spitfire Memorial Building (www.spitfire-museum.com) houses an excellent Battle of Britain display. Both are located close to the airport.

2. Thanet Allied Aircrew Memorial, unveiled 18 July 1997 and Allied Air Forces Memorial Garden, unveiled 30 June 2001.

3. Plaque in airport terminal.

4. Jolly Farmer Inn, Manston includes memorabilia.

The RAF's first operational jet unit, 616 Squadron, was at Manston in late 1944 as part of the anti V-1 defences. (616 Squadron records)

# MARWELL HALL

**UTM/Grid:** OS map 185–SU510210
**Lat/Long:** N50°59.26 W001°16.55

**County:** Hampshire

**Nearest Town:** Eastleigh 3 miles to south-west

## HISTORY

The Southampton area was noteworthy in World War Two for its aircraft factories and workshops, the most famous connection, of course, being Supermarines and the Spitfire; however, other aircraft companies were involved in this work and one of these, Cunliffe-Owen with their factory in the Swaythling district, decided to acquire an airfield site beyond the boundaries of the city. Marwell Hall, some three miles away, was owned by the company's managing director and he decided to create a grass strip on the estate. This strip was ready for use by September 1941 and the first aircraft, Spitfires, one of the many contracts that Cunliffe-Owen had, duly arrived. A series of twenty Robin hangars had been built in the nearby wood and the Air Transport Auxiliary provided pilots to ferry the new aircraft to their destinations, the initial hops from Southampton to Marwell Hall being made by Company pilots. The arrangement worked well, despite some problems with the length and direction of the grass runway.

The range of aircraft types varied as the company undertook production and modification work, the latter including British fighters and bombers as well as American types. According to those who worked here, the sight of a four-engined bomber taking-off from this constrained airfield was always 'interesting.'

In early 1944 the work was transferred back to the main site, as the German air threat had all but ceased; however, the airfield and hangars continued to be used – by Air Service Training – for design and modification work, although very little flying took place. All this came to an end in 1945; although Marwell had a final burst of aviation activity when Wilmott and Manser Experimental Aircraft took up residence this was very short-lived and the two fields that had been joined to create the runway reverted to being two fields.

Marwell Hall is now the site of a zoo and there is little left, other than at least one Robin hangar in good condition, plus the traces of other hangars.

## UNITS

No based units

# MERSTON (Station 356)

**County:** West Sussex

**UTM/Grid:** OS map 197–SU885030
**Lat/Long:** N50°49.09 W000°44.30

**Nearest Town:** Chichester 2½ miles to north-west

Spitfires were Merston's main occupants for most of its operational period.

## HISTORY

The plan of Merston shows that airfield construction sometimes had to take account of existing structures rather than removing them – the kink in the perimeter track around the nurseries on the west side of the airfield being a classic example. Merston was the earliest wartime airfield built in Sussex, having been surveyed in 1939 as a satellite for Tangmere, less than three miles away. Land was requisitioned the same year and construction work began, few problems being encountered other than waterlogging of the grass airfield – this necessitated additional drainage and opening of Merston was delayed to 1941. The airfield was given a number of dispersals and fighter pens, plus a number of Blister hangars (on the north side), but facilities were limited as, at this stage, it was only intended to house a single fighter-squadron. The airfield finally opened in spring 1941 and the Spitfires of 145 Squadron moved in at the end of

May, although two months later they were replaced by the similarly-equipped 41 Squadron. Fighter Command was now on the offensive and Merston's Spitfires flew fighter sweeps and escort missions. Merston was still suffering from waterlogging and this appears to be the reason for no aircraft being in residence over the winter. In spring 1941 the airfield was live once more and was soon housing Spitfires again, with two units in residence for part of the time. The airfield was also chosen as the location of one of No.11 Group's Air Sea Rescue Flights, this Lysander-equipped unit forming early in 1941 and moving to Westhampnett in November. Spitfires remained Merston's main occupants for the next two years, although for a period in 1942 they carried unusual markings, as the airfield was used by the 307th Fighter Squadron of the 31st Fighter Group, which also meant the airfield became Station 356 of the

## AIRFIELD DATA DEC 1944

| | | | |
|---|---|---|---|
| Command: | RAF Fighter Command | Runway surface: | Sommerfeld Track |
| Function: | Operational Satellite | Hangars: | 6 × Over Blister |
| Runways: | 045 deg 1,592yd | Dispersals: | 20 × Single-Engine |
| | 135 deg 1,400yd | Personnel: | Officers – 79 (one WAAF) |
| | | | Other Ranks – 1,123 (60 WAAF) |

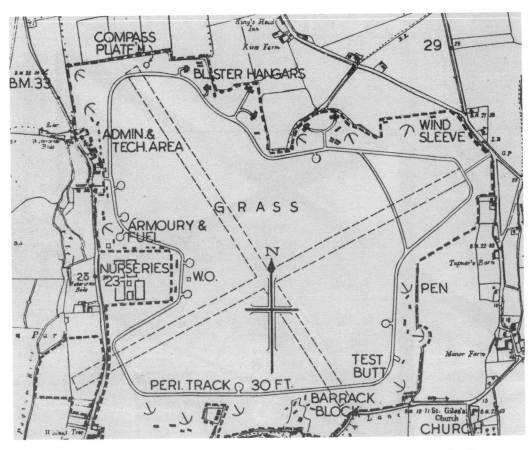

USAAF. It was a short-lived episode and, with the departure of the Americans, the airfield was temporarily closed for further development, the main element of which was the laying of two Sommerfeld Track runways along with additional hardstands – essentially giving Merston the same operating surfaces as an ALG.

With this latest development complete, Spitfires returned, but the airfield was also used by 184 Squadron with its RP-equipped Hurricane IVs, pilots making use of the coastal ranges to practise with their new – and not easy to aim – weapon. The Hurricanes were soon replaced by Typhoons, again for trials, but on this occasion they didn't stay long. The

Canadians of the Digby Wing were also fleeting visitors and were followed by No.124 Airfield with its three Typhoon squadrons. This Wing operated a mix of RP and bombing, both roles requiring additional training, although the squadrons also flew operational sorties. The Wing departed on 31 December for Odiham, but was back again two weeks later and stayed until 1 April 1944, the pace of operations steadily increasing as Allied fighter-bombers worked their way through the extensive target list in and around Normandy. A Free French Spitfire Wing moved in from Perranporth and, with their Spitfire IXs, flew fighter sweeps as well as training for, and flying, fighter-bomber missions. No.421 Repair and

The 'ready room' for 247 Squadron – yet another tent – August 1943.

Salvage Unit was based at Merston for the intensive period of mid-May to mid-June 1944, to work with the Typhoons of No.135 (Selsey) and No.145 (Merston) Wings. The French Wing moved to Funtingdon in mid-June, their place being taken by an ADGB Wing of three Spitfire IX squadrons, whose personnel had barely time to find their billets before they moved out again, leaving Merston for No.142 Wing. This final use of the airfield lasted for six weeks, after which the airfield was, perhaps surprisingly, abandoned and its runways removed. The airfield was kept under Care and Maintenance, however, and there was a final period of activity from March to May 1945, with use by No.103 Wing for Air Disarmament Units. Even then the airfield was not finally abandoned as, in November, it was loaned to the Admiralty for storage, although this, too, soon ended and Merston was at last left to return to its original condition.

## UNITS

### HQ Units at Merston

| | | |
|---|---|---|
| No.124 Airfield | 9 Oct 1943–31 Dec 1943 | 181, 182, 247 Sqn |
| No.145 Airfield/ (French) (F) Wing | 14 Apr 1944–22 Jun 1944 | 329, 340, 341 Sqn |

### 1939–1945

| | | |
|---|---|---|
| 41 Sqn | 28 Jul 1941–16 Dec 1941; 1 Apr 1942–15 Jun 1942 | Spitfire |
| 80 Sqn | 22–27 Jun 1944 | Spitfire |
| 118 Sqn | 24 Aug 1943–20 Sep 1943 | Spitfire |
| 130 Sqn | 27 Jun 1944–3 Aug 1944 | Spitfire |
| 131 Sqn | 14 May 1942–22 Aug 1942 | Spitfire |
| 145 Sqn | 28 May 1941–28 Jul 1941 | Spitfire |
| 174 Sqn | 12 Jun 1943–1 Jul 1943 | Typhoon |
| 181 Sqn | 8 Oct 1943–1 Apr 1944+ | Typhoon |
| 182 Sqn | 12 Oct 1943–31 Dec 1943; 23 Jan 1944–1 Apr 1944 | Typhoon |
| 184 Sqn | 31 May 1943–12 Jun 1943 | Hurricane |
| 229 Sqn | 24–28 Jun 1944 | Spitfire |
| 232 Sqn det | May–Aug 1942 | Spitfire |
| 247 Sqn | 11 Oct 1943–1 Apr 1944+ | Typhoon |
| 274 Sqn | 22–28 Jun 1944 | Spitfire |
| 303 Sqn | 27 Jun 1944–9 Aug 1944 | Spitfire |
| 329 Sqn | 17 Apr 1944–22 Jun 1944 | Spitfire |
| 340 Sqn | 17 Apr 1944–22 Jun 1944 | Spitfire |
| 341 Sqn | 14 Apr 1944–22 Jun 1944 | Spitfire |
| 402 Sqn | 7 Aug 1943–19 Sep 1943; 27 Jun 1944–8 Aug 1944 | Spitfire |
| 412 Sqn | 19 Jun 1942–24 Aug 1942 | Spitfire |
| 416 Sqn | 9 Aug 1943–19 Sep 1943 | Spitfire |
| 485 Sqn | 21 May 1943–1 Jul 1943 | Spitfire |
| ASRF | ?1941–15 Nov 1941 | Lysander |
| 84 Gp CF det | 7 Apr 1944–12 May 1944 | |

### USAAF Units

| | | |
|---|---|---|
| 307th FS | 24 Aug 1942–Oct 1942? | Spitfire |

# MIDDLE WALLOP
# (HMS *Flycatcher*)

**County:** Hampshire

**UTM/Grid:** OS map 185–SU305393
**Lat/Long:** N51°08.43 W001°34.05
**Nearest Town:** Andover 6 miles to north-east

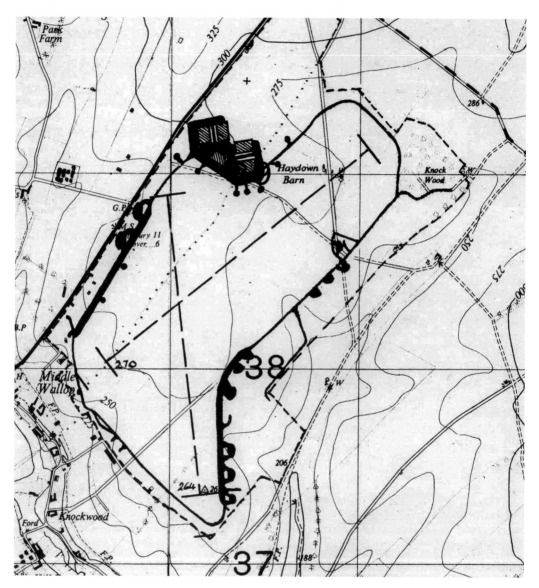

## HISTORY

Planned as a bomber airfield, as part of the RAF's 1930s Expansion Plan, Middle Wallop came under No.11 Group Fighter Command control while it was still being built. The airfield was designed for two bomber squadrons and was to have a grass operating-surface of roughly oval shape with a group of 'C'-type hangars on the northern side, along with the usual array of brick workshops and accommodation, the latter being of the 'H-block variety'. Sub-soil conditions were considered reasonable and drainage work

# AIRFIELD DATA DEC 1944

| Command: | RAF Fighter Command | Runway surface: | Sommerfeld Track |
|---|---|---|---|
| Function: | Sector | Hangars: | 16 × Blister, 4 × C |
| Runways: | 242 deg 1,780 × 50yd | Dispersals: | 8 × Standard Twin |
| | 185 deg 1,600 × 50yd | Personnel: | Officers – 110 (17 WAAF) |
| | | | Other Ranks – 2,142 (282 WAAF) |

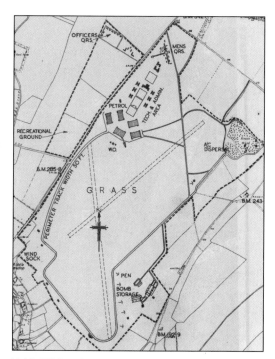

Middle Wallop plan dated early 1950s.

was soon completed, as was the general preparation of the flying surface – hence its use prior to building work being completed. A concrete perimeter-track was laid, linking the dispersals and the hangar area, whilst a bomb dump was built in the south-east corner.

Flying training commenced in April 1940, with No.15 Flying Training School's Oxfords arriving in the middle of the month and remaining for two months, by which time the airfield had also received its first operational unit, with the arrival of the Hurricane-equipped 601 Squadron. The Squadron was soon engaged on escort work, a role that was subsequently taken on by a number of squadrons that rotated through Wallop in the summer of 1940. With the re-organization of Fighter Command, Middle Wallop was allocated to the newly formed No.10 Group to become a Sector Airfield and, as the Battle of Britain approached, the airfield was home to 234

and 609 Squadrons flying Spitfires and 604 Squadron flying Blenheims. Night-fighter operations subsequently became a major part of the station's operations, with 604 Squadron enjoying a great deal of success, especially when re-equipped with the Beaufighter; the unit was to remain at the airfield for over two years, Middle Wallop's longest-serving resident. During the Battle of Britain, Middle Wallop was one of the airfields targeted by the Luftwaffe and it was attacked a number of times during August, with some damage and casualties.

Various fighter-units continued to use the airfield on both day and night operations until January 1944 and, during this time, the airfield also saw use by specialist units, two of the unsuccessful ideas being the aerial-minelaying Harrows of No.420 Flight and the Turbinlite Havocs of No.1458 Flight. Throughout these middle years of the war, Middle Wallop was an active fighter-station with various squadrons and aircraft types; the airfield received a number of improvements during this period including lengthening of the grass strips and additional accommodation. In autumn 1943 the airfield was transferred to the Americans for use by the IXth Air Force, its HQ element moving in to the airfield – with the operational unit, the 67th Tactical Reconnaissance Group, arriving at the end of the year. However, not all of this Group's squadrons were present at any one time and the first to become operational from Wallop were the 12th and 107th squadrons. By spring, four squadrons were engaged on reconnaissance over Europe, flying sorties that were an essential pre-requisite to the invasion. The Group's diverse fleet of aircraft remained operational throughout the invasion period and finally moved to the Continent in the first week of July.

Passing back to No.10 Group, the station then received two Mosquito night-fighter squadrons, both of which also flew anti-*Diver* patrols with some success. The number of aircraft was increased in September with the arrival of No.3501 Servicing Unit, whose task it was to carry out servicing and minor repair on aircraft flown back from operational squadrons in France and then return them to active duty. At any one time this unit could have between fifty and eighty aircraft being worked on – one of those many unsung units that played important roles

245 Squadron operated Hurricanes from Middle Wallop
from December 1941.

within the Allied air forces.

The December 1944 survey showed that both
Sommerfeld Track runways could be extended, but
only by a few hundred yards and no comment was
made as to the ease or advisability of this work; however, no additional work was undertaken before the
end of the war. Between February 1945 and April
1946 the airfield was in the hands of the Royal Navy
as HMS *Flycatcher* and acted as a training base for
Mobile Air Operations Bases (MAOB) for possible
deployment to the Far East. A number of other Fleet
Air Arm units used the airfield before it was paid off
from naval service on 10 April 1946. It was back to
the RAF once more and more fighter operations, a
single Spitfire squadron taking up residence, but in
early 1948 the army began to use the site for Air
Observation Post (AOP) training and Austers
became the main occupants. It was still an RAF airfield and, in addition to units providing army support,
it also housed other squadrons and organizations,
including, from the mid-1950s, a number of units
involved with the development of the helicopter for
military uses, the Joint Helicopter Experimental Unit
perhaps being the most significant. The nature of the
aircraft being flown and the increased use of helicopters meant that there was no need to develop hard
runways and Middle Wallop retained its grass surface
and almost rustic feel.

The airfield was eventually transferred to the newly
formed Army Air Corps (AAC) on 1 October 1958
and has remained at the forefront of AAC activity
ever since, with a major training role as well as being
home to operational squadrons. A great deal of development work has taken place over the last thirty years
in terms of infrastructure, with buildings being modified or new ones constructed, but much of the airfield
retains its World War Two appearance. The airfield
(EGVP) now declares two grass-strips, 09/27 at
around 1,000 yards and 18/36 at 1,180 yards, and one
of its main current tasks is training aircrew on the

army's new WAH-64 Apache attack-helicopters.

The Museum of Army Flying is well worth a visit
for, although it is not specific to Middle Wallop, its
exhibits of aircraft and other displays tell the fascinating story of 'army aviation' – and of course the
connection with the airfield. Furthermore, it is situated on the edge of the airfield and from the car park
or picnic site there is an excellent view of current
activities at this home of the Army Air Corps.

## DECOY SITES

| Q | Houghton | SU331343 |
|---|---|---|

## UNITS

### HQ Units at Middle Wallop

| | | |
|---|---|---|
| No.121 Airfield | 28 Feb 1943–5 Apr 1943 | 19, 182, 247 Sqn |
| IXth FC | 30 Nov 1943–Jul 1944 | |
| XIXth ASC | 4 Jan 1944–1 Feb 1944 | |
| IXth ASC | 1 Feb 1944–15 Feb 1944 | |
| No.62 Group | 2 Jul 1946–21 Jan 1948 | |
| AAC | 1970–current | |

### 1939–1945

| | | |
|---|---|---|
| 1 RCAF Sqn | 21 Jun 1940–3 Jul 1940 | Hurricane |
| 16 Sqn | 1–29 Jun 1943 | Mustang |
| 19 Sqn | 1 Mar 1943–4 Apr 1943 | Spitfire |
| 23 Sqn det | 12–25 Sep 1940 | Blenheim |
| 32 Sqn | 15 Dec 1940–16 Feb 1941 | Hurricane |
| 56 Sqn | 29 Nov 1940–17 Dec 1940 | Hurricane |
| 93 Sqn | 7 Dec 1940–6 Dec 1941 | Havoc |
| 125 Sqn | 30 Jul 1944–18 Oct 1944 | Mosquito |
| 151 Sqn | 16 Aug 1943–17 Nov 1943 | Mosquito |
| 164 Sqn | 8 Feb 1943–19 Jun 1943 | Hurricane |
| 169 Sqn | 21 Jun 1943–19 Sep 1943 | Mosquito |
| 182 Sqn | 1 Mar 1943–5 Apr 1943 | Typhoon |
| 234 Sqn | 13 Aug 1940–11 Sep 1940 | Spitfire |
| 236 Sqn | 14 Jun 1940–4 Jul 1940 | Blenheim |
| 238 Sqn | 20 Jun 1940–14 Aug 1940; | Hurricane |

Harrow II, complete with Shark Mouth, of 93 Squadron at
Wallop, early 1941. (Andy Thomas)

The Hurricanes of 56 Squadron spent two weeks here at the end of 1940.

| | 10–30 Sep 1940 | |
|---|---|---|
| 245 Sqn | 19 Dec 1941–26 Oct 1942 | Hurricane |
| 247 Sqn | 1 Mar 1943–5 Apr 1943 | Typhoon |
| 400 Sqn | 27 Oct 1942–14 Jan 1943+ | Mustang |
| 406 Sqn | 8 Dec 1942–31 Mar 1943 | Beaufighter |
| 414 Sqn | 1–20 Feb 1943; | Mustang |
| | 9 Apr 1943–25 May 1943 | |
| 418 Sqn | 29 Jun 1944–27 Aug 1944 | Mosquito |
| 456 Sqn | 30 Mar 1943–17 Aug 1943 | Mosquito |
| 501 Sqn | 4–25 Jul 1940; | Hurricane, |
| | 24 Aug 1942–19 Oct 1942 | Spitfire |
| 504 Sqn | 19 Oct 1942–30 Dec 1942 | Spitfire |
| 537 Sqn | 2 Sep 1942–25 Jan 1943 | Havoc, |
| | | Hurricane |
| 601 Sqn | 1–17 Jun 1940 | Hurricane |
| 604 Sqn | 26 Jul 1940–7 Dec 1942 | Blenheim, |
| | | Beaufighter |
| 609 Sqn | 5 Jul 1940–29 Nov 1940 | Spitfire |
| 15 FTS | 20 Apr 1940–1 Oct 1940 | Harvard, |
| | | Oxford |
| 420/1420 Flt | 29 Sep 1940–7 Dec 1940 | Harrow |
| FEE | 23 Apr 1941–1 Aug 1941 | Wellington |
| 1458 Flt | 6 Dec 1941–8 Sep 1942 | Havoc |

## USAAF units:
### 67th TRG
| | |
|---|---|
| Squadrons: | 12th TRS, 15th TRS, 30th PRS, 107th TRS, 109th TRS |
| Aircraft: | P-38, P-51/F-6, P-38/F-5 |
| Dates: | Dec 1943–Jul 1944 |
| First mission: | Dec 1943 |
| Last mission: | May 1945 (from bases in Germany) |

### Post-1945
| | | |
|---|---|---|
| 63 Sqn | 1–3 Sep 1946; | Spitfire |
| | 30 Oct 1946–5 Jan 1948 | |
| 288 Sqn | 16 Mar 1953–30 Sep 1957 | Spitfire, |
| | | Balliol |
| 651 Sqn | 1 Nov 1955–1 Apr 1957 | Sycamore, |
| | | Auster |

| | | |
|---|---|---|
| 657 Sqn | 19 Jan 1948–1 Nov 1955 | Auster, Hoverfly, Sycamore |
| FC CRS | Dec 1945–Sep 1957 | Spitfire, Oxford, Balliol |
| 62 Gp CF | 10 Sep 1946–7 Jan 1948 | |
| 227 OCU | 6 Jan 1948–1 May 1950 | Auster |
| 1901 Flt | 1 Feb 1948–21 Feb 1952 | Auster |
| 1900 Flt | 1 Dec 1948–Nov 1951; | Auster |
| | Mar 1953 | |
| 1962 Flt | 1 Sep 1949–10 Mar 1957 | Auster |
| AOPS | 1 May 1950–3 Apr 1953 | Auster |
| 1906 Flt | 1 May 1950–20 Mar 1957; | Hoverfly, |
| | ?–1 Sep 1957 | Skeeter |
| 1912 Flt | 15 Aug 1951–14 Jul 1952; | Auster |
| | Oct 1956–Dec 1956 | |
| 1913 Flt | 12 Jun 1951–30 Aug 1951; | Auster |
| | Feb 1955–Sep 1956 | |
| LAS | 3 Apr 1953–1 Sep 1957 | Auster |
| CFS HF | 8 Mar 1954–18 Jun 1955 | various |
| JEHU | 1 Apr 1955–31 Jan 1960 | Sycamore, Whirlwind |
| 1915 Flt | 6 Mar 1956–3 Apr 1956 | Auster |

**FAA Units**
| | | |
|---|---|---|
| 700 Sqn | 23 Nov 1945–1 Apr 1946 | Avenger, Barracuda |

## MEMORIALS

The on-site Museum of Army Flying includes material relating to Middle Wallop. (www.flying-museum.org.uk)

Austers, the Army Air Corps and Middle Wallop – the combination that gave the airfield its place in British aviation history. This particular line-up was at one of the Station's air displays in the late 1990s.

# NEEDS OAR POINT

**County:** Hampshire

**UTM/Grid:** OS map 196–SZ402978
**Lat/Long:** N50°46.23 W001°25.53
**Nearest Town:** Lymington 5 miles to west

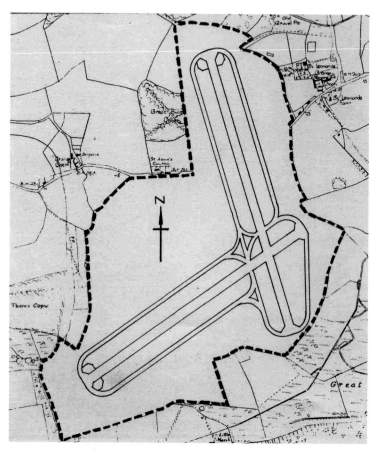

## HISTORY

Needs Oar Point was selected for development by the 1942 survey team and was one of a number of Advanced Landing Grounds in Hampshire being prepared for use by tactical aircraft. Some recent publications show it as 'Ore' but the RAF records use 'Oar'. The site, just north of the Great Marsh and very near the coast, overlooking the Solent and the Isle of Wight, was reasonably straightforward to develop and, during the early part of 1943, hedges and ditches were cleared or covered – concrete culverts over field ditches being one of the few tell-tale signs remaining at the sites of these ALGs – and two Sommerfeld Track runways were laid. The site was ready by summer 1943 but was not chosen as one of those to which aircraft would deploy for field trials, so

it was temporarily returned to agriculture. During the winter of 1943–44, further development work took place so that, by spring 1944, the airfield was complete to full ALG-standard, with surfaced perimeter-tracks linking the runways, dispersal points (in this case thirty-six Sommerfeld Track areas) and four Blister hangars.

The first squadrons of No.146 Airfield arrived on 10 April 1944 and, by the end of the month, Needs Oar Point was home to four squadrons of Typhoons. Accommodation for the over-1,000 personnel was in tents, as the whole idea was for the Airfield/Wing to be fully mobile and self-contained, although a number of farm buildings were requisitioned. With four squadrons, the Wing had over 100 aircraft on

Pilots of 257 Squadron pose with Typhoon EK172.

back damaged or not coming back at all. It was a short period of activity, however, and in the first few days of July the Wing moved out of Needs Oar Point. From organized chaos and the roar of Sabre engines to a return of peaceful Hampshire coastline in a matter of days, as there was no further need of the ALG once the tactical aircraft had moved to the Continent.

In the December 1944 survey the airfield is listed as de-requisitioned, this having taken place the previous month, and most of its infrastructure was removed, to leave little trace of a few months in 1944 when this airfield played a role in one of the most important campaigns of World War Two.

## UNITS

### HQ Units at Needs Oar Point

| | | |
|---|---|---|
| No.146 Airfield/(F) Wing | 10 Apr 1944–8 Jul 1944 | 193, 197, 257, 266 Sqn |

### 1939–1945

| | | |
|---|---|---|
| 193 Sqn | 11 Apr 1944–3 Jul 1944 | Typhoon |
| 197 Sqn | 10 Apr 1944–3 Jul 1944 | Typhoon |
| 257 Sqn | 10 Apr 1944–2 Jul 1944 | Typhoon |
| 266 Sqn | 10–27 Apr 1944; 6 May 1944–29 Jun 1944 | Typhoon |

strength and it must have been an impressive sight with this number of Typhoons dispersed around the airfield. Operations commenced immediately and the 'Tiffies' used rockets, bombs and guns to attack targets in and around Normandy, as part of the softening-up process for the invasion. It is hard to visualize the intensity of a typical day's operations in June 1944, when as many as 200 sorties might be mounted from an airfield such as this – with some aircraft coming

The ALG only had a three-month operational career but in that time its Typhoons played a significant role in the D-Day campaign.

# NEWCHURCH

**County:** Kent

**UTM/Grid:** OS map 188–TR045315
**Lat/Long:** N51°02.45 E000°55.15
**Nearest Town:** Ashford 7 miles to north-west

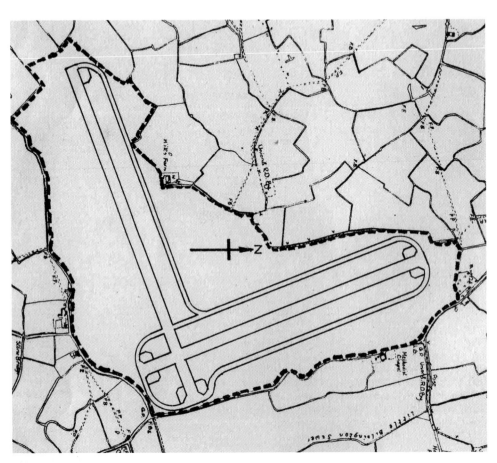

## HISTORY

Newchurch was one of the series of Advanced Landing Grounds constructed on Romney Marsh, the land area acquired being one of the smallest, and the two runways were laid in an 'L'-shape that was pretty much mirrored by the airfield boundary. The survey team identified this flat area just west of Newchurch village in early 1942 and approvals had been given by the end of the year for construction. Work was straightforward and, after removing fences, burying power lines and filling or bridging ditches, the Airfield Construction Squadron laid two Sommerfeld Track runways of standard lengths. According to some records, the airfield was given a decoy site at Burmarsh – if this is correct then it was an unusual arrangement.

The airfield was complete by late spring and the two Spitfire squadrons of No.122 Airfield moved in on 2 July 1943 to evaluate the airfield and practise mobile operations. As usual, accommodation was in tents and, other than a few requisitioned buildings, all personnel worked and lived in these primitive conditions to prepare them for the situation they would face when the invasion eventually took place. The squadrons continued their escort and fighter-sweep activities, the Wing swapping one squadron and adding a third to bring it up to standard three-squadron strength. No major problems were discovered with the airfield or the mobile operations, other than the, by then well-known, problem of tyre

# AIRFIELD DATA DEC 1944

| | | | |
|---|---|---|---|
| Command: | RAF Fighter Command | Runway surface: | Sommerfeld Track |
| Function: | Advanced Landing Ground | Hangars: | 4 × Enlarged Over Blister |
| Runways: | 260 deg 1,600yd | Dispersals: | nil |
| | 350 deg 1,400yd | Personnel: | Other Ranks – Tented camp |

damage from the Sommerfeld Track. There was no intention of over-wintering at the ALGs and the Wing moved out in late-October to the more comfortable surroundings of Detling. The construction team moved back in and, over the next few months, completed the perimeter track, although Newchurch's east/west runway was only given a single perimeter-track, as well as erecting four Blister hangars. Unusually for this second build-phase, no surfaced-dispersals were laid, it being deemed that the grass surfaces were capable of taking the strain.

The airfield re-opened in April, when the Tempests of No.150 Airfield arrived, although one of the units, 56 Squadron, initially operated Spitfires and Typhoons. The Wing was soon in action, the Tempests undertaking offensive sweep- and escort-missions, whilst 56 Squadron soldiered on with its Spitfires (eventually receiving its Tempests in late-June – too late for D-Day but just in time for the Wing to take on a new threat, the V-1 flying bomb). Newchurch's role in anti-*Diver* was significant and this period of the airfield's history was certainly its most interesting, especially when the Tempest took on the role of engaging the V-1s at night. It was a hectic period and the Wing scored a number of successes by day and night. The Tempests eventually left in late-September and Newchurch was declared surplus to requirements. The airfield was still listed as a Fighter Command ALG in the December 1944 survey but with the usual remark for ALGs of 'de-requisitioned'. The runway tracking was lifted and the Blister hangars removed and these Kent fields returned to agriculture, leaving no real trace of their important wartime role.

## DECOY SITE

Burmarsh            TR100310

## UNITS

### HQ Units at Newchurch

| | | |
|---|---|---|
| No.125 Airfield | 2 Jul 1943–12 Oct 1943 | 19, 132, 184, 602 Sqn |
| No.150 Airfield/(F) Wing | 28 Apr 1944–19 Sep 1944 | 3, 56, 486 Sqn |

### 1939–1945

| | | |
|---|---|---|
| 3 Sqn | 28 Apr 1944–21 Sep 1944 | Tempest |
| 19 Sqn | 2 Jul 1943–18 Aug 1943 | Spitfire |
| 56 Sqn | 28 Apr 1944–23 Sep 1944 | Spitfire, Typhoon, Tempest |
| 132 Sqn | 2 Jul 1943–12 Oct 1943 | Spitfire |
| 184 Sqn | 18 Aug 1943–12 Oct 1943 | Hurricane, Spitfire |
| 486 Sqn | 29 Apr 1944–19 Sep 1944 | Tempest |
| 602 Sqn | 13 Aug 1943–12 Oct 1943 | Spitfire |

## MEMORIALS

Newchurch is recorded on the New Forest Airfield memorial at Holmsley South.

New Romney was unique amongst ALGs in that t housed a Tempest Wing; groundcrew prepare a 3 Squadron Tempest for its next mission.

July 1944 and Tempest pilots study the next mission in this posed pubic relations shot.

# NEW ROMNEY (Honeychild)

**County:** Kent

**UTM/Grid:** OS map 189–TR089275 (Littlestone), TR063269 (Honeychild)
**Lat/Long:** N51°00.15 E000°56.15
**Nearest Town:** New Romney

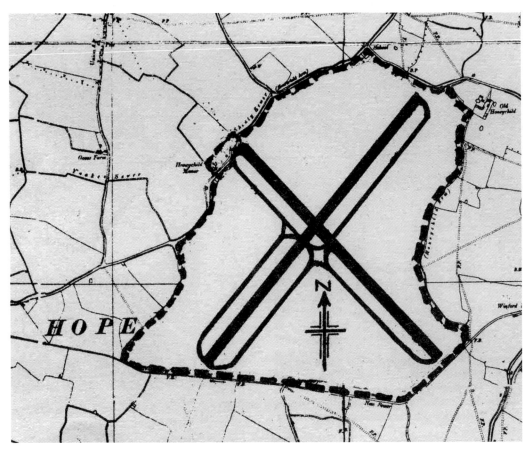

## HISTORY

There have been two distinct airfield sites within a few miles of this village: New Romney/Littlestone in World War One and New Romney/Honeychild in World War Two. The World War One airfield, two miles north-east of the village, was selected late in the war, in response to the need for additional train-ing-facilities near the important coastal ranges. First use of the Landing Ground was in August 1917, when No.3 (Auxiliary) School of Aerial Gunnery formed here; the airfield was reasonably well equipped with hangars, workshops and other build-ings. The School operated a variety of types and the output of students increased during the year as more courses arrived. Littlestone remained busy into 1918

and, on 9 March, the School changed its name to No.1 (Observers) School of Aerial Gunnery and operated at both New Romney and Dymchurch (Hythe), although it moved most of its assets to the former in November. A hectic pace of training con-tinued to the end of the war but, within weeks of the end of hostilities, the School had been greatly reduced in size and it was soon announced that the airfield would close. The School finally moved out in autumn 1919 and the first phase of military opera-tions at New Romney was over.

The site at Littlestone was brought back into use, or at least made available to use, during the 1920s as an Emergency Landing Ground for civil aircraft and,

## AIRFIELD DATA DEC 1944

| | | | |
|---|---|---|---|
| Command: | RAF Fighter Command | Runway surface: | Sommerfeld Track |
| Function: | Advanced Landing Ground | Hangars: | 4 × Blister |
| Runways: | NE/SW 1,600 × 50yd | Dispersals: | 3 × Refuelling, 1 × MT |
| | NW/SE 1,375 × 50yd | Personnel: | Other Ranks – Tented camp |

A Typhoon of 181 Squadron comes to grief in a drainage ditch, October 1943.

as such, the 'airfield' came under the control of the Directorate of Civil Aviation. There is no record of any emergency landings by civil aircraft, but some use was made by private owners. By the mid-1930s the airfield was no longer required and it passed out of use.

During the 1942 survey for Advanced Landing Grounds the initial choice fell on New Romney/ Dymchurch, but this was subsequently rejected and a new site in the same area was selected as an alternative. A 400-acre site near St Mary-in-the-Marsh was picked in summer 1942 and was subsequently developed as New Romney airfield, the alternate name Honeychild being taken from Honeychild Manor, requisitioned at the same time. Construction of the ALG was straightforward, despite the number of small streams that criss-crossed the site, and two Sommerfeld Track runways were laid across the old

field system. As with Newchurch, this was one of the few ALGs to be given a decoy site, in this case at Romney Salts just to the south-east.

It was not long before the cross-shaped runways received their first users, Typhoons of No.124 Airfield arriving from Appledram in early July. Within days, the tented camps had become well established and the squadrons were in action flying fighter-bomber missions over Europe. The airfield held up well, other than some damage to the runways, and the squadrons had a good work-out in their new role as a mobile Wing. Having satisfied the requirements, the Wing moved out in early October and New Romney went into the second phase of development, during which perimeter track and three refuelling-hardstands were laid and four Blister hangars erected. This work was complete by spring 1944, but the airfield saw no further operational use as it was designated a reserve ALG. A number of aircraft did use it for emergency landings during summer 1944 and, as with all the reserve ALGs, a handling party was stationed here for just this eventuality. With the Allies safely ashore in Normandy and squadrons moving across the Channel, there was no need for the ALGs and a closure programme was started in September, New Romney being abandoned in late-November. The runways and other tracked areas were lifted and the Blister hangars removed as peace returned to these Kentish fields.

181 Squadron was one of three squadrons in No.124 Airfield; this posed bombing-up shot (note the airmen admiring the WAAF driver) is probably not at New Romney.

There is now no significant trace of New Romney airfield, other than a few visible differences in the hedges and ditches that had once been removed or bridged.

## DECOY SITES

| Q | Romney Salts | TR064223 |
|---|---|---|

## UNITS

### HQ Units at New Romney

| No.124 Airfield | 2 Jul 1943–9 Oct 1943 | 181, 182, 247 Sqn |
|---|---|---|

### Pre-1919

| 3 SoAG | 1 Aug 1917–9 Mar 1918 |
|---|---|
| 1 (O) SofAG | 1 Nov 1918–Sep 1919 |

### 1939–1945

| 181 Sqn | 2 Jul 1943–8 Oct 1943 | Typhoon |
|---|---|---|
| 182 Sqn | 2 Jul 1943–12 Oct 1943 | Typhoon |
| 247 Sqn | 10 Jul 1943–11 Oct 1943 | Typhoon |

## MEMORIALS

Yes

# ODIHAM

**County:** Hampshire

**UTM/Grid:** OS map 186–SU740491
**Lat/Long:** N51°14.08 W000°56.38
**Nearest Town:** Basingstoke 6 miles to north-west

Odiham, September 2002.

## HISTORY

The first use of what later became RAF Odiham took place in the late-1920s, when an area of land at Down Farm was acquired for use as a Summer Camp location – its nearness to Aldershot and the Salisbury Plain ranges being one of the factors in this decision. The first such camp took place in 1926, when two Army Co-operation units, 4 and 13 squadrons, moved in for a few weeks, complete with tented camp and temporary Bessonneau hangars. In the dry and pleasant conditions of a Hampshire summer the Landing Ground was delightful and when the search for true airfield sites was underway in the early 1930s it seemed logical to expand this summer camp location. More land was acquired and work began in 1934 on an Expansion Period airfield, complete with 'C'-type hangars and the usual range of brick buildings. The contractors, Lindsey Parkinson Ltd, handed the airfield over in December 1936 and RAF Odiham was allocated to No.22 Group.

Odiham was designed to house three Army Co-operation squadrons and, by February 1937, the first two squadrons for No.50 (AC) Wing had arrived, eventually being joined by the third a year later. All three squadrons took part in a wide range of exercises with the army and honed their skills in the art of Army Co-operation, for which the delightful Audax was an excellent aircraft, although by the late-1930s this biplane was very out of date. As the war approached, the re-equipment programme reached Odiham and all three squadrons received new aircraft, 53 Squadron acquiring Blenheims, whilst 4 and 13 squadrons acquired Lysanders. The airfield was improved by the addition of concrete runways in early 1939, the airfield surface having proved problematical for all but the lightest of aircraft types. The Wing was assigned to the Expeditionary Force and duly moved to France in autumn 1940, but Odiham was not left empty as more AC squadrons arrived,

## AIRFIELD DATA DEC 1944

| | | | |
|---|---|---|---|
| Command: | RAF Fighter Command | Runway surface: | Concrete and wood-chippings |
| Function: | Forward Airfield | Hangars: | 6 × Blister, 3 × C |
| Runways: | 102 deg 1,700 × 50yd | Dispersals: | 29 × Spectacle, 6 × Blenheim, 5 × Frying Pan |
| | 045 deg 1,400 × 50yd | Personnel: | Officers – 200 (7 WAAF) Other Ranks – 1,600 (69 WAAF) |

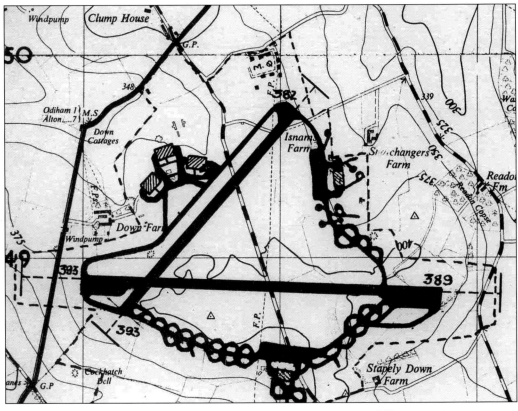

This 1950s plan reflects the wartime shape of Odiham, the only new additions being the ORPs.

bringing with them biplane types such as Hectors that had only recently been taken out of front-line service. However, all the squadrons duly re-equipped whilst continuing to exercise with the army. This was pretty much the pattern for the first year of the war, although a new role was acquired in mid-1940 with the arrival of French and Belgian pilots and a variety of French aircraft that had escaped from the advancing Germans. They were here to train and then join RAF squadrons and a Fighter Training Squadron was formed, which, in November, became the Franco-Belgian Flying Training School. The school, primarily equipped with Magisters, remained to June 1941,

when it disbanded; this left Odiham with two operational units: 400 Squadron, which had formed from 110 (RCAF) Squadron in March 1941, and 13 Squadron, which returned in July. The airfield had already undergone an improvement phase in early 1941 but, later in the year, was extended and improved again, most effort being expended on the runways.

Operational flying remained the main flying activity from Odiham for the rest of the war, various changes of squadron taking place during 1942 and 1943, with the main type being the Mustang. As part of the general re-organization of units for D-Day,

Odiham's moment of glory: the Royal Review of July 1954 was an impressive collection of RAF aircraft.

Odiham became part of Fighter Command on 1 June 1943, a change that also included the three Mustang-squadrons becoming No.123 Airfield, with the role remaining that of Tactical Reconnaissance (Tac/R). Combat ops continued as before, but the squadrons left later in the year, being replaced by a variety of flying and non-flying units; amongst the latter the most significant was No.511 Forward Repair Unit, whose task was the repair and return to service of a wide range of aircraft types, for which they used some of the existing hangars, as well as a number of additional T.2 hangars. Seldom do ground units get a mention in brief histories but some, such as the FRUs, played a major role in maintaining front-line aircraft strength; this FRU was eventually disbanded in November 1944 – and in the intervening period Odiham had continued its tradition of hosting numerous units for short periods of time. It was No.128 Wing's three Mustang-squadrons that were operating out of Odiham on D-Day itself, but Spitfires and Typhoons had been using the airfield in recent months. With the Recce Wing gone, the final burst of operational activity for 1944 came with No.147 Wing and its two Mosquito units, although only a few night patrols over the Continent were flown before this unit, too, departed.

The latter months of the war were unusually quiet for Odiham and, on 7 June 1945, the station was transferred to Transport Command for use by No.46 Group; the Dakotas of 233 Squadron began to arrive the following day and, for the next year, Odiham's units, with a number of changes, flew a transport

Autogyro under trials at Odiham, probably 1937.

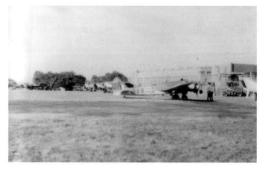

Blenheims of 13 Squadron; the Squadron spent two periods at Odiham.

September 1961 and 66 Squadron reforms with the Belvedere.

shuttle to and from the Continent. From November 1945 the station had been under the control of No.120 (RCAF) Wing and it was they who eventually handed it back to No.11 Group on 28 June 1946 to become part of Fighter Command. Three fighter-squadrons duly moved in and before long Odiham was home to the first Vampire Wing; until July 1959 Odiham was a busy and happy jet-fighter base, housing in turn various Marks of Vampire, Meteor, Hunter and Javelin. However, the most spectacular activity during this period was, of course, the Royal Review held on 15 July 1954, when the airfield was literally covered in aircraft, whilst an equally impressive formation flew by – the total number of aircraft on show that day was almost 1,000, an amazing total and an awesome sight.

The departure of the fighter squadrons in July 1959 was followed by a short period in Care and Maintenance before the airfield once more joined Transport Command, opening as a No.38 Group station, and indeed HQ for that Group, on 15 February 1960. By May two units were in residence: 225 Squadron with Sycamores and Whirlwinds and 230 Squadron with Pioneers and Twin Pioneers. A few weeks later the Belvedere Trials Unit was formed here to bring this twin-rotor heavy helicopter into service, the BTU then becoming the nucleus of 66 Squadron the following year. This set Odiham on the path that it still follows as one of the RAF's pre-eminent helicopter bases. Over the next forty years various squadrons came and went at Odiham and virtually every rotary type with which the RAF has been involved spent at least some time here; indeed, more than that, for Odiham has often been home to the trials unit responsible for introducing a new type to service, as well as performing a training role for helicopter crews. Most of the squadrons have been

involved in active operations and in recent years Odiham has supported virtually every UN and NATO operation involving British forces.

## DECOY SITES

| Q | Froyle | SU726435 |
|---|--------|----------|

## UNITS

### HQ Units at Odiham

| Unit | Dates | Squadrons |
|------|-------|-----------|
| No.50 (AC) Wing | Dec 1936–21 Sep 1939 | 4, 13, 53 Sqn |
| No.35 Wing | 28 Jun 1943–15 Aug 1944 | |
| No.123 Airfield | 23 Jun 1943–20 Sep 1944 | 2, 168, 170, 268 Sqn |
| No.130 Airfield | 7 Aug 1943–15 Nov 1943 | 268, 330, 331 Sqn |
| No.124 Airfield | 31 Dec 1943–13 Jan 1944 | 175, 181, 182 Sqn |
| No.128 Airfield/ (RCAF) (F) Wing | 19 Feb 1944–29 Jun 1944 | 168, 400, 414, 430 Sqn |
| No.129 Airfield | 2–22 Apr 1944 | 414, 430 Sqn |
| No.130 (R) Wing | 12 May 1944–7 Jul 1944 | |
| No.147 (NF) Wing | 20 Dec 1944–8 Jan 1945 | 264, 604 Sqn |
| No.120 (RCAF) (TR) Wing | 12 Nov 1945–30 Jun 1946 | 435, 436, 437 Sqn |
| No.38 Group | 17 May 1960–15 May 1972 | |

### 1919–1938

| Unit | Dates | Aircraft |
|------|-------|----------|
| 4 Sqn | 16 Feb 1937–2 Oct 1939 | Audax, Hector, Lysander |
| 13 Sqn | 16 Feb 1937–2 Oct 1939; 14 Jul 1941–1 Aug 1942 | Audax, Hector, Lysander, Blenheim |
| 53 Sqn | 8 Apr 1938–18 Sep 1939 | Hector, Blenheim |

### 1939–1945

| Unit | Dates | Aircraft |
|------|-------|----------|
| 2 Sqn | 10 Aug 1943–22 Jan 1944; 27 Jun 1944–29 Jul 1944 | Mustang |
| 4 Sqn | 7 Aug 1943–15 Sep 1943; 6 Oct 1943–15 Nov 1943; 27 Jun 1944–16 Aug 1944 | Mustang; Spitfire |
| 13 Sqn | 14 Jul 1941–1 Aug 1942 | Lysander, Blenheim |
| 59 Sqn | 9 Jun 1940–3 Jul 1940 | Blenheim |
| 63 Sqn det | 31 Dec 1942–19 Feb 1943 | Mustang |

| 96 Sqn | 24 Sep 1944–12 Dec 1944 | Mosquito |
| 168 Sqn | 18 Nov 1942–20 Sep 1943;<br>31 Mar 1944–29 Jun 1944 | Mustang |
| 170 Sqn | 26 Jun 1943–20 Sep 1943 | Mustang |
| 171 Sqn | 11 Jul 1942–25 Aug 1942 | Tomahawk |
| 174 Sqn | 6 Dec 1942–1 Mar 1943 | Hurricane |
| 175 Sqn | 14 Jan 1943–19 Mar 1943 | Hurricane |
| 181 Sqn | 31 Dec 1943–13 Jan 1944 | Typhoon |
| 182 Sqn | 31 Dec 1943–5 Jan 1944 | Typhoon |
| 184 Sqn | 6–11 Mar 1944;<br>3–23 Apr 1944 | Spitfire,<br>Typhoon |
| 225 Sqn | 11 Oct 1939–9 Jun 1940 | Lysander |
| 233 Sqn | 8 Jun 1945–15 Aug 1945 | Dakota |
| 239 Sqn | 18 Nov 1942–6 Dec 1942 | Mustang |
| 247 Sqn | 31 Dec 1943–13 Jan 1944 | Typhoon |
| 264 Sqn | 21 Dec 1944–8 Jan 1945 | Mosquito |
| 268 Sqn | 31 May 1943–15 Sep 1943;<br>8–15 Oct 1943;<br>27 Jun 1944–10 Aug 1944 | Mustang;<br>Typhoon |
| 271 Sqn | 30 Aug 1945–5 Oct 1945 | various |
| 400 Sqn | 1 Mar 1941–27 Oct 1942;<br>18 Feb 1944–1 Jul 1944 | Lysander,<br>Tomahawk |
| 412 Sqn | 6 Mar 1943–7 Mar 1943 | Spitfire |
| 414 Sqn | 19–28 Feb 1944;<br>1 Apr 1944–15 Aug 1944 | Mustang,<br>Spitfire |
| 430 Sqn | 1 Apr 1944–29 Jun 1944 | Mustang |
| 437 Sqn det | 1 Aug 1945–17 Nov 1945 | Dakota |
| 604 Sqn | 4–31 Dec 1944 | Mosquito |
| 613 Sqn | 2 Oct 1939–29 Jun 1940 | Hind,<br>Hector,<br>Lysander |
| 614 Sqn | 9 Jun 1940–1 Sep 1940 | Lysander |
| 110 Sqn RCAF | 9 Jun 1940–1 Sep 1940 | Lysander |
| GMDC | Jul 1940–Oct 1940 | |
| ATF | 1 Apr 1940–1 Jul 1940 | Cierva C.30,<br>C.40 |
| Franco-Belgian<br>ATS | 28 Oct 1940–9 Jun 1941 | Magister |
| 8 AACU | Nov 1940–1941 | |
| 4 ADF | 20 Oct 1943–25 Nov 1943 | |
| 1516 Flt | 17 Sep 1944–1 Sep 1945 | Oxford |
| 1 ADF | 14 Feb 1945–4 Jun 1945 | |

## Post-1945

| 7 Sqn | 1 Sep 1982–date | Chinook |
| 18 Sqn | 27 Jan 1964–1 Jan 1965;<br>4 Aug 1969–31 Aug 1970;<br>4 Aug 1981–6 Aug 1983 | Wessex,<br>Chinook |
| 26 Sqn | 1 Jun 1962–1 Mar 1963 | Belvedere |
| 33 Sqn | 14 Jun 1971–date | Puma |
| 46 Sqn | 15 Aug 1954–15 Jul 1959 | Meteor,<br>Javelin |
| 54 Sqn | 28 Jun 1946–27 Apr 1953; | Vampire, |

Chinook of 7 Squadron; the airfield is now the RAF's main Support Helicopter base.

| | 29 Jul 1953–13 Jul 1959 | Meteor,<br>Hunter |
| 66 Sqn | 15 Sep 1961–26 May 1962 | Belvedere |
| 72 Sqn | 1 Feb 1947–22 Mar 1950;<br>15 Nov 1961–16 Apr 1981 | Vampire,<br>Belvedere,<br>Wessex |
| 130 Sqn | 23 Jul 1946–1 Feb 1947 | Spitfire |
| 225 Sqn | 23 May 1960–15 Nov 1963 | Whirlwind |
| 230 Sqn | 30 May 1960–14 Jan 1964;<br>1 Jan 1965–10 Mar 1965;<br>25 Nov 1966–10 Mar 1969;<br>1 Jan 1972–14 Oct 1980 | Twin<br>Pioneer,<br>Whirlwind,<br>Puma |
| 247 Sqn | 27 Jun 1946–27 Apr 1953;<br>29 Jul 1953–31 Dec 1957 | Vampire,<br>Hunter,<br>Meteor |
| 436 Sqn | 4 Apr 1946–22 Jun 1946 | Dakota |
| BTU | 4 Jul 1960–15 Sep 1961 | Belvedere |
| 38 Gp CF | 17 May 1960–15 May 1972 | various |
| 38 Gp SU | 26 Jun 1962–1 Dec 1964 | |
| TCF | 1 Jan 1963–Aug 1964 | Twin<br>Pioneer |
| Wessex TU | 1 Jul 1963–27 Jan 1964 | Wessex |
| 1310 Flt | 23 Jul 1964–1 Sep 1964 | Whirlwind |
| SRCU | Aug 1964–1 Jul, 1967 | Belvedere,<br>Wessex |
| HOCF | 1 Jul 1967–1 May 1971 | Wessex,<br>Puma |
| ATS | 1 May 1971–1 Jan 1972 | Wessex |
| 240 OCU | 29 Dec 1971–1 Oct 1993 | Wessex,<br>Puma |
| SHTTU | 1993– | |

## MEMORIALS

Bell in church acquired by 4 Sqn at Gallipoli in 1923.

# PENSHURST

**County:** Kent

**UTM/Grid:** OS map 188–TQ522442
**Lat/Long:** N51°10.6 E000°10.5
**Nearest Town:** Tonbridge 4 miles to north-east

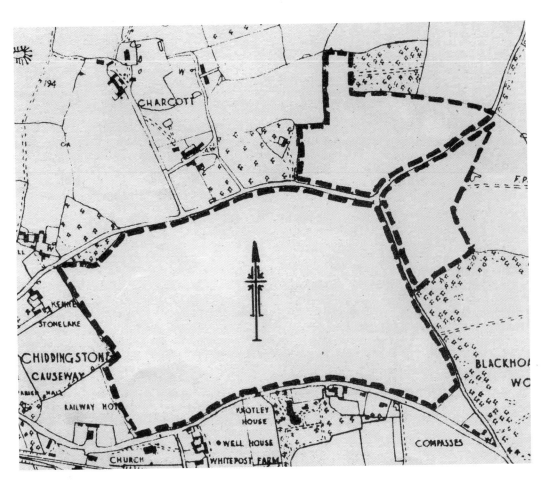

## HISTORY

Penshurst was one of those delightful grass-airfields that dotted southern England and had both a military and civil use – enhanced in this case by a backdrop provided by Knotley House. The site, some two miles north of the village after which it was named, was first used in the latter part of World War One, when a 72-acre area was adopted as a Landing Ground for instructional purposes. The sole occupant during this period was No.2 Wireless School, which formed here in November 1917 and used a small fleet of DH6 aircraft for a one-week course of instruction in W/T procedures. In addition to the lush grass landing-ground, two hangars, each 130ft × 60ft, were erected and

personnel accommodated in tents, a few wooden huts or in local buildings; no doubt the officers were entertained in the Hall. The school was reasonable busy and the airfield was also used as storage depot for wireless material. Run-down started when the war ended; the school finally disbanded in March 1919, leading to closure and dismantling of the airfield.

There appears to have been some private use of the field in the late-1920s and early 1930s (when it was also a polo pitch), although records are scant; it was not until the middle of World War Two that the military returned. Tomahawks of 268 Squadron spent a few days here in August 1941, so the airfield must

# AIRFIELD DATA DEC 1944

| | | | | |
|---|---|---|---|---|
| Command: | RAF Fighter Command | | Runway surface: | Grass |
| Function: | Landing Ground | | Hangars: | nil |
| Runways: | N/S 800yd | | Dispersals: | nil |
| | E/W 400yd | | Personnel: | Officers – 26 |
| | 270 deg 2,000 × 50yd | | | Other Ranks – 166 |

have been at least temporarily re-activated by then, although it was never much more than a grass strip and no significant development took place. Penshurst's World War Two usage was limited to Army Co-operation units and, after this brief visit by Tomahawks, the main type to use this strip was the Auster, with 653 Squadron taking up residence in September 1942. A number of other Auster units used Penshurst before it was finally abandoned in March 1945.

## UNITS

### Pre-1919

| | | |
|---|---|---|
| 2 WS | 8 Nov 1917–23 Mar 1919 | various |

### 1939–1945

| | | |
|---|---|---|
| 268 Sqn | 4–8 Aug 1941 | Tomahawk |
| 653 Sqn | 7 Sep 1942–17 Aug 1943; | Auster |
| | 17 Sep 1943–27 Jun 1944 | |
| 661 Sqn | 27 Jun 1944–7 Aug 1944 | Auster |
| 664 Sqn | 2 Feb 1945–23 Mar 1945 | Auster |

# PORTSMOUTH

**County:** Hampshire

**UTM/Grid:** OS map 196–SU670035
**Lat/Long:** N50°49.6 W001°03.0
**Nearest Town:** Portsmouth centre 2 miles to south-west

The camouflaged Airspeed factory on the edge of Portsmouth airfield.

## HISTORY

On 2 July 1932, the municipal airport for Portsmouth opened on a 275-acre site two miles from the city centre, fulfilling an ambition that dated back to the early 1920s. The airfield comprised a large, well-drained grass area with one large hangar and a terminal building and, although a commercial service was soon in operation, it was the arrival of the aircraft manufacturer Airspeed later in the year that was to prove more significant. Over the next few years a variety of carriers, such as Jersey Airlines, and private flying operations, such as the Yapton Aero Club, used Portsmouth but with mixed fortunes. With the out-break of World War Two the airport was requisitioned by the Air Ministry, all civil flying stopped and the technical staff re-organized to form Portsmouth Aviation, which, in due course, undertook repair and overhaul of a variety of RAF aircraft. This became part of the Civil Repair Organization and was one of three CRO companies at Portsmouth, the bulk of the work being component manufacture, in addition to the building of Oxfords and Kirby Cadets.

When Airspeed had moved to Portsmouth it was a struggling company but, on 26 June 1934, the

The Airspeed Oxford – the 'Oxbox' – was one the most important training aircraft of World War Two.

Airspeed Envoy made its first flight and the fortunes of the company were about to change. The twin-engined Envoy was aimed at the civil market and acquired a few orders, but of greater importance was the decision to develop a dual-controlled version: the Airspeed Oxford was duly born and the first true prototype flew on 19 June 1937. By the time first deliveries were made that November, the factory complex was being extended to cope with an increasing number of orders; the creation of this excellent trainer coincided with the RAF's desperate late-1930s Expansion Programme. The 'Oxbox', along with the Anson, was to play a central role in aircrew training for World War Two; for that reason alone, Airspeed and the Portsmouth factory deserve a place in British aviation annals. A number of other Airspeed designs emerged before the design team was moved to Hatfield, this move in part being dictated by an attack on Portsmouth on 11 July 1940; although little damage was caused, it was considered too risky to keep the valuable design team in place, although other elements, such as the drawing office, remained at Portsmouth.

By the time production ceased, in July 1945, the factory had produced 4,411 Oxfords and, in addition, had undertaken work on the Horsa glider, including flight trials. Production didn't end after the war and Airspeed was able to convert the Oxford into a successful six-seat passenger-aircraft, achieving a market for converted Oxfords and new-build aircraft. In the early 1950s the Airspeed name was lost when it officially became part of de Havilland and the factory worked on aircraft such as the Ambassador (which bore the Airspeed title), as well as a number of DH products, such as the Comet and Vampire. The factory was eventually closed in the mid-1960s.

Interest in re-developing the city's commercial airport continued post-war and, when the site was de-requisitioned in June 1949, commercial operations returned with a number of small airlines. For the next twenty years the airport was moderately successful but, in the absence of hard runways, it was always going to struggle and by the late-1960s all the significant carriers had moved their operations elsewhere. By 1970 the council was determined to close the airport and this finally happened on 31 December 1973; a sad end to a once-important aircraft-manufacturing site and a civil airport that could have been a success if the right levels of political interest and investment had been available.

A number of airfield buildings, including the control tower and terminal, survive but the grass airfield itself has now vanished under development.

## UNITS

### 1939–1945

| | | |
|---|---|---|
| 163 GS | 1944–Sep 1946 | Cadet |

# PULBOROUGH (Parham Park)

**County:** West Sussex

**UTM/Grid:** OS map 197–TQ072147
**Lat/Long:** N50°55.3 W000°28.6
**Nearest Town:** Storrington 1 mile to south-east

## HISTORY

This 1930s private airfield, sometimes known as Parham Park, was requisitioned in July 1940 as a dispersal/Emergency Landing Ground for Tangmere. There is little record of usage but some suggestion that it may also have been used by Air Observation Post Austers in the latter part of the war.

# RAMSGATE

**County:** Kent

**UTM/Grid:** OS map 179–TR375673
**Lat/Long:** N51°21.3 E001°24.6
**Nearest Town:** Northern outskirts of Ramsgate

## HISTORY

There was no significant military use of this small airfield adjacent to Ramsgate, but it was allocated to Manston as a scatter field in 1940, with that airfield's fighters making use of the site from time to time. There had been a Landing Ground authorized for the Ramsgate area in World War One for Home Defence use, but nothing appears to have been done and the first definite presence of aviation was in the 1930s. As a private airfield, Ramsgate Airport, the site was used by the Thanet Aero Club and it also hosted a number of RAF Summer Camps, as well as being part of the Civil Air Guard. With the scatter-field requirement at an end after the Battle of Britain, Ramsgate Airport was taken out of use and obstructed.

The airport eventually re-opened in 1953 and a number of commercial operators used the site between this date and 1968, when it finally closed its doors.

## UNITS

No specific units

# REDHILL

**County:** Surrey

**UTM/Grid:** OS map 187–TQ300475
**Lat/Long:** N51°12.54 W000°08.22
**Nearest Town:** Redhill 2 miles to north-west

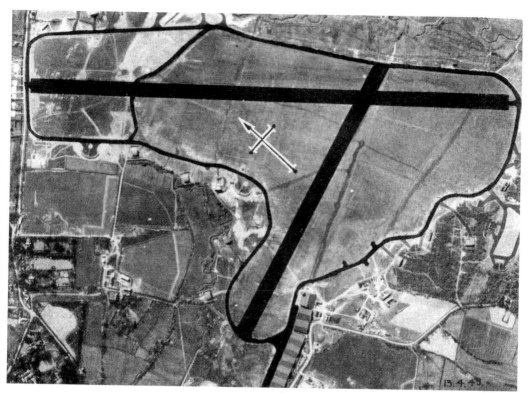

## HISTORY

Another of the pre-war flying-training bases in this region, Redhill was home to No.15 EFTS at the outbreak of war. The airfield had been developed in the 1930s for private flying, the Redhill Flying Club being the main user, although it was also used by Imperial Airways as an alternate for London/Croydon Airport. An ERFTS had formed here in July 1937 for pilot training, using a variety of aircraft including Moths and Harts. The School was renamed in September 1939, as all such schools were, but it continued to be operated by British Air Transport Ltd. The location and facilities – which included a variety of small 'civil' hangars and other buildings – were considered suitable for training to continue after the start of the war and the school was now primarily using Magisters, although a number of Battles were acquired in early 1940, when it incorporated the Polish Grading and Testing Flight. The EFTS was soon so busy that a Relief Landing Ground was

required and, in January 1940, authority was given to requisition land at Bysshe Court, west of Lingfield. However, in March, this plan was cancelled and Redhill was allocated Penshurst as an RLG. With the threat of German attack on airfields in southern England, the decision was taken to move training units to less vulnerable locations and the EFTS duly moved, in June 1940, to Kingstown, Carlisle.

Redhill now passed into full RAF control and became an operational station, its first occupants being 16 Squadron's Lysanders, although this was for only a few weeks. This pattern of short-term deployments was to hold true for the airfield for the rest of the war, as a large number of fighter squadrons operated from its grass surfaces. Various improvements were made to the airfield: a hardened perimeter track was laid, from which dispersal points sprang, and a number of Blister hangars were erected. On-base accommodation was always in short supply, so use

# AIRFIELD DATA DEC 1944

| | | | |
|---|---|---|---|
| Command: | RAF Fighter Command | Runway surface: | Army Track |
| Function: | Operational | Hangars: | 9 × Civil, 8 × Blister |
| Runways: | 087 deg 1,567yd | Dispersals: | 12 × Frying Pan (50ft), 12 × Blenheim |
| | 019 deg 1,057yd | Personnel: | Officers – 30 |
| | | | Other Ranks – 333 |

*No WAAF accommodation was available and use was made of requisitioned property.*

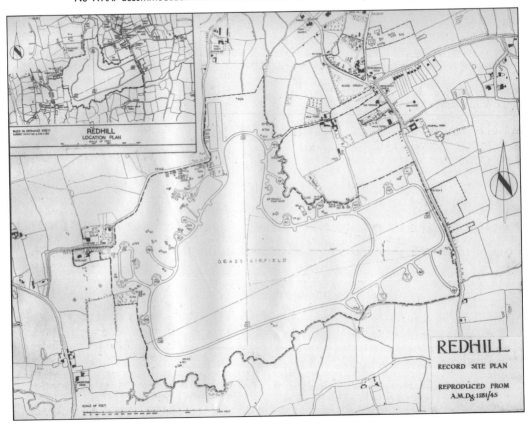

had to be made of local buildings, either requisitioned or under contract. The grass airfield was also extended, in order to give longer runs for types such as the Blenheim, but it was always a restricted area.

Spitfires were the commonest type to be seen at Redhill and, at times, the airfield was very busy: for example, when five squadrons were based here for the August 1942 Dieppe operation. At some point, probably during 1943, the grass strips were converted to surfaced strips by adding Army Tracking. In early 1943 'Z Group' formed at Redhill for *Spartan*, the major exercise designed to test concepts of army support and squadron mobility, for which purpose the HQ of No.83 Group also formed and operated at Redhill in April. However, the main fighter period

Gladiator of 615 Squadron at Redhill in May 1940.
(Andy Thomas)

was over by late-1943, although a number of Mustang squadrons used Redhill into early 1944, and the remainder of its war was spent with support units: the most significant of these was the Support Unit for No.83 Group, part of the 2nd Tactical Air Force. This type of GSU had an important role to play in converting pilots to type and, thus, providing a steady stream of replacement pilots to the tactical squadrons. Other flying units at Redhill in 1944 and 1945 were responsible for supporting anti-aircraft units, either as calibrators or 'targets'. These latter roles continued to the end of the war but, by late-1945, the RAF had little further interest in Redhill. However, in 1948, British Air Transport was once more operating an RAF contract, as No.15 RFS, using a small number of instructors for reserve-pilot training. At the same time private flying had returned to Redhill and, when the RFS disbanded the future of the airfield lay with this commercial activity. Private flying recommenced in 1947 but was suspended in 1954 as it appeared that the airfield was not viable. However, flying returned in 1959 with the Tiger Club and, the following year, Bristow Helicopters.

Redhill carved a niche for itself not only with private owners and clubs but also with a number of specialist helicopter-operators, the most significant of which was Bristow. The airfield later became well known for its international helicopter show – Helitech – although in recent years this has moved to Duxford. Redhill Aerodrome (EGKR) (www.redhillaerodrome.com) retains much of its wartime layout and is still grass with hard taxiways; there are three marked-strips – two oriented 08/26, the longest being 900 yards, and one 01/19 at 850 yards. As it is a busy helicopter location there is also a heli-strip and a number of heli-pads.

Spitfire of 457 Squadron at dispersal; the Squadron spent two months here in 1942.

## Decoy Sites

| Q | Lower Beeding | TQ236299 |
| Q | South Godstone | TQ336476 |

## Units

### HQ Units at Redhill

| No.50 (AC) Wing | 9 Jun 1940–6 Aug 1940 | 4, 13 Sqn |
| No.83 Gp | 1–23 Apr 1943 | |
| No.126 Airfield | 4 Jul 1943–6 Aug 1943 | 401, 411, 412 Sqn |
| No.39 (R) Wing | 1 Aug 1943–1 Apr 1944 | 231, 400, 414 Sqn |

### 1939–1945

| 1 Sqn | 1 May 1941–1 Jul 1941 | Hurricane |
| 16 Sqn | 2–29 Jun 1940 | Lysander |
| 66 Sqn | 10–13 Aug 1943 | Spitfire |
| 116 Sqn | 5 Sep 1944–2 May 1945 | Oxford, |
| | | Anson |
| 131 Sqn | 16 Aug 1943–17 Sep 1943 | Spitfire |
| 219 Sqn | 12 Oct 1940–10 Dec 1940 | Blenheim, Beaufighter |
| 231 Sqn | 15 Oct 1943–15 Jan 1944 | Mustang |
| 258 Sqn | 1–14 Jun 1941 | Hurricane |
| 287 Sqn | 20 Jan 1945–3 May 1945 | various |
| 303 Sqn | 15–20 Aug 1942 | Spitfire |
| 310 Sqn | 16–21 Aug 1942 | Spitfire |
| 312 Sqn | 1–8 Jul 1942; 16–20 Aug 1942 | Spitfire |
| 340 Sqn | 1–7 Apr 1942 | Spitfire |
| 350 Sqn | 31 Jul 1942–23 Sep 1942 | Spitfire |
| 400 Sqn | 15 Oct 1943–2 Dec 1943; 30 Dec 1943–18 Feb 1944 | Mustang |
| 402 Sqn | 31 May 1942–29 Jun 1942; 6 Jul 1942–13 Aug 1942 | |
| 414 Sqn | 15 Oct 1943–3 Nov 1943 | Mustang |
| 416 Sqn | 23 Sep 1942–1 Feb 1943+ | Spitfire |
| 421 Sqn | 23 Mar 1943–17 May 1943+ | Spitfire |
| 452 Sqn | 21 Oct 1941–14 Jan 1942 | Spitfire |
| 457 Sqn | 23 Mar 1942–31 May 1942 | Spitfire |
| 485 Sqn | 1 Jul 1941–21 Oct 1941 | Spitfire |
| 504 Sqn | 14 Aug 1943–19 Sep 1943 | Spitfire |
| 602 Sqn | 14 Jan 1942–4 Mar 1942; 13 May 1942–17 Jul 1942 | Spitfire |
| 611 Sqn | 20 Jul 1942–23 Sep 1942 | Spitfire |
| 110 Sqn RCAF | 5 Jul 1940–1 Sep 1940 | Lysander |
| 15 ERFTS | 1 Jul 1937–3 Sep 1939 | various |
| 15 EFTS | 3 Sep 1939–2 Jun 1940 | Magister, Battle |
| 83 Gp CF | 8 Apr 1943–15 Apr 1944 | |
| 83 Gp SU | 1 Mar 1944–25 Jun 1944 | |
| 1310 Flt | 18 May 1944–25 Jun 1944 | Anson |
| 1 ADF | 12 Oct 1944–14 Feb 1945 | |
| 4 OADU | 22 May 1944–26 Jun 1944 | Anson |

### Post-1945

| 15 RFS | 1 Apr 1948–20 Jun 1945 | Tiger Moth |

# ROCHESTER

**County:** Kent

**UTM/Grid:** OS map 178–TQ744646
**Lat/Long:** N51°21.2 E000°30.2
**Nearest Town:** Rochester 2½ miles to north-west

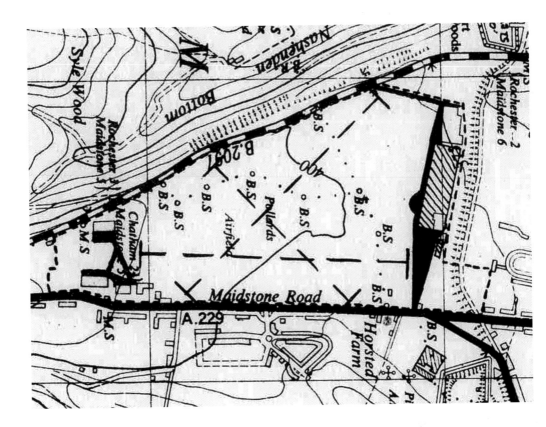

## HISTORY

Rochester Airport sits on a 400ft hill overlooking the River Medway and 500 years ago this was a vital area for the defence of Britain, the naval dockyards at Chatham being one of the main bases for the 'wooden walls' of the Royal Navy, England's main defence. Sixty years ago Kent was at the heart of the Battle of Britain and, as Rochester Airport was home to the Shorts aircraft factory, it was very much on the Luftwaffe target list.

In 1913, aircraft manufacturer Short Bros acquired land near the bridge at Rochester and, by the following year, their Cuxton Works was turning out one of the best floatplanes of World War One, the Short 184.

The end of the war brought a sudden end to the lucrative military contracts and the company turned its attention to producing buses and cars, as well as continuing to maintain its interest in aviation. However, with its track record of floatplanes, Short Bros continued to develop maritime types and, by the early 1930s, the flying-boat business was given a boost with the success of the Empire Class boats – from which would grow the Sunderland, one of Coastal Command's main types for World War Two.

Shorts were also involved in land-based aircraft and, in 1933, an opportunity arose to acquire an aerodrome at Rochester, when the council purchased land on the ride above the city for a Municipal Airport. A lease was offered to Short Bros on the condition that private and commercial flying was permitted, to which the company readily agreed. The first hangar was erected the following year, after which development was rapid, with hangars and other buildings sprouting on the triangular site. Other companies moved in, as did private owners, and by 1938 the well-established airfield was quite busy, especially so when No.23 ERFTS formed in April that year for RAF and, from July, Fleet Air Arm training, using a variety of

Short Cromarty flying boat at the Shorts works.

aircraft types. The training unit departed when war broke out the following year and, truly, it was never an appropriate location, as Shorts had become increasingly busy since the four-engined Stirling made its first flight on 14 May 1939 – a disaster as the aircraft crashed on landing. Despite this setback, the Stirling was the first of Bomber Command's new 'heavies' to enter service and it played an important part in the development of the Command's offensive capability – reason enough for Rochester to have a place in the annals of World War Two.

Meanwhile, the airfield had received its first accurate attack by the Luftwaffe when, on 15 August 1940, the bombers destroyed a number of aircraft and production facilities. The damage was great enough – and the continued threat real enough – for production of this important bomber to be dispersed to other airfields and, for almost two years, Rochester was reasonably quiet in terms of flying activity, its main role being that of an emergency airfield. However, by 1942, the threat of attack had receded and production was geared up once more; by the end of the war the Rochester factory had produced 536 Stirlings. During the immediate post-war period the factory produced one new prototype – the Sturgeon – before it was closed and all work transferred to the Belfast facility.

March 1946 brought a return of RAF training, with the arrival of No.24 EFTS from Sealand, using Tiger Moths for pilot training and becoming No.24 Reserve Flying School in May 1947. A number of other training and military units used the airfield during this period and, in 1954, Shorts re-started aircraft work, although this was for modification work on a range of types, such as Beaufighters and Mosquitoes. By 1959 the aircraft work was over but three years later a new aerospace company took over the factory; Marconi Avionics went on to have a long association with Rochester Airport, including some flying operations.

Commercial flying resumed in the 1950s and, by the early 1960s, Channel Airways had established a number of routes; however, the constraints placed on airfields during the 1960s meant that Rochester was no longer suitable and all such operations had ceased by 1967. Private flying continued, as did the presence of Marconi and a number of other companies. The airfield lease reverted to the council in 1979 and for a while it looked as if they would close the airfield. There was a reprieve when a consortium led by Marconi took on management of the site. For the past twenty years the airfield has never been totally secure, with some local pressure for its closure: the latest consultation paper suggesting development for other uses was debated in 1999. The aerospace company involvement eventually became BAE and they still occupy part of the site. Management is now in the hands of Rochester Airport plc and the main basis of the airfield is that of private flying and flying training. Rochester Airport (EGTO) operates two main grass-strips – 02/20 at 830 yards and 16/34 at around 800 yards – but its future is still not certain and recently only a temporary lease extension has been granted.

## DECOY SITES

| Q | Chatham | TQ779638 |

## UNITS

### 1919–1938

| 23 ERFTS | 1 Apr 1938–3 Sep 1939 | various |

### 1939–1945

| 16 Gp CF | 3 Sep 1939–1941 | |
| 168 GS | 1944–1949 | Cadet |

### Post-1945

| 24 EFTS | 1 Mar 1946–7 May 1947 | Tiger Moth |
| 24 RFS | 7 May 1947–31 Mar 1953 | various |

## MEMORIALS

EE Lightning ZF581, painted as a 56 Sqn aircraft, was dedicated as a gate guard on 15 Oct 2003, the ceremony being performed by ex-test-pilot Jimmy Dell.

The Stirling bomber was the first of Bomber Command's new four-engined 'heavies' to enter service.

# SELSEY

**County:** West Sussex

**UTM/Grid:** OS map 197–SZ865957
**Lat/Long:** N50°45.08 W000°46.24
**Nearest Town:** Chichester 5 miles to the north

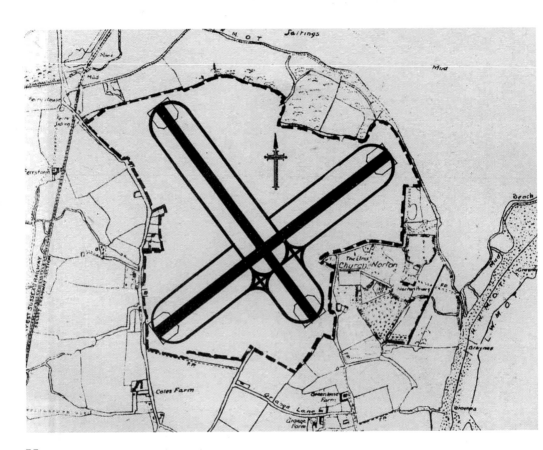

## HISTORY

A 1930s private airfield, Selsey was included in the 1942 survey for Advanced Landing Grounds and was duly requisitioned in July that year. Work started in early 1943 and the construction unit had few problems, other than the usual filling of ditches and removing of hedges to make room for two runways laid out in the preferred cruciform pattern. A number of local buildings were requisitioned, such as Norton Priory for use as a HQ, but, as with all ALGs, the basic concept was one of mobile operations and tents were to be the main accommodation. The initial phase of construction was over by spring 1943 and in late-May/early June the Spitfires of 65 Squadron and the Typhoons of 245 Squadron arrived from Fairlop. As part of the re-organization of tactical air-power, the squadrons became No.121 Airfield and for the

next few weeks tested their capability for mobile operations by operating from the minimal facilities of Selsey. Both squadrons soon departed and the airfield entered its second phase of construction with perimeter tracks, Sommerfeld Track hardstands and Blister hangars being provided. Selsey ALG re-opened in spring 1944, in time to receive its next units, the three Spitfire squadrons of No.135 Airfield. The Spitfire IXs were soon operating as fighter-bombers over Europe as part of the growing Allied air offensive and, whilst this remained their primary role in the D-Day period, they, like most Spitfire units, flew defensive beachhead patrols on 6 June itself and for the next few weeks; indeed, they were one of the few fighter-units to see the Luftwaffe on D-Day and 349 Squadron claimed a number of successes. When the

# AIRFIELD DATA DEC 1944

| | | | |
|---|---|---|---|
| Command: | RAF Fighter Command | Runway surface: | Sommerfeld Track |
| Function: | Advanced Landing Ground | Hangars: | 4 × Extra Over Blister |
| Runways: | 045 deg 1,400yd | Dispersals: | Temporary Sommerfeld Track hardstands |
| | 135 deg 1,250yd | Personnel: | Other Ranks – Tented camp |

Spitfire IX MH358 of 65 Squadron at Selsey, September 1943. (Andy Thomas)

The mixed (many French) aircrew of 340 Squadron, part of No.145 (French) Wing.

Location plan showing the concentration of airfields in this area.

Wing departed at the end of June its place was taken by the Free French No.145 Wing, also equipped with Spitfires; this unit maintained the same sortie pattern as its predecessor and operated from Selsey until early August. By mid-August everyone had gone but, unusually for an ALG, the airfield was not finally released until the war ended.

## UNITS

### HQ Units at Selsey

| | | |
|---|---|---|
| No.121 Airfield | 31 May 1943–1 Jul 1943 | 65, 245 Sqn |
| No.135 Airfield/(F) Wing | 11 Apr 1944–30 Jun 1944 | 222, 349, 485 Sqn |
| No.145 (French) (F) Wing | 1 Jul 1944–6 Aug 1944 | 329, 340, 341 Sqn |

### 1939–1945

| | | |
|---|---|---|
| 33 Sqn | 6–19 Aug 1944 | Spitfire |
| 65 Sqn | 31 May 1943–1 Jul 1943 | Spitfire |
| 74 Sqn | 17–24 Jul 1944 | Spitfire |
| 222 Sqn | 11 Apr 1944–30 Jun 1944; 6–19 Aug 1944 | Spitfire |
| 245 Sqn | 1–30 Jun 1943 | Typhoon |
| 329 Sqn | 1 Jul 1944–6 Aug 1944 | Spitfire |
| 340 Sqn | 1 Jul 1944–14 Aug 1944 | Spitfire |
| 341 Sqn | 1 Jul 1944–6 Aug 1944 | Spitfire |
| 349 Sqn | 11 Apr 1944–30 Jun 1944; 6–19 Aug 1944 | Spitfire |
| 485 Sqn | 7 Apr 1944–30 Jun 1944; 7–19 Aug 1944 | Spitfire |

## MEMORIALS

Plaque on a plinth at the ALG as part of a heritage trail.

# SHOREHAM

**UTM/Grid:** OS map 198–TQ203055
**Lat/Long:** N50°50.09 W000°17.24
**Nearest Town:** Western edge of Shoreham

**County:** West Sussex

26.2.43.

S. RLY.

## HISTORY

The civil airport at Shoreham was opened on 20 June 1911 and is still active today as a busy south-coast airport, for private flying and limited commercial-operations. Located on the west side of the town and near the coast, the airfield comprised a large grass-area bounded to the south by the main railway line and to the east by the river Adur, the former providing a backdrop for the series of sheds that were soon erected on site and the latter doing nothing to help the waterlogging problem that plagued Shoreham for much of its history. The airfield saw a number of private operators and flying schools, including the Avro Flying School, use its grass over the next few years and it made the news for its part in a number of air events. However, in August 1914, it was requisitioned by the War Office for military use as a training base, the initial hope being to use the established training-schools. This proved impractical and, in

January 1915, the airfield became home to No.3 Reserve Squadron and it was this unit that dominated Shoreham for the next three years. As usual with these training units, it operated a diverse fleet of types, with at least thirteen types, from Maurice Farman Shorthorns to Sopwith Camels, being recorded. Pupil pilots flew a short course and were then despatched to specialist schools or direct to squadrons, depending on how desperate was the need for pilots. At least two operational units, 14 Squadron and 86 Squadron, formed here, both taking part of the training-squadron strength as their nucleus of aircraft and experience. No.14 Squadron formed on 3 February 1915 and, after a few weeks of training, moved to Hounslow prior to being shipped out to the Middle East, whilst 86 Squadron didn't form until 1 September 1917 and departed the same month for Wye. In May 1916 the Reserve Squadron

## AIRFIELD DATA DEC 1944

| Command: | RAF Fighter Command | Runway surface: | Grass |
|---|---|---|---|
| Function: | Operational Satellite | Hangars: | 4 × Over Blister |
| Runways: | NW/SE 1,200yd | Dispersals: | 4 × Single-engine, 2 × Twin-engine |
| | NE/SW 1,150yd | Personnel: | Other Ranks – 614 |
| | 270 deg 2,000 × 50yd | | |

Hurricanes of 3 Squadron operated from Shoreham during the Dieppe Raid of August 1942.

had also given birth to a second Reserve Squadron, although this was only a nucleus, as this unit was destined for service overseas.

Having trained a great many pilots at Shoreham, No.3 Training Squadron, as it was by then, departed in July 1918, its place being taken by the South Eastern Area Flying Instructors School, this unit running short courses using Avro 504s and Service types. A third operational squadron passed through Shoreham when 94 Squadron spent a few weeks here in mid-1918, continuing its training before equipping with the SE5a and moving to France. The Flying Instructors School closed in March 1919 and the last squadrons had disbanded by early 1920. The final two units, 82 and 123 Squadrons, were also designated as Nos. 1 and 2 Squadrons of No.1 Wing, Canadian Air Force; they had moved to Shoreham from Upper Heyford as part of the post-war plan for the Canadian Air Force. A change of plan led to the disbandment of the Wing and its squadrons and the final closure of Shoreham at the end of 1921.

A new airfield was established, close to the original site in 1926, for civil flying by the Southern Aero Club and, over the next decade, improvements were made and other organizations began to use what had become a well-established airfield.

In the immediate pre-war period Shoreham became home to No.16 E&RFTS (Elementary and Refresher Flying Training School) and a flying club – both of which were closed at the outbreak of war. The airfield was subsequently used to support civilian air-routes operated by neutral countries – for example, KLM, Sabena and DDL – in order to keep them clear of Croydon. This role had ended by June 1940 and Shoreham was requisitioned by the Air Ministry for use as an advanced airfield by squadrons of the Tangmere Sector.

The Fighter Interception Unit arrived in August and was joined in October by No.422 Flight, another night-fighter outfit. This was short-lived and, by early 1941, the airfield was being improved and extended, waterlogging still being a major problem. The airfield was extended to the west and a number of new buildings, including Blister hangars, were

Lysander of 225 Squadron, one of a number of Lysander units to use this south-coast airfield.

erected. It is surprising that, given Shoreham's exposed coastal position, it received little attention from the Luftwaffe, although a hit-and-run raider destroyed one of the old hangars.

The next permanent occupants were the Lysanders of the Air-Sea Rescue Flight and this role was one that Shoreham held for some time, the Flight growing into a detachment of 277 Squadron with Lysanders and Walruses, the former being replaced by Defiants the following year. Other units used the airfield during this period, including fighter detachments supporting the August 1942 Dieppe operation. The ASR detachment remained Shoreham's main unit, but the airfield's strength was boosted in April 1943 with the creation of No.7 Anti-Aircraft Practice Camp (AAPC); this gave the airfield a new role – training RAF Regiment gunners, with Lysanders providing the banner towing; the unit was re-designated No.1631 Flight in June. The Flight moved out in December and a few months later the main grass runway, 03/21, was given a metal-track surface to ease the problems of wear and tear and waterlogging. Shoreham had also been receiving an increasing number of battle-damaged aircraft diverting to the first usable airfield – the American heavy-bombers causing a particular problem. In addition to its ASR and APC work, the airfield also played host from time to time to fighter detachments, for both training and operations. After an intensive phase in the D-Day period, the ASR aircraft being kept particularly busy, Shoreham entered a run-down period

from August 1944, the Station Headquarters being disbanded in September, and the airfield was reduced to Care and Maintenance. However, January 1945 brought a new lease of life with the arrival of a detachment from the Central Fighter Establishment, but this was very short-lived and Shoreham was pretty much deserted.

Shoreham was transferred to the Ministry of Civil Aviation on 12 March 1946 and it had no further military involvement; nevertheless, in the almost sixty years since then, Shoreham Airport has been a fascinating place, with its variety of flying clubs, private owners, commercial operations and, most interestingly, as home to Miles Aircraft. The aircraft manufacturers moved in during the early 1950s and a number of new designs made first flights from the Sussex airfield, sadly none of which were a great success commercially. Miles was absorbed by Beagle Aircraft and a new factory was erected for production of types such as the Beagle B.206. Sadly this venture, too, collapsed in 1970 but Shoreham survived and eventually prospered as private flying entered a growth phase. From 1971 the airfield was Shoreham Municipal Airport and, ten years late, it was at last given a hard runway when 03/21 was surfaced. Shoreham Airport (EGKA) is now operated by the Brighton, Hove and Worthing Joint Municipal Airport Committee and remains a very active airfield with one asphalt runway and two grass-strips – the notes for the airfield still carry the warning that 'after heavy rain standing water may persist on grass areas'.

# UNITS

## Pre-1919

| | | |
|---|---|---|
| 14 Sqn | 3 Feb 1915–May 1915 | Longhorn |
| 81 Sqn | 2 May 1919–28 Jan 1920 | Dolphin |
| 82 Sqn | 15 Feb 1919–May 1919 | FK8 |
| 86 Sqn | 1–17 Sep 1917 | various |
| 94 Sqn | 27 Jul 1918–19 Aug 1918 | various |
| 123 Sqn | 31 Mar 1919–5 Feb 1920 | DH9a |
| 3 RS | 21 Jan 1915–15 Jul 1918 | various |
| 21 RS | May 1916 | various |
| SEA FIS | Jul 1918–31 Mar 1919 | various |

## 1919–1938

| | | |
|---|---|---|
| 16 ERFTS | 3 Jul 1937–3 Sep 1939 | |
| 6 CANS | 26 May 1938–15 May 1939 | Anson |

## 1939–1945

| | | |
|---|---|---|
| 3 Sqn | 14–21 Aug 1942 | Hurricane |

| | | |
|---|---|---|
| 225 Sqn det | Jul 1940–Jul 1941 | Lysander |
| 245 Sqn det | Dec 1941–Oct 1942 | Hurricane |
| 253 Sqn | 24–30 May 1942 | Hurricane |
| 277 Sqn det | 22 Dec 1941–7 Oct 1944 | Lysander, Walrus, Defiant |
| 345 Sqn | 26 Apr 1944–16 Aug 1944 | Spitfire |
| 667 Sqn det | Dec 1943–Dec 1945 | various |
| 1422 Flt | 14 Oct 1940–9 Dec 1940 | Hurricane |
| ASRF | May 1941–9 Jul 1941; 15 Oct 1941–22 Dec 1941 | Lysander |
| 11 Gp TTF | 20 May 1941–1 Dec 1941 | Lysander |
| 1488 Flt | 1 Dec 1941–9 Feb 1942 | Lysander |
| 7 AAPC | 21 Apr 1943–17 Jun 1943 | Lysander |
| 1631 Flt | 17 Jun 1943–1 Dec 1943 | Defiant, Lysander |
| 1497 Flt | 3 Jul 1943–18 Oct 1943 | Lysander |
| CFE det | 15 Jan 1945–? Mar 1945 | |

# SOBERTON

**County:** Hampshire

**UTM/Grid:** OS map 196–SU620155
**Lat/Long:** N50°56.41 W001°07.33
**Nearest Town:** Bishop's Waltham 4 miles to west

## HISTORY

Soberton airfield was named after the village less than one mile to the north and was laid out in 1940 as a scatter field for Gosport. The 150-acre site near Broom Farm was little more than a group of large fields and had two marked landing-strips oriented north/south and north-west/south-east. There is no record of usage of the airfield during the war, but it remained on the RAF's books and was listed in 1944 as an Emergency Landing Ground and again in the early 1950s for air-dropping trials by the Transport Command Development Flight, as well as a forced-landing field, the latter by Air Service Training at Hamble. It appears to have gone out of use in the late-1950s and been returned to agriculture.

# SOMERTON

**County:** Isle of Wight

**UTM/Grid:** OS map–SZ488944
**Lat/Long:** N50°44.9 W001°18.6
**Nearest Town:** Cowes one mile to north

## HISTORY

In April 1916, flight trials commenced at the new airfield of Somerton on a landplane derivative of the successful Short 184 floatplane; development by White & Co, an Isle of Wight boat builders, led them to develop the airfield close to Cowes – and also to construct a factory in the adjacent fields. They were also building standard Short 184s and these were towed down the river to the East Cowes slipway. White's were not the only users of Somerton and local manufacturer S E Saunders used the airfield for flight testing of Avro 504s. Both manufacturers also developed ideas of their own, although with limited success. The end of the war brought an almost immediate end to aircraft production here, although the airfield (known as Wight to the RAF) remained in use for a short while, a detachment from the RAF's School of Aerial Co-operation having been in residence since September 1918 to work with coastal batteries. The station was finally closed in August 1919.

There may have been some use of the site in the early 1920s for private flying and, by the early 1930s, it was certainly in use by Saunders-Roe as a flight test and delivery airfield. Spartan Aircraft took over the Somerton works in 1931 and produced a number of aircraft, such as the Cruiser, also forming Spartan Air Lines to demonstrate the use of the aircraft. True commercial operations commenced in 1933, with links to Birmingham and Bristol by Railway Air Services. With the outbreak of World War Two it remained in use, primarily for visitors to Saunders-Roe, who still owned the airfield.

Post-1945, the main operator was Somerton Airways but, despite improvements to the airfield by new owners Morgan Aviation in 1948, the main runway being increased to 3,600ft but still grass and an agreement with BEA to operate feeder services to Portsmouth and Southampton, the future for Somerton was always bleak. In January 1951, Hamble's Air Service Training purchased the lease for the airfield but a reduction in the number of students meant that little use could be made of the airfield and it was once more put up for disposal. The land was acquired by Plessey as a factory site and all flying came to an end.

# STAPLEHURST

**County:** Kent

**UTM/Grid:** OS map 188–TQ810432
**Lat/Long:** N51°09.38 E000°35.2
**Nearest Town:** Maidstone 8 miles to north-west

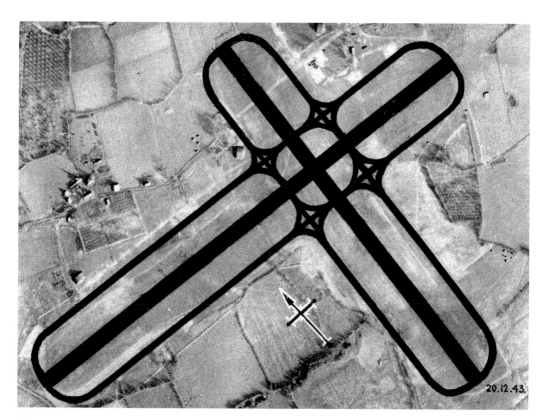

20.12.43.

## HISTORY

Staplehurst was one of a series of Advanced Landing Grounds in Kent, the selection of which took place in 1942, when the RAF was looking at its future requirements for airfields suitable for fighter and fighter-bomber wings of up to three squadrons. Development commenced in January 1943, with a construction unit arriving to prepare the airfield approaches and surfaces and lay two Sommerfeld Track runways. As with all the ALGs, accommodation was to be in tents, although a number of buildings near the airfield were requisitioned. The three squadrons of a Canadian Spitfire Wing, equipped with VBs, flew in at the end of the first week in August 1943 from Redhill and operated from here for two months, departing to Biggin Hill in mid-October. During their time at Staplehurst, the Canadians flew escort and fighter-bomber missions. It was pilots from this Wing that performed the infa-

mous stealing of two Spitfires from Ashford during an evasion exercise! When the Canadians departed, the airfield went into the second phase of construction, during which runways were repaired and strengthened, and perimeter tracks and hardstands were laid although, unlike at most ALGs, no Blister hangars were erected. This work was complete by spring and April 1944 saw the arrival of the IXth Air Force's 363rd Fighter Group from Rivenhall, the Group's P-51s carrying out bomber escort and, as D-Day approached, fighter-bomber missions. The intense operations of early June placed a strain on the airfield but the Mustangs moved to France, to Maupertus, on 1 July, leaving Staplehurst all but deserted. The Sommerfeld Track was lifted and the airfield was de-requisitioned, being handed back for agriculture in January.

# AIRFIELD DATA DEC 1944

| | | | |
|---|---|---|---|
| Command: | RAF Fighter Command | Runway surface: | Sommerfeld Track |
| Function: | Advanced Landing Ground | Hangars: | nil |
| Runways: | 100 deg 1,400yd | Dispersals: | 70 × Sommerfeld |
| | 010 deg 1,100yd | Personnel: | Other Ranks – Tented camp |

Pilots of the 363rd FG; this shot may be when they have moved to France after D-Day.

## UNITS

### HQ Units at Staplehurst

| | | |
|---|---|---|
| No.126 Airfield | 6 Aug 1943–13 Oct 1943 | 401, 411, 412 Sqn |

### 1939–1945

| | | |
|---|---|---|
| 401 Sqn | 7 Aug 1943–13 Oct 1943 | Spitfire |
| 411 Sqn | 7 Aug 1943–13 Oct 1943 | Spitfire |
| 412 Sqn | 8 Aug 1943–14 Oct 1943 | Spitfire |

### USAAF Units

**363rd FG**

| | |
|---|---|
| Squadrons: | 160th, 161st, 162nd FS |
| Aircraft: | P-51 |
| Dates: | Apr 1944–1 Jul 1944 |
| First mission: | 23 Feb 1944 (from Rivenhall) |

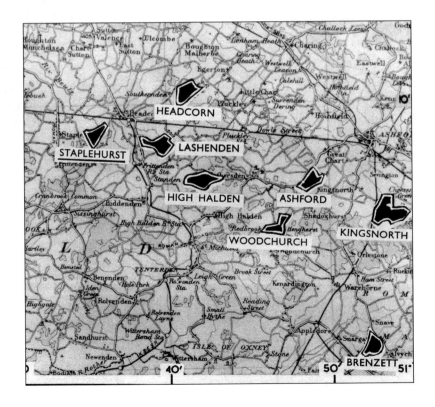

# STONEY CROSS

**UTM/Grid:** OS map 195–SU246113
**Lat/Long:** N50°54.45 W001°39.08
**Nearest Town:** Southampton 11 miles to east

**County:** Hampshire

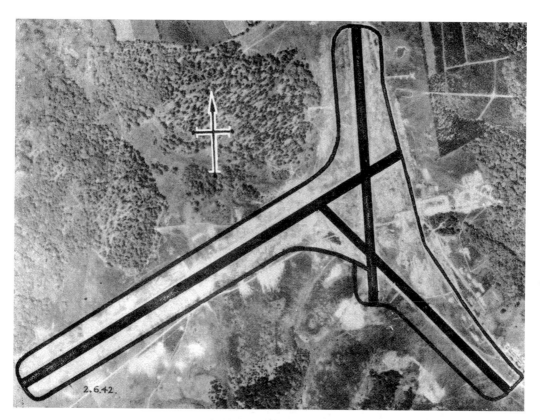

2.6.42.

## HISTORY

Situated on a plateau area west of Southampton, the airfield at Stoney Cross had a varied history and an unusual layout, in part a reflection of its varied usage. The origins of the airfield are a little unclear but it appears to have been laid out as an emergency airfield or satellite by 1942. However, in that year, the decision was taken to improve the airfield and, on 9 November 1942, Stoney Cross re-opened as an Army Co-operation airfield, the Mustangs of 239 Squadron arriving in January the following year. With the formation of No.123 Airfield in February and the arrival of its third squadron in March, the AC Wing was complete, although the same could not be said for the airfield. The main contractor, Wimpey, was still working on the runways – an unusual layout because of the terrain – and other infrastructure and, having taken part in Exercise *Spartan*, the Wing departed to

leave the constructors to finish their work. In June the airfield was transferred to Fighter Command, although it was actually intended for airborne-forces use. The first of the new units, 297 Squadron, moved in from Thruxton in August and, with its Albemarles and Whitleys, undertook a variety of training exercises followed by a number of operations. In November, the squadron gave birth to a new unit, 299 Squadron, and together they began intensive training in day and night paratroop-drops. For some time the Americans had also been using the airfield, including the erection of Hadrian gliders, and, with the departure of the RAF units, the airfield was vacated for use by a new American unit.

The three P-38 squadrons of the 367th Fighter Group moved in during the first week of April and, early the following month, commenced operations.

## AIRFIELD DATA DEC 1944

| | | | |
|---|---|---|---|
| Command: | RAF Transport Command | Runway surface: | Concrete and wood-chippings |
| Function: | Parent Station No.116 Wing | Hangars: | 6 × Blister, 3 × T.2 |
| Runways: | 250 deg 2,000 × 50yd | Dispersals: | 30 × Frying Pan (125ft), 21 × Frying Pan (100ft), 11 × Special Loop |
| | 328 deg 1,520 × 50yd | Personnel: | Officers – 176 (12 WAAF) |
| | 188 deg 1,400 × 50yd | | Other Ranks – 2,270 (383 WAAF) |

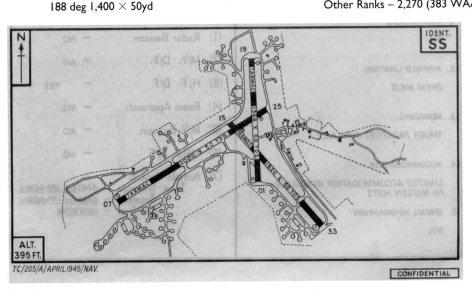

TC/203/A/APRIL 1945/NAV.

Fighter and fighter-bomber missions were flown at an increasing rate as D-Day approached and, on the day itself, the Lightnings were tasked with combat patrol – but they were soon back on fighter-bombing. In early July the Group moved to Ibsley, although a few days later they went on to France. Their place at Stoney was taken by the 387th Bomb Group. The B-26 Marauders of the 387th Bombardment Group had arrived in England in June 1943 and, as part of VIIIth Bomber Command, had commenced operations in August. However, the 387th was transferred to the 9th Air Force and took over Stoney Cross from the P-38s in mid-July 1944. The four squadrons of Marauders were dispersed around the, now quite extensive, airfield and maintained a high level of operations, especially in the period around D-Day. The Group moved to Maupertus on 1 September and the airfield returned to RAF control. The December 1944 survey showed that only runway 32 could be extended, to 2,230yd, but this was 'not recommended as it entails the diversion of the Ringwood to Romsey road'.

The rest of the airfield's career was spent as a transport base, although a detachment of the Heavy Glider Conversion Unit and a number of RAF Regiment squadrons also spent time here. Two Wellington transport squadrons formed in November and Stoney became home to No.116 Wing. The Wellingtons gave way to Dakotas in January and Stirling transports arrived to equip 46 Squadron. Over the next few months aircraft and squadron changed but the Station remained busy, as transport was at a premium. The end of the war did not immediately affect Stoney's pace of operations but it was only a temporary reprieve and only 46 Squadron was left by the end of the year. They eventually moved to Manston in October 1946 and the airfield was put into Care and Maintenance. It was finally declared surplus to requirements in January 1948 and, in the 1950s, was taken over by the Forestry Commission.

Whilst all the main buildings have long vanished, there are substantial traces of perimeter track and dispersals, the former in use as roads and the latter as parking areas now that Stoney Cross is open to the public as a park.

## UNITS

### HQ unit at Stoney Cross
No.123 Airfield       Apr 1943          26, 175, 239 Sqn

### 1939–1945

| | | |
|---|---|---|
| 26 Sqn | 27 Feb 1943–7 Apr 1943 | Mustang |
| 46 Sqn | 9 Jan 1945–11 Oct 1946 | Dakota |
| 175 Sqn | 1 Mar 1943–8 Apr 1943 | Hurricane |
| 232 Sqn | 25 Jan 1944–14 Feb 1945 | Spitfire |
| 239 Sqn | 25 Jan 1943–7 Apr 1943 | Mustang |
| 242 Sqn | 15 Nov 1944–9 Dec 1945 | Spitfire |
| 296 Sqn | 25 Jun 1943–15 Oct 1943 | Albemarle |
| 297 Sqn | 1 Sep 1943–14 Mar 1944 | Albemarle |
| 299 Sqn | 4 Nov 1943–15 Mar 1944 | Ventura, Stirling |
| 1552 RATS | 5 Feb 1946–13 Apr 1946 | Oxford |

### USAAF Units
#### 387th BG

| | |
|---|---|
| Squadrons: | 556th BS, 557th BS, 558th BS, 559th BS |
| Aircraft: | B-26 |
| Dates: | Jul 1944–1 Sep 1944 |
| First mission: | Aug 1943 |
| Last mission: | Apr 1945 (from Clastres) |

#### 367th FBG

| | |
|---|---|
| Squadrons: | 392nd FS, 393rd FS, 394th FS |
| Aircraft: | P-38 |
| Dates: | 5 Apr 1944–6 Jul 1944 |
| First mission: | 9 May 1944 |
| Last mission: | 8 May 1945 (from Frankfurt/ Eschborn) |

The airfield site is now a park; a display panel records its wartime history.

## MEMORIALS

The memorial plaque gives a short history of the airfield alongside a site plan and the badges of the three main users – RAF, USAAF and Airborne.

# SWINGFIELD

**County:** Kent

**UTM/Grid:** OS map 179–TR240448
**Lat/Long:** N51°09.45 E001°12.15
**Nearest Town:** Dover 5 miles to south-east

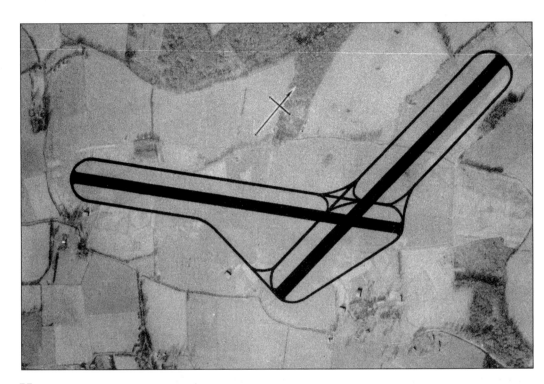

## HISTORY

Swingfield was surveyed in 1942 for use as an Advanced Landing Ground and work commenced in early 1943. However, the new airfield occupied part of an Emergency Landing Ground that had been allocated for use from 1916 to 1918 by 50 Squadron for Home Defence duties. There is no record of this Class 2 Landing Ground being used, although it is likely that aircraft did make occasional use of the site, if only to test it out. With the end of the war, the site reverted to fields and was all but forgotten. There may have been some use of fields in this vicinity in 1940 during the Dunkirk operations, it being suggested that Swordfish operated from here during June 1940. It was as an ALG, however, that Swingfield's record is most secure but, even then, it was an unusual airfield.

Work on the site was slow but, by early summer 1943, two Sommerfeld Track runways had been laid along with two Blister hangars, construction being complete by mid-June. There was no immediate requirement for the airfield and it was not chosen as one of the test ALGs; therefore it was released for grazing whilst further construction work took place. This involved laying perimeter tracks and dispersals (all on the south and east side). Although the original intention was for Swingfield to receive a fighter-bomber Wing for the D-Day period, this plan was changed and the airfield saw only intermittent use during these hectic months of 1944. It was not until August that it truly entered operations – and then as a Coastal Command airfield for use by No.157 (General Reconnaissance) Wing, which comprised 119 Squadron and 819 Squadron. Both units were tasked with anti-shipping work, the Swordfish of 819 specializing in night attack on E-Boats. Most ALGs were daytime only and no provision was made for night flying – so 819 arranged an ad hoc flarepath. The two squadrons moved out to Bircham Newton on 2 October and Swingfield was left abandoned.

The December 1944 survey showed that three run-

## AIRFIELD DATA DEC 1944

| | | | |
|---|---|---|---|
| Command: | RAF Fighter Command | Runway surface: | Sommerfeld Track under grass |
| Function: | Advanced Landing Ground | Hangars: | 4 × Blister |
| Runways: | N/S 1,400 × 52yd | Dispersals: | 50 × Hardcore and gravel |
| | NE/SW 1,600 × 52yd | Personnel: | Other Ranks – Tented camp |
| | 270 deg 2,000 × 50yd | | |

The Fairey Albacore was operated by 119 Squadron as part of a GR Wing in late 1944.

ways, all over 2,000 yards long, could be laid out but that the work would entail 'demolition of a cottage, a farm and building and a garage'. The airfield remained on the books as a Fighter Command ALG until late-April 1945, when it was finally de-requisitioned and returned to agriculture.

## UNITS

**1939–1945**

| | | |
|---|---|---|
| 119 Sqn | 9 Aug 1944–2 Oct 1944 | Albacore |

**FAA Units**

| | | |
|---|---|---|
| 819 Sqn | 7 Aug 1944–2 Oct 1944 | Swordfish |

# TANGMERE

**County:** West Sussex

**UTM/Grid:** OS map 197–SU910060
**Lat/Long:** N50 50.49 W000°42.26
**Nearest Town:** Chichester 2½ miles to west

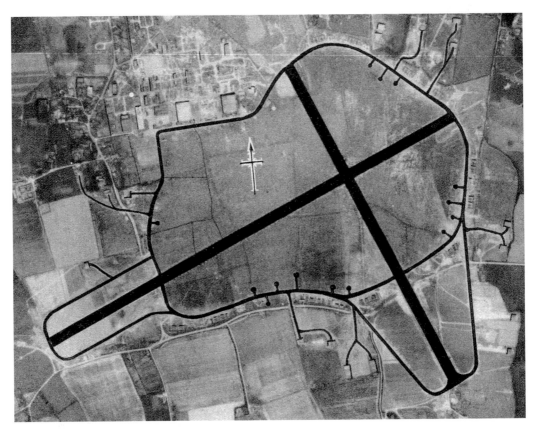

## HISTORY

Tangmere was first used as a Landing Ground in the latter months of World War One, a 200-acre site near Bayley's Farm being requisitioned in September 1917. Development began immediately and the first aircraft arrived at the still incomplete airfield in March the following year, when 92 Squadron moved in with its Pups from Chattis Hill. The squadron stayed until July, when it moved over to France, but Tangmere had already been allocated for development as a Training Depot Station for the United States Air Service and was scheduled to receive Handley Page bombers, for which large hangars were under construction. In the interim, another RAF unit, No.61 TDS, formed here from No.40 Training Squadron but, in September, the Americans took over, personnel arriving from Ford in November.

However, with the end of the war – and still no Handley Page bombers – they soon departed, leaving Tangmere to the RAF TDS. The airfield was quite impressive, as it had a large landing-area, needed for the heavy bombers, and no less than seven General Service Belfast Truss hangars, plus one 'Handley Page shed'. Tangmere's training role continued into 1919, but with a reduced number of students, the airfield was also used for disbanding squadrons returning from France. By late-1919 all flying activity had ceased and the airfield was closed the following year, although retained on the Air Ministry Books.

Tangmere saw little use in the inter-war period, despite the fact that it had re-opened on 1 June 1925 for use by Coastal Area (forerunner of Coastal Command) as a storage facility. The following year

219 Squadron aircrew take a few moments rest; the
Squadron had a Beaufighter detachment here from
October 1940.

the airfield received its first active squadron, when 43
Squadron arrived in December 1926 from Henlow.
This Gamecock-equipped fighter squadron was
joined by 1 Squadron in November 1927 and
Tangmere was very much an operational fighter
station, the role for which it is best remembered.
Both squadrons subsequently operated Siskins and
Furys and Tangmere was considered to be a good
posting; the airfield itself underwent a number of
developments – especially during the early 1930s
when Expansion Period activity included upgrading
existing airfields as well as building new ones. By the
late-1930s the RAF was desperately trying to increase
its strength, the usual expedient being to create new
squadrons from a nucleus provided by an existing
squadron; at Tangmere 1 Squadron gave birth to 72
Squadron (22 February 1937) and 43 Squadron gave
birth to 87 Squadron (15 March 1937). Further
changes to both squadron and airfield infrastructure
took place over the next two years, including the
presence of Coastal Command Ansons, but by the
outbreak of war it housed two Hurricane squadrons
and, for much of the next year or so, this was to be its
usual complement; although, at times, three fighter-
units were in residence, most squadrons rotated
through the airfield, staying a matter of weeks or a
few months.

By the time of the Battle of Britain, Tangmere was
a major Fighter Command station and housed
a Sector Operations Room; it also controlled a
number of satellite airfields, the main one being
Westhampnett. Tangmere was very much a front-
line fighter-station in the Battle and its squadrons
achieved a fine record – but its importance was also
recognized by the Luftwaffe and it was on the receiving end of a number of attacks. Stukas carried out an
effective attack on 16 August, causing damage to
hangars, buildings and the airfield surface, as well as
killing thirteen people and destroying more than ten
aircraft. This was not the only attack on the airfield

in 1940–41 but it was the most effective and, in an
attempt to prevent a repeat performance, two decoy
sites were laid out.

The night-fighter defences of the area were boosted
by additional units operating from Tangmere, including the FIU; the latter had been at Tangmere for some
time but had lost most of its Blenheims in the August
attack. The airfield also acquired, in 1941, a
Turbinlite Havoc unit, as yet another attempt to
boost the RAF's ability to tackle the increasing night
attacks by the Luftwaffe. Throughout this period
fighter squadrons came and went, as Tangmere played
its part in both night defence and daylight offence,
with the Spitfire squadrons flying an increasing number of offensive sweeps and bomber escorts. During
the winter of 1941–42, the airfield facilities were
improved by the addition of asphalt runways and sixteen Blister hangars.

The next intensive period was August 1942, with
the Ibsley Wing's three squadrons operating from
Tangmere for Operation *Jubilee*, the Dieppe raid. The
rotation of squadrons continued over the next two
years and this was always a busy airfield; in addition
to its based fighter-units, it also played host to a variety of specialist units, including Air-Sea Rescue, as
well as being used as a forward-deployment base for
specific operations. Typhoons had first operated from
Tangmere in October 1942 and for the next few
months this aircraft type dominated operations from
the West Sussex airfield, the 'Tiffies' initially operating as fighters but increasingly taking on the fighter-
bomber role, attacking shipping and targets in
Occupied Europe. Their replacement by a Spitfire
Wing in late-1943 was temporary as, the following
February, the airfield became home to No.146
Airfield with three Typhoon squadrons. The departure of this Wing in April was followed by the arrival
of two Spitfire Wings, which meant that, at one
stage, Tangmere was operating six Spitfire squadrons.
This was part of the final shifting of units pre-D-Day
and the 'Spits' were intensively engaged on fighter
sweeps, escorts and bombing missions; Tangmere

Formation of Siskins of 43 Squadron.

## AIRFIELD DATA DEC 1944

| | | | |
|---|---|---|---|
| Command: | RAF Fighter Command | Runway surface: | Asphalt |
| Function: | Sector Station, Night Fighter | Hangars: | 10 × Over Blister, 6 × Extra Over Blister |
| Runways: | 255 deg 1,950 × 50yd | Dispersals: | 14 × Single-engine |
| | 170 deg 1,600 × 50yd | Personnel: | Officers – 242 (17 WAAF) |
| | | | Other Ranks – 4,156 (748 WAAF) |

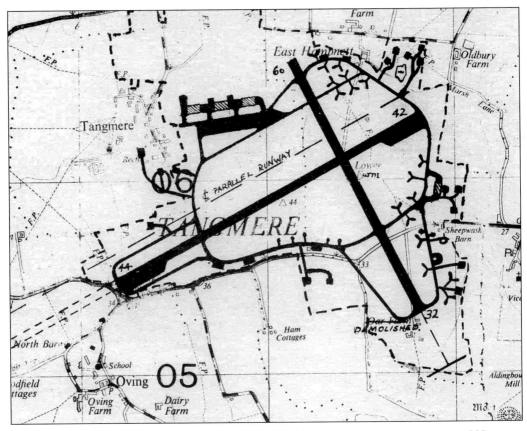

This 1950s plan still reflects the wartime layout, although the airfield shows some post-war changes, such as ORPs.

must have been a truly hectic place! Having met with some success in the days after the initial Allied landings, both Wings deployed to France in mid-June, amongst the first RAF units to cross the Channel. They were immediately replaced by two more Spitfire Wings and, whilst the pace of operations had slackened somewhat, they were nevertheless kept busy; both departed in July to be replaced by the three squadrons of No.145 Wing. They stayed a matter of days before moving to France, a routine followed by No.135 Wing, the next temporary occupants of Tangmere. With the operational squadrons gone,

Tangmere was suddenly very quiet, although it was probably used by the Group Support Unit of No.83 Group, which had moved into Westhampnett in November 1944. The December 1944 airfield survey showed that, with the demolition of four houses, the two runways could be extended, with the main runway increasing to 3,300 yards.

In January 1945, the Central Fighter Establishment took up residence and, along with the Naval Air Fighting Development Unit (787 Squadron), these two units brought a truly amazing array of aircraft types to Tangmere. This fascinating period was

No.1 Squadron operated Hurricanes and Spitfires from Tangmere.

The Ibsley Wing at Tangmere in August 1942.

Servicing a visiting Stirling, March 1944.

Tempest V of the Fighter Interception Unit, 1945. (Andy Thomas)

short-lived and within a year the airfield was back in the fighter game with a new Tangmere Wing, the build-up eventually creating the new Fighter Command standard Wing of day- and night-fighter units. The airfield underwent further development, partly to make it more suitable for jet operations, as the Meteor now became the standard type. One unusual aspect was the construction of a number of T.2 hangars, there being plenty of these World War Two stalwart 'tin sheds' available. Meteors dominated the airfield for a decade and it was one such plane that gained Tangmere the first of its clutch of speed records. On 7 September 1946, Group Captain E M Donaldson achieved 616mph (991km/h) in a Gloster Meteor IV; a record beaten on the same date in 1953 when Neville Duke set a new record of 727.63mph (1,171km/h) in the prototype Hawker Hunter – flown from Tangmere. Fighter operations ceased in the late-1950s and Tangmere passed to No.90 (Signals) Group, becoming home to a number of Canberra squadrons. The Canberras left in 1963 and the station passed to No.38 Group of Transport Command, but they did not base a flying unit at the airfield, the only flying being that by the SAR Whirlwind detachment

of 22 Squadron, plus some gliding activity. The airfield was reduced to Care and Maintenance on 14 December 1970 and, whilst retained for a further ten years, for much of which time the Gliding School continued to operate, its fate was sealed and it was finally put up for auction in 1979.

Although much of the two runways remain, used as roads by the industrial site that now occupies the airfield, the majority of buildings, other than some hangars and married quarters, have gone. The Control Tower stares forlornly across fields and aircraft (of the model variety) fly off the still-impressive stretch of concrete that formed the apron in front of the hangars. The site is well worth a visit, as it houses the excellent Tangmere Military Aviation Museum (www.tangmere-museum.org.uk) with its collection of aircraft and extensive display of memorabilia, much of it relating to Tangmere.

## DECOY SITES

| | | |
|---|---|---|
| Q | Colworth | SU926027 |
| Q/K | Gumber | SU958120 |

Wellington XIII NB855 of the FIU, summer 1945.
(Andy Thomas)

## UNITS

### HQ Units at Tangmere

| | | |
|---|---|---|
| No.146 Airfield | 31 Jan 1944–Feb 1944 | 183, 197, 257 Sqn |
| No.126 Airfield/ (RCAF) (F) Wing | 15 Apr 1944–16 Jun 1944 | 401, 411, 412 Sqn |
| No.127 Airfield/ (RCAF) (F) Wing | 17 Apr 1944–14 Jun 1944 | 403, 416, 421 Sqn |
| No.132 (Norwegian) (F) Wing | 21 Jun 1944–6 Aug 1944 | 66, 331, 332 Sqn |
| Sqn No.134 (Czech) (F) Wing | 19–23 Aug 1944 | 310, 312, 313 Sqn |
| No.145 (French) (F) Wing | 6–19 Aug 1944 | 329, 340, 341 Sqn |
| No.135 (F) Wing | 19–23 Aug 1944 | 222, 349, 485 Sqn |

### Pre-1919

| | | |
|---|---|---|
| 92 Sqn | 17 Mar 1918–2 Jul 1918 | Pup, SE5a |
| 93 Sqn | 19 Mar 1918–17 Aug 1918 | various |

### 1919–1938

| | | |
|---|---|---|
| 14 Sqn | 1 Jan 1919–4 Feb 1919 | cadre only |
| 25 Sqn | 26 Apr 1920–28 Sep 1922; 3 Oct 1923–22 Aug 1939+ | Snipe, Grebe, Siskin, Fury, Demon, Gladiator |
| 32 Sqn | 5 Mar 1919–8 Oct 1919 | cadre only |
| 40 Sqn | 13 Feb 1919–4 Jul 1919 | cadre only |
| 41 Sqn | 10 Feb 1919–8 Oct 1919 | cadre only |
| 42 Sqn det | Mar 1938–Sep 1938 | Vildebeeste |
| 43 Sqn | 12 Dec 1926–18 Nov 1939 | Snipe, Gamecock, Siskin, Fury |
| 72 Sqn | 22 Feb 1937–1 Jun 1937 | Gladiator |
| 84 Sqn | 12 Aug 1919–8 Oct 1919 | cadre only |
| 87 Sqn | 15 Mar 1937–7 Jun 1937 | Fury |
| 148 Sqn | 17 Feb 1919–4 Jul 1919 | cadre only |
| 207 Sqn | 22 Aug 1919–8 Oct 1919 | cadre only |

| | | |
|---|---|---|
| 217 Sqn | 7 Jun 1937–25 Aug 1939+ | Anson |
| 61 TDS | 15 Dec 1918–20 Jun 1919 | Avro 504, F2b, Camel |
| 61 TS | 20 Jun 1919–Dec 1919 | |

### 1939–1945

| | | |
|---|---|---|
| 1 Sqn | 23 Jul 1940–9 Sep 1940; 1 Jul 1941–8 Jul 1942; 30 Apr 1946–1 Jul 1958+ | Hurricane; Spitfire, Meteor |
| 17 Sqn | 19 Aug 1940–2 Sep 1940 | Hurricane |
| 23 Sqn det | Mar 1941–Aug 1942 | Havoc |
| 25 Sqn | 10–12 May 1940 | Blenheim |
| 26 Sqn | 6 Oct 1944–8 Dec 1944+ | Spitfire |
| 33 Sqn | 3–17 Jul 1944 | Spitfire |
| 41 Sqn | 17 Aug 1942–11 Oct 1942+; 12 Apr 1943–21 May 1943; 4 Oct 1943–11 Mar 1944 | Spitfire |
| 43 Sqn | 31 May 1940–8 Sep 1940; 16 Jun 1942–1 Sep 1942 | Hurricane, |
| 56 Sqn det | May 1942–Jun 1942 | Typhoon |
| 65 Sqn | 29 Nov 1940–26 Feb 1941 | Spitfire |
| 66 Sqn | 3 Jul 1942–20 Aug 1942+; 8–9 Oct 1942; 22 Jun 1944–6 Aug 1944 | Spitfire |
| 74 Sqn | 3–17 Jul 1944; 6–20 Aug 1944 | Spitfire |
| 82 Sqn det | Aug 1939–Mar 1943 | Blenheim |
| 91 Sqn | 4 Oct 1943–8 Feb 1944 | Spitfire |
| 92 Sqn | 10 Oct 1939–30 Dec 1939 | Blenheim |
| 96 Sqn det | Oct 1942–Aug 1943 | Beaufighter |
| 118 Sqn | 3–7 Jul 1942; 16–24 Aug 1942 | Spitfire |
| 124 Sqn | 25 Sep 1942–29 Oct 1942 | Spitfire |
| 127 Sqn | 23 Jul 1944–6 Aug 1944+ | Spitfire |
| 129 Sqn | 28 Feb 1943–13 Mar 1943 | Spitfire |
| 130 Sqn | 3–11 Aug 1944 | Spitfire |
| 131 Sqn | 22 Aug 1942–24 Sep 1942 | Spitfire |
| 141 Sqn | 23 Jun 1942–10 Aug 1942 | Beaufighter |
| 145 Sqn | 10 Oct 1940–23 Jul 1940; 9 Oct 1940–28 May 1941 | Hurricane |
| 161 Sqn det | Oct 1943–Jun 1945 | various |
| 164 Sqn | Sep 1942–Jan 1943; 25 Mar 1946–26 Apr 1946 | Spitfire |
| 165 Sqn | Aug 1942–29 Mar 1943 | Spitfire |
| 168 Sqn det | Jul 1942–Nov 1942 | Tomahawk |
| 170 Sqn det | Jun 1943–Sep 1943 | Mustang |
| 183 Sqn | 4 Aug 1943–18 Sep 1943; 1 Feb 1944–15 Mar 1944 | Typhoon |
| 197 Sqn | 28 Mar 1943–10 Apr 1944+ | Typhoon |
| 198 Sqn | 16–30 Mar 1944 | Typhoon |
| 213 Sqn | 7 Sep 1940–29 Nov 1940 | Hurricane |
| 219 Sqn det | Oct 1940–Jun 1942 | Beaufighter |
| 222 Sqn | 19–26 Aug 1944 | Spitfire |
| 229 Sqn | 22–24 Jun 1944 | Spitfire |
| 238 Sqn | 16 May 1940–20 Jun 1940 | Spitfire |
| 257 Sqn | 3 Feb 1944–10 Apr 1944 | Typhoon |
| 266 Sqn | 23 Mar 1944–10 Apr 1944; 9–10 Sep 1944 | Spitfire, Typhoon |
| 268 Sqn det | Jun 1943–Sep 1943 | Mustang |
| 302 Sqn | 18–21 Sep 1943 | Spitfire |

| | | |
|---|---|---|
| 310 Sqn | 22–30 Jun 1944 | Spitfire |
| 312 Sqn | 29 Jun 1944–4 Jul 1944 | Spitfire |
| 313 Sqn | 22 Jun 1944–4 Jul 1944 | Spitfire |
| 329 Sqn | 6–19 Aug 1944 | Spitfire |
| 331 Sqn | 22 Jun 1944–6 Aug 1944 | Spitfire |
| 332 Sqn | 21 Jun 1944–6 Aug 1944 | Spitfire |
| 340 Sqn | 14–19 Aug 1944; 3–6 Sep 1945 | Spitfire |
| 341 Sqn | 6–19 Aug 1944 | Spitfire |
| 349 Sqn | 19–26 Aug 1944 | Spitfire |
| 401 Sqn | 18 Apr 1944–18 Jun 1944 | Spitfire |
| 403 Sqn | 18 Apr 1944–16 Jun 1944 | Spitfire |
| 411 Sqn | 16 Apr 1944–19 Jun 1944 | Spitfire |
| 412 Sqn | 24 Aug 1942–23 Sep 1942; 15 Apr 1944–18 Jun 1944 | Spitfire |
| 416 Sqn | 17 Apr 1944–16 Jun 1944 | Spitfire |
| 421 Sqn | 18 Apr 1944–16 Jun 1944 | Spitfire |
| 485 Sqn | 19–31 Aug 1944 | Spitfire |
| 486 Sqn | 29 Oct 1942–31 Jan 1944 | Typhoon |
| 501 Sqn | 27 Nov 1939–10 May 1940; 3–7 Jul 1942; 8–10 Oct 1942; 21 Jun 1943–30 Apr 1944+ | Hurricane, Spitfire |
| 534 Sqn | 2 Sep 1942–25 Jan 1943 | Havoc, Boston, Hurricane |
| 601 Sqn | 30 Dec 1939–7 Sep 1940+ | Blenheim, Hurricane |
| 605 Sqn | 27 Aug 1939–11 Feb 1940 | Gladiator, Hurricane |
| 607 Sqn | 1 Sep 1940–10 Oct 1940 | Hurricane |
| 609 Sqn | 16–21 Mar 1944 | Typhoon |
| 614 Sqn det | Jun 1940–Mar 1941 | Lysander |
| 616 Sqn | 26 Feb 1941–9 May 1941; 3 Sep 1942–29 Oct 1942 | Spitfire |
| 1455 Flt | 7 Jul 1941–2 Sep 1942 | Havoc |
| CFE | 4 Sep 1944–1 Oct 1944; 15 Jan 1945–1 Oct 1945 | various |
| EAF | 17 Jan 1945–Nov 1945 | German types |
| NFDW | 15 Jul 1945–1 Oct 1945 | Mosquito, Beaufighter |

**FAA Units**

| | | |
|---|---|---|
| 787 Sqn det | 27 Oct 1945–16 Nov 1945 | various |
| 823 Sqn | 25 Sep 1942–1 Jun 1943+ | Albacore |

**Post-1945**

| | | |
|---|---|---|
| 22 Sqn det | Jun 1956–Apr 1974 | Whirlwind |
| 29 Sqn | 25 Nov 1950–14 Jan 1957 | Mosquito, Meteor |
| 34 Sqn | 1 Aug 1954–15 Jan 1958 | Meteor, Hunter |
| 43 Sqn | 11 Feb 1949–11 Nov 1950 | Meteor |
| 69 Sqn | 19 Apr 1947–16 May 1947 | Mosquito |
| 74 Sqn | 1–8 Jul 1950 | Meteor |
| 85 Sqn | 11 Oct 1945–16 Apr 1947+ | Mosquito |
| 98 Sqn | 19 Apr 1963–1 Oct 1963 | Canberra |
| 115 Sqn | 25 Aug 1958–1 Oct 1963 | Varsity |

| | | |
|---|---|---|
| 208 Sqn det | Jan 1958–Mar 1959 | Hunter |
| 222 Sqn | 2 Oct 1946–1 May 1948+ | Meteor |
| 245 Sqn | 25 Aug 1958–19 Apr 1963 | Canberra |
| 587 Sqn | 1–15 Jun 1946 | Vengeance, Spitfire |
| 38 Gp SU | 1 Dec 1964–14 Dec 1970 | |

## MEMORIALS

The memorial stone at Tangmere is in poor condition and, whilst one of the earliest series of memorials, is poor recognition of the airfield's history.

1. Stone on village green, inscribed:

> This stone erected by local subscription in 1970 commemorates Tangmere Airfield famous in two World Wars and in the forefront of the Battle of Britain 1940. It was manned by Royal Air Force squadrons whose valiant memory is recorded for all to see at the church of St Andrew Tangmere.

2. The nearby Bader Arms pub has a good collection of photos.
3. Tangmere Military Aviation Museum.
4. Kneelers and calendar of remembrance in Tangmere church.

# THORNEY ISLAND

**County:** Hampshire

**UTM/Grid:** OS map 197–SU760025
**Lat/Long:** N50°49.05 W000°55.25
**Nearest Town:** Emsworth 2 miles to north,
Portsmouth 6 miles to west

Aerial view of Thorney in 1945; note the burnt-out hangar from the 1940 attack.

## HISTORY

Located on the large, flat (average 15ft above sea level) oval island after which it takes it name, Thorney Island was one of the great wartime Coastal Command airfields. The selection of the airfield site is purported to lie in the investigation of a crash in 1933, in which Sergeant William Molesworth Hodge was killed (Fury K2073) – *see* memorial entry. From the outset, this Expansion Period airfield was planned to be large and impressive, capable of holding three or four squadrons and, as such, its 1,450 acres were carefully prepared and no less than six 'C'-Type hangars, in pairs, were built, along with the standard administrative, technical and accommodation facilities. Other than the tiny village of West Thorney (on the east of the island!), around which the perimeter

track and dispersal eventually kinked, there were few buildings on the island other than isolated farmhouses. At low tide the area on either side of the island became mud flats through which the Emsworth and Thorney Channels ran and from which a good harvest of shellfish could be obtained.

Construction was slower than expected, but the airfield eventually opened on 3 February 1938, No.16 Group of Coastal Command, with two Vildebeeste squadrons – the RAF's main torpedo bomber – taking up immediate residence. Within a matter of weeks the airfield had been transferred to No.17 (Training) Group, the first of what was to become a sequence of flying-training periods for the station, with the formation of the School of General Reconnaissance,

## AIRFIELD DATA DEC 1944

| Command: | RAF Coastal Command | Runway surface: | Tarmac |
|---|---|---|---|
| Function: | Operational Parent | Hangars: | 17 × Extra Over Blister, 6 × C |
| Runways: | 057 deg 1,700 × 50yd | Dispersals: | 42 × 120ft diameter |
| | 015 deg 1,630 × 50yd | Personnel: | Officers – 349 (19 WAAF) |
| | 120 deg 1,350 × 50yd | | Other Ranks – 3,795 (489 WAAF) |

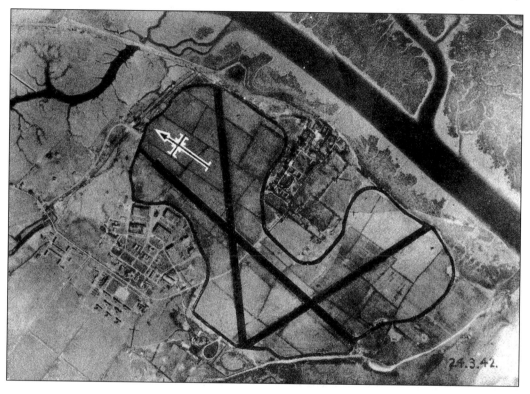

tasked with training 200 GR pilots a year. The operational Group was back in control by November, Thorney's location being considered ideal for anti-shipping strikes and coastal patrols. There was some moving of units; 42 Squadron departed and the Anson-equipped 48 Squadron arrived. It was with Ansons and Vildebeestes, both unsuitable combat types, that Thorney entered the war, one of its main roles being anti-submarine warfare. The School of GR moved out in April 1940 and for the remainder of the war Thorney Island was used by a variety of maritime squadrons, most of which stayed for a few weeks or months, or simply deployed to Thorney to use it as an advanced base for a specific operation. For a few months in mid-1940, the airfield was home to No.3 General Reconnaissance Unit and its unusual Wellingtons with their mine-exploding rings.

Virtually every Coastal Command operational type used the station over the next few years, as Thorney's units undertook anti-shipping missions that varied from routine patrols to dramatic pre-planned attacks on enemy shipping. It was inevitable that such an exposed and easy-to-find major airfield would receive visits from the Luftwaffe and the first of these came in August, the most effective taking place on 18 August when Stukas damaged two hangars – one of which remained a burnt-out shell until after the war – and a number of other buildings, as well as destroying a number of aircraft. The raiders, however, were handled roughly by fighters on the way in and out of the area, losing a number of aircraft. At this stage Thorney was also operating fighters, in the shape of Blenheims of 235 Squadron.

Attacks on the airfield continued into 1941,

February 1938 and the RAF's main torpedo bomber – the lumbering Vildebeest!

Swordfish of 836 Squadron were one of a number of FAA units to operate from this Coastal Command base.

11 May 1942 and a Hudson of 59 Squadron makes a successful wheels-up landing – or did the pilot forget to lower the wheels?

June 1946; Thorney was home to Coastal Command's two-squadron Strike Wing.

prompting improvements to the decoy site at West Wittering with the addition of dummy aircraft (Blenheims) and a flare path. The decoy was some three miles south-east of Thorney but, given the nature of the geography of the real target, it is not surprising that there are no recorded incidents of West Wittering being attacked. Thorney Island was very much in the offensive game and its squadrons attacked shipping as well as enemy ports – always a hazardous mission – and other land targets. It was also home to Air Sea Rescue aircraft, the main unit being 280 Squadron. Hudsons, Beauforts and Blenheims were the main types up to 1944, at which time the changing of units brought new types, such as the Fortress and the Mosquito, to join Thorney's battle. By this time the appearance of the airfield had changed, as three surfaced runways had been laid in 1942, along with extended perimeter-tracks leading to large circular dispersals, the main areas being to

the north and west, as well as seventeen Extra Over Blister hangars. Other than the later addition of Operational Readiness Platforms at each end of the main north/south runway, this pattern was pretty much maintained to the end of the airfield's life.

In addition to its continuing coastal role, Thorney had two periods when it was used by single-engined fighters; the first of these was July–August 1942, when Spitfire squadrons operated from the airfield before, during and after the Dieppe raid; the second came two years later, when the airfield was virtually emptied of Coastal Command units to make way for Typhoon squadrons involved in the D-Day campaign. The first Typhoons arrived in March and the airfield was now a 2nd Tactical Air Force station; soon it was home to two Typhoon Wings – No.123 and No.136 – which involved some swapping of units but gave two squadrons per Wing. Thorney Island's four Typhoon squadrons played a full and active part in the attacks on enemy installations, such as radar sites and barracks, in the days leading up to D-Day, after which they roamed Normandy attacking German road and rail transport, as well as supporting the ground troops. With the departure of the 'Tiffies' in mid-June, the airfield became home to the three Mosquito squadrons of No.140 Wing and

Refuelling a Meteor of 500 Squadron, 1948.

Battle of Britain day at Thorney Island, September 1949.

June 1949; Thorney's short period as a home to a Meteor fighter Wing.

Training base 1950s; Valettas at dispersal for No.2 Air Navigation School.

the offensive, day and night, against the enemy in and around Normandy continued unabated. The Wing remained at Thorney until February 1945, during which time it supported most major ground operations, including Arnhem in September 1944, as well as mounting the type of special pinpoint raids for which the Mosquito and its crews were duly famous.

Coastal units had not abandoned the airfield during this TAF period but, with the departure of No.140 Wing to the Continent, Thorney was once more primarily coastal-oriented. The diverse collection of types operated by the Air Sea Warfare Development Unit (ASWDU) had arrived in January and aircraft numbers increased as more Fleet Air Arm units made use of Thorney. The war ended with a variety of units in residence, primarily involved in trials work or Air-Sea Rescue. However, Coastal Command decided to base its main Strike Wing – of two squadrons – at Thorney Island and, in May 1946, Mosquito units arrived to convert to the Brigand, being joined in November by the Torpedo

Training Unit. Delays in the Brigand and a change of mind over future strategy saw the disbandment of the Strike Wing in autumn 1947.

The station was transferred to No.11 Group of Fighter Command on 15 December 1947 and the first fighters arrived a few weeks later; the intention was to form a Wing equipped with Meteors and, by July 1948, three such squadrons were in place. It was during this period that the ORPs were added to the main runway but the fighter period was brief, with the Wing moving to Waterbeach in May 1950. From the latest jets, Thorney reverted to lumbering Ansons and Wellingtons with its transfer to No.21 Group of Flying Training Command and the arrival of No.2 Air Navigation School. During the twelve years that the Hampshire airfield churned out navigators, a number of aircraft types were used but, by the late-1950s, the school was operating the Valetta and the Varsity as its flying classrooms. Air-Sea Rescue also returned during this period, in the shape of Sycamore helicopters, with 22 Squadron from February 1955. The ASR unit subsequently re-equipped with Whirlwinds and stayed at Thorney – on and off – until January 1976, by which time the Nav School was long gone. With the departure of the school in 1962, the station was transferred to No.38 Group of Transport Command and, as

Thorney Island in Army hands, September 2002.

the new unit was No.242 OCU from Dishforth, the station's training role continued. The OCU operated a number of types during its lengthy tenure at Thorney, starting with the Hastings and Beverley and ending with the Hercules and Andover, having also trained crews on the Argosy. Thorney was also home to one operational transport unit, 46 Squadron, from 1970 to 1975. With the disbandment of the squadron and the move of the OCU to Lyneham, Thorney was left with just the Whirlwinds of 22 Squadron; they, too, left in January 1976 and on 31 March this once great RAF station closed its doors.

It was not until 1982 that a new military use was found for the airfield, when it was transferred to the army, under whose control it is now Baker Barracks of the Royal Artillery. Some flying still takes place, although this is mainly recreational gliding and that very modern aspect of military aviation the UAV (Unmanned Aerial Vehicle).

## Decoy Sites

Q/K      West Wittering      SZ770983
*Provided with decoy Blenheims and a flare path in early 1941.*

## Units

### HQ Units at Thorney Island

| | | |
|---|---|---|
| No.123 Airfield/ (RP) Wing | 1 Apr 1944–17 Jun 1944 | 198, 609 Sqn |
| No.136 Airfield/ (F) Wing | 6 Apr 1944–17 Jun 1944 | 164, 183, 193 Sqn |
| No.20 (F) Wing | 9 Apr 1944–May 1944 | |
| No.140 (B) Wing | 18 Jun 1944–6 Feb 1945 | 21, 464, 487 Sqn |

### 1919–1939

| | | |
|---|---|---|
| 22 Sqn | 10 Mar 1938–8 Apr 1940 | Vildebeeste |
| 42 Sqn | 11 Mar 1938–18 Aug 1939+ | Vildebeeste |
| SoGR/1 SoGR | 4 Apr 1938–26 Apr 1940 | Anson |

### 1939–1945

| | | |
|---|---|---|
| 21 Sqn | 18 Jun 1944–6 Feb 1945 | Mosquito |
| 22 Sqn | 25 Jun 1941–28 Oct 1941; 1–16 Feb 1942 | Beaufort |
| 42 Sqn | 28 Apr 1940–1 Mar 1941 | Beaufort |
| 48 Sqn | 28 Sep 1938–10 Oct 1938; 25 Aug 1939–16 Jul 1940 | Anson, Beaufort |
| 53 Sqn | 24 Nov 1940–20 Mar 1941; 29 Apr 1943–25 Sep 1943 | Blenheim; Whitley |
| 59 Sqn | 3 Jul 1940–17 Jan 1942+; 29 Aug 1942–6 Feb 1943; 27 Mar 1943–11 May 1943 | Blenheim, Hudson, Liberator, Fortress |
| 86 Sqn | Jan 1942–Mar 1942; 1 Aug 1942–18 Mar 1943 | Beaufort, Liberator |
| 129 Sqn | 30 Jul 1942–25 Sep 1942 | Spitfire |
| 130 Sqn | 16–20 Aug 1942 | Spitfire |
| 131 Sqn | 24 Sep 1942–7 Nov 1942 | Spitfire |
| 143 Sqn | 11 Jun 1942–27 Jul 1942 | Blenheim |
| 164 Sqn | 16 Mar 1944–18 Jun 1944+ | Typhoon |
| 183 Sqn | 1 Apr 1944–18 Jun 1944 | Typhoon |
| 193 Sqn | 16 Mar 1944–6 Apr 1944 | Typhoon |
| 198 Sqn | 6 Apr 1944–18 Jun 1944+ | Typhoon |
| 217 Sqn | 29 Oct 1941–6 Mar 1942 | Beaufort |
| 220 Sqn det | Oct 1943–Jun 1945 | Fortress |
| 233 Sqn | Aug 1941–12 Jul 1942 | Hudson |
| 235 Sqn | 10 Jun 1940–4 Jun 1941 | Blenheim |
| 236 Sqn | 4 Jul 1940–8 Aug 1940 | Blenheim |
| 248 Sqn | 8–16 Apr 1940; 30 May 1946–1 Oct 1946 | Blenheim; Mosquito |
| 278 Sqn | 15 Feb 1945–15 Oct 1945 | Spitfire |
| 280 Sqn | 12 Dec 1941–10 Feb 1942; 30 Oct 1944–21 Jun 1946 | Anson, Warwick |
| 404 Sqn | 15 Apr 1941–20 Jun 1941 | Blenheim |
| 407 Sqn | 8 May 1941–8 Jul 1941; 18 Feb 1942–31 Mar 1942 | Blenheim, Hudson, Wellington |
| 415 Sqn | 20 Aug 1941–11 Apr 1942; 16 May 1942–5 Jun 1942; | Beaufort, Hampden, |

The area between the hangars is dotted with Spitfires (and a Mosquito) – but note the two destroyed hangars.

|  |  |  |
|---|---|---|
|  | Sep 1942–Jul 1944 | Wellington, Albacore |
| 455 Sqn det | Apr 1944–Oct 1944 | Beaufighter |
| 464 Sqn | 18 Jun 1944–7 Feb 1945 | Mosquito |
| 487 Sqn | 18 Jun 1944–5 Feb 1945 | Mosquito |
| 489 Sqn | 8 Mar 1942–5 Aug 1942 | Blenheim, Hampden |
| 547 Sqn | 25 Oct 1943–14 Jan 1944 | Wellington |
| 609 Sqn | 1 Apr 1944–18 Jun 1944 | Typhoon |
| 612 Sqn | 18 Aug 1942–23 Sep 1942 | Whitley |
| 1 CACF/U | 15 Sep 1939–18 May 1940 |  |
| 3 GRU | 24 May 1940–26 Jul 1940 | Wellington |
| 1431 Flt | 4–19 Sep 1940 | Maryland |
| 2 ATC | Nov 1941–16 Jun 1943 |  |
| 83 Gp SU | 25 Sep 1944–3 Nov 1944 |  |
| CCFC | ?–1 Sep 1945 |  |
| ASWDU | 1 Jan 1945–26 May 1948 |  |
| ECIF | 14 Jan 1945–31 Dec 1945 |  |

**FAA Units**

| 703 Sqn | 19 Apr 1945–25 May 1948 | Avenger |
|---|---|---|
| 704 Sqn | 20 Jun 1945–2 Dec 1945 | Mosquito |
| 810 Sqn | 1 Feb 1945–8 Apr 1945 | Barracuda |
| 812 Sqn | 11 Sep 1940–12 Jan 1941+ | Swordfish |
| 816 Sqn | 2 May 1941–4 Jun 1941 | Swordfish |
| 819 Sqn | 23 Sep 1942–28 Oct 1942 | Swordfish |
| 822 Sqn | 19 Jan 1945–14 Apr 1945 | Barracuda |
| 854 Sqn | 7–27 Aug 1944 | Avenger |
| 855 Sqn | 3–7 Aug 1944 | Avenger |

**Post-1945**

| 22 Sqn | 15 Feb 1955–26 Jan 1976 | Sycamore, Whirlwind |
|---|---|---|
| 36 Sqn | 1 Oct 1946–15 Oct 1947 | Mosquito |
| 42 Sqn | 1 Oct 1946–15 Oct 1947 | Beaufighter |
| 46 Sqn | 9 Sep 1970–29 Aug 1975 | Andover |
| 56 Sqn | 2 Feb 1948–3 May 1948; 23 Jun 1948–10 May 1950 | Meteor |
| 63 Sqn | 5 Jan 1948–14 May 1948; 29 Jun 1948–10 May 1950 | Spitfire, Meteor |
| 80 Sqn | 4–11 Feb 1948; 10 May 1948–5 Jun 1948 | Spitfire |

| 222 Sqn | 28 Jun 1948–9 May 1950 | Meteor |
|---|---|---|
| 254 Sqn | 6 May 1946–1 Oct 1946 | Beaufighter, Mosquito |
| ASWDU | 1945–26 May 1948 |  |
| 1 TTU | Nov 1946–1947 | Beaufighter |
| 2 ANS | 15 May 1950–15 Jan 1962 | Anson |
| 242 OCU | 29 Jan 1962–31 Oct 1975 | various |
| ATF | 9 Sep 1970–1 Nov 1970 | Andover |

## MEMORIALS

Various memorabilia in St Nicholas's church, West Thorney, plus plaque with inscription:

> In September 1933 the pilot of a Fury aircraft of No 1 Fighter Squadron crashed at this spot. Representatives of the RAF who came to investigate the crash observed the unique suitability of the adjoining land as an airfield and their recommendation subsequently resulted in the building of this aerodrome. He died not in battle yet not in vain.

Memorial plaque for the crash that is reported to have led to the construction of Thorney Island airfield.

# WESTHAMPNETT (Goodwood) (Station 352)

**County:** West Sussex

**UTM/Grid:** OS map 197–SU875075
**Lat/Long:** N50°51.30 W000°45.30
**Nearest Town:** Chichester 2 miles to south

Aerial view of Goodwood airfield September 2002.

## HISTORY

In 1938, land was acquired for an Emergency Landing Ground on behalf of the fighter station at Tangmere; although the area acquired from the Duke of Richmond's Goodwood Estate was left as little more than a cleared field until early 1940, when it was uprated to the status of a satellite airfield. When Westhampnett re-opened in July, the Hurricanes of 145 Squadron moved in from Tangmere, the airfield being designed for use by a single fighter-squadron. Battle was joined straight away, as the Channel war – the opening phase of the Battle of Britain – involved the squadrons of No.11 Group in some intense combats, with mixed results. In mid-August, 145 changed places with 602 Squadron, under Dowding's plan to rotate squadrons in the No.11 Group area. The hectic pace of operations continued as the Battle of Britain reached its climax and matters were not helped by poor conditions at Westhampnett – the airfield was plagued with waterlogging problems

as the autumn rains arrived and the tented accommodation was less than satisfactory. Over the next eighteen months a number of fighter squadrons used this Kent airfield and, during that time, the airfield was gradually improved. During the winter of 1940–41 the waterlogging problem was eased by the addition of a surfaced perimeter-track and dispersals. Nissen huts sprang up for multiple uses, from workshops to accommodation, although nearby Shopwyke Hall was taken over as the Officers' Mess and additional hangars, of various Blister types, were constructed. By mid-1941 the airfield's squadrons, with the norm now being for two to be based at Westhampnett, were taking part in offensive operations and escorts, with Spitfires remaining the main type flown from here.

A change of ownership came in July 1942, when the USAAF's 31st Fighter Group took the airfield on as Station 352. However, as this unit was equipped with Spitfires, little else changed and the first

## AIRFIELD DATA DEC 1944

| | | | |
|---|---|---|---|
| Command: | Fighter Command | Runway surface: | Grass |
| Function: | Operational Satellite, Tangmere sector | Hangars: | 7 × Over Blister, 1 × Extra Over Blister, 1 × T.1 |
| Runways: | NW/SE 1,400yd | Dispersals: | 32 × Single-engine, 19 × Twin-engine |
| | WNW/ESE 1,100yd | | |
| | NE/SW 1,000yd | Personnel: | Officers – 91 |
| | | | Other Ranks – 1,326 (55 WAAF) |

squadron to arrive, the 309th, flew its initial missions as part of the Tangmere Wing. With a second squadron, the 308th, in place from late-August and with the third squadron at Merston, the 31st FG began to operate as an independent unit. However, they left in autumn en route for North Africa and the station was returned to the RAF. The Spitfire VIs of 616 Squadron moved in for operations against high-flying German aircraft, although they were joined by 131 Squadron and both flew offensive *Circus* and *Rhubarb* operations. Various units continued offensive operations, the norm now being for a Wing of three squadrons, either Spitfires or Typhoons, to operate from this grass airfield that was originally intended for a single squadron. The pace of activity increased as D-Day approached but the Spitfire Wing that arrived in April 1944 as part of this build-up left at the end of the month and, for the next few months, Westhampnett's sole operational unit was the Typhoon-equipped 184 Squadron.

When the V-1 campaign started, the airfield's strength was temporarily increased by Spitfires for anti-*Diver* patrol, but this was short-lived, although the airfield subsequently housed a series of Spitfire squadrons tasked with the usual routine of offensive patrols and escort. However, most operational activ-

Hurricane of 145 Squadron at Westhampnett in 1940.

ity was over by September 1944 and the airfield was used by No.83 Group Support Unit until February the following year. The GSU's were interesting units, as they were responsible for a variety of tasks, including operational training/conversion and providing replacement pilots and aircraft for front-line squadrons – an instant source of 'combat ready' pilots to keep units at full strength. The final wartime occupants were Air Disarmament Units of SHAEF (Supreme HQ Allied Expeditionary Force).

In July 1945 the Naval Air Fighting Development Unit (NAFDU) moved in from Tangmere and continued to operate its diverse fleet as part of the Central Fighter Establishment. However, this fascinating unit had departed for West Raynham by the end of the year, and on 13 May 1946 Westhampnett was closed. Parts of the airfield infrastructure were removed but the perimeter track was developed into the Goodwood motor-racing circuit. The track had a life of almost sixty years but its main period of action was over by 1965, although special race days – including the 'Festival of Speed' – still take place. In 1958, authority had been given for the central grass-area to be used as an as airfield once more and, whilst the original idea was for race-goers and owners to use the strip, it gradually became a vibrant General Aviation airfield. As Chichester (Goodwood) Aerodrome (EGHR), the airfield is operated by Goodwood Road Racing (www.goodwood.co.uk), has four grass-strips and is home to a variety of private owners and a number of clubs.

## UNITS

### HQ Units at Westhampnett

| | | |
|---|---|---|
| No.121 Airfield | Oct 1943–1 Apr 1944 | 174, 175, 245 Sqn |
| No.129 Airfield/(FB) Wing | 22 Apr 1944–28 Jun 1944 | 441, 442, 443 Sqn |

### 1939–1945

| | | |
|---|---|---|
| 41 Sqn | 16 Dec 1941–1 Apr 1942; 21 Jun 1943–4 Oct 1943; 28 Jun 1944–3 Jul 1944 | Spitfire |
| 65 Sqn | 7 Oct 1941–22 Dec 1941 | Spitfire |
| 91 Sqn | 28 Jun 1943–4 Oct 1943 | Spitfire |
| 118 Sqn | 15–24 Aug 1943; 29 Aug 1944–25 Sep 1944 | Spitfire |
| 124 Sqn | 29 Oct 1942–7 Nov 1942; 9 Aug 1944–25 Sep 1944 | Spitfire |
| 129 Sqn | 29 Aug 1941–1 Nov 1941; 22 Dec 1941–6 Jul 1942 | Spitfire |
| 130 Sqn | 19–27 Jun 1944 | Spitfire |
| 131 Sqn | 7 Nov 1942–22 Jan 1943 | Spitfire |
| 145 Sqn | 23 Jul 1940–14 Aug 1940 | Hurricane |
| 167 Sqn | 21 May 1943–12 Jun 1943 | Spitfire |
| 174 Sqn | 10 Oct 1943–21 Jan 1944; 4 Feb 1944–1 Apr 1944 | Typhoon |
| 175 Sqn | 9 Oct 1943–1 Apr 1944 | Typhoon |
| 184 Sqn | 23 Apr 1944–17 Jun 1944 | Typhoon |
| 245 Sqn | 10 Oct 1943–1 Apr 1944 | Typhoon |
| 302 Sqn | 23 Nov 1940–7 Apr 1941 | Hurricane |
| 303 Sqn | 19–27 Jun 1944; 9 Aug 1944–25 Sep 1944 | Spitfire |
| 340 Sqn | 7 Apr 1942–28 Jul 1942 | Spitfire |
| 350 Sqn | 3 Jul 1944–8 Aug 1944 | Spitfire |
| 402 Sqn | 19–27 Jun 1944 | Spitfire |
| 416 Sqn | 25 Jun 1942–7 Jul 1942 | Spitfire |
| 441 Sqn | 1–12 Apr 1944 | Spitfire |
| 442 Sqn | 1–23 Apr 1944 | Spitfire |
| 443 Sqn | 8–22 Apr 1944 | Spitfire |
| 485 Sqn | 2 Jan 1943–21 May 1943 | Spitfire |
| 501 Sqn | 30 Apr 1943–17 May 1943; 12–22 Jun 1943; 2 Jul 1944–2 Aug 1944 | Spitfire, Typhoon |
| 602 Sqn | 13 Aug 1940–17 Dec 1940 | Spitfire |
| 610 Sqn | 15 Dec 1940–29 Aug 1941; 20 Jan 1943–30 Apr 1943 | Spitfire |
| 614 Sqn det | Mar 1941–Jul 1941 | Lysander |
| 616 Sqn | 9 May 1941–6 Oct 1941; 29 Oct 1942–2 Jan 1943; | Spitfire |
| ASRF | 15 Nov 1941–30 Nov 1941 | Lysander |
| 83 Gp SU | 3 Nov 1944–22 Feb 1945 | |

### FAA Units
787 Sqn

### USAAF Units
**31st FG**

| | |
|---|---|
| Squadrons | 307th FS, 308th FS, 309th FS |
| Aircraft | Spitfire |
| Dates | 1 Aug 1942–8 Nov 1942 |
| First mission: | 29 Aug 1942 (but had flown with RAF since July) |
| Last mission: | 9 Oct 1942 |

## MEMORIALS

1. To the 31st FG.
2. Statue of Douglas Bader unveiled 9 Aug 2001 in front of the flying club; Bader flew his last wartime mission from here, during which he collided with a Bf109 and was taken prisoner.

# WEST MALLING

**County:** Kent

**UTM/Grid:** OS map 178–TQ680555
**Lat/Long:** N51°16.3 E000°24.4
**Nearest Town:** Maidstone 5 miles to east

West Malling vanishes under housing and industry; June 2003.

## HISTORY

The first airfield in the West Malling area was a small (47-acre) Class 2 Landing Ground, known as Kings Hill, close to the railway station. This site was in use from the middle years of the war but there is little detail, other than its possible allocation to 143 Squadron. The military lost interest with the end of the war, but the same rough area was used in the 1930s by the Maidstone School of Flying and Kent Aeronautical Services. By 1932 the site was known as Maidstone Airport and the main operator was Malling Aviation.

West Malling was requisitioned by the RAF on the outbreak of war, although the first squadron did not move in until June 1940 – the Lysander-equipped 26 Squadron. They were joined the following month by the Defiants of 141 Squadron and it was from here, on July 21, that the Defiants took-off for the mission

on which they were decimated by German fighters – one of the final proofs that the turret-fighter concept was misplaced for a daylight fighter. Nevertheless, Malling's main role became that of a satellite for Kenley and it was used as an advance airfield by Kenley and Biggin Hill. Fighter units flew from there during the Battle of Britain and it was on the receiving end of Luftwaffe attacks in August and September. The August attacks put it out of action for some time and fighter operations did not resume fully until October, with the arrival of 66 Squadron with Spitfires. By 1941 the station was 'specializing' in night-fighter operations, using Defiants, Beaufighters and Turbinlite Havocs. The airfield's grass surface provided adequate runs for the fighter types and, during the first two years of the war, a number of hangars were erected, including one 'J'-

## AIRFIELD DATA DEC 1944

| | | | |
|---|---|---|---|
| Command: | Fighter Command | Runway surface: | Concrete (264), Sommerfeld Track (004) |
| Function: | Forward Airfield (Night Fighter), Biggin Hill Sector | Hangars: | 16 × Blister, 1 × J |
| | | Dispersals: | 13 × Frying pan, 12 × Temporary, 4 × Blenheim, 3 × Single-engine |
| Runways: | 264 deg 2,000yd | | |
| | 004 deg 1,660yd | Personnel: | Officers – 68 |
| | | | Other Ranks – 1,344 |

*All WAAF accommodation requisitioned.*

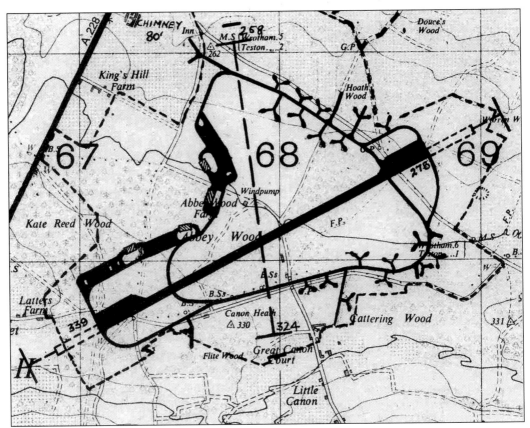

This 1950s plan shows various developments from the 1944 data, with longer runways, ORPs and other parking areas.

type and sixteen Blisters of various types. However, in order to provide a true all-weather strip, Sommerfeld Track was laid on both strips, with one subsequently being given a hard surface, and the overall airfield area was increased to provide longer runs and to cater for the increasing number of aircraft using the airfield – up to five squadrons were in residence during some periods. However, the most notable incident occurred on 16 April 1943, when a number of Fw190s mistook West Malling for a friendly airfield in Europe: one landed and was captured, one was destroyed when it attempted to take-off again and one crashed nearby (a fourth crashed near Staplehurst).

Day- and night-fighter units continued to use the Station until August 1944, when it was closed for major reconstruction, its final period of operations before this being a significant contribution to the

Fighter-bomber operations by Spitfires were a stock-in-trade role for units operating from the airfield in World War Two; this is not a West Malling picture.

Mosquito XIII HK419 of 96 Squadron, December 1943.

Spitfire pilots of 80 Squadron, West Malling July 1944. (Jerry Jarrold)

85 Squadron parades with its Meteors.

anti-flying-bomb defences. The reconstruction included the concreting of the 2,000ft runway, 26/08, and the airfield eventually re-opened in June 1945, when it became the main centre for the rehabilitation of PoWs returning from Germany.

After the war, the Station remained a fighter base, first arrivals being the Spitfires of 287 Squadron, although they were soon followed by other units and aircraft. Jets arrived in May 1946 with 500 (County of Kent) Squadron and, over the next few years, Meteors, Vampires and Javelins operated from here with a variety of squadrons, although Malling did not receive the standard three-squadron Wing. Indeed, the airfield was without a unit in the late-1950s until 85 Squadron moved back in for a final spell, before departing again in September 1960. No further flying units used the airfield and, in August 1964, it was reduced to Care and Maintenance. However, it re-opened the following year for use by a US Navy communications unit, operating such types as the Convair C-131. This unit remained for two years but then moved to Blackbushe. This was not quite the end of flying, as No.618 Volunteer Gliding School

moved in from Manston – and remained for thirty years, by which time the airfield had passed out of RAF hands, closure occurring in 1967. Kent County Council acquired the site in 1970 and many of the buildings were turned into offices and an industrial park. To those interested in aviation, the airfield is perhaps best known for its 1980s staging at the Great Warbirds Airshows. Sadly, these are now long past and the airfield site has undergone major development as an industrial and technical park, along with housing areas. The developers have kept many of the buildings and old H-block accommodation buildings are now well-equipped office blocks.

## DECOY SITES

| Q | Collier Street | TQ700464 |
| Q | Hammer Dyke | TQ642463 |

## UNITS

### 1939–1945

| 3 Sqn | 14 May 1943–11 Jun 1943 | Typhoon |
| 19 Sqn det | Feb 1941–Aug 1941 | Spitfire |
| 26 Sqn | 8 Jun 1940–3 Sep 1940 | Lysander |
| 29 Sqn | 27 Apr 1941–13 May 1943; | Beaufighter; |
| | 1 May 1944–19 Jun 1944 | Mosquito |
| 32 Sqn | 5 May 1942–14 Jun 1942; | Hurricane |
| | 7 Jul 1942–10 Sep 1942+ | |
| 41 Sqn | 19–28 Jun 1944 | Spitfire |

As a 1950s fighter base West Malling housed all the classics, such as this Javelin of 85 Squadron.

| | | |
|---|---|---|
| 64 Sqn | 6–25 Sep 1943 | Spitfire |
| 66 Sqn | 30 Oct 1940–7 Nov 1940 | Spitfire |
| 80 Sqn | 5 Jul 1944–29 Aug 1944 | Spitfire, Tempest |
| 85 Sqn | 13 May 1943–1 May 1944; 21 Jul 1944–29 Aug 1944 | Mosquito |
| 91 Sqn | 23 Apr 1944–21 Jul 1944 | Spitfire |
| 96 Sqn | 8 Nov 1943–20 Jun 1944 | Beaufighter, Mosquito |
| 124 Sqn | 20 Sep 1943–18 Mar 1944 | Spitfire |
| 130 Sqn | 5 Aug 1943–18 Sep 1943 | Spitfire |
| 133 Sqn det | Feb 1942–May 1942 | Spitfire |
| 141 Sqn | 11–25 Jul 1940 | Defiant |
| 157 Sqn | 21 Jul 1944–29 Aug 1944 | Mosquito |
| 234 Sqn | 5 Aug 1943–16 Sep 1943 | Spitfire |
| 255 Sqn det | Sep 1941–Mar 1942 | Beaufighter |
| 264 Sqn | 14 Apr 1941–1 May 1942 | Defiant |
| 274 Sqn | 5 Jul 1944–17 Aug 1944 | Spitfire |
| 287 Sqn | 10 Sep 1945–15 Jun 1946 | Tempest, Spitfire |
| 316 Sqn | 4–11 Jul 1944 | Spitfire |
| 322 Sqn | 20 Jun 1944–21 Jul 1944 | Spitfire |
| 350 Sqn | 7–19 Sep 1943 | Spitfire |
| 409 Sqn | 14 May 1944–19 Jun 1944 | Beaufighter |
| 410 Sqn | 20 Oct 1943–8 Nov 1943 | Mosquito |
| 485 Sqn | 16–22 Aug 1942 | Spitfire |
| 486 Sqn | 10–29 Oct 1942 | Typhoon |
| 531 Sqn | 8 Sep 1942–25 Jan 1943 | Havoc, Boston, Hurricane |
| 610 Sqn | 19–27 Jun 1944 | Spitfire |
| 616 Sqn | 3–7 Jul 1942 | Spitfire |
| 1421 Flt | 31 Oct 1940–6 Nov 1940 | Hurricane, Spitfire |
| 1452 Flt | 7 Jul 1941–8 Sep 1942 | Havoc |
| 1528 Flt | 14 Apr 1942–7 Dec 1942 | Master |

**Post-1945**

| | | |
|---|---|---|
| 14 Sqn | 29 Sep 1947–4 Jun 1948 | Mosquito |
| 25 Sqn | 5 Sep 1946–30 Sep 1957+ | Mosquito, Vampire, Meteor |
| 29 Sqn | 29 Oct 1945–25 Nov 1950 | Meteor |
| 85 Sqn | 16 Apr 1947–18 Sep 1957+ 5 Jun 1959–6 Sep 1960 | Meteor Javelin |
| 153 Sqn | 28 Feb 1955–17 Sep 1957 | Meteor |
| 247 Sqn | 1–12 Jun 1946; 7–16 Sep 1946 | Vampire |
| 500 Sqn | 10 May 1946–10 Mar 1957 | Mosquito, Spitfire, Meteor |
| 567 Sqn | 26 Apr 1946–15 Jun 1946 | Spitfire |
| 1 AEF | 12 Sep 1959–10 Sep 1960 | |
| 618 VGS | 9 Jan 1965–Mar 1995 | |

## MEMORIALS

A very impressive memorial was unveiled in June 2003. A series of engraved marble plaques depict the Station history, along with a fine bronze sculpture of fighter pilots running towards the airfield. The inscriptions give an outline history of the station and include unit plaques and engravings of aircraft types operated from the airfield.

The impressive memorial at West Memorial comprises a series of plaques plus the figure of a pilot.

# WINKTON

**County:** Hampshire

**UTM/Grid:** OS map 195–SZ165975
**Lat/Long:** N50°46.6 W001°46.0
**Nearest Town:** Bournemouth 5 miles to south-west

## History

The area to the north-east of Bournemouth proved popular with the surveyors in 1942, when they were hunting for locations at which to construct Advanced Landing Grounds, and Winkton was one of a clutch of such sites. A roughly rectangular area to the east of the village of Sopley was chosen and work commenced, in early 1943, on the construction of a standard ALG complete with two tracked runways but very little else. The usual clearing of hedges and filling of ditches, plus closure of one minor road, caused few problems and the airfield was ready by the planned date of September 1943. It was not, however, used as one of the evaluation ALGs and was released for grazing until brought back into service the following spring. By this time the airfield had been improved, with perimeter tracking linking the runways.

Although originally intended for RAF use, Winkton was allocated to the IXth Air Force and, on 5 April 1944, the 404th Fighter-Bomber Group arrived with three squadrons of P-47s. Having been re-designated as a Fighter Group, despite the fact that the fighter-bomber role remained its primary task, the 404th flew its first missions on 1 May and, from that date on, played an active role in the pre-D-Day campaign. When maximum-effort missions were mounted, as many as fifty Thunderbolts might take part, which must have been an impressive site for anyone leaning over the hedge at Winkton. It was always planned that these tactical Groups would

move to Europe at the earliest opportunity and the 404th duly vacated their Hampshire field on 6 July, moving to Chapelle. Like most of the ALGs, the site was rapidly abandoned and its infrastructure – such as it was – removed for possible re-use on the Continent. By the end of the year the site had been officially de-requisitioned and it was soon returned to agriculture, leaving little trace of its brief but intensive military occupation.

## Units

**1939–1945**
**USAAF Units**
**404th FG**

| | |
|---|---|
| Squadrons: | 506th FS, 507th FS, 508th FS |
| Aircraft: | P-47 |
| Dates: | 4 Apr 1944–6 Jul 1944 |
| First mission: | 1 May 1944 |
| Last mission: | May 1945? (from Fritzlar) |

P-47 of the 404th FG, Winkton's only operational unit.

# AIRFIELD DATA DEC 1944

| Command: | Fighter Command | Runway surface: | Sommerfeld Track/PSP |
|---|---|---|---|
| Function: | Advanced Landing Ground | Hangars: | 4 × Blister |
| Runways: | N/S 1,600 × 50yd | Dispersals: | 80 × Sommerfeld Track |
| | E/W 1,400 × 50yd | Personnel: | Other Ranks – Tented camp |
| | 270 deg 2,000 × 50yd | | |

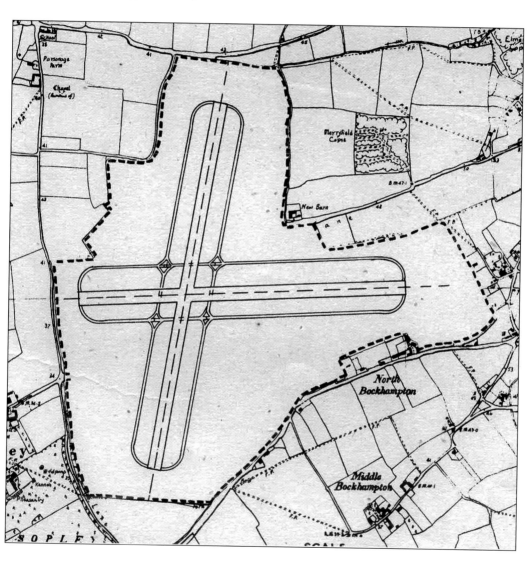

# WISLEY

**County:** Surrey

**UTM/Grid:** OS map 187–TQ075575
**Lat/Long:** N51°18.4 W000°27.6
**Nearest Town:** Woking 5 miles to west

## HISTORY

Wisley was opened in 1943 as a relief field for the Vickers Weybridge factory, which was three miles to the north and, by this time, was very busy and in need of additional space. The airfield was given little in the way of facilities, as it was originally intended to be a simple flying-strip for flight testing, with aircraft hopping over from the Weybridge site, although some also came by road. A number of hangars and other buildings were erected as Wisley gradually became the main flight-test centre for Vickers-Armstrong. Amongst the military work undertaken at the airfield was a series of flight trials on a Me163 Komet.

In the post-war period the grass surface became inadequate for the new generation of aircraft and a single 7,500ft hard-runway was laid in 1952, a major investment but one that was important, as the Company was working on the Valiant. Over the next twenty years the Wisley site was an important part of the British aircraft industry and witnessed a number of significant events. However, it was located between Heathrow and Gatwick and, as commercial aviation at these civil airports boomed in the 1960s, it was decided that Wisley was not suitable for further

Wisley 1977; the size of he apron can be appreciated from the VC-10 that looks almost lost. (BAe via Aldon Ferguson)

use. In 1973 the decision was taken by British Aircraft Corporation, the successors to Vickers, to close the airfield.

The concrete runway is still there, although many of the buildings have gone, but there are development plans for a housing estate on part of the site.

Valiants and Valettas make an imposing site at Wisley in 1956. (M P Marsh via Aldon Ferguson)

# WOODCHURCH
# (Station 419)

**County:** Kent

**UTM/Grid:** OS map 189–TQ945365
**Lat/Long:** N51°05.7 E000°46.6
**Nearest Town:** Ashford 5 miles to north-east

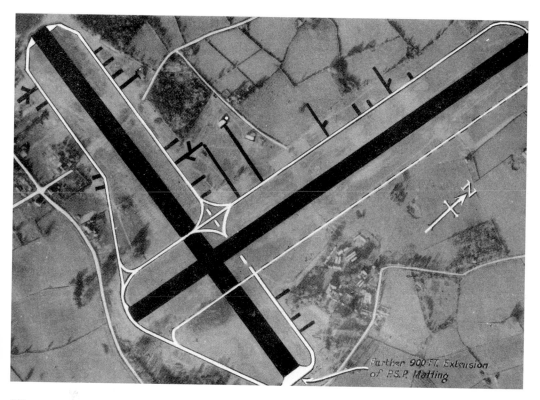

Further 900 FT. Extension of P.S.P. Matting

## HISTORY

The area around Ashford, in Kent, was the site of numerous Advanced Landing Grounds but Woodchurch was slightly unusual, in that it was constructed for light-bomber rather than fighter-bomber use, the main difference being the provision of a larger bomb-dump. The site was one of those chosen in the 1942 survey round and on which work commenced in early 1943. Preparation of the site turned out to be more difficult than expected and the main strip had to be constructed somewhat shorter than the standard length. As usual, little else was provided and accommodation was in tents, although a number of huts were also available. With Sommerfeld Track runways in place, the airfield was complete by summer 1943 and the two Mustang squadrons of No.39 (Recce) Wing arrived on 28 July from Dunsfold, the light-bomber plan having been changed. This detachment remained in place to mid-October, being joined in the last few weeks by a third squadron, and,

whilst operational sorties were flown during this period, it was also an opportunity to evaluate the airfield and the squadrons. There were a few problems but nothing significant and the Wing duly moved out to its winter quarters. Woodchurch underwent a second phase of development that saw Sommerfeld Track perimeter-tracking and dispersals laid down – and, indeed, a third phase by American engineers, when the airfield was allocated to the USAAF for fighter-bomber use. The engineers extended the main runway to 5,000ft, using PSP, to cater for the heavier P-47, and the number of dispersals was increased to the USAAF standard of seventy.

On 4 April 1944, the P-47s of the 373rd Fighter Group arrived at Station 419, this being their first duty-station in England. Under the command of Colonel William H Schwartz Jr, the Group flew its first combat mission only five weeks later, a fighter sweep in the Normandy area. The three squadrons of

# AIRFIELD DATA DEC 1944

| | | | |
|---|---|---|---|
| Command: | Fighter Command | Runway surface: | Sommerfeld Track/PSP |
| Function: | Advanced Landing Ground | Hangars: | Nil |
| Runways: | 010 deg 1,600yd | Dispersals: | 70 × Sommerfeld Track |
| | 110 deg 1,667yd | Personnel: | Other Ranks – Tented camp |
| | 270 deg 2,000 × 50yd | | |

The 373rd FG's Thunderbolts spent three months at Woodchurch.

the 373rd were kept busy with escort and ground-attack missions: like most of the Thunderbolt units, specializing in the latter, especially after the D-Day landings. With the Allies ashore in Europe, the tactical squadrons moved across the Channel, the 373rd moving to Tour-en-Bessin on 4 July, although the rear element did not leave Woodchurch until the end of the month. Authority was given to remove runway matting for use elsewhere and the site was de-requisitioned later in the year. By early 1945 all significant trace of the ALG had vanished.

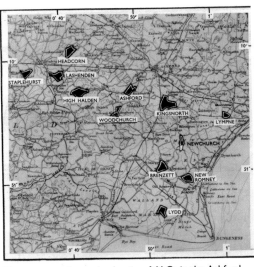

The area map shows the density of ALGs in the Ashford area.

## UNITS

### HQ Units at Woodchurch:

| | | |
|---|---|---|
| No.128 Airfield | 28 Jul 1943–15 Oct 1943 | 231, 400, 414 Sqn |
| No.39 Wing | 11 Aug 1943–13 Oct 1943 | |

### 1939–1945

| | | |
|---|---|---|
| 231 Sqn | 28 Jul 1943–15 Oct 1943 | Mustang |
| 400 Sqn | 28 Jul 1943–15 Oct 1943 | Mustang |
| 414 Sqn | 5–15 Oct 1943 | Mustang |

### USAAF Units

### 373rd FG

| | |
|---|---|
| Squadrons: | 410th FS, 411th FS, 412th FS |
| Aircraft: | P-47 |
| Dates: | 4 Apr 1944–30 Jul 1944 |
| First mission: | 8 May 1944 |
| Last mission: | 4 May 1945 (from Lippestadt) |

# WORTHY DOWN
## (HMS *Kestrel*, HMS *Aerial II*)

**County:** Hampshire

**UTM/Grid:** OS map 185–SU470351
**Lat/Long:** N51°06.47 W001°19.42
**Nearest Town:** Winchester 4 miles to south

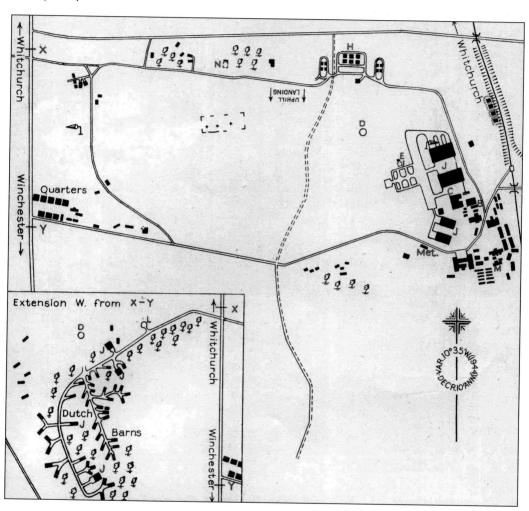

## HISTORY

Worthy Down is an airfield name barely known except amongst aviation historians, yet this Hampshire station was in use from the latter part of World War One into the 1950s and, during the inter-war years, was one of the main bomber stations in the Wessex Area. The original site, which occupied Winchester Racecourse, was acquired in August 1917 for a training establishment, the Wireless and Observer School. However, the extensive (480-acre) area took longer to develop than anticipated and

involved some ground work and the construction, much of it by the Canadian Pioneer Corps, of a number of buildings and six large aeroplane-sheds of modified General Service type, along with instructional blocks and accommodation. Worthy Down opened, still far from complete, in August 1918, for the Artillery and Infantry Co-operation School, although this underwent a couple of name changes during its time here, finally becoming the School of Army Co-operation. The School had an impressive

58 Squadron pose with one of their Virginias in 1935.

collection of aircraft, with almost 100 aircraft of three main types on strength, the RE8 being the most numerous, as this was one of the main types then employed for the Army Co-operation role. The end of the war brought a rapid run-down and Worthy Down, still not complete to the original plan, bade farewell to the school in March 1920. The airfield was not closed, however, and, for the next few years, was used as a flying satellite by Flowerdown and the Electrical and Wireless School.

Operational flying returned in 1924, with the formation of 58 Squadron as a bomber unit; this squadron spent the next twelve years here, initially operating the Vimy but re-equipping with the Virginia in December 1925 and subsequently operating six versions of this visually impressive but lumbering 'heavy' bomber. They were joined in April 1927 by the Virginia-equipped 7 Squadron from Bircham Newton and, together, the Worthy Down bomber-

Wing developed new bomber tactics and participated in countless exercises – all of which 'proved' the superiority of the bomber weapon! Further work on buildings, mainly barracks, and general improvements, mainly airfield surface and drainage, took place in the late-1920s and early 1930s and Worthy Down took on the appearance of a permanent RAF Station. The mid-1930s saw the creation of two new bomber units through the expedient of splitting existing units, 7 Squadron giving birth to 102 Squadron and 58 Squadron giving birth to 215 Squadron, although both 'new-borns' departed in 1936, as indeed did their parents. The airfield then became home to three other bomber squadrons within No.2 Group of the new Bomber Command, but these units, with a variety of bomber types, had all departed by May 1938, as Worthy Down had been allocated to Coastal Command in April that year. Despite the fleeting presence of a number of Anson squadrons, the main role for the airfield was as a shore base for Fleet Air Arm ship-borne units, first of which were the Nimrods and Ospreys of 800 Squadron. The station duly became HMS *Kestrel* on 24 May 1939, by which time it had housed a number of units, including the Fleet Air Arm Pool and the usual wide variety of naval aircraft. The arrival of No.1 Air Gunners School, with its three flying squadrons, made Worthy a busy station and, to this, training for TAGs was added, in late-1939, that of No.1 TSR being responsible for providing replacement crews and keeping trained-crews current. Operational squadrons continued to appear at, or form at, Worthy Down and, in

October 1929 and 5 Squadron receive the Minot Trophy.

common with most Naval Air Stations, it played host to a sometimes bewildering array of units, most of which stayed only short periods.

With the Luftwaffe's attempts to destroy RAF airfields in summer 1940, Worthy Down was on the receiving end of one ineffective raid on 15 August, its location near the south coast having attracted attention. The station was hit twice more in August – 19 and 25 – but again with little result. One unusual lodger-unit, located in two Blister hangars from December 1940, was Supermarine's Spitfire flight-testing, moved here for safety following attacks on the Southampton area. A second unusual site was the 'crop' of Dutch Barn aircraft-sheds, forty-eight of them, that sprang up in a field adjacent to the airfield and were used for aircraft storage. The TAG School continued to be very active and, until its closure in 1943, was responsible for training hundreds of aircrew. Although the FAA moved in other training units and also a number of trials and evaluations units, the most interesting aspect of Worthy Down, for much of this wartime period, rested with the work being carried out on Spitfire flight-testing; this not only involved new variants, including the Seafire, but modifications such as arrestor gear. Flight testing eventually moved to High Post in March 1944, leaving Worthy Down to the FAA units.

The airfield remained active, but at a slow pace following the end of the war, until Worthy was reduced to Care and Maintenance in November 1947 and closed on 9 January 1950. However, this was not the end and, in June 1952, the airfield reopened as HMS *Aerial II*. During the early 1950s usage by the FAA, the main landing-strip was oriented 090/270 degrees as a grass strip 1,920ft by 120ft but, as the resident unit was the non-flying Air Electrical School, the runway was only used by visitors. It was a short-lived second life and the navy once more closed Worthy Down on 1 November 1960, handing the site to the army – making it one of the few airfields to have been used by all three services. The army didn't want it as an airfield and, instead, it became HQ of the Army Pay Corps. Following a major rebuild, which saw the end of many of the original buildings including the hangars, the new site opened in 1961.

## DECOY SITES

| | |
|---|---|
| Micheldever | SU510390 |

## UNITS

### 1919–1938

| | | |
|---|---|---|
| 7 Sqn | 7 Apr 1927–3 Sep 1936 | Virginia |
| 35 Sqn | 20 Aug 1936–20 Apr 1938 | Gordon, Wellesley |
| 49 Sqn | 8 Aug 1936–14 Mar 1938 | Hind |
| 58 Sqn | 1 Apr 1924–13 Jan 1936 | Vimy, Virginia |
| 102 Sqn | 1 Oct 1935–3 Sep 1936 | Heyford |
| 207 Sqn | 20 Aug 1936–20 May 1938 | Gordon, Wellesley |
| 215 Sqn | 1 Oct 1935–14 Jan 1936 | Virginia |
| ACS | 19 Sep 1918–23 Dec 1919 | BE2c, RE8 |
| SoAC | 23 Dec 1919–8 Mar 1920 | various |
| 1 EWS | Dec 1919–11 Mar 1927 | various |
| 1 AACU | 24 May 1937–16 Sep 1937 | |

### 1939–1945

| | | |
|---|---|---|
| SUAS | Oct 1942–Dec 1945 | |

### FAA Units

| | | |
|---|---|---|
| 700 Sqn | 7 Nov 1944–23 Nov 1945 | Master |
| 734 Sqn | 14 Feb 1944–21 Aug 1945 | Whitley |
| 739 Sqn | 14 Sep 1943–5 Oct 1944 | various |
| 755 Sqn | 24 May 1939–31 Oct 1944 | various |
| 756 Sqn | 6 Mar 1941–1 Dec 1942 | Proctor, Tiger Moth |
| 757 Sqn | 24 May 1939–15 Aug 1939; 6 Mar 1941–1 Dec 1942 | various |
| 763 Sqn | 15 Dec 1939–11 Mar 1940; 4–8 Jul 1940 | Swordfish, Albacore |
| 800 Sqn | 7 Jul 1938–2 Oct 1939+ | Skua, Gladiator, Roc |
| 803 Sqn | 21 Nov 1938–30 Apr 1939+ | Skua, Roc |
| 806 Sqn | 1 Feb 1940–28 Mar 1940; 26 May 1940–11 Jun 1940 | Skua, Roc |
| 808 Sqn | 1 Jul 1940–5 Sep 1940 | Fulmar |
| 815 Sqn | 9 Oct 1939–5 Feb 1940 | Swordfish |

### Post-1945

| | | |
|---|---|---|
| SUAS | Sep 1946–18 Oct 1946 | |

### FAA Units

| | | |
|---|---|---|
| 848 Sqn | 9 Nov 1959–10 Mar 1960 | Whirlwind |

During World War Two the airfield was in the hands of the Fleet Air Arm, amongst the units to use the airfield was 803 Squadron with Skuas.

# World War One Airfields and Landing Grounds

## ALL HALLOWS

**County:** Kent
**UTM/Grid:** OS map 178–TQ832775
**Lat/Long:** N51°28.0 E000°16.3
**Nearest Town:** Chatham 8 miles to south-west

### HISTORY

All Hallows was a small (32-acre) Class 3 Landing Ground on the Isle of Grain and, as such, saw very little use during World War One. The grass landing area was given no facilities and, other than the few tents and the occasional presence of aircraft, it was little different to the surrounding fields. It appears to have been used by aircraft from Eastchurch.

## BEMBRIDGE

**County:** Isle of Wight
**UTM/Grid:** OS map 196–SZ642887
**Lat/Long:** N50°41.7 W001°05.5
**Nearest Town:** Ryde 3 miles to north-west

### HISTORY

Although the present airfield at Bembridge has no military background, there was a World War One seaplane station at Bembridge Point. This was established in 1915 as a sub-unit for Calshot and initially comprised little more than a slipway at Bembridge Harbour (then known as Brading Harbour), with an adjacent hard stand. By November 1916, the station was home to a detached flight of four Short 184 RNAS floatplanes and facilities had been improved to include two seaplane sheds and a number of huts, although accommodation was a local hotel (the Spithead Hotel) for officers, whilst naval ratings lived in the nearby coastguard station. The number of aircraft increased in order to cover the patrol areas from the Isle of Wight; the RAF took over in April 1918 and, in May, No.412 (Seaplane) Flight formed, becoming part of 253 Squadron in August. The following month it was joined by No.413 Flight, again part of 253 Squadron. These Flights operated the Short 184, but with some use of the Campania and Hamble Baby. Patrols continued to the end of the war and Bembridge remained in use to May 1919, when the Squadron disbanded. The seaplane station was not finally disposed of until some time in 1920.

### UNITS

**Pre-1919**

| | | |
|---|---|---|
| 412 Flt | 20 May 1918–May 1919 | Short 184, Campania |
| 413 Flt | 15 Sep 1918–Nov 1918 | Short 184 |

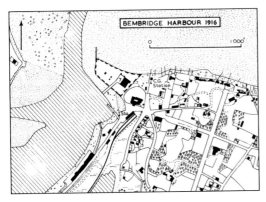

The Short 184 as the main type operated from Bembridge; this is not a Bembridge shot. (Ray Sturtivant)

# CAPEL (Folkestone)

**County:** Kent
**UTM/Grid:** OS map 179–TR260389
**Lat/Long:** N51°06.3 E001°13.6
**Nearest Town:** Folkestone 2 miles to south-west

The SS12 at Capel August 1915.

## HISTORY

Airships were one of the Admiralty's main weapons in the war against German submarines during World War One and Capel was one of a number of sites along the south coast and Thames estuary chosen for development into an airship station. The site at Capel le Ferne (now best known for its impressive memorial to the Battle of Britain) was acquired in early 1915 and, despite the fact that construction was still underway, the Station opened on 8 May 1915. Three airships were housed here in purpose-built sheds, although the airships themselves, the ex-army *Beta, Delta* and *Gamma* were by no means ideal, but new ships – the SS series – were already under development. The site eventually became the main assembly- and test-station for the SS series, although

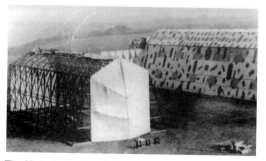

The SS sheds dominated the landscape.

the inauspicious arrival of SS1 – it crashed on approach – was perhaps not the best of starts!

The three airship sheds, modified as the larger airships came into service, continued to dominate this cliff-top site, although a number of workshops and accommodation huts were built on the east side, whilst the officers used Abbots Cliff House. In addition to its task of maintaining coastal anti-submarine patrols, for which it had three of four airships on call, Capel also undertook design and construction work on airships and kite balloons, making it an important Admiralty Station during this period.

The RAF took over the station in April 1918 but little else changed – other than the official change of name to Folkestone. During this last year of the war, Capel had an operational strength of between five and seven airships, mostly of the SSZ (SS–Zero) type. The end of the war brought a rapid end to Folkestone and within a few months the site had closed.

A final burst of military activity occurred during World War Two when the site was used for a wireless station. Although none of the site's buildings survive, the concrete bases of the airship sheds can still be seen.

Satellite moorings were used at Godmerstone Park (TR049504) and Wittersham (TQ886281); these sites were in use from early 1918 and it was standard practice for Capel to maintain one airship at each mooring. With the end of the war both were immediately abandoned.

# DOVER

**County:** Kent
**UTM/Grid:** OS map 179–TR335432-TR326414
**Lat/Long:** N51°07.30 E000°120
**Nearest Town:** All within 2 miles of Dover

Typically for World War one the Dover airfields a variety of types; the BE series would have been present at the landing grounds although this BE2e is not a Dover shot.

## HISTORY

Whilst Dover and aviation is perhaps best remembered for cross-Channel flights and especially that first flight by Blériot in July 1909, there were three distinct military flying-stations in the immediate vicinity of Dover, all active during World War One: these were located at Guston Road, Marine Parade and St Margarets. These are covered below in chronological order.

## DOVER (Guston Road) (TR325430)

The Admiralty was an early advocate of aviation and, in 1911–1912, was searching for suitable locations at which to construct Naval Air Stations; their eye fell on a site at Dover, to the north-east of the town, for an airfield with the dual purpose of defending the port and providing a staging post for the route to France. A 55-acre site not far from Fort Burgoyne was mapped out in summer 1913 and construction work began. The airfield had progressed little by the outbreak of war, but in December 1914 it received its first operational detachment, although the aircraft of 2 Squadron RNAS were joined and then replaced by those of 1 Squadron RNAS. As with the RFC's airfield at nearby Swingate Down, units based at

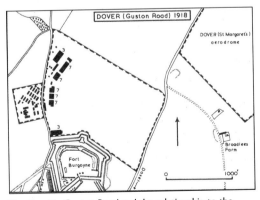

Plan showing Guston Road and the relationship to the St Margarets airfield.

Guston Road had the dual task of working-up to operational status and maintaining a defence flight against German air attack. The RNAS was, however, a very aggressive force and it was not long before offensive sorties were being flown: an attack mounted on the German naval facilities at Ostend and Zeebrugge on 17 February 1915, albeit with little success, was one of a number of such efforts. However, Guston Road's primary task was that of training and a number of squadrons formed here and either remained for training or departed to other airfields for the same purpose. This remained the situation even after the RAF had taken control in April 1918, although the operational role had also increased.

The airfield had maintained the Dover Defence Flight for some time, whose black-painted aircraft were part of the Home Defence network but also flew maritime patrols. It was the latter role that took the airfield into the last few months of the war and beyond; from August 1918, the DH9s of No.491 Flight became part of 233 Squadron and were tasked with anti-submarine and coastal patrols, this work occupying them until the end of the war. The move of the Flight to Walmer in January 1919 meant the end of Guston Road and it was closed early the following year.

## UNITS

**Pre-1919**

| | | |
|---|---|---|
| 1 Sqn RNAS | 29 Dec 1914–Feb 1915 | various |
| 2 Sqn RNAS det | 24 Dec 1914–2 Jan 1915; 10 Feb 1915–Jun 1915 | TB.8 |
| 491 Flt | 25 May 1918–1 Mar 1919 | DH9, Sopwith 1½ Strutter |

# DOVER (St Margarets/ Swingate Down) (TR335432)

Located two miles north-east of Dover, this field had seen some private flying and was thus considered a suitable site at which to construct a landing ground for the RFC as a final land-stage in England before hopping across the Channel to France. It was first used for this purpose in August 1914, when aircraft of the first three squadrons destined for France – 2, 3 and 4 Squadrons RFC – passed through; the latter left a small detachment at St Margarets to act as a defence and patrol unit, although this only stayed a month before it, too, had gone to France. The last of the available 'front-line' squadrons had transited by October and the airfield entered a temporary lull during which improvement work was undertaken.

By spring 1915 the airfield had been given wooden hangars and huts and in May the next unit, 15 Squadron, appeared, being retained as a training and replacement unit, as well as fulfilling a Home Defence role. The training role for Dover/St Margarets, which was also referred to locally as Swingate Down or Langdon, increased as more units arrived, including the temporary presence of the Machine Gun School. When this left in November 1915 the airfield was used to form two reserve squadrons, one of which, No.13 Reserve Squadron, remained to become the airfield's main training unit for the next eighteen months. The unit operated the usual diverse range of types, although Avro 504s and BE2 variants were in a majority. This reserve squadron gave birth to a number of similar units at Dover and, when it finally departed in June 1917, it changed places with No.62 Training Squadron (all Reserve Squadrons having become Training (Ex-Reserve) Squadrons) at Yatesbury. Further changes of training took place and a number of operational squadrons also passed through the airfield, on either work-up or detached to fulfil a training role.

When the RFC assumed responsibility for Home Defence, Dover was a logical location for a dedicated Home Defence unit and on 15 May 1916 the BE2c-equipped 50 Squadron had been formed here. This was short-lived and the squadron departed in

October to its new bases, leaving Swingate Down to its growing training role. Further expansion of facilities took place during 1917, with five substantial hangars, an aircraft-repair shed and other buildings, and by spring 1918 the airfield had become No.53 Training Depot Station with a notional establishment of twenty-four Avro 504Ks for initial training and twenty-four Camels for advanced training. Accidents, including running over the cliffs (!), were still all too common, despite various improvements to the landing area. The TDS continued its role to autumn 1918 but, in October, it became the School for Marine Operational Pilots and its aircraft establishment concentrated on the DH9.

By February 1919 the school had closed and this once vibrant training airfield was no longer required, the airfield being de-requisitioned the following year. However, parts of the site were retained for storage and, although this was short-lived, the site was not abandoned. In 1938 active military occupation returned and Dover became part of the vital network of Chain Home radar stations. It remained a radar site into the post-war period and, after it was no longer required for military use, the towers were retained for civil use.

## UNITS

### HQ Units at Swingate Down

No.6 Wing   30 Aug 1915–8 Sep 1916

### Pre-1919

| | | |
|---|---|---|
| 2 Sqn | 12–13 Aug 1914 | BE2, RE1 |
| 3 Sqn | 12–13 Aug 1914; | various, |
| | 2 May 1919–15 Oct 1919 | cadre only |
| 4 Sqn det | 13 Aug 1914–20 Sep 1914 | BE2c |
| 5 Sqn | 14–15 Aug 1914 | Avro 504 |
| 7 Sqn det | Sep 1914–Oct 1914 | various |
| 9 Sqn | 23 Jul 1915–12 Dec 1915 | various |
| 15 Sqn | 11 May 1915–23 Dec 1915 | various |
| 27 Sqn | 10 Dec 1915–1 Mar 1916 | various |
| 49 Sqn | 15 Apr 1916–12 Nov 1917 | various |
| 50 Sqn | 15 May 1916–23 Oct 1916 | Be2c, BE12 |
| 58 Sqn | 22 Dec 1917–10 Jan 1918 | FE2b |
| 110 Sqn | 12–26 Nov 1917 | various |
| 212 Sqn | 7 Mar 1919–9 Feb 1920 | DH9a |
| MGS | 3 Oct 1915–27 Nov 1915 | various |
| 12 RS | 15–16 Nov 1915 | various |
| 13 RS | 27 Nov 1915–1 Jun 1917 | various |
| 20 RS | 1 Feb 1916–24 Jul 1916 | various |
| 62 TS | 1 Jun 1917–1 May 1918 | various |
| 64 RS | 7–14 Apr 1917 | various |
| 65 TS | 25 Nov 1917–15 Jul 1918 | various |
| 53 TDS | 15 Jul 1918–15 Oct 1918 | Avro 504, |
| | | Camel, DH9 |
| SMOP | 15 Oct 1918–1 Feb 1919 | DH9 |

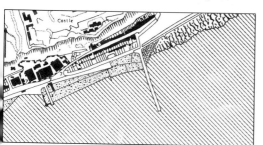

# DOVER (Marine Parade) (TR326414)

It was probably logical that Dover would acquire a seaplane base but, unlike other sites where such a base could be co-located with the landplane field, this was not the case at Dover, as both airfields were on top of the cliffs. In response to the growing U-boat threat, two RNAS seaplanes, both Wright navy-types, were despatched to Dover and located in the harbour – and the navy promptly requisitioned the skating rink on Marine Parade as a shed for the aircraft! A slipway was built and Dover/Marine Parade was in business. It was a far from ideal site and it was not long before the operational task had been taken over by other stations, although Dover was retained as a training and repair depot. Additional buildings were erected along the Parade, as was a second slipway, and new naval seaplane-pilots spent four weeks at Dover before transferring to the main operational station at Dunkirk. These roles, including modification and development work, continued until the RAF took over in April 1918, by which time an increased operational requirement to counter the German U-boats in the Channel meant that 233 Squadron based its No.407 Flight, operating Short 184s, at Marine Parade. The Flight remained in place after the war but eventually disbanded in May 1919, although the buildings at Marine Parade may have been out of use before that date. Marine Parade was also home to HQ No.5 Group from April 1918 to May 1919, this command organization having administrative responsibility for units in the Kent and Dunkirk area, for which it also operated an advanced HQ at Spycker Camp.

Dover Harbour continued to appear in the RAF's list of seaplane alighting areas into the 1930s, but it was never again a permanent station.

## UNITS

### HQ Units at Marine Parade
No.5 Gp    1 Apr 1918–15 May 1919

### Pre-1919
407 Flt    20 May 1918–31 Mar 1919    Short 184

## MEMORIALS

The Dover area has a number of aviation memorials:

1. Stone outline of Blériot monoplane to mark the end point of the historic cross-Channel flight, inscribed: 'After making the first Channel flight by aeroplane Louis Blériot landed at this spot on Sunday 25th July 1909. This memorial was presented to the Aero Club of the United Kingdom by Alexander Duckham.'
2. Statue of C R Rolls on Marine Parade, inscribed: 'Charles Stewart Rolls – the first man to cross the Channel and return in a single flight, June 2nd 1910.'
3. Window in St Mary's church (near the castle) depicting high-speed launch and Walrus with airmen in dinghy, inscribed: 'In memory of all ranks of the Allied Air Forces and Air-Sea Rescue and Marine Craft Sections of the Royal Air Force who perished in the seas throughout the world during the Second World War.'
4. Granite plinth at Swingate Down, inscribed: 'The Royal Flying Corps contingent of the 1914 British Expeditionary Force consisting of Nos.2, 3, 4 & 5 Squadrons flew from this field to Amiens between 13 & 15 August 1914.'

The SS2 in its shed at Dover in April 1915.

# DYMCHURCH (Hythe/Palmarsh)

**County:** Kent
**UTM/Grid:** OS map 189–TR127330
**Lat/Long:** N51°03.4 E001°02.0
**Nearest Town:** Hythe 2½ miles to north-east

## HISTORY

By 1917 this airfield on the edge of Romney Marsh was a major training facility for the Royal Flying Corps, as home to the School of Aerial Gunnery. The site had been in use since early 1915 and, in November, the Machine Gun School moved in from Dover – but at this stage there was no airfield; aircraft operated from Lympne, whilst the HQ was in Hythe at the Imperial Hotel. Renamed the School of Aerial Gunnery on 3 September 1916, the increased usage of the ranges in this area made it desirable to establish a landing ground, although first use of the chosen site at Dymchurch (hence one of the names for the airfield, although it was also known as Hythe and Palmarsh) was by the Kite Balloon Section. In a confusing series of decisions on the future of the School it was decided that the unit, now renamed No.1 (Auxiliary) School of Aerial Gunnery, needed a proper well-equipped aerodrome and an area close to the balloon site was acquired and developed. The new airfield gained an impressive line-up of Bessonneau hangars along with various huts for technical and instructional use. The airfield was ideally situated adjacent to the training ranges but it paid a price, in that the weather factor and surface conditions were far from ideal, leading to a spate of accidents, although most training airfields at this period had poor accident records. The length of course was usually only two weeks, just enough to introduce observers to the principles of aerial gunnery before passing them on to their squadrons or next stage of training. Another change of name was made in March 1918, when the 'Auxiliary' was changed to 'Observer', but this had no effect on the actual work being carried out. In November the unit moved to New Romney and Dymchurch became an emergency field, a number of aircraft taking advantage of its nearness to the ranges. The airfield was finally abandoned early the following year and, having been dismantled, was put up for disposal in 1920. Little now remains of this once busy and important airfield.

The location remained on RAF files and it was one of the World War One airfields examined in 1942 for possible development as an ALG, although there is some debate as to whether or not it was the old site or simply an area near Dymchurch that was the subject of study; either way, no action was taken.

## UNITS

**Pre-1919**

| | |
|---|---|
| MGS | 27 Nov 1915–13 Sep 1916 |
| SoAG | 3 Sep 1916–Jan 1917 |
| 1 (A)SoAG | Jan 1917–9 Mar 1918 |
| 1 (O) SoAG | 9 Mar 1918–1 Nov 1918; ? 1919–14 Feb 1919 |

# EASTBOURNE

**County:** East Sussex
**UTM/Grid:** OS map 198–TQ625015
**Lat/Long:** N50°47.5 E000°18.1
**Nearest Town:** Eastbourne 2 miles to south

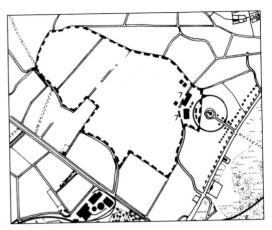

## HISTORY

The airfield at Eastbourne was amongst the earliest in England when the Eastbourne Flying School (also known as the Fowler Flying School) opened its doors on December 1911. This private venture was the brainchild of Frederick Fowler, who had acquired the assets of a flying school at Beaulieu and moved them to a 50-acre site just north of Eastbourne on Willingdon Level. Fifteen months later, the Eastbourne Aviation Company was formed and a site on the Crumbles was turned into a seaplane factory. With the outbreak of World War One the airfield was acquired by the Admiralty, who had already been involved with the site since 1913, having leased part of the airfield and subsidized the development of facilities.

This was essentially two sites: the training airfield, which, as the Naval Flying School, was extended by acquiring neighbouring land, and the Crumbles factory, at which production was increased to meet wartime demand. This production was not, however, of seaplanes but of types such as the BE2c and Avro 504, although it also acted as a repair facility for RNAS aircraft. The factory prospered with war contracts but, as the war neared its end, this work slumped and, despite attempts to find new work, the factory was closed in 1924.

By 1915 the training airfield had become a busy and fascinating place, with large numbers of RNAS pilots undertaking initial flying-training on a wide variety of aircraft types – a far from ideal situation for a training establishment. The aircraft types were rationalized and, by mid-1916, the airfield was home to Maurice Farmans and Curtiss Jennys, although other types were also present for use by the instructors or visitors.

The AIR 1 plan for 1916 shows a small oval of land, less than 1,000 yards across at its longest run, with a small clutch of buildings on the east side.

Indeed, Eastbourne was never an ideal airfield in some respects, as the surface area was poor, due to numerous small ditches, many of which had to be boarded over.

When the RAF took over the site in 1918, upon absorbing the RNAS, the training routine continued, with the Naval Flying School initially becoming No.206 Training Depot Station. However, No.54 Training Squadron was transferred to Eastbourne from Castle Bromwich and a week later the two units became No.50 Training Depot Station. The TDS was primarily tasked with training crews for day-bomber units and, to achieve this, it used a mixed fleet that included the Avro 504, F2b, DH6, DH9 and Camel. The number of trainees decreased in the latter weeks of the war and, by late-1918, the TDS was much reduced in size. It appears to have moved from Eastchurch in summer 1919 and was certainly established at Manston by early autumn. The airfield reverted to its former owners but, despite some interest in pleasure flying, it was not possible to attract enough business and it was closed in 1920, returning once more to agriculture.

## UNITS

**Pre-1919**

| | | |
|---|---|---|
| NFS | Aug 1914–Nov 1916; | various |
| | May 1917–Apr 1918 | |
| 206 TDS | 1 Apr 1918–15 Jul 1918 | various |
| 54 TS | 6–15 Jul 1918 | various |
| 50 TDS | 15 Jul 1918–mid-1919 | various |

# FORELAND

**County:** Isle of Wight
**UTM/Grid:** OS map–SZ654877
**Lat/Long:** N50°41.1 W001°04.5
**Nearest Town:** Adjacent to Bembridge

## HISTORY

The seaplane station at Bembridge Point had been established in 1915 when it became apparent that aircraft based on the Isle of Wight would be useful additions to the coastal patrols designed to counter German submarine operations. This same rationale led to the establishment of a landplane station in the same rough area at Foreland's 51-acre site. The landing ground was laid out during early 1918 at Lane End and was referred to as New Bembridge as well as Foreland; it may even at one stage have been called Brading (as was the Bembridge seaplane station!) Very few facilities were provided, other than a number of Bessonneau hangars, with unit personnel accommodated in the local area. Equipped with the DH6, two Special Duty Flights (511 and 512) formed at Brading in June 1918, moving to Foreland in August, as part of No.75 Wing and effectively elements of 253 Squadron. Anti-submarine patrols

were maintained to the end of the war but, with the Armistice, there was no further need of this landing ground and by early 1919 it had been abandoned.

## UNITS

**Pre-1919**

| | | |
|---|---|---|
| 511 Flt | 8 Aug 1918–Jan 1919 | DH6 |
| 512 Flt | 8 Aug 1918–Jan 1919 | DH6 |

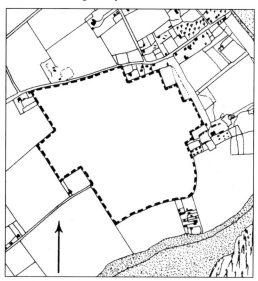

# GORING-BY-SEA

**County:** Sussex
**UTM/Grid:** OS map 199 – TQ114036
**Lat/Long:** N50°49.2 W000°25.2
**Nearest Town:** Worthing 2 miles to south-east

## HISTORY

This 168-acre site was acquired in late-1917/early 1918 for development into one of the series of Training Depot Stations allocated for the United States Air Service. However, it was one of the last to go into construction and it is believed that no significant work had commenced before the end of the war.

# GRAIN (Port Victoria)

**County/State:** Kent
**UTM/Grid:** OS map 178–TQ890753
**Lat/Long:** N51°26.7 E000°43.1
**Nearest Town:** Sheerness 3 miles to east

The Grain PV2 was one of a number of aircraft designed at the Grain/Port Victoria airfield, although most were little more than experimental. (Peter Green)

## HISTORY

The Medway Estuary has played a key part in Britain's defences since the Middle Ages and in the early years of aviation a site on the west shore (almost opposite Sheerness), not far from the junction with the Thames, was chosen as a seaplane station by the Admiralty. The site was commissioned on 30 December 1912, making it one of the earliest naval air-stations, and a series of hangars (sheds as they were then known), slipways and other buildings were constructed over the next few years; although some existing buildings, including a run of Coastguard cottages, were taken over. This new location was variously known as the Isle of Grain, or simply Grain, and Port Victoria. Almost at once the station was used for trials work; this was the early days of seaplanes and the RNAS needed somewhere to develop and test this new type of machine. It was not long before the assembled experts were designing their own aircraft, the Experimental Armament Section having been established here in late-1915, along with a Seaplane Test Flight and an Experimental Construction Section. Together they became the Marine Experimental Aircraft Depot.

In addition to evaluating production types, for example, deck-landing trials with Sopwith Pups using a marked-out area on the airfield before the real thing was tried on a ship, the Depot modified aircraft to make them more suitable for the naval role. The first Port Victoria designation (PV.1) was applied to a modified Sopwith Baby, the first of a series of PV 'designs' from 1916 to the end of the war. Most of these aircraft were new designs with specific naval-requirements in mind; the PV.7 Grain , for example, was a single-seat fighter design having a very small wing-span, only 18ft, to make it suitable for use on small destroyers. Unfortunately, very few of these designs proved satisfactory and, whilst they provided useful information, they were not production machines.

The 1916 plan shows two slipways and a jetty with a line of sheds and other buildings running parallel to the coast, whilst the roughly rectangular landing-ground was about 2,500ft × 1,500ft. Photographs of machines at Grain illustrate a, perhaps, useful aspect of the Station's work, that of armament development and experiment, as well as the navalization of aircraft through the addition of floatation systems. This was, without doubt, a fascinating station during World War One and, although it played little direct part in operations, other than a number of anti-Zeppelin patrols (by the Nore War Flight) in the early years of the war, it did play a significant role in developing naval aviation. By the end of the war Grain had grown to a sizeable station and it retained its trials role into the early 1920s, finally closing its doors (or should that be slipways) on 17 March 1924, when the, by then, Marine Aircraft Experimental Unit moved to Felixstowe.

There is no trace of this important airfield and a large power-station occupies the approximate area of the site.

## UNITS

**Pre-1919**

| | |
|---|---|
| Experimental Flt | Apr 1916–1918 |
| Seaplane Design Flt | Dec 1916–1918 |
| Design Flt | Mar 1917–1918 |
| MAES | May 1918–Mar 1924 |

*The precise title of the main unit(s) changed from time to time and all had been absorbed into the Marine Aircraft Experimental Station by May 1918, although this too later changed its name.*

# KINGSNORTH

**County:** Kent
**UTM/Grid:** OS map179–TQ810725
**Lat/Long:** N51°25.4 E000°36.1
**Nearest Town:** Rochester 5 miles to south-west

## History

Not to be confused with the World War Two Kingsnorth ALG – also in Kent but in a different part of the county – this Kingsnorth was an important naval airship-station thirty years previously. With the establishment of military air-arms in 1912, the Admiralty formed a Naval Airship Branch, always something of a Cinderella service compared with aeroplanes but important nonetheless. Work began on building an airship station in one of the heartlands of the Royal Navy, the Medway, close to Chatham naval base. An area of land near the village of Hoo, and not from the air station at Grain, was chosen for development and work commenced on building the necessary infrastructure.

Kingsnorth was commissioned in April 1914 with building work still underway and three months later was part of the Royal Naval Air Service, the airship branch having been absorbed into the RNAS; by August and the outbreak of war, one airship – the *Astra Torres* – was on site, soon joined by *Perseval*.

These two airships carried out patrols along the Thames and into the Channel. The Station was also given a developmental role and was called on to provide an anti-submarine airship – and given only a few weeks to come up with a workable design. The 'SS' (Submarine Scout) type of airship first flew in early 1915 and was, in essence, a BE2c aircraft-fuselage suspended beneath a Willows gas-envelope. This seemingly Heath-Robinson arrangement proved workable and was duly put into production! Experienced airship-staff moved in from Farnborough to help work on other designs, the next one being the 'C' (Coastal) type, using an established envelope-type and with a cabin comprising two Avro 504 front-fuselages bolted together. In recognition of its pre-eminent position in respect of naval airships, Kingsnorth also took on the task of training crews, and the Station's facilities, dominated by the massive airship-sheds, were further developed and a large number of buildings were erected. The Station retained its dual role of airship development and production, and training for the rest of the war; a number of other designs were forthcoming. Trials also took place on how best to use airships and other developmental work, all of which justified Kingsnorth's reputation as a centre of excellence for airships. However, the end of the war brought it all to a rapid end and, in a post-war environment that saw more future for aircraft than airships, Kingsnorth closed in 1919, being finally dismantled the following year.

The SS7 at Kingsnorth; a good view of the 'gondola (a BE2 fuselage!).

# LEYSDOWN
# (Shellbeach)

**County:** Kent
**UTM/Grid:** OS map–TR040698
**Lat/Long:** N51°23.4 E000°55.9
**Nearest Town:** Leysdown-on-Sea ½ mile to north-west

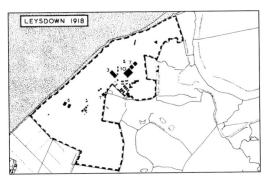

## HISTORY

Leysdown is one of a number of sites in Kent competing for the title of 'first aerodrome', its claim resting on the creation in 1909 of an airfield alongside the aircraft-construction sheds erected by Short Brothers. It all started when a local balloon enthusiast, Griffith Brewer, persuaded Shorts to undertake licence building of Wright Flyers at Leysdown. They acquired a patch of marshy land and started to build a number of sheds for aircraft assembly, whilst other sheds were erected by members of the Aero Club. As this was taking place in 1909–1910 there is, indeed, some justification for calling Leysdown the first planned airfield. All was not well, however, and the site soon proved inadequate as a flying ground. A number of aircraft did fly from here, but by early 1910 Shorts had moved their main facility to Eastchurch. This was not the end of Leysdown and development work continued, primarily on floatplanes.

A second lease of life came in 1917, with the need to expand military training-facilities, for which Leysdown was well placed due to the presence of coastal ranges. The site had already been used as an ELG by Eastchurch, but it was now developed into a training airfield in its own right. A number of buildings were erected, including two Bessonneau

hangars, and aircraft of the Gunnery School from Eastchurch moved in. This unit became the Pilots & Observers Aerial Gunnery and Aerial Fighting School on 1 April 1918, when it came under RAF control. It was, however, a short life; although by late-summer 1918 the Marine Observers School had taken over at Leysdown. This, too, was short-lived but the airfield remained in military hands to administer the nearby ranges and to act as an emergency field for aircraft using the range. From January 1932 to November 1937 the airfield was also a satellite for the Air Armament School.

The range commitment continued in World War Two and there was a plan to form No.9 Anti-Aircraft Practice Camp at Leysdown in May 1943, the flying element to be No.1633 Flight, but this appears to have been cancelled before any action was taken. The military retained the site into the 1970s and final disposal did not take place until 1981!

## UNITS

**Pre-1919**
MOS　　　Aug 1918–Sep 1919

**1919–1938**
AAS　　　Jan 1932–Nov 1937

# NEWHAVEN

**County:** East Sussex
**UTM/Grid:** OS map–TQ454002
**Lat/Long:** N50°47.0 E000°03.7
**Nearest Town:** North-west outskirts of Newhaven

## HISTORY

RNAS Newhaven opened in May 1917, as part of the Admiralty's attempts to increase the anti-submarine patrols by the RNAS following an increase in German submarine activity. A stretch of beach adjacent to Newhaven port was chosen and a wooden slipway was laid across the beach. A hardstand was built for the aircraft and other facilities included a number of hangars plus various wooden sheds, although none of these were for accommodation, both officers and men being billeted locally. As with the other seaplane sites on the mainland, this was a sub-station for Calshot and it was allocated four Short 184 floatplanes, although this was later increased to six. When the RAF took over the site in April 1918 there were plans for more permanent facilities and an adjacent landing ground, but little progress had been made before the war ended. Since May, Newhaven had been home to No.408 Flight, this being later joined by No.409 Flight and both becoming part of 242 Squadron when it formed in August within No.10 Group. It was rare for these anti-submarine patrols to see the enemy but, on 7 July 1918, one of the squadron's Short 184s delivered an accurate attack on a surfaced submarine; the single bomb exploded close to its target but it was not credited as destroyed. In terms of the hundreds of hours of such patrols flown by the RNAS and RAF aircraft it was a rare moment of excitement – and frustration.

The squadron disbanded in May 1919 and the station closed by the end of the year.

## UNITS

**Pre-1919**

| | | |
|---|---|---|
| 408 Flt | May 1918 – May 1919 | Short 184, Campania |
| 409 Flt | May 1918 – Nov 1918 | Short 184 |

# POLEGATE

**County:** East Sussex
**UTM/Grid:** OS map 199–TQ581035
**Lat/Long:** N50°49.6 E000°14.6
**Nearest Town:** Eastbourne 3½ miles to south-east

## HISTORY

The airship station at Polegate was opened on 6 July 1915, having been chosen for development earlier in the year. A 142-acre site was acquired just south of Polegate village, but the seemingly suitable meadowland proved to be a problem for the constructors due to waterlogging. By the end of the year three SS-type airships were stationed at the still-incomplete station, their main role being anti-submarine patrols along the Sussex coast. A second airship-shed was erected in 1916 and a fourth SS-type blimp added; the SS40 *Black Ship* was put together at Polegate – its nickname came from the fact that it was painted black for secret operations over Europe. The station's main role remained that of anti-submarine patrols and, over the next two years, improved airships entered service and Polegate became an important station within Portsmouth Command, as evidenced by almost continual development, with new buildings springing up, including a large number of huts for accommodation.

In April 1918 the RAF took over but nothing changed in respect of the operational role, with the airships remaining under the control of the Admiralty.

For part of the war, Polegate had operated two out-stations Slindon (SU952104) and Upton. Slindon, sited north-east of Chichester, was used as a mooring out-station from April 1918 and up to two SSZ airships operated from this site in Eartham Wood. The second mooring out-station, Upton saw similar usage.

The end of the war meant that Polegate's airships were no longer required and the station was closed in 1919, with most of the buildings being removed shortly afterwards.

Two SS airships in A Shed at Polegate, October 1916.
(Jack Bruce)

# RUSTINGTON

**County:** West Sussex
**UTM/Grid:** OS map–TQ058020
**Lat/Long:** N50°48.5 W000°30.0
**Nearest Town:** Littlehampton 2 miles to west

## HISTORY

Named after the nearby village, Rustington appears to have come into use as a day-only Landing Ground in 1917, for use by aircraft operating in the villages that abounded in this part of Sussex. Records are poor but the field appears to have been little more than that and, as no units were based here, there is no movement record. The following year the site was proposed for development as a Training Depot Station, to help meet the growing need for training bases. A site of roughly 160 acres was earmarked for use by the United States Air Service for bomber training and work commenced on construction of sheds suitable for the Handley Page 0/400 bombers. Work was brought to an end when the war ended and, in October 1919, the site was in the process of being dismantled and the land was returned to its original owners.

# SHEERNESS

**County:** Kent
**UTM/Grid:** OS map 178–TQ913742 and TQ932748
**Lat/Long:** N51°26.1 E000°45.0 and N51°26.4 E000°46.7
**Nearest Town:** Located at Sheerness

## HISTORY

During World War One, Sheerness was the location for two aviation establishments, one for the Admiralty and one for the Royal Flying Corps. The Navy had long had an association with the port of Sheerness and, indeed, in January 1912 a ship (HMS *Africa*) anchored off the naval base of HMS *Actaeon* had been the scene of the first aeroplane flight from the deck (or rather a platform over a gun turret) of a British warship. This feat was performed in a Short 184 by Lieutenant Charles Samson, one of that impressive breed of early naval aviators, and, whilst it had little immediate impact on naval planning, it was very much the start of sea-borne naval aviation; but it has to be remembered that, in these early days, naval aviation was very much a land-based affair. The Admiralty's subsequent interest in Sheerness came in 1917, with the establishment of a kite-balloon training establishment on a 75-acre site near Mile Town (TQ913742) south of the dockyard. No.1 Balloon Training Base (SE) was duly formed to handle the training of balloon observers who had already been through the basic course at the Roehampton Depot. The Navy used kite balloons aboard ships as an 'over the horizon' observation system and Sheerness was soon providing a steady steam of trained observers. The Station was provided with five canvas balloon-sheds and a number of huts for other uses, but it was never a very developed site. This training role continued to the end of the war and the RAF, who had assumed control in April 1918, finally handed the site back to the Admiralty in September 1919.

The Royal Flying Corps Landing Ground was further to the east (TQ932748) near Marine Town and was established as an Emergency Landing Ground, probably from early 1917. It was given virtually no facilities other than a minimal cleared operating-area and was primarily intended for use by Home Defence aircraft, this part of Kent and Essex being covered by 37 Squadron's various detached flights. The following year it was also available for day use by aircraft operating in the Sheerness ranges; although records for this type of site are poor and despite the fact that there are no recorded incidents of it being used, it almost certainly witnessed a landing or two.

# SOUTHBOURNE

**County:** West Sussex
**UTM/Grid:** OS map–SU763065
**Lat/Long:** N50°51.2 W000°55.0
**Nearest Town:** Chichester 6 miles to east

## HISTORY

The need for airfields to enable the build-up of American air strength for the Western Front had led to the development of a number of sites in southern England: Southbourne was one such site. A 247-acre area was chosen in late-1917 for a bomber Training Depot Station using the HP 0/400 and, as usual with such sites, the plan was impressive, with a series of large aeroplane-sheds, including a Handley Page erection-shed, along with a variety of other buildings and huts. As it was intended for large bombers, the landing ground itself was levelled and treated and Southbourne would have been an impressive airfield had it been completed. However, by the Armistice, work, although advanced, was not complete and the site was put up for disposal.

# TELSCOMBE CLIFFS

**County:** Sussex
**UTM/Grid:** OS map 198–TQ406017
**Lat/Long:** N50°47.8 W000°00.4
**Nearest Town:** Brighton 7 miles to west

## HISTORY

The site at Telscombe Cliffs was developed in late-1916 in response to German airship raids on the Portsmouth area and was one of three Landing Grounds allocated to the newly formed 78 Squadron. The squadron formed at Newhaven on 1 November and, as usual with Home Defence squadrons at this period, was equipped with a mix of BE2c and BE12 aircraft. The Landing Ground was little more than a 1,500ft square of rough grass, although it was also given two Bessonneau hangars. Accommodation for squadron personnel was mainly tents, although some lucky ones – mainly the officers – acquired local billets. It was an unproductive and uncomfortable time for the squadron and they moved to Sutton's Farm in mid-September 1917, where they also re-equipped with better aircraft. Telscombe Cliffs became an Emergency Landing Ground, although since 27 August it had also been home to No.13 Aircraft Acceptance Park. The AAP remained in residence to March 1918, although it is not certain how busy it was during this time. With the departure of the AAP, Telscombe was allocated to a new role as one of a number of airfields housing special-duty flights for coastal patrol work. No.514 (SD) Flight formed as part of 253 Squadron in June 1918, within No.10 Group, and operated DH6 aircraft along the coast and in support of coastal shipping, the primary purpose being anti-submarine patrol. The airfield was given a double wooden-shed to house the six or so DH6s, but little else changed at what remained a basic field. The Flight became part of 242 Squadron in August 1918, but nothing else changed in terms of the missions flown between this date and the end of the war. Neither 514 Flight nor Telscombe long survived the war's end; the Flight disbanded in January (the rest of the Squadron – whose home base was Newhaven – followed in May) and the airfield had reverted to its original owners by spring.

## UNITS

**Pre-1919**

| | | |
|---|---|---|
| 78 Sqn | Nov 1916–20 Sep 1917 | BE2c, BE12 |
| 514 Flt | 7 Jun 1918–20 Jan 1919 | DH6 |

# THROWLEY

**County:** Kent
**UTM/Grid:** OS map–TQ991535
**Lat/Long:** N51°14.7 E000°51.1
**Nearest Town:** Faversham 5 miles to north

SE5a of 143 Squadron at Throwley. (Peter Green)

## HISTORY

Throwley was developed in late-1916 as one of the new landing grounds created for the RFC with its adoption of responsibility for the Home Defence role. Situated on the North Downs near Throwley Forstal, hence the name, an area of some 87 acres was taken over and the BE2Cs of 50 Squadron took up residence from October. This squadron had become the main HD unit in this part of Kent and, as was usual in this scenario, established flights at a number of locations, Throwley becoming home initially to 'C Flight', as well as making use of other landing grounds on an 'as required' basis. In July the following year, this detachment was joined by 112 Squadron, this unit having formed (out of 'B Flight 50 Squadron) on 25 July 1917 at Detling. This became the most significant unit at Throwley and remained in residence to June 1919, having operated Pups, Camels and Snipes. By this stage of the war the main air-threat to Britain was from the German strategic-bombers rather than Zeppelins but very few raids were mounted and, even when the enemy did appear, the defending fighters had little success. Indeed, the only accredited victory for a Throwley aircraft came on 19 May 1918, when Capt C Brand shot down a Gotha G.IV of Kaghol 3.

As far as the airfield itself was concerned, it was developed from the usual 'field with a few tents and requisitioned buildings' to a somewhat more established look, complete with a set of Bessonneau hangars and a number of other buildings. By 1918 this building programme included a hutted camp for accommodation, along with various technical buildings and hangars. On 1 February 1918 a new unit was formed, when 143 Squadron was created from a nucleus of 112 Squadron, although, rather than using the established types of that unit, the new squadron equipped with Armstrong Whitworth FK8s; however, after less than two weeks, the squadron moved to Detling. In May, the Pups and Camels of 188 (Night) Training Squadron arrived from East Retford and continued their training role to March 1919. The pace of activity at Throwley had slowed with the end of the war the previous November and, by early 1919, this once-busy airfield was all but deserted. In October that year, it was transferred to the Ministry of Munitions but there is no record of it being used. The site subsequently reverted to agriculture and aviation ended – except that in mid-1940 the same rough area around Cadman's Farm was allocated as an emergency landing-ground and dispersal field for Detling. It does not, however, appear to have been used.

## UNITS

**Pre-1919**

| | | |
|---|---|---|
| 50 Sqn det | Oct 1916–Mar 1918 | BE2, BE12 |
| 112 Sqn | 30 Jul 1917–13 Jun 1919 | Pup, Camel, Snipe |
| 143 Sqn | 1–14 Feb 1918 | Various |
| 188 (N) TS | 5 May 1918–1 Mar 1919 | Pup, Camel |

# TIPNOR

**County:** Hampshire
**UTM/Grid:** OS map 196–SU638034
**Lat/Long:** N50°49.6 W001°05.8
**Nearest Town:** Southern area of Portsmouth Harbour

## HISTORY

Tipnor was chosen as a kite-balloon site within Portsmouth harbour, a major naval facility with plenty of warships for which kite balloons were required. The small (12-acre) site was opened in 1917 and was given a row of six balloon-sheds, along with a hydrogen-producing plant and a variety of other buildings. When the RAF took over in April 1918 it became No.15 Kite Balloon Base under the control of Calshot, although operationally it remained part of Portsmouth Command. It was never a satisfactory situation for the RAF and Tipnor was one of the sites handed back to the Admiralty in summer 1919, although they, too, had no real use for the site other than as a range.

# WALMER

**County:** Kent
**UTM/Grid:** OS map 189–TR375493
**Lat/Long:** N51°11.6 E001°23.9
**Nearest Town:** Deal 2 miles to north

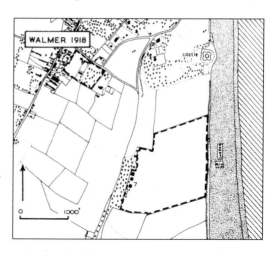

## HISTORY

Walmer has long been associated with the defence of England's coastline, an impressive castle being part of a chain of such fortifications in the sixteenth century. The creation of a Landing Ground, just south of the castle, in May 1917, was connected with protecting shipping using one of the great anchorages – The Downs – and the Walmer Defence Flight was established with a mix of aircraft types from BE2c to Pup. The airfield covered some fifty-seven acres on Hawkshill Down and was equipped with Bessonneau hangars, these being later replaced by three wooden aeroplane-sheds and wooden huts for accommodation, along with a number of requisitioned buildings. The Flight's main role was protecting shipping but, like all 'fighter flights', it was also engaged in Home Defence and met with some success against the German daylight bombers.

The airfield's defensive capability increased in autumn 1917 with the arrival of two front-line units, 3 (Naval) and 4 (Naval) Squadrons, although both were technically here to rest and recover from operations in France. Indeed, this proved to be a hectic few months, with a number of units passing through and the Walmer Flight becoming part of the newly formed 6 (Naval) Squadron, with HQ at Dover. The departure by early 1918 of naval aviation was soon made up for by the arrival of RAF aircraft, a mixed bag of aircraft types that eventually included Camels, DH9s and Short 184s. The Flight was one of three that became elements of 233 Squadron when that unit formed on 31 August, the other two being based at Dover. Operations continued to the end of the war, coastal patrols being the main work, and there was even a short detachment to bases across the Channel at the end of the year. However, although much of 233 Squadron gathered at Walmer in early 1919, there was no future for the squadron and it disbanded on 15 May. The airfield had also been used as a detachment location for another Dover unit –

No.2 Observer School – and this was the last unit to leave Walmer, probably in summer 1919. The airfield was soon forgotten, although a memorial was erected in 1920, one of the first such tributes, to those who had served at Walmer during World War One.

With the area returned to agriculture there was little trace of the airfield, although the approximate area was used during World War Two as an RAF MT location.

## UNITS

**Pre-1919**

| | | |
|---|---|---|
| 233 Sqn | Aug 1918–May 1919 | various |
| 471 Flt | 14 Jun 1918–25 Oct 1918;<br>Jan 1919–17 Mar 1919 | Camel |
| 491 Flt | Jan 1919–Mar 1919 | DH9 |

**RNAS**

| | | |
|---|---|---|
| 3 (Naval) Sqn | Nov 1917–Jan 1918 | |
| 4 (Naval) Sqn | Dec 1917–Mar 1918 | |
| 6 (Naval) Sqn | Jan 1918 | |
| 8 (Naval) Sqn | Mar 1918 | Camel |
| Walmer DF | May 1917–Jan 1918 | |
| 2 OS det | Sep 1918–Sep 1919 | |

## MEMORIALS

A memorial was erected in August 1920 by the Countess of Beauchamp to those who had lost their lives flying from Walmer. The thatched well-head fell into disrepair but the accompanying plaque was moved to another site.

# WESTGATE

**County:** Kent
**UTM/Grid:** OS map 179–TR328705
**Lat/Long:** N51°23.1 E001°20.7
**Nearest Town:** Margate 1½ miles to east

Short 184s at Westgate, 1918. (Ray Sturtivant)

## HISTORY

Westgate was one of a series of Admiralty Landing Grounds around the Thames Estuary, a vital area for naval operations and, as such, in need of the latest technology – aeroplanes – to provide coastal patrols. The site at St Mildred's Bay, Westgate-on-Sea was opened on 1 August 1914, but was little more than a flat area behind the gently sloping beach across which seaplanes were dragged. Like many of these early naval establishments this was an ad hoc unit that had to use borrowed aircraft and achieved little. By late-summer there was little activity from Westgate but the site was given slipways, a hangar and a few other buildings, and St Mildred's Hotel was requisitioned for accommodation. By the end of the year there was a permanent detachment of two seaplanes and it had been decided to extend the site by creating a larger airfield on the cliff-top slightly to the east. The primary purpose of the new site was Home Defence, still an Admiralty responsibility, and 'A Flight' of 2 (Naval) Squadron arrived in April 1915. Despite the limited facilities at Westgate, little more than a few wooden hangars and sheds, and the poor performance of the aircraft types then in use for Home Defence, the airfield was soon playing its part in the night war against German airships.

This dual role continued into 1916 but the new Landing Ground was not ideal and the decision was taken in July to move the landplane War Flight to Manston. The move was motivated by a string of accidents at Westgate and a recommendation that it should be closed as unsuitable; whilst this was agreed, it brought a rebuke from the Treasury that 'considerable saving of public money would apparently have been affected if the disadvantages attaching to Westgate had been foreseen before the Station was built there'.

The seaplane base remained active and, although the aircraft types changed over the next two years, the basic tasks remained the same. This continuity was also evident when the RAF took over the site

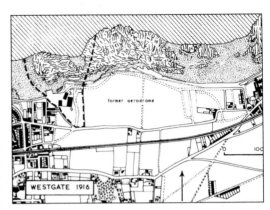

WESTGATE 1916

when it formed on 1 April 1918, although the following month the flying unit became No.406 (Seaplane) Flight, which in turn became an element of 219 Squadron in July. This was a mixed unit with two seaplane Flights, both of which were at Westgate, and three landplane Flights with HQ at Manston. The seaplane element was equipped with the Short 184 and Fairey IIIb, although other types were also used, and remained operational after the war. It seems likely that both Flights survived into late-1919 and possibly until the Squadron disbanded in February 1920. The seaplane station closed on 7 February 1920 and was immediately put up for disposal.

## UNITS

**Pre-1919**

| | | |
|---|---|---|
| 2 (Naval) Sqn | | |
| 219 Sqn | 22 Jul 1918–Feb 1920 | |
| 406 Flt | 25 May 1918–Feb 1920? | Short 184 |
| 442 Flt | Nov 1918–Feb 1920 | Fairey IIIb |

# WYE

**County:** Kent
**UTM/Grid:** OS map 189–TR044478
**Lat/Long:** N51°11.6 E000°55.4
**Nearest Town:** Ashford 4 miles to south-west

## HISTORY

Yet another of the small airfields situated in the Ashford area, Wye occupied a site of fewer than 100 acres and was allocated to the training role; in July 1916 the first unit, No.20 Training (ex-Reserve) Squadron, arrived from Dover with its mix of aircraft, primarily BE2Cs, RE8s and Avro 504s. In the same month a new unit was formed, when a nucleus of this unit was used to create 61 Squadron; however, the new unit does not appear to have been allocated any aircraft of its own and, in late-August, was absorbed into 63 Squadron, which had formed at Stirling in July. As at all these airfields, facilities remained poor and the Bessonneau hangars were the most impressive structures on site; most personnel lived in tents, although officers managed to find local billets. With the need to increase the number of pilots for deployment to France, there was continual expansion at training stations and Wye spawned a number of additional Training (ex-Reserve) Squadrons: No.50 RS formed and departed in December 1916 and No.66 did the same in May. As part of major re-organization of No.6 Training Wing, Wye was emptied of units; this may, in part, have been because the airfield was allocated to a new Anglo-American training organization as part of the plan to deploy US Army Air Corps squadrons to France. A certain amount of building work appears to have taken place during 1917, including new hangars, technical buildings and accommodation. In the meantime, 65

Squadron arrived at Wye from Wyton in late-May 1917, but its initial purpose was work-up for deployment to France and it was not allocated its own aircraft until July, when it equipped with Camels. In October, the squadron moved to La Lovie in France. The previous month had seen the arrival of 86 Squadron from Shoreham; it, too, had arrived with a view to carrying out training and work-up, although, in this instance, any plan to deploy overseas was changed and in December the squadron moved to Northolt.

Finally, in December 1917, the new training unit was established, No.42 RS being given the task of providing pilot training, which, from mid-1918, included American students.

The unit maintained this task to February 1919, although, from the latter part of 1918, the run-down in strength had begun leading to disbandment on 1 February. The RAF, as it now was, had not finished with Wye and the same month brought 3 Squadron to the airfield – but it was only a cadre unit, pending final decisions on which squadrons would survive the massed disbandment after the war. The Squadron moved to Dover in May (and survived).

## UNITS

### Pre-1919

| | | |
|---|---|---|
| 61 Sqn | 5 Jul 1916–24 Aug 1916 | no aircraft |
| 65 Sqn | 29 May 1917–24 Oct 1917 | Camel |
| 86 Sqn | 17 Sep 1917–16 Dec 1917 | various |
| 20 RS | 24 Jul 1916–1 Jun 1917 | various |
| 50 RS | 7–14 Dec 1916 | various |
| 51 RS | 8 Jan 1917–14 May 1917 | various |
| 66 RS | 1–10 May 1917 | various |
| 42 RS | 16 Dec 1917–1 Feb 1919 | FK3, Avro 504, BE2 |

### 1919–1938

| | | |
|---|---|---|
| 3 Sqn | 15 Feb 1919–2 May 1919 | cadre only |

# Abbreviations

All aspects of military aviation are crammed with abbreviations, especially when it comes to the designations of units. The following abbreviations have been used in this series, especially in the unit tables. This list is by no means exhaustive – at a rough estimate a complete list would run to 20,000-plus abbreviations! However, it does include the abbreviations most relevant to this series. There is an element of logic the reader can apply where an abbreviation is not listed; for example, 'CU' is most commonly used for Conversion Unit, hence a WCU could be a Wellington Conversion Unit. The down-side of this logic is that it could also be Washington or Wessex and so context – i.e. which is most likely – must also be taken into account.

| | | | |
|---|---|---|---|
| AAC | Army Air Corps | AONS | Air Observer and Navigator School |
| AACU | Anti-Aircraft Co-operation Unit | AOP | Air Observation Post |
| A&AEE | Aeroplane and Armament | AOS | Air Observers School |
| | Experimental Establishment | APC/S | Armament Practice Camp/Station |
| AAF | Auxiliary Air Force | APF | Air Pilotage Flight |
| AAP | Aircraft Acceptance Park, Air | ARD/S | Aircraft Repair Depot/Station |
| | Ammunition Park | ARW | Air Refuelling Wing |
| AAS | Air Armament School | ASF | Aircraft Servicing Flight |
| AASDF | Anti-Aircraft Special Defence Flight | ASP | Air Stores Park |
| ABTF | Air Bomber Training Flight | ASR(F) | Air Sea Rescue (Flight) |
| AC | Army Co-operation | ASRTU | ASR Training Unit |
| ACCS | Airborne Control and Command | ASS | Air Signallers School |
| | Squadron | ASU | Aircraft Storage Unit |
| ACHU | Air Crew Holding Unit | ASW | Anti-Submarine Warfare |
| ACIS | Air Council Inspection Squadron | ATA | Air Transport Auxiliary |
| ACS/W | Airfield Construction | ATC | Armament Training Camp, Air |
| | Squadron/Wing | | Traffic Control, Air Training Corps |
| AD | Air Division | ATDU | Air Torpedo/Transport Development |
| ADF/U | Aircraft Delivery Flight/Unit | | Unit |
| ADGB | Air Defence of Great Britain | ATF | Autogiro Training Flight |
| AEF | Air Experience Flight | ATP | Advanced Training Pool |
| AF | Air Force | ATW | Airship Training Wing |
| AFDS/U | Air Fighting Development | AW | All-Weather |
| | Squadron/Unit | AWDS | All-Weather Development Squadron |
| AFEE | Airborne Forces Experimental | AWFCS | All-Weather Fighter |
| | Establishment | | Combat/Conversion Squadron |
| AFS/U | Advanced Flying School/Unit | | |
| AGS | Air Gunnery School | BAD | Base Air Depot |
| AHU | Aircrew Holding Unit | BAFO | British Air Forces of Occupation |
| AIEU | Armament and Instrument | BANS | Basic ANS |
| | Experimental Establishment | BAS | Beam Approach School |
| AIS | Air Interception School | BATF | Beam/Blind Approach Training |
| ALS | Air Landing School | | Flight |
| AMC | Air Mobility Command | BBBLEE | Bomb Ballistics and Blind Landing |
| AMSDU | Air Ministry Servicing Development | | Experimental Establishment |
| | Unit | BB(M)F | Battle of Britain (Memorial) Flight |
| AMU | Aircraft Modification Unit | BBU | Bomb Ballistics Unit |
| ANS | Air Navigation School | BC | Bomber Command |

| | | | |
|---|---|---|---|
| BCBRU | BC Bombing Research Unit | E(R)FTS | Elementary (and Refresher) Flying Training School |
| BCDU | BC Development Unit | | |
| BCFU | BC Film Unit | | |
| BCIS | BC Instructors School | FAA | Fleet Air Arm |
| BCMS | BC Missile School | FB | Fighter-Bomber, Flying Boat |
| BDE | Balloon Development Establishment | FBDF | Flying Boat Development Flight |
| BDU | Bombing Development Unit | FBS/W | Fighter-Bomber Squadron/Wing |
| BFTS | Basic Flying Training School | FC | Fighter Command; Ferry Command |
| BG | Bombardment Group, Bomb Group | FC CRS | Fighter Command Control and Reporting School |
| BGF/S | Bombing and Gunnery Flight/ School | | |
| | | FCPU | Ferry Command Preparation Unit |
| BLEU | Blind Landing Experimental Unit | FEE | Fighter Experimental Establishment |
| BS | Bombardment Squadron, Bomb Squadron | FFU | Film Flight Unit |
| | | FG | Fighter Group |
| (BS) | Bomber Support | FIDO | Fog Investigation Dispersal Operation |
| BSDU | Bomber Support Development Unit | | |
| BW | Bombardment Wing, Bomb Wing | FIS | Flying Instructors School |
| | | FIS/W | Fighter Interception Squadron/Wing |
| CAACU | Civilian AACU | FIU | Fighter Interception Unit |
| CAEU | Casualty Air Evacuation Unit | FLS | Fighter Leaders School |
| CBCS/F | Coastal Battery Co-operation School/Flight | Flt | Flight |
| | | F(P)P/U | Ferry (Pilots) Pool/Unit |
| CBE | Central Bomber Establishment | FRS | Flying Refresher School |
| CBW | Combat Bomb Wing | FSS | Flying Selection Squadron |
| CC | Coastal Command | FTF/U | Ferry Training Flight/Unit |
| CDTF | Coastal Defence Training Flight | FTS | Flying Training School |
| CF/U | Conversion Flight/Unit; Communications Flight/Squadron | FW | Fighter Wing |
| | | FWS | Fighter Weapons School |
| CFE | Central Fighter Establishment | FWTS | Fixed Wing Test Squadron |
| CFS | Central Flying School | | |
| CGS | Central Gunnery School | GC/S | Gliding Centre/School |
| CLE/S | Central Landing Establishment/School | GCF | Gunnery Co-operation Flight |
| | | GIF/S | Glider Instructors Flight/School |
| CNS | Central Navigation School | GMDC | Groupe Mixte de Combat |
| CPF | Coast(al) Patrol Flight | GOTU | Glider OTU |
| CRO | Civilian Repair Organization | GPR | Glider Pilot Regiment |
| CSF | Central Servicing Flight | GR&ANS | General Reconnaissance and Air Navigation School |
| CSE | Central Signals Establishment | | |
| CSDE | Central Servicing Development Establishment | GRF/U | Gunnery Research Flight/Unit |
| | | GSEU | Glider Storage and Erection Unit |
| CTTO | Central Trials and Tactics Organization | GTF | Gunnery Training Flight |
| | | GTS | Glider Training School/Squadron |
| | | GWDS | Guided Weapon Development Squadron |
| deg | degrees | | |
| det | detachment | | |
| DF | Development Flight | HAS | Hardened Aircraft Shelter |
| DFCS | Day Fighter Combat School | HC | Home Command |
| DFLS | Day Fighter Leaders School | HCU | Heavy Conversion Unit |
| DUC | Distinguished Unit Citation | HD | Home Defence |
| DWI | Directional Wireless Installation | HDF | Halifax Development Flight |
| | | HG | Heavy Glider |
| EAB | Engineer Aviation Battalion | HGCU | Heavy Glider Conversion Unit |
| EAC | Enemy Aircraft Circus | HQ | Headquarters |
| ECU | Experimental Co-operation Unit | HSF | High-Speed Flight |
| EF | Experimental Flight | HSL | High Speed Launch |
| EGS | Elementary Gliding School | HT | Heavy Transport |

| | | | |
|---|---|---|---|
| HTF | Heavy Transport Flight | OAF/PU | Overseas Aircraft Ferry/Preparation Unit |
| IDE | Instrument Design Establishment | OADU | Overseas Aircraft Delivery Unit |
| IE | Initial/Immediate Establishment/Equipment | OATS | Officers Advanced Training School |
| | | OCF/U | Operational Conversion Flight/Unit |
| IRF/S | Instrument Rating Flight/Squadron | OEU | Operational Evaluation Unit |
| IRMB | Intermediate Range Ballistic Missile | OG | Observation Group |
| ITF/S | Instrument Training Flight/Squadron | ORTU | Operational Refresher Training Unit |
| ITW | Initial Training Wing | OS | Ordnance Survey |
| | | OTU | Operational Training Unit |
| JASS | Joint Anti-Submarine School | | |
| JATE | Joint Air Transport Establishment | (P)AFU | Pilot Advanced Flying Unit |
| JCF/U | Jet Conversion Flight/Unit | PAS/U | Pilotless Aircraft Section/Unit |
| JEFTS | Joint Elementary Flight Training School | PDC | Personnel Despatch Centre |
| | | PFF | Pathfinder Force |
| JEHU | Joint Experimental Helicopter Unit | PFU | Practice Flying Unit |
| | | PoW | Prisoner of War |
| KES | Kestrel Evaluation Squadron | PRDE/U | Photographic Reconnaissance Development Establishment/Unit |
| KF | King's Flight | | |
| | | PRF/U | Pilot Refresher Flight/Unit |
| LAIS | Low Attack Instructors School | PRU | Photographic Reconnaissance Unit |
| LAS | Light Aircraft School | PRG | Photographic Reconnaissance Group |
| LCF/S | Lightning Conversion Flight/Squadron | PSP | Pierced Steel Planking/Plating |
| | | PTS | Parachute Training School |
| LFS | Lancaster Finishing School | | |
| LG | Landing Ground | QF | Queen's Flight |
| LRDU | Long Range Development Unit | QRA | Quick Reaction Alert |
| LRF | Long Range Fighter | | |
| LUAS | London University Air Squadron | RAAF | Royal Australian Air Force |
| | | RAuxAF | Royal Auxiliary Air Force |
| MA | Midland Area | RAE | Royal Aircraft Establishment |
| MAC | Military Airlift Command | RAFC | Royal Air Force College |
| MAEE/U | Marine Aircraft Experimental Establishment/Unit | RAFO | Reserve of Air Force Officers |
| | | RAFVR | Royal Air Force Volunteer Reserve |
| MC | Maintenance Command | RAS | Reserve Aeroplane Squadron |
| MCS | Metropolitan Communications Squadron | RASC | Royal Army Service Corps |
| | | RATS | Radio Aids Training Flight |
| MCU | Mosquito Conversion Unit | RC | Reserve Command |
| METS | Multi-Engine Training Squadron | RCAF | Royal Canadian Air Force |
| MOS | Marine Observers School | RCM | Radio Counter Measures |
| MT | Motor Transport | RE | Royal Engineers |
| MTU | Mosquito Training Unit; Mobile Training Unit | RFC | Royal Flying Corps |
| | | RFTS | Refresher Flying Training School |
| MU | Maintenance Unit | RFU | Refresher Flying Unit |
| | | RLG | Relief Landing Ground |
| NA | Northern Area | RNAS | Royal Naval Air Service |
| NATO | North Atlantic Treaty Organization | RNZAF | Royal New Zealand Air Force |
| NCS | Northern Communications Squadron | ROC | Royal Observer Corps |
| | | RRE | Radar Research Establishment |
| NF | Night Fighter | RSU | Repair and Salvage Unit |
| NFF | Night Flying Flight | RS | Radio School |
| NFDW | Night Fighter Development Wing | RWE | Radio/Radar Warfare Establishment |
| NFLS | Night Fighter Leaders School | RWTS | Rotary Wing Test Squadron |
| NTU | Navigation/Night Training Unit | | |
| NZ | New Zealand | SAC | Strategic Air Command |
| | | SAD | Strategic Air Depot |

| | | | |
|---|---|---|---|
| SA(O)EU | Strike Attack (Operational) Evaluation Unit | SWA | South-West Area |
| SC | Support Command; Strike Command, e.g.: | SWO | School for Wireless Operators |
| SCBS | Strike Command Bombing School | T | Training |
| SCF | Signals Co-operation Flight | TAF | Tactical Air Force |
| SD (F) | Special Duties (Flight) | T/VASF | Transit/Visiting Aircraft Servicing Flight |
| SDU | Signals Development Unit | TAW | Tactical Airlift Wing |
| SEF | Special Experimental Flight | TC | Transport Command |
| SF | Station Flight | TCF | Transport and Communications Flight |
| SFTS | Service Flying Training School | | |
| SFU | Signals Flying Unit | TCG/S/W | Troop Carrier Group/Squadron/Wing |
| SHORAD | Short Range Air Defence | | |
| SHQ | Station Headquarters | TDF/S | Torpedo Development Flight/Section |
| SHTTU | Support Helicopter Trials and Tactics Unit | TDS | Training Depot Squadron/Station |
| SLAIS | Specialist LAIS | TDY | Temporary Duty |
| SLG | Satellite Landing Ground | TEU | Tactical Exercise/Evaluation Unit |
| SMT | Square-Meshed Track | TFF/U | Target Facilities Flight/Unit |
| SOG | Special Operations Group | TFU | Telecommunications Flying Unit |
| SOM | Secret Organizational Memoranda | TRE | Telecommunications Research Establishment |
| Sqn | Squadron | | |
| SRCU | Short-Range Conversion Unit | TRS/W | Tactical Reconnaissance Squadron/Wing |
| SRW | Strategic Reconnaissance Wing | | |
| STC | Strike Command | TTF | Target Towing Flight |
| STF/S | Seaplane Training Flight/Squadron | TTS | Torpedo Training Squadron |
| SU | Support Unit | TTTE | Tri-national Tornado Training Establishment |
| Schools | N.B. the 'o' is often omitted or used in full 'of': | TU | Training Unit |
| SoAC | School of Army Co-Operation; Airfield Construction | TW(C)U | Tornado/Tactical Weapons (Conversion) Unit |
| SoACCA | School of Aerial Co-operation with Coastal Artillery | UAS | University Air Squadron |
| SoAG | School of Air Gunnery | UN | United Nations |
| SoAN | School of Air Navigation | US(A)AF | United States (Army) Air Force |
| SoAP | School of Air Pilotage | | |
| SoAS | School of Air Support | VC | Victoria Cross |
| SoASR | School of Air Sea Rescue | VE | Victory in Europe |
| SoAT | School of Air Transport | VGS | Volunteer Gliding School |
| SoFC | School of Fighter Control; Flying Control | VR | Volunteer Reserve |
| SoGR&AN | School of General Reconnaissance & Air Navigation | WA | Western Area |
| | | WAAF | Women's Auxiliary Air Force |
| SoL(A)W | School of Land (Air) Warfare | WEE | Wireless/Winterization Experimental Establishment |
| SoMR | School of Maritime Reconnaissance | | |
| SoNC | School of Naval Co-operation | W&O | Wireless and Observers |
| SoP | School of Photography | WRS | Weather Research Squadron |
| SoRF/T | School of Refresher/Flying Training | WS | Wireless School |
| SoSF | School of Special Flying | WTP | Wireless Testing Park |
| SoTT | School of Technical Training | WTS | Washington Training Squadron |